# THE ARABS

# THE ARABS

Their History, Aims and
Challenge to the Industrialized World

ঋ১৯

## THOMAS KIERNAN

Little, Brown and Company    Boston • Toronto

FIRST EDITION

T 11/75

LIBRARY OF CONGRESS CATALOGING IN PUBLICATION DATA

Kiernan, Thomas.
  The Arabs.

  Includes index.
  1.  Arabs.  2.  Jewish-Arab relations.
DS36.7.K53   909'.04'927   75-19303
ISBN 0-316-49201-9

*Designed by Janis Capone*

*Published simultaneously in Canada*
*by Little, Brown & Company (Canada) Limited*

PRINTED IN THE UNITED STATES OF AMERICA

77-1537

For Samantha.
And for Annie, who made her.

*The enemy of my friend*
*is my enemy;*
*The enemy of my enemy*
*is my friend.*

— AN OLD ARAB PROVERB

# CONTENTS

## Part IV

# FOREWORD

A book — any book — should speak for itself, explain itself, justify itself. No prefatory conceits can make more of a book than that which it contains and means. This book, then, is about what it says it is: the Arabs.

Nevertheless, a word about its genesis. In 1973 I was witness to a debate in the United States between official spokesmen for Israel and for what was then being called "the Arab cause." I must say that as usual the debate was resoundingly won by the Israeli. It was won, however, not on the basis of facts or truth, but on style, technique and rhetoric. It occurred to me that the Arab spokesman's failure was due simply to the fact that he had used the wrong code words and slogans while the Israeli had used all the right ones. Both twisted the facts they had marshaled to support their respective arguments. But that is an acceptable component of the debating art, if you can call debate an art. The outcome of the proceeding rested not on which adversary bent the facts less; it was won simply on the basis of how articulately the bent facts were presented.

Yet the Arab made what I thought was an interesting, even conciliatory, point. "The problem in the Middle East," he said, "is like a glass of water in which the level of the water is halfway from the top of the glass. To some, the glass is half full. To others it is half empty. Most responsible Arabs acknowledge this. But the Jews, they cannot. They can only see the glass in one way. If they see it as half full, then they cannot see it as also half empty."

The analogy was lost on most of the pro-Israeli audience, but I liked its symmetry and thought it worth investigating. As someone who had a certain intimacy with the Jewish approach to the question, I felt the Arab spokesman was right in this characterization of the Israeli perspective. What I then felt compelled to learn was whether he was right in his characterization of the Arab approach.

I later mentioned my impression to a very high-placed Arab acquaintance. "I don't know who's right and who's wrong in this," I said. "I don't even know if there is a right and wrong. But I do know that you Arabs are not getting your message across to the outside world. I would like to find out what that message is, and I would like to write a book about it."

He jumped at my suggestion, offering to use his considerable influence within the Arab world to arrange for me to interview its highest-level notables.

"I will not write propaganda," I said. "I will simply try to present the Arab point of view as it is presented to me. I will try to be fair and honest, but the book will not be a conduit for Arab rhetoric. If it is known that you cooperated or helped me, it might prove an embarrassment to you."

"I don't care what you write," he replied, "as long as it is accurate. I wouldn't expect you to write Arab propaganda. But so long as you don't set out to write anti-Arab propaganda, I will do everything I can to ensure that you see as many people as you feel you need to. All I would hope is that you let America see the Arab people as we are. Don't apologize for us, don't defend us. But don't attack us either."

I thought that an eminently reasonable proposition. And so this book.

# THE ARABS

# PROLOGUE

## JOURNAL: *"The Arabs Are Different from You and I"*

"STAY IN THE TRUCK!" shouted Albricht, the red-bearded Dutch UN driver. Not more than a hundred yards ahead of us Israeli jets were pummeling the innards of the Palestinian refugee camp at Nabatieh in the Mount Hermon foothills of southern Lebanon.

The jets' arrival had coincided with ours. As Albricht swung the white Land Rover onto the dirt track leading into the camp, he lifted his foot from the throttle and said, "Listen!"

At first it was not so much a noise as a feeling, a feeling that the sun-baked air around us was compressing in our ears. A calm-before-the-storm feeling. Then came an unfamiliar hissing sound. Albricht, more experienced in these things, had sensed it first, and as the Land Rover slowed into its own dust a look of profound worry painted itself on his ruddy face.

"What is it?" I said. I was thinking flat-tire. Then I felt it, heard it, too.

Before he had a chance to answer the sound exploded over us. The camouflaged jets had come from behind us, streaking low up a long crease from the south, hugging its contours so that their roar was swallowed by the hills. Suddenly the Land Rover shook violently and the jets' oily tailpipes filled our windshield. There must have been a dozen of them. As their thunder assailed our ears they banked as one and hurtled skyward, weaving out of their tight box formation and spiraling into a long rising column.

I watched, transfixed. It was early summer of 1974. I had been traveling around the Middle East off and on since the previous February, gathering material for this book. I had met with kings, princes, sheikhs, presidents and ministers. I had visited battlefronts, oilfields, deserts and cities throughout Arabdom and in Israel. I had listened to war talk until it was coming out of my ears. I had seen much of the destructive aftermath of the recent war* and its ongoing post-ceasefire hostilities, but I had yet to witness the Middle East conflict at first hand. On this boiling June day, my time, it seemed, had come.

"Phantoms," said Albricht, peering as intently as I at the column of jets as they grew smaller in the translucent haze overhead.

"What are they up to?" I asked.

"I don't know," he said. There was a quiver in his voice, and his knuckles grew white on the steering wheel. "Could be a raid. God, don't let it be a raid!"

I had met Albricht the night before at the bar of the St. Georges Hotel in Beirut. I'd just finished an interview with a high Lebanese government official in a corner of the hotel's lobby and, feeling pleased with its results, stopped at the bar for a nightcap. Albricht, nursing a whiskey, politely excused himself and inquired after my trade. He had seen me talking to the Lebanese, had noted the tape recorder. Was I a journalist?

From there our conversation expanded. I learned that he worked for UNRWA (United Nations Relief Works Agency), the organization that administered the Palestinian refugee camps throughout the Arab Middle East. He told me he had been at Ein al Helweh — the largest camp in Lebanon — the month before when a massive Israeli air attack killed more than a score of people and wounded hundreds of others. Describing the horrors he'd witnessed, he then casually mentioned that he was going to be driving south the next morning on a UN errand. He had to stop at Ein al Helweh with a load of vaccine and then go on to Nabatieh — another camp raided a month earlier — to pick up some documents.

It cost me three whiskeys, but I finally persuaded him to take me along. It was against all rules and regulations, he protested. He could get in a great deal of trouble. However.

On the drive down the Lebanese coast the next morning our talk was mostly about the respective merits of the Arab and Israeli causes. At heart Albricht was a pacifist and by principle a neutral. But sixteen months of daily exposure to the squalor and pathos of Lebanon's 250,000 Palestinian refugees had forged in him a sympathy for the Arab — or at least the Palestinian — cause.

* The Yom Kippur War, according to Israel; the Ramadan War, according to the Arabs; the 1973 October War, according to Western commentators.

"Don't forget," he said after showing me around Ein al Helweh, on the outskirts of the port of Saida, "I'm a Dutchman. We Dutch did a great deal for the Jews during the Nazi period. We have a tradition of helping the Jews that goes back to the Inquisition. And look what Holland did last October. It refused to accede to the Arabs' demands that it publicly repudiate Israel. So it got the oil embargo worse than any other country, even yours. Even I agree with Holland's stand."

His face clouded over as we drove southeast toward Nabatieh, a distance of about fifteen miles inland from Saida. "But what the Jews here have done to these people," he continued, "well, you can see for yourself. It is not very nice."

I had already been through camps in Jordan and around Beirut, and I agreed that what I saw was not very nice. And I'd endlessly heard the party line from both sides of the issue: The camps and the refugee problem were creations of the Jews (from the Arab side); the camps and the refugee problem were creations of the Arabs (from the Israeli side). I commented to Albricht on the fruitless circularity of the conflict and wondered whether any possibility existed within the limits of human reason that might jar the dispute off its track and bring about a new approach to the problem.

Albricht shrugged as he maneuvered the Land Rover through a swarm of refugee kids playing about the stiffened corpse of a donkey by the roadside.

I thought about my two young sons, probably playing that very moment not fifty miles away in a comfortable seaside suburb of Tel Aviv. After the divorce of their parents they had gone to Israel with their mother, lived there for almost two years, then returned every summer thereafter, bringing back with them each time to their home in America a stronger, if still juvenile, Zionist resolve and coloration. Their bedroom in New York grew thick with the souvenirs of Israeli warrior righteousness — rocket casings, Uzi models, posters of attacking Phantoms, miniature Israeli paratroop boots. They were being raised to be soldiers for Israel — in mind, if not in body. And their minds were uncluttered by the vexations caused by exposure to both sides of an issue.

I mentioned them to Albricht. He was intrigued. "They live in Israel?"

"They did," I said. "Now they only spend their summers there."

"They're Jews?"

"Of course."

"And you?"

"After a fashion."

"So what are you doing over on this side of the fence?"

"There's an old saying in America attributed to Abraham Lincoln," I answered. "You know who he was?"

"One of your prime ministers, no?"

"Sort of. We call them presidents."

"Ah yes," Albricht nodded. "Like this Nixon fellow." Nixon had just concluded his lavishly publicized tour of the Middle East following the American-orchestrated ceasefire agreements between Israel and Syria.

"Well," I said, wondering how to explain the difference between a Lincoln and a Nixon to a Dutchman, "not exactly like Nixon. But anyway, Lincoln was supposed to have said that the best way to turn an enemy into a friend is to get to know him. When you live among Jews in America you find yourself automatically accepting the fact that the Arabs are evil, that they're your enemy. But then you begin to wonder why. Simply because they continually threaten Israel . . . ?"

"Ah," Albricht said, "the oil. It is the oil that makes you reconsider the Arabs, eh?"

"No," I replied, "not necessarily the oil. Not the embargo. But the fact that I still consider myself a Jew. That's what makes me want to reconsider them. So, following Lincoln's prescription, I am here trying to get to know them."

"Well," said Albricht, turning the Land River onto the curving dirt road that led into the Nabatieh camp, "I can tell you this about the Arabs . . ." It was then that he lifted his foot from the throttle and said, "Listen!"

Now he was shouting, "Stay in the truck!" Shortly after the Israeli jets had blasted over us and soared skyward, forming into a single tight column that disappeared into the high haze, they reappeared from a different quadrant, to our right, the column spread out now. The lead plane slanted steeply down toward the center of the camp. When it was about a thousand feet from the ground it flattened out and puffs of smoke blossomed under its droopy, swept-back wings.

"Rockets!" exclaimed Albricht. "It *is* a raid." He jammed the gear into reverse and hastily backed the Land Rover to the intersection we'd just turned from.

I looked back, then forward again as the first explosives went off ahead of us. The lead plane was curving gracefully upward, and a second diving jet was now etched against the washed-out blue of the sky.

The Land Rover was still in reverse as the second pair of explosions ripped through a large cement-block building a hundred yards ahead of us. I saw a body fly out of the ball of smoke and flame, legs spinning away from torso, and said, "Jesus!"

Suddenly the Land Rover came to a jarring halt, its hood angled upward. In his panic Albricht had backed us right through the intersection into a deep drainage ditch. Muttering curses in Dutch, he ground the gear into first and raced the engine, but we didn't move. We were caught, we discovered later, on a rock.

A third jet was diving in and this one seemed closer. It fired its rockets and a second later a building off to the right, through a stand of scrub pine, was enveloped in gleaming white flame.

"My God," Albricht shouted, still struggling with the gears, "phosphorus!"

The fourth jet came in low. The pilot evidently had a change of mind about releasing his rockets. Instead he banked sharply and was suddenly angling straight at us, a hundred feet off the ground.

Now it was my turn to panic. I wrestled with the door handle, mindlessly trying to get out of the Land Rover. By the time I got the door open the Israeli jet was past us, its roar rattling my ears and shaking my bones. For a split second I was sure the roar was the sound of an exploding rocket. Then I felt Albricht gripping my shoulder. "Stay in the truck!" he shouted.

From behind us came a real explosion. The jet had fired its rockets into a building about fifty yards to our rear. The concussion turned the glass at the back of the Land Rover into a sheet of crackle.

"Stay in the truck!" Albricht cried again. "We've got markings on the roof. They should leave us alone."

My panic subsided. Now I was simply scared. The attack continued, but smoke from the initial explosions began to engulf us, obscuring the sky and making it impossible to see what was happening. The smoke was acrid, smelling of cordite and seared metal. "What if they can't see us?" I shouted to Albricht over another explosion.

He shrugged resignedly. "We go poof!"

Still another explosion, this one closer — a sudden gleam of white light through the smoke, followed by a loud crump and a strong tremor that shook the Land Rover.

"Another phosphorus!" said Albricht. "If one of those hits us no one will know we've been here."

We were both crouched below the Land Rover's open windows. The explosions began to recede. Intermixed with the whines of the jets and the din of the impacting bombs and rockets we began to hear the cries and screams of human voices.

Then, as suddenly as a summer thunderstorm ends, the raid was over. The explosions stopped. The fearful sound of the jets had vanished. Now all we heard were the voices — some moaning, some shrieking, some shouting, some jabbering in incomprehensible Arabic. Some were distant, some close by.

The smoke around us was thinning. I ventured a peek through the side window and was stunned by what I saw. A human figure materialized out of the gloom, an eerie, unintelligible, gurgling chant issuing from what were once its lips. Stumbling, weaving, then falling to its knees and crawling, it crept toward us. It was a child — girl or boy I couldn't tell — and its charred skin was literally melting, leaving a trail of viscous fluid in its wake. Its face had no recognizable features. The top of its skull shone through the last layer of scorched membrane on its head. Not more than ten yards from us it fell onto its side, its kneecaps exposed like the yolks of poached eggs. It twitched once or twice in the dust, gave a final wheeze, then went still in the puddle of molten flesh that formed around it in the dust.

Next to me, Albricht was being sick. I tasted my own vomit in my throat and might have followed suit except for a sudden, even more terrifying, distraction.

A camouflaged armored car bounced out of the thinning smoke — a comic bathtub on wheels. My sense of its ridiculousness was abruptly altered when it skidded to a stop in front of us. The twin barrels of its lethal machine guns slowly spun to point at us.

Albricht recovered quickly. He leaned out the window and shouted something in Arabic. From within the buttoned-up vehicle came a reply — muffled, but clearly angry.

Again Albricht shouted, and there was panic in his voice. We heard a laugh from inside the armored car, then a stream of sing-song chatter.

"What's going on?" I demanded.

He ignored my question and shouted something further in Arabic. Suddenly the hatch at the top eased open and a helmeted head popped out. It belonged to the commander of the vehicle, a swarthy man with a black moustache. Incongruously, he was wearing dark wraparound sunglasses beneath his helmet so that his eyes were invisible. He shouted something at

Albricht, then barked a command back into the vehicle. The barrels of the machine gun wavered for a moment, then moved an inch to the right. Now, instead of being trained on Albricht, they were zeroed in on me.

Something in the demeanor of the man made me realize he meant business. I had a vision of myself being plucked apart by machine gun bullets, my remains dumped in an anonymous grave. No one knew I was here. I would simply have vanished.

The prospect of dying did not bother me so much as the notion of disappearing without a trace. The blind urge to flee again overcame me. Albricht must have sensed it, because he hissed, "Don't move. If you try to run they'll kill you."

"It looks like they're going to kill me anyway. Who are they?"

"Palestinians. The Palestinian army. They think we guided the Israeli planes here."

"Us?" I exclaimed.

"They say the Israelis used this truck to sight on the camp. They think we parked here deliberately."

"Can't they see we're stuck here?" I said.

Albricht nodded, then leaned out the window and shouted, again in Arabic, to the man in the armored car. He gesticulated with his arms, pointing to the underside of the Land Rover. The Palestinian shouted something back. A heated discussion followed, during which several foot soldiers toting carbines trotted up behind the armored car. The man in the turret issued an instruction and the soldiers — wearing U.S. Marine combat fatigues — approached us, their weapons at the ready. The man in the turret then shouted an order at Albricht.

"Open your door slowly," he said to me, looking straight ahead. "Then get out and stand with your hands over your head."

I did as instructed while Albricht carried out the order on his side of the Land Rover. Three soldiers surrounded me, one of them with his gun in my back. Small men, they looked mean and capable of anything. One of them said something to me.

"I'm sorry," I said, feeling foolish, "I don't really understand Arabic."

The soldier thrust the barrel of his carbine into my midsection and jabbered at me again. "They want to see your identification," Albricht called over to me.

"All I've got is my passport. It's in my bag." I pointed into the back of the Land Rover where my shoulder bag was stashed. One of the soldiers reached in and dragged it out. Protruding from the top was my tape recorder. When the soldiers saw it they grew excited. One of them pulled it out and held it up for the man in the armored car to see.

"They think it's a homing device," Albricht said over the roof of the Land Rover. "My God, I knew I should not have brought you here."

"Tell them it's only a tape recorder."

Albricht called out to the man in the turret. A siren wailed in the distance, and in a few moments a white ambulance with a red crescent on its side careened past us into the dirt road leading to the camp. As it shifted gears it ran over the charred corpse lying in the middle of the track. There was a sickening *splat*, and the corpse divided in two at the midsection.

A breeze had come up and was blowing the smoke from the fires away from us. Looking up the road I could see dozens of figures staggering about. Another siren approached.

While Albricht and the Palestinian commander argued about my tape recorder, my mind wandered. I thought about home — about the woman pregnant with my child, about whether the corn had yet pushed through the gravelly soil of our garden, about whether the special trip insurance I had taken out at the beginning of my journey in New York would be honored in the event of my death here in the parched wasteland of Lebanon (wasn't there some exclusion concerning an act of war?). Then I thought about my two sons — were they in Israel or not at this moment? — and the irony of it all: to have almost, if inadvertently, been killed by the Israelis, only to have escaped and now to face death at the hands of the Arabs. And then another memory rose to the surface of my mind — of the time a few months earlier in California when, as a lark, I had had my fortune told by a woman who claimed to be prescient and who took me through a tea leaf ritual. She knew nothing about me. But of the sixty or so items she remarked upon, many had to do with me finding myself in great difficulty in the desert. She advised me to give up my plans to go to desert places — how did she know I had such plans? — and followed that counsel with the prediction of a male death in the family.

The memory was hardly reassuring, but I was unable to dwell on it. My attention was jerked back to the matters at hand by a glob of spittle in my eye, issued from the mouth of the Palestinian soldier babbling hysterically in front of me.

I wiped the spit away with the sweat-soaked sleeve of my shirt and suppressed the urge to smash my fist into the little man's face. The suppression was made easier by the carbine he was waving at me.

"I just told them you are an American," Albricht called over to me.

"Thanks a lot," I said. "Now all you have to do is tell them I'm a — you-know-what."

"They want to know what you do here."

"Say I'm a journalist, that I'm writing a book about them."

Before Albricht had a chance to convey this information a jeep bearing a stand-up machine gun skidded to a stop in front of us. The soldiers who'd been harassing me pulled away and snapped to attention. The uniformed man in the jeep's passenger seat — also wearing dark sunglasses — was obviously some sort of senior commander. He stepped out of the jeep, tall, whip-lean, moustached, face heavily scarred, treacherous looking. He conferred with the man in the turret of the armored car, than fielded my tape recorder as it was tossed down to him and examined it. He looked at me suspiciously, then said something to Albricht in Arabic.

As Albricht replied, the man approached me. "You can drop your arms," he said in English.

"Thank you," I said, after recovering from my surprise.

He began to question me with elaborate politeness. I told him the reason for my presence there and mentioned the names of some of the Palestinian Liberation Organization leaders I had interviewed in Beirut during the previous week.

"I have always had the greatest respect for writers," he said, his accent redolent of a British public school. "I used to do a bit of it myself. I trust you understand the reasons for my men's suspicions of you."

I nodded.

He swept his arm toward the smoking rubble in the distance. "Put that in your book," he said, and then turned to stare hard at me. "You will let the world know what the Zionist pigs do to us, to our women and children. No?"

This was not the time to start arguing about who did what to whom. "I intend to present the facts," I said.

"These are the facts!" he insisted, again pointing to the camp. "These are the only facts." His scarred cheek twitched dangerously. "And let your readers know where all this death comes from. From America. American planes. American rockets. American bombs. You will do that, will you not?"

Albricht had come around the Land Rover and was standing behind the man. He widened his eyes at me, silently exhorting me to agree with the demand. Complete agreement obviously would be our passport out of there.

"I will do my best to present all the facts I can," I ventured.

The man continued to gaze at me sternly from behind his dark glasses. I could just barely make out his eyes. In one, the socket was blank.

He handed me the tape recorder, turned and gave an order to the soldiers, then said something to Albricht in Arabic. Albricht nodded, trotted around to the driver's side of the Land Rover and got in. The soldiers surrounded the Land Rover and rocked it off the stone on which it was caught. Albricht motioned for me to get back in. While I did so the armored car trundled off toward the camp, followed by the jeep carrying the man who had questioned me. The crisis was obviously over, and I trembled with relief.

"Who is he?" I asked Albricht.

"I do not know his true name," he replied, his own voice quivering. "They call him Colonel X. He is in charge of the Liberation army garrison here." Albricht put the Land Rover in gear and started again up the dirt road toward the camp, carefully skirting the charred corpse scattered now in oozing pieces across the track.

"What are we doing?" I said.

"We must go in to inspect the damages. I will have to make a report."

The center of the camp was chaos. We pulled up next to the ambulance that had come in earlier. Two women — burned, one without an arm below the elbow — were lying in the back moaning in pain. There were no attendants about. In the dust around the ambulance lay other bodies — an elderly man, two girls, several young men, two in fatigue uniforms — some still, unconscious, others writhing and screaming. From the nearby buildings and huts, shattered and smoking, came more shrieks and wails. A truck lay on its side, charred and smoldering, a few yards away. Next to it was a disembodied human leg, a sandal still on its foot.

"Stay here," Albricht said as he got out of the Land Rover. "If anyone asks you questions, do not say you are American. They will kill you. Say you are Australian or British, if anything. With the UN. I'll be back in a few minutes."

"But look at all these people," I said, indicating the bodies strewn about the ambulance. "Why isn't anyone taking care of them?"

"There are no doctors here," he said.

"So what about the ambulance crew?"

"They are not medical people." With that he strode off toward the camp's administration building.

One of the wounded girls who had been lying unconscious stirred in the dust. Most of her black robe had been burnt away, revealing seared flesh. She had been lying on her back, one of her legs bent under her at a crazy angle. Now she tried to turn over, uttering a long scream that dissolved into an incoherent whimper.

I jumped out of the Land Rover and ran over to her. I had no idea what I could possibly do except try to calm her, comfort her. I knelt and slipped my arm under her neck. She groaned and began to shiver, her eyes looking up into mine beseechingly. She must have been nineteen or twenty. The smell of her burnt flesh and hair was sickening; I could feel my bare forearm turn slippery with the ooze of her blood. As I held her head up I reached down with my other arm and tried to straighten out her leg. She recoiled in pain, and as I brought the leg out from under her I could see that her entire hip was torn away. I stared for a moment at the gleam of bone and blood. I had her thigh straightened out, but her lower leg was still awry and I couldn't reach it while still holding her head. I tried to gently pull her rearward a few inches, hoping the leg would drag out straight, but as I did so a stream of blood began to spurt from her hip.

I let her head down and, still on my knees, tore off my shirt. While I was trying to fashion a tourniquet I heard shouting behind me. I turned and saw an old man, with a legless child in his arms, chattering at me. I shook my head and returned my attention to the girl. The man came around to the other side of the girl and sank to his knees in the dust, facing me.

"*Tabeeb?*" he said. "*Tabeeb, tabeeb!*"

I looked up at him and shrugged to convey my lack of comprehension.

"*Tabeeb!*" he said more sharply. "*Dok-tor?*"

"No, no, I'm not a doctor." I said. The girl's blood was spattering my chest.

"*Dok-tor, dok-tor!*" he shouted, and then said something in Arabic, holding the child out toward me. The two legs were neatly severed at midthigh.

I shook my head again. Unnoticed by me, the ambulance attendants had returned. I heard the engine start and looked up to see the ambulance driving away, still with only the two women in back.

"Hey!" I shouted. "Wait a minute!"

I jumped to my feet and chased it a few yards, but it was already well away from me and gathering speed. The driver obviously had no intention of stopping. He was back on the dirt road and heading out of the camp. In his dust he had left the cluster of bodies still writhing and moaning on the ground.

When I turned back to the girl I went dumb with disbelief. The old man had set the child down and was kneeling over the girl, feebly but zealously pounding a large rock against her skull. Several uninjured people had gathered round and were watching, indifferent. When the man had turned the girl's face into a bloody pulp he dropped the rock, gathered up the child, and approached me, again holding out the body and saying, now with a toothless smile, "Dok-tor?"

The child's eyes were wide open and staring blankly ahead at nothing. The stumps of his thighs were blood and gristle, but no blood flowed from them. He was already dead. I brushed past the man and knelt by the girl. She, it was obvious, was also dead.

The man with the child followed me and nudged me in the back with his foot. Around him stood the group of onlookers, all staring at me expectantly.

"I'm not a doctor, goddamnit!" I yelled, getting to my feet and trying to get by them. They all moved with me, blocking my way.

"Dok-tor, dok-tor," said the old man, still smiling and offering the child.

"*Tabeeb*," said one of the men next to him.

"*Muta assef*," I said in my rudimentary Arabic, "*ana la tabeeb.*" That should have been enough of an approximation to get across the message that I wasn't a doctor. It was. The looks on the faces of the group grew surly. The man with the child started to shout angrily at me in Arabic. His companions advanced threateningly.

"He is dead," I said, pointing to the child. I tried to remember the Arabic word for "dead," but couldn't. So I pantomimed it. "He is dead. I'm sorry. *Muta assef.*"

The group looked at the boy's eyes and exchanged glances of recognition. They broke into a babble of Arabic, every other word of which seemed to be "Allah." I used the opportunity to slip away and return to the Land Rover.

Another ambulance arrived, but instead of stopping to collect the injured it weaved its way past them and drove further into the camp. I felt no desire to make myself conspicuous again by trying to hail it down, so I got back into the Land Rover, pulled out my tape recorder, and began describing the scene as more injured people and corpses were brought out of the smoking ruins and deposited in the dusty clearing.

In a little while Albricht returned, accompanied by an Arab man dressed in a scruffy sport shirt and slacks, his eyes shielded by the ubiquitous wraparound sunglasses. The Arab was holding a white bloodstained towel to his right shoulder. Only when he followed Albricht to the driver's side of the Land Rover did I notice that he carried a pistol in his hand.

He motioned Albricht into the truck, then came around to my side and barked something at me. Albricht responded sharply in Arabic. The man argued back, raising his pistol and pointing it across me at him.

"What's going on?" I said.

"He's forcing me to take him to the hospital in Saida," Albricht said. "He wants you out. I said you come with us."

"Who is he?"

"Never mind," Albricht said, then spoke again to the Arab.

The Arab now pointed the pistol at me and motioned me out of the Land Rover.

"Listen," I said, "I'll get out. We've had enough trouble."

"No, stay where you are," said Albricht. He quickly removed the key from the ignition switch and put it in his mouth, then said something further to the Arab, pointing to the rear of the truck. By now a group of people had gathered round.

The Arab shrugged. He opened the door on my side and motioned me into the back with the pistol. "Go ahead," said Albricht.

I climbed over the seat and settled myself in the back. The Arab took my place, then pointed the pistol at Albricht and shouted, "*Al mustashfa!*"

I recognized the Arabic word for "hospital." As he said it the onlookers crowding around the door — all with wounds of one kind or another — struggled to get into the Land Rover. The Arab tried to beat them away with the pistol. But it was too much of a strain on his injured shoulder. So he fired the pistol into their midst.

One of the men sagged backwards with a groan, a bright red stain spreading over his shirt. The others backed off as the Arab screamed at them. He slammed the door shut, then turned to Albricht and shouted again. "*Al mustashfa!*" Albricht nodded obediently and started up the Land Rover. Soon we were out of the camp and on the road back to Saida.

The trip passed without a word spoken by anyone, but it was at least without any further incident. Albricht deposited the Arab at the small hospital in Saida and then pointed the Land Rover north toward Beirut.

We were quiet most of the way, both of us lost in our thoughts — me, for one, savoring the relief I felt at being safely on the road back to a hot shower and a cooling drink.

A stop at an army roadblock outside Beirut airport brought conversation back. Albricht learned from the Lebanese officer in charge that there was talk of an Israeli attack on the airport — another reprisal for the recent Palestinian guerrilla raids from Lebanon into northern Israel.

"Good material for your book, eh?" he said as we were waved through the roadblock.

"I guess so," I said. "The Palestinians — that's what it's all about when you come right down to it."

"Palestinians, Arabs," said Albricht, "they're all the same."

"There's one thing that astonished me," I said. I described what I'd seen at Nabatieh while he'd been gone from the Land Rover — the old man killing the wounded girl so as to get the undivided attention of someone he thought to be a doctor, the ambulance leaving without the injured, the Arab shooting at his wounded compatriots to ensure himself an unencumbered trip to the hospital.

"I mean," I went on, "in the last few months I've talked to a lot of Arabs — high and low, all walks of life, different countries. I've been wined and dined by some, castigated and insulted by others. Which is fine, because it allowed me to see the Arab character at work, in all its variety. But what I saw today, this kind of reflexive recourse to violence, this lack of any reverence for human life — among themselves, mind you, not toward outsiders — well, it kind of . . ."

"That sounds odd," Albricht said, "coming from an American. You should understand violence better than anyone."

"Yes," I agreed, "the capacity for violence is very much a part of the American character. No doubt about it. But what I've seen in the Arab character is different. It's a capacity for cruelty. Not just cruelty itself, for we are also capable of cruelty. Every group of people I've ever come across is. What I mean is the way Arab cruelty is expressed. It is institutionalized. It expresses itself indifferently, impersonally, without any apparent meditation or premeditation. It's reflexive, automatic. I've seen it time and time again in my travels, in the way people treat each other in their normal, everyday relationships. When it's not actually physical you don't take too much notice of it. It's there, you feel it like an undercurrent in everything that goes on between people. But since it's not directed at you it's of no great importance. But today I saw it in its fullest expression, you might say. In all its impersonal, almost stoic grandeur. And it makes me wonder: Are these people the key to our future, to the destiny of the Western world?"

"You have just," said Albricht, "stumbled on the first law that every Westerner must observe when dealing with the Arabs — the number one law."

"What is that?"

"Simply this. The Arabs are different from you and I."

# PART ONE

# 1.

# HISTORY: *In the Beginning*

THE WORLD'S LONG TRADITION of violence, war, death and political and religious struggle found its origins in the harsh sand, rock and occasional verdancy of what we today call the Middle East. Fragments of our planet's earliest recorded history have survived to attest to that fact, while anthropologists and archeologists have gone even further back into time to unearth similar evidence.

It is from our anthropologists and archeologists that we are best able to trace the probable origins of human life in the Middle East. Much anthropological conclusion rests in the realm of scientific hypothesis and educated guesswork. There still remain conflicting theories, and nothing has been proven to the absolute satisfaction of all who have been involved in the search. Nevertheless it is a more or less accepted conclusion among most that man, as we know him today, first came into existence either within the region of the modern Middle East or on its African periphery.

The basic theoretical conflict lies in the question: Where did this original version of man come from? Did he evolve within the confines of the region — in the Nile River valley, as some say, or in the valley between the Tigris and Euphrates rivers of Mesopotamia (today's Iraq), as others claim? Or did he originate in the Arabian peninsula or in East Africa, as still others insist, and then migrate to the Nile and Tigris-Euphrates regions?

Whichever (and these are not the only theories), archeological findings have proven that man as far back as the Paleolithic era inhabited both the Nile and the Tigris-Euphrates valleys. Many anthropologists who have studied the fossilized skeletal remains dug up from the Nile delta agree that its first inhabitants most likely did not migrate there from elsewhere. Comparisons of their skull formations with those found elsewhere — in Arabia, for instance, and in central Africa — reveal sharp measurable differences that support the anthropologists' contentions that the people of the Nile originated there.

Similar findings relate to the people of the Tigris-Euphrates valley. The question becomes, then: Which of these two civilizations was older, the Egyptian or the Mesopotamian?

To this day the question remains unanswered, but a large body of anthropological opinion holds to the claim that human life originated in these two areas of the Middle East and then spread north, east, south and west.

Other experts insist that the inhabitants of the Nile and the Tigris-Euphrates were predated by peoples who evolved either in northwest or in central-eastern Africa. Those who favor the northwest Africa theory explain that these people migrated eastward, still in Paleolithic times, and invaded the area of ancient Egypt, forming a rudimentary tribal civilization in the Nile delta and valley. In succeeding generations branches of this civilization are said to have spread farther eastward, passing through the Sinai Peninsula. From there some sallied north and east into the fertile lands of the Levant (the easternmost coastal areas of the Mediterranean) and the Tigris-Euphrates valley, while others drifted south into the Arabian peninsula.

Those who favor the central-eastern Africa theory claim that these peoples, Nubians, emigrated across the Red Sea and into the Arabian peninsula, and then spread north in succeeding waves to the Nile and the Tigris-Euphrates.

There are still other scholars who grant the probability of both theories being correct. From there they hypothesize that the migrating peoples from northwest Africa eventually encountered and intermingled with the migrating east Africans. Out of this encounter gradually evolved a new, mixed civilization that became the matrix for the future peoples of the ancient Middle East.

Still others do a variation on this theme. They accept the various migration hypotheses, but aver also that the ancient Egyptian and Mesopotamian peoples evolved and existed on their own, along with perhaps one or two other peoples in southwest Asia. Thus, through the processes of migration and cross-fertilization between and among these six or seven peoples in prehistoric times, there evolved a matrix that was much more of a "mixed salad" than supposed by others.

The most commonly accepted theory today holds that the ancient population of the Nile valley probably did exist on its own.* But man did not simply evolve in one place. Centuries — indeed, millennia — of man's prehistoric origins and evolution remain cloaked in mystery. What appears likely, though, is that at some point in time the Arabian peninsula became a kind of crossroads of early migrating populations — or better put, a collecting place. As these populations intermingled and expanded over hundreds of centuries, the peninsula, like a reservoir, overflowed, sending forth succeeding waves of emigrants northward — the only direction in which they could go inasmuch as the peninsula was surrounded east, south and west by water.

It is generally believed that the first wave took place around 3500 B.C. The nomadic emigrants are thought to have emerged from the Arabian desert and discovered the lands of what is today known as the Fertile Crescent.†

Although this theory of the early history of the Middle East is European in origin, most knowledgeable Arab historians subscribe to it. The conventional wisdom is that during this first northern migratory wave the emigrants split off into groups, one heading northwestward to settle among the ancient Egyptians of the Nile valley, the second traveling in a more northerly direction to settle along the valley of the Jordan River in what eventually came to be known as Palestine, and the third journeying northeasterly to reach the rich valley of Mesopotamia between the Tigris and Euphrates.

Although these first emigrants are assumed to have been an admixture of northwest Africans, east Africans and probably Asians, they have generally come down through history known exclusively as Semites. "Semite" is an eighteenth-century German anthropological coinage which was originally invented to denote a group of people according to the language they spoke. Since its emergence it has often been used, and is used to this day — erroneously — as a biological designation, to describe a "race" or subrace of people. There is no evidence to support the contention that the peoples who came out of the Arabian peninsula were of a single biological unity. Indeed,

---

* The study of ancient Egyptian hieroglyphics supports this view, as does the analysis of skeleton fossils.

† That more-or-less continuous arc of territory beginning at the Nile valley and extending northeastward through Israel, Lebanon and Syria, then bending southeastward through Iraq and along the Tigris and Euphrates rivers to their termination in the delta above the Persian Gulf.

the evidence is to the contrary. What bound them together was the apparent fact that they had all developed while in Arabia a mutual language, one that had regional and tribal variations but a common root.

The most significant aspect of their early thrust out of Arabia is thought to have been their intermingling with the ancient Egyptians of the Nile valley: Out of this integration the highly civilized Egyptian dynasty is believed to have emerged. Also the earliest recorded language known to us, the Semitic Akkad, developed during this period.

About a thousand years later, around 2500 B.C., a second wave of emigrants spread north from the reservoir of Arabia. With this outpouring the history of the Middle East begins to become more certain. By the time of the second wave Egyptian culture, having had a thousand years to develop, was well established along the Nile. In the east, Mesopotamian civilization was not far behind. Between, in the area of the Jordan valley, progress was considerably slower.

It was probably for this reason that the major portion of the second migratory wave gravitated as it did into the area of the Jordan. At the head of the wave was a Semitic group known as the Canaanites, which established itself as the dominant culture in the lowlands between the Jordan River on the east and the Mediterranean and Sinai desert to the west and south. The land area of Canaanite settlement corresponded to what later became Palestine.

The Canaanites were followed by the linguistically Semitic Amorites, who settled the lands to the north and east in what today corresponds to Syria and Lebanon. The Amorites also fragmented eastward to the lower reaches of the Tigris and Euphrates, where they intermingled with the Mesopotamians to eventually produce separate but similar cultures that came to be known as Babylonian and Assyrian.

Hence, by about the year 2000 B.C. there were strategically entrenched in the Middle East five Semitic groups, each with a variation in their language, but all basically Semitic in culture, custom and tradition.

The third wave out of Arabia began about 1500 B.C. and consisted of groups which became known as the Phoenicians, the Aramaeans and the Hebrews. All zeroed in on the area around Canaan. The Phoenicians sliced out a length of Amorite-dominated Mediterranean coastline (in what today corresponds to Lebanon) above Canaan and established themselves as seafarers. The Aramaeans wrested another portion of Amorite territory east of Canaan, in what is today Syria and northern Jordan, and became a significant subcultural component of the region, eventually sending tendrils eastward into Mesopotamia.

It is over the question of the Hebrews and their role in the evolving Semitic Middle East of the time that the greatest amount of historical heat has been generated down through the centuries. I will trace that role in greater detail further on. For now, let us leave the Hebrews as simply another of those nomadic Semite tribes which periodically issued from the crowded sands of Arabia to carve a niche for themselves in the more fertile regions of the north. It is true that they were apparently able to establish a foothold for themselves in the land of Canaan about 1400 B.C., but their arrival upon the scene was probably of less immediate consequence than that of their fellow Arabian tribes, the Phoenicians and the Aramaeans.

This migratory tide was by no means the end of the expansion of the Middle East. Another thousand years later, about 500 B.C., the Palmyrans and Nabateans emerged from Arabia to establish themselves. In the meantime the already long-established Semitic cultures had spread out and intermixed, and had created political entities, legal systems, moral ideals, and patterns of industry, commerce and trade that became the template upon which much of the world's later civilization would be formed. The core of the Middle East had become the Fertile Crescent, ranging from Egypt in the west to Mesopotamia in the east. In turn, this core became the core of the world.

By about 2000 B.C. the region was the world's center of agricultural production and industrial and mercantile activity. The peasant soil-tenders supplied the manufacturing and trading cities with food, while skilled craftsmen made products for markets both near and far. Commerce developed at first along the rivers, then spread across overland caravan and sea routes to more distant lands. The cities of the northern Middle East — Memphis, Haran, Nineveh, Babylon, Ur — became the hubs of trade routes reaching far into Europe, Asia and Africa. For many centuries the region, as a center of agriculture and industry and as a nexus of trade routes, enjoyed a most favorable geographical position for economic prosperity.

Directly related to the geographic attractiveness contributing to the prosperity and cultural progress of the region, however, were certain distinct drawbacks. The caravan and sea routes became avenues of invasion accessible to outsiders. The caravan routes crossed arid and semiarid wastelands suitable only to wandering tribes, who increasingly became a threat to the agrarian populations of the Fertile Crescent. As well, the great wealth accumulating in the cities became a constant temptation to the emerging Indo-European civilizations to the north and to the Persian and Mongolian civilizations to the east.

To maintain the order and security necessary to the continuance of the region's prosperity, centers of political power gradually evolved in the pre-biblical Middle East along with concomitant military might. The Egyptians developed a national state, the Sumerians a group of city-states. Out of these grew separate Egyptian and Mesopotamian empires which began to strive, one against the other, for domination over the Fertile Crescent. Ironically, the wars between these imperial dynasties did more than anything else to undermine the region's security and independent prosperity.

It was while the Egyptians and the Mesopotamians waged their centuries-long struggle that two other civilizations were in the process of development on opposite sides of the Middle East. By the sixth century B.C. the Persians in Asia, to the southeast, and the Greeks in Europe, to the northwest, had gained political control over their respective regions. Having also secured control of the land and sea trade routes to the Orient, the Persians then enlisted the Egyptians and Phoenicians in a struggle against Greece to wrest control of the routes to Europe.

The wars that followed are known in our history books as the Persian Wars. Neither side predominated, and the resulting impasse created a situation that was untenable for all concerned and particularly galling to the ruling classes in both the Persian Empire and the Greek city-states. The Greeks presented themselves as fighting to preserve the democratic ideals of Hellenism against the totalitarianism of the "barbarian" Persians, but the actual stake was the control of the Middle East, with its prosperous and advanced industries and its well-traveled intercontinental trade routes.

The impasse was resolved in 331 B.C. by Alexander the Great. After acquiring power over the Greek city-states, he quickly conquered Egypt and overran the Persian Empire in an effort to create his own imperial state extending through the Middle East to central Asia. His success was rapidly sabotaged by the struggle for power among his successors. From the time of Alexander's death in 323 B.C. until its Roman conquest nearly two hundred years later, the Middle East was the focal point of rivalries between the Ptolemaic dynasty of Egypt, the Seleucids of Asia Minor and the Macedonians of southern Europe.

By now the region was well into the time of recorded history. Within the framework of the great struggles, first between the Egyptian and Mesopotamian dynasties, then between the Persians and the Greeks — and accompanied by continuing migrations from the south — the cultural and political face of the Middle East began to change. Kingdoms and subkingdoms were formed and quickly swallowed up in the metronomic ebb and flow of war between East and West. New states evolved out of old ones, only to disappear in a century or two — transformed into still newer states or incorporated into larger kingdoms and empires. The only cultural aspect that remained constant was the language. Although the language of the area developed numerous variants with time — Akkadian, Amorite, Babylonian, Syriac, Canaanite, Phoenician, Hebrew, Aramaic, Nabatean, Palmyran — it remained basically Semitic in root and was the principal vehicle of the region's cultural integrity in the face of foreign invasions.

In the meantime the land that had been periodically delivering the peoples who were developing the Fertile Crescent was not without its own cultural progress. Much of very early life in the Arabian peninsula is, of course, lost to us due to the lack of any known record-keeping. Yet the conjecture of classical historians and anthropologists suggests that life and civilization flowered there with a color and intensity not even matched in the north.

The center of this civilization appears to have been along the southernmost extremities of the peninsula, especially in the western portions, at the conjunction of the Red Sea and the Indian Ocean (in the area of the Yemens of today). The proximity of this area to the coast of East Africa lends credence to the theory that at least one component of ancient man evolved in eastern or central Africa and migrated to Arabia.

Life in coastal southwestern Arabia developed over the span of several millennia from a primitive tribal existence into a civilization that featured a proliferation of monarchical government institutions, a highly complex society and intense commercial activity. Several states seem to have succeeded each other and to have coexisted, and as civilization crept north along the semifertile coast of the Red Sea the way of life became stable and cultivated.

Hemming in the coast to the east was a long spine of mountainous terrain that ran the entire length of the southern half of the peninsula. Beyond the mountains lay a vast, forbidding desert plateau that stretched across the peninsula for nearly a thousand miles to the Gulf of Persia. This desert would play as central a role in the development of the Middle East in ancient times as it does today.

The populations that spread northward along the Red Sea coast from Yemen were basically town and village kingdoms. As these early populations expanded they became at the same time sedentary and self-enclosed. Space and resources could not support the expansion, so from each the overflow gradually expelled itself into the desert. The overflow may or may not have encountered a similar overflow pouring westward out of Asia; again, theories abound on this. Whether it did or not, a new kind of society began to form — tribal, nomadic, animal-tending, and eventually highly inbred.

The society expanded through the centuries, breaking up into subsocieties that pushed farther northward through the Arabian desert to secure space for their wanderings. As they spread through the peninsula some of them infiltrated back to the coast to intermingle with the agrarian and urban kingdoms, transforming themselves into primitive farming and craft groups and acquiring modicums of the civilization of the day. Others stayed in the desert, remaining untainted by the sophistication of the coast and developing a highly ritualized way of life based on exotic religious ideals, tribal values and the struggle for survival.

All through this time the Arabian peninsula was continuing to fill up with migrating peoples from elsewhere and with now-indigenous populations. Growing space limitations along the coast, the tyranny of established governments and kingdoms, droughts and famines in the settled areas — all contributed to forcing more and more people into the desert. Tribal society expanded in turn, becoming more biologically and culturally diffuse as it was pushed farther and farther northward. The time finally came when Arabia could no longer hold all its peoples, and it was then that the first tribes burst out of the northern reaches of the desert and made for the region of the Fertile Crescent, to be followed periodically by succeeding waves of tribal migration.

Once the northern tier of the Middle East was settled and industry, agriculture, commerce, long-distance trade and war were firmly established as features of life, a trend toward reciprocal communication and cultural interchange developed between the increasingly civilized societies of the north and both the tribal and civilized ones of the south. The Arabian peninsula was a strategically convenient highway to southern Asia and Africa, and caravan routes were opened up across the desert. The desert tribes became the suppliers of camels for these routes, and depending on their dispositions became the protectors or raiders of the caravans. In southern Arabia, meanwhile, and in Yemen, coastal civilization was still thriving. The principal commodities produced there were aromatic spices — frankincense, labdanum, myrrh. Soon they were being shipped north to the Mediterranean basin.

The spice trade quickly became the structural foundation on which the progress of the civilized societies of southern Arabia rested. All a society's efforts — led by a ruling monarch, supported by an executive of elders and spiritually inspired by the particular society's gods — were directed to the production and shipment of spices. The prosperity that resulted produced even richer and more cultivated societies — evidence of which comes to us through the southern Arabian epigraphs that have survived the period. The epigraphs tell us much about the organization of public life in these societies, about their religious practices, their family structures (which appear to have been monogamous), and their economies and laws.

As the camel-breeding nomads of Arabia became important to the maintenance of the caravan routes they began to spread from the Arabian desert into the more northerly arid reaches of the Middle East — the Egyptian, Sinai and Syrian deserts. And as their presence began to impress itself upon the consciousness of the settled peoples of the Fertile Crescent — the nomads were not only camel breeders and herders, after all; they were also raiders and pillagers — they started to acquire a special identity in the minds of the natives.

This identity first expressed itself (as far as we know) in an Assyrian inscription of 853 B.C., in which the Assyrian king, Shalmaneser III, told of his battle with a coalition of mutinous princes and nomad chieftains. Prominent among the latter was one Gindibu, who was described as an "Aribi" and was accused of contributing a thousand of his camels to the rebellion.

From that date until about 550 B.C. the word "*aribi*" was found frequently in the inscriptions and writings that appeared in the region of the Fertile Crescent. The word was invariably used in reference to desert peoples in general and to specific nomad individuals and tribes who came from the southern deserts (Arabia) in particular. One Assyrian inscription from about 700 B.C. indicates that the Aribi were considered not much better than slaves. Another of a slightly later date describes punitive campaigns waged against the Aribi in retaliation for their preying on certain caravans.

None of these writings mentions anything about Arabia itself. Nor do surviving early southern Arabian epigraphs indicate that the inhabitants of what we today call Arabia thought of themselves as living in a place so named. However, there *are* references in these epigraphs to *aribi* and linguistic variations thereof. They were invariably applied to the nomads of the inland desert to distinguish them from the sedentary inhabitants of the coastal regions, who were the authors of the epigraphs. It is safe to say then — though not with dogmatic certainty — that the southern Arabians did not think of themselves as *aribi*.

In the languages of the time the word *"aribi"* and its variations derived from an ancient Semitic root implying nomadism: *'abar,* or "to pass." (It is from this root that the word "Hebrew" is also derived.) The English word "Arab," of course, comes from the Semitic *aribi* and its variations, so it seems clear that the original Arabs were those camel-herding, wandering nomads of the Arabian desert who filtered northward into the Fertile Crescent anywhere from 2000 to 1000 B.C.

After about 550 B.C., around the time of the Persian invasion, the word *"aribi"* dropped out of the literature and tablature of the Fertile Crescent. The peoples of the area, large and small, retained their own particular cultural identities — Egyptian, Canaanite, Hebrew, Phoenician, Assyrian, Babylonian, etc. — each speaking its own version of the basic Semitic language and each struggling to retain its own cultural integrity as the shock waves of war and invasion rolled through the region.

The successive invasions of the Persians and the Greeks in the last few centuries B.C., however, brought about a renewal and expansion of the identity that was eventually to become known as Arab. Ancient cuneiform tablets reveal that the Persians called the large peninsula across the Persian Gulf "Arabaya." This designation undoubtedly passed to the conquering Greeks, for the word "Arabia" occurs for the first time in Greek writings. Herodotus, followed by later Greek and Latin writers, extended the terms "Arabia" and "Arab" to eventually include all the desert areas of the Middle East inhabited by people who spoke Semitic languages.

Thus the word "Arab," and indeed its concept, came out of the Middle East into Asia and Europe as a tightly specific designation for a type of people, and was fed back a few centuries later with a considerably broader connotation. The process would prove important in the still-later crystallization of the word into an almost mystical symbol of a people's own perception of itself.

The nearly two hundred years of struggle over the Fertile Crescent following the death of Alexander the Great in 323 B.C., between the Ptolemaians, the Seleucids and the Macedonians, were mirrored by considerable internal turmoil. The seeds of Greek culture and civilization had been scattered throughout the region. As they sometimes integrated but more often clashed with residual Semitic values and attitudes, they produced an expanding local political consciousness that expressed itself in rebellion and insurrection.

The arrival of the Romans temporarily put an end to much of this. Successors of the Greeks as rulers of Mediterranean Europe, the Romans proceeded to spread the tendrils of their empire throughout the Fertile Crescent. By 64 B.C. Rome had a firm hold on the Middle East, its armies quelling local rebellions with swift, often brutal, dispatch and its proconsuls administering home rule with an iron hand.

During these roughly four thousand years of Middle East development — from the evolution of its prehistoric inhabitants, through the progressive migratory waves from the south, to the succession of military invasions from the north and east — the largely Semitic nature of the indigenous population persevered. Operating, of course, was a continuous process of biological transformation as separate Semitic cultures first integrated and assimilated, then became exposed to Persian, Greek, Roman and other genetic infusions. And not only did the invading foreigners impose their biological influence, they also grafted onto the native Semitic consciousness their respective religious and political ideas, their customs and traditions, and their ethnological aspirations. Nevertheless, mainly through the commonality of language and native lore, the Semitic character of the land was firmly established.

# 2.

# HISTORY: *Enter God*

MOST OF OUR KNOWLEDGE about the character and nature of the peoples of the Middle East up until about 1000 B.C. comes to us, as we have seen, through anthropological hypothesis and archeological artifact. The first comprehensive written record of the region was a series of narrative tales, most of which are believed to have been refined and codified through the folklore of one of the peoples of the region and put into literary form between about 700 and 500 B.C. This record is what today we call the Bible.* Its authors were the people who organized the idea of a single God, an idea that did more than anything else to give much of the world, and all of the Middle East, its present-day character. The people were called, variously, Abramites (after the man who, having heard "the voice of the Lord," supposedly originated the idea), Hebrews (after the version of the Semitic language they spoke), Negebites (after the desert area west of the Jordan River in which they first settled), Israelites (after their belief in a single God), and Judahites (after a later name given to the region of the Negeb desert), or Judaeans. Subsequently scattered throughout the world, their biological or spiritual descendants have come down through history known as Jews.

Thus far the Bible's supposedly divine inspiration and especially its accounts of earliest times remain beyond the reach of archeological and anthropological validation. But these two sciences, along with allied disciplines,

---

* I use the word "Bible" in the Jewish sense. It is the equivalent of what Christians are accustomed to calling the Old Testament. Jews, of course, do not recognize the New Testament as being part of the Bible.

have endowed its testimony of later times with more than a little credibility. Hence the Bible can be considered a reasonably certain social and political history of the Middle East — albeit one seen from a narrow ethnological focus — from about 1000 to 100 B.C. It is, of course, the only extensive written history we have.

But as much as archeology and anthropology validate the Bible, the Bible serves to confound the theories of these sciences (the most popular ones are described in Chapter 1) vis-à-vis the emergence of various civilizations and cultures in the Middle East. You will recall that the conventional anthropological wisdom holds that the Fertile Crescent was populated by succeeding waves of migrant tribes issuing from the Arabian peninsula, perhaps encountering and intermingling with cultures possibly already established in Egypt and Mesopotamia, perhaps not. Among these tribes were supposed to have been the Hebrews, who (the theory goes) invaded the land of the earlier established Canaanites about 1500 B.C. and gained a foothold there. Again, evidence to support the theory is provided by the fact that, as I have mentioned, the word "Hebrew" derives from the Semitic *'abar*, which means "to pass." From this root (as we have also seen) came the word *"aribi,"* which in ancient Middle Eastern times referred to the nomadic camel-herding tribes that had come from the Arabian peninsula. Thus among anthropologists it has long been popularly supposed that the Hebrews were simply another of those nomadic tribes drifting north from the Arabian desert — "passers-through" — who by dint of settlement in a fertile region transformed themselves over a period of generations into an agrarian society.

This theory retains an agreeable symmetry until it is held up against biblical accounts about the life of the Hebrews. The Bible provides no indication whatsoever that the Hebrews were ever desert nomads, or that they even came out of Arabia. Indeed, evidence for the contention that they were not nomads can be readily deduced from the way the Bible recounts their enforced sojourn in the Sinai desert, purported to be the time and place of the birth of their formal religion, Judaism.

The Hebrews' sojourn in the desert while traveling from Egypt to Canaan was, according to the biblical account, their most terrifying ordeal as a people — even more terrifying than their prior servitude in Egypt. The reason it was such an ordeal could have been because they simply weren't accustomed to the desert. It is logical to assume that had they had their origins in the Arabian desert only a century or two before, as the popular anthropological theory contends, they should not have found it such a travail.

The explicit descriptions of the Hebrews' inability to exist in the desert, suggesting a lack of any nomadic background, are buttressed by internal evidence from the Bible. It shows even more graphically that within their memory the Hebrews were never anything but a sedentary people. If the Bible is compared to classical Arabic literature — which, like much of the Bible, was actually written down generations later by a people remembering its mythological past — the Arabic tales, even in recall, show unmistakable evidence of a desert existence. Everything in the language — metaphors, similes, themes, indeed the actual vocabulary — is redolent of the nomadic desert life of the authors' Arabian ancestors. The Bible in contrast reveals the opposite: Its language, images and conceits are wholly reflective of a life of farming and animal husbandry — a basically sedentary life.

So, then, who were the Hebrews if not tribal nomads from Arabia? And where did they originate, these people whose descendants claim legitimate primacy over a sliver of embattled land in the modern Middle East?

Unfortunately, all we have to go on, aside from anthropological theory, is the Hebrews' own elliptical account, as written down by their descendants centuries — perhaps even a millennium or more — after the fact.

It begins, of course, in Genesis with the creation of the world by a single, omnipotent, judgmental God. For that reason it is impossible to determine at what point in the account, if any, that which is largely mythological ends and that which is factual begins.* For our purposes we should remember that the narrative was written not for the edification of the rest of the known world at the time but for the promotion of a sense of cohesiveness, commonality and singularity within the people from whom it emanated and to whom it was directed.

* When I say this I am in no way unmindful of the fact that for well over two thousand years hundreds of millions of people have derived their spiritual sustenance from faith and belief, both personal and institutionalized, in various interpretations of what I choose to call the Bible's mythological content; and that hundreds of millions still do. It is certainly not my desire in this book to condescend to or in any other way offend the individual reader's religious faith or lack thereof. But to write from a particular religious or theological point of view would be tantamount to excluding or minimizing the worth of other points of view, religious and otherwise, and would automatically mar the objectivity I am trying to achieve. What I wish to do in these pages is to deal in at least minimally verifiable history. Thus, that which is not minimally verifiable falls in my view into the category of mythological history. Although my particular personal views on the matter cannot help but emerge as the book progresses, it is not my intention to attempt to proselytize the reader in my beliefs. Therefore I have no interest in denying the existence of God, or affirming it. As we shall see, the *notion* of God and all that flows from it play a primary role throughout the evolution of the Middle East. The question of whether God exists or not is largely irrelevant.

The Bible tells us that the founding ancestor of the Hebrews was a Mesopotamian named Abram, born and raised in the city of Ur, which was close to the northern Arabian desert in the southern part of Mesopotamia. Ur was a large city of its time, a junction of trade routes that stretched from the Mediterranean across the northern desert into Asia. It was a religious center as well. It was dominated by a large temple devoted to the worship of the moon god; numerous shrines devoted to other gods were also conspicuous.

About 2000 B.C., when Abram was a grown man, his father Terah decided to move out of Ur. He took the family northwest along the Euphrates until they came to the even more flourishing city of Haran, at the top of the Fertile Crescent. Haran was the center of moon-god worship as well as a hub of the rich caravan trade. Terah settled his family there and became wealthy. In time he died, leaving Abram in charge of the family.

Some time later, for reasons the Bible never makes clear, Abram received a revelation in the form of a voice speaking to him from above and beyond. The voice said:

Get thee out of thy country, and from thy kindred, and from thy father's house, unto a land that I will shew thee:

And I will make of thee a great nation, and I will bless thee, and make thy name great; and be thou a blessing:

And I will bless them that bless thee, and him that curseth thee will I curse: and in thee shall all the families of the earth be blessed. (Genesis xii, 1–3).

Abram perceived this command as coming from the voice of God. Not *a* god, but God. The civilizations of the Middle East had created dozens of regional religions, but all were dominated by the worship of many gods — human, animal, planetary, geographical and so on. To each god was attributed a particular role in the scheme of things. Each was responsible for certain events the causes of which could not otherwise be explained, and within three different regional religions there might be three different gods that accounted for what was essentially the same phenomenon. (Thus, in Babylon the moon governed the fortunes of the crops, while in southern Arabia it was the caps of the waves off the coast and in Canaan the snakes of the desert that bore the responsibility.) By Abram's time the more sophisticated Sumerians of Mesopotamia had reduced their principal gods to three: Anu (Heaven), Ea (Abyss) and Bel (Earth). The Mesopotamians believed that their kings or rulers were agents of the gods. The ancient Egyptians, on the other hand, believed their kings were gods incarnate whose divine power was not to be challenged.*

Although the Egyptians worshiped many gods, by about 2000 B.C. — the time of Abram's revelation — they had firmly developed the notion of a single God that reigned above all the others. This God, the Eternal God, was unknown and invisible to man except as perceived through his creative powers and superior will. In their sacred *Book of the Dead* it was written that "man does not know the name of God," and in the "Hymn of Amon" (Amon, meaning "hidden one," being the God of gods of the Thebians of Egypt) that "the name of God is unknown to the people." These statements suggest that the Egyptians believed in an omniscient, omnipotent supreme being about which a mere human could not possibly hope to learn until he passed on into eternity. An inscription found in the Pyramids of Onas, built about 1800 B.C., states that "the Creator is above and beyond our human power of perception." Before praying for wisdom or advice, the supplicant prefaced the prayer with: "Oh Almighty God, Master of the Heavens and the Earth, Creator of All, My God and Maker, please illuminate my sight, grant me the wisdom to grasp your glory and permit my ears to comprehend your message." At the core of the Egyptians' religious beliefs, then, was a monotheistic concept.

Too, their God of gods was a judgmental one. The Egyptians also believed that the soul never died, but rather lived on in eternity and would one day be called to account for its life on earth. The deceased would be rewarded for his good behavior or punished according to the severity of his nongood conduct. On the final day of judgment, all forms of accepted social and moral behavior would be part of the person's final defense. As one stood before the deciding Court of Osiris, one would be evaluated by the Forty Judges and make the following oath:

Oh, my God, here I stand before you living in truth. I was not unjust towards anyone. I did not break any promise or swear. Neither did I desire my neighbor's wife, nor another's money. I did not lie, nor disobey the divine commandments. I tried not to harm any slave or master, nor cause anyone to go hungry, to cry, or to kill, nor did I incite another to commit murder. I did not betray anyone, steal, or take anything which I did not rightfully earn. I respected the dead, did not violate the

---

* This difference in approach perhaps accounts for the fact that the development of Egyptian culture was relatively stable, whereas the Mesopotamian civilization had many upheavals, often causing one group of people to fade out of existence entirely, enabling others to become more prominent until they too were challenged by newer groups.

pure, did not sell wheat for a greater profit than was otherwise permitted by the law of the land, nor cheat anyone in its weight. I did not disobey the orders for land irrigation, nor destroy anything that was planted in the soil. I did not snuff the burning candles from the temples, other public buildings, or from the streets, nor did I disturb any religious gathering. I did not prevent animals from grazing and have always respected truth and justice. I did not exact of any worker more than was expected of him, nor speak against anyone not in my presence. I have always respected my priest and have striven to do as many good deeds as possible, within my power. I have given food to the hungry, water to the thirsty, clothing to the naked and provided shelter to strangers. I have been a father to those who were fatherless, an aid for the widowed, an eye for the blind, an ear for the deaf, a tongue for the mute, an arm for the limbless. I was a rod for the old to depend upon, and a refuge for the miserable.

This oath is, of course, an English vulgarization that has come down to us from the earliest Egyptian mythologies, but it reflects the ideals of the social ethics that prevailed during the existence of the ancient Egyptian societies. The similarity between the oath's moral imperatives and those of the Ten Commandments, which appeared at a much later time, are so obvious that they need no further attention drawn to them.

There were several distinct societies in ancient Egypt, with several distinct versions of the one basic evolving religion of the land. One of the earliest societies known to us was that which lived at Ain Shams, at the head of the Nile delta near today's Cairo. It is quite probable that Ain Shams was the birthplace of the monotheistic concept that eventually infused Egyptian religious practice. It appears that the people who originally inhabited the place (some time about 4000 B.C., as has best been determined) believed, in trying to understand the existence of the world around them, that in the beginning there was only a great mass of darkness and a great mass of water, in between which there was space. They called space No, and decided that an Eternal God inhabited it. This God created the universe and organized it, particularly extracting the land from the water and the sky from the darkness. He then caused himself to appear in many forms (whence the ancient belief that God exists in everything), the foremost of which was the sun. This all-powerful God was thus called Ra, which meant "sun" in the ancient language. By so naming the creator, they did not mean to assert that God was the sun itself; they merely saw the sun as the foremost symbol of God's power.* To them, God was the Creator of all life. Without him, life could

* Accordingly, they named their community Ain Shams, which meant "Well of the Sun."

not exist. In this sense, then, God was accepted as the abstract Supreme Being behind all creation.

But the nature of the times and the traditions of the people were such that the existence of a single, abstract God without any visible personal relationship to them was inconceivable. Whether the society of Ain Shams worked up from the original tribal worship of numerous gods to the concept of a single God or worked down from the original concept of a single God to the worship of numerous gods is unclear, but given the times and the traditions it would be safe to assume that it was the former. How, then, to explain the existing gods — gods who had been the objects of worship long before the realization of a single God?

The explanation was simple: God, the Creator of all things, had created the intermediate gods — again, as symbols of his power and presence. From this explanation flowed an extensive and complex theology in which the multiplicity of earlier gods was condensed into eight. Four were male and four were female, and the eight were grouped or married into four pairs.* Some took human form, some animal, some combinations of both. But all were considered expressions of the One God; they represented various aspects of his nature.

Next to God himself, the most important god was Osiris. Whereas the other gods represented various visible expressions of the One God's creative will (for instance, Tefnut represented fire and heat, without which life could not be sustained; Geb symbolized the earth; Seth encompassed the desert and the sandstorms which plagued the area), Osiris symbolized eternity. It was Osiris to whom God assigned the task of judgment over the souls who passed from the earth. Thus the symbol of Osiris was worshiped with the most reverence and fervency.

The people of Memphis, a few miles upriver from Ain Shams, were also basically monotheistic. They named their prime God "Ptah." The people of Hermopolis called their God "Thoth" and introduced the notion of divine determinism in all things. The people of Thebes, in the Upper Nile valley to the south, called their God "Amon," but reduced the nine symbols of his nature devised at Ain Shams to three: Amon-Mott-Khonshu. These three gods constituted one Almighty God who manifested himself in three distinctive characteristics but as a single unity.

* Shu and Tefnut, Geb and Nut, Osiris and Isis, and Seth and Nephthys — male and female respectively. The original God, being the most powerful and the originator of all life, required no association with other gods and thus remained separate and apart from all the others. His all-encompassing nature, however, made Him the ninth god.

So it was, then, that by about 2000 B.C. — the time of Abram's revelation in the northern Mesopotamian city of Haran — the concept of a single judgmental God as the creator of all things had probably spread well across the land of the Fertile Crescent. Two thousand years of trade and traffic between Egypt and Mesopotamia (where notions of heaven and hell had taken form within the concept of the tripartite God of the Sumerians) could not have helped but disseminate and integrate the various established and evolving religious interpretations of existence of the different regions. Nor could it have helped but generate exciting new ideas — whether through visionary experience or rational thought processes.

The Bible tells us that Abram heeded the revelation he received. He and his nephew Lot gathered up families, servants and possessions and set out to the southwest, undoubtedly following a well-traveled trade route toward Egypt. After some time they found themselves in the land of the Canaanites, midway between Mesopotamia and Egypt. While passing through, Abram is said to have had another revelation, which came in the following form: "Unto thy seed will I give this land" (Genesis xii, 7).

Since the fertile lands of the area were already well inhabited by the Canaanites, Abram and his small family of travelers were forced into the arid, hilly country of the South, known as the Negeb. There was little in the way of sustenance here, however, as a drought was on the land, so the band struck its tents and moved on across Sinai into the fertile valley of the Nile — Egypt. Settling there, the aged Abram* became very rich in cattle, silver and gold, while Lot acquired wealth in flocks and tents.

Upon relief of the drought some years later Abram, Lot and their group returned to Canaan and settled near the oasis town of Bethel. They continued to prosper with their sheep and cattle, but their herds grew so large that it soon became evident that there was not enough land to sustain them. Thereupon Abram and Lot decided to split up. Lot moved his people and herds eastward across the Jordan River to the city of Sodom while Abram remained at Bethel.

Years passed. Abram continued to receive visits from God along with reassurances of divine rewards, provided he remain righteous and heed the word of the Lord at all times.

Abram had everything but a child — his wife Sarai was evidently barren — and this was what he desired most. He requested such a blessing

---

* Abram is said to have been in his late seventies when he passed through Canaan. This was in the days when men were said to live for hundreds of years.

from God, decrying the possibility of having no blood heir and having to pass his inheritance on to one of the faithful servants born in his house. God responded enigmatically:

> This shall not be thine heir; but he that shall come forth out of thine own bowels shall be thine heir.
> . . . Look now toward heaven, and tell the stars, if thou be able to number them . . . : So shall thy seed be.
> . . . Unto thy seed have I given this land, from the river of Egypt unto the great river, the river Euphrates (Genesis xv, 4–18).

Still no child appeared. Finally Sarai suggested that her husband couple with her favorite handmaiden, a woman they had picked up in Egypt named Hagar. Abram did so and Hagar produced a son whom Abram, at the behest of God, named Ishmael.

But Ishmael was not to be Abram's heir. When Abram was ninety-nine years old God again made an appearance and declared that the time had come for the two to make a covenant. First God ordered Abram to change his name to Abraham, Sarai, hers to Sarah. Then said the Lord:

> And I will give unto thee, and to thy seed after thee, the land wherein thou art a stranger, all the land of Canaan, for an everlasting possession; and I will be their God. . . .
> And I will bless her [Sarah], and give thee a son also of her . . . and she shall be a *mother* of nations. . . . and thou shalt call his name Isaac: and I will establish my covenant with him for an everlasting covenant, *and* with his seed after him (Genesis xvii, 8–19).

Thus, with the birth of Isaac, was the line of succession in this unique birthright established. Abraham had obviously been "chosen" by the Lord to be the human patriarch of the one true nation of the one and only True God. God warned that the times ahead would often be difficult. But he promised that the rewards of their faith in and obedience to him — the keeping of their covenant — would be plentiful. They would not only gain the rightful ownership of all the land he had promised, but would enjoy health, prosperity and favorable treatment in eternity.

There followed centuries of adventure and misadventure — through Isaac; through his sons Jacob and Esau (Jacob becoming heir to Isaac); and through Jacob's twelve sons,* particularly Joseph, who was sold into slavery in Egypt by his brothers but who rose to become a powerful and well thought of ruler under the Pharaoh there. The forgiving Joseph eventually brought his father and family — numbering now no more than seventy — out of once-again drought-stricken Canaan to Egypt. The Israelites, including Joseph and his Egyptian family, settled in Goshen, multiplied exceedingly over several hundred years, and prospered under the friendly Pharaohs. The families of each of Jacob's (Israel's) twelve sons developed into separate tribes that were held together by the covenant between God and Abraham.

Eventually there arose a new Pharaoh over Egypt who had not known of Joseph's friendly relationship with former kings. He disliked the idea of all these foreign people, with their strange ideas about God and their different language, in his land. It seemed to him that soon there would be more Israelites than Egyptians in the land of Egypt. He needed their labor but did not want their numbers to increase, so he delivered them into slavery and ordered certain genocidal measures — namely, that every future son born to the Israelites be drowned in the Nile.

There was a woman of the tribe of Levi who had already given birth to a son, Aaron, and a daughter, Miriam. Now she gave birth to another son, and when the Pharaoh's soldiers came looking for newborn Israelite males to take to the river she hid the infant in the reeds bordering the stream. There the child was discovered by a daughter of the Pharaoh, who named him Moses and raised him in the palace as though he were a royal prince.

Moses grew up knowing he had been born of the tribe of Levi. From the Egyptians he learned much of the arts and sciences unknown to the Hebrew-speaking Israelites, but he never forgot who his people were. Although living in luxury, every instinct told him he was one of the children of Israel — those simple farmers and husbandrymen now toiling relentlessly in servitude to his benefactor the Pharaoh — whose God was the only True God.

---

* It was during the time of Jacob that God appeared again to repeat the promises made to his grandfather Abraham and father Isaac, that from them and from Jacob would come a people to whom the land of Canaan would everlastingly belong. Then God said, "Thy name shall be called no more Jacob, but Israel: for as a prince hast thou power with God . . ." (Genesis xxxii, 28). Thus the twelve sons of Jacob — indeed the entire group of people living under Jacob's rule — were to become known as the "children of Israel," and eventually, the Israelites. The twelve sons were Reuben, Simeon, Levi, Judah, Issachar, Zebulun, Gad, Asher, Dan, Naphtali, Joseph and Benjamin. Each was to establish his own family, giving birth to the "twelve tribes of Israel."

As he grew to manhood he would often leave the palace to circulate among his own people. On one occasion he saw an Egyptian overseer beating an Israelite slave. Moses reacted instinctively, forgetting his years of regal upbringing. He killed the overseer and hid his body in the sand.

But word got out, and the Pharaoh ordered Moses arrested and put to death. Moses fled Egypt and traveled deep into the wilderness for refuge. There, at an oasis, he met a group of sheep-herding Midianites. He was invited to stay with one of the group's families, that of a man named Jethro. Not only did he accept the invitation, he married one of Jethro's daughters — Zipporah — and sired two sons.

Although Moses, a man of culture, lived as a simple shepherd far away from Egypt for many years, he never forgot the enslaved and beleaguered Israelites. Neither did their God. The Lord heard the agony of their cries and saw their dreadful burden. He remembered his covenant with Abraham, with Isaac, and with Jacob, and he resolved to set his people free and get them back to the promised land of Canaan.

A man would have to be found who was capable of leading them. Moses, a man of the tribe of Levi and one who knew both the Israelites and the Egyptians well, might be such a leader. Thus one day did Moses, still in the wilderness, lead his flock to the far side of the desert in search of greener pastures. As he grazed his flock at the foot of a mountain called Horeb he was astonished to see a nearby bush burst into flame and to continue burning without dwindling to ash. With fearful curiosity Moses approached the fiery shrub and was astounded to hear a voice emanate from it. It was the voice of God directing him to return to Egypt and lead the Israelites out of their bondage.

Moses did as God said. Using magical powers temporarily bestowed on him by the Lord, he managed to persuade the Pharaoh to release the Hebrews. Then he announced to them, invoking the name of their God, that he had been sent to lead them back to the promised land of Canaan. The Israelites — there were six hundred thousand of them now — were doubtful, but they consented.

It was a terrible, seemingly never-ending journey through the bone-dry wilderness, and the people turned into a complaining, squabbling mob that constantly threatened to mutiny. Only a succession of miracles, demanded of the Lord by Moses at the direst times, managed to keep them together.

In the third month of their journey they came to the place where Moses had earlier seen the burning bush and received his command from God. Here again God spoke. He put on a display of trumpets, flame and earthquake on Mount Horeb to show the multitude of Israelites that he was watching over them and would continue to do so provided they kept the covenant. The people were convinced. Then the Lord summoned Moses to the mountaintop. There he delivered to him ten commandments and a code of lesser rituals, rules and laws that the Israelites would thereafter be absolutely required to follow in the course of their daily lives and in the observance of their religious ceremonies — *if* they wished to keep the covenant. God also told Moses to inform the people that as a reward for their righteous observance of his laws he would lead them into the land of Canaan and gradually drive out all its inhabitants until all the land belonged to them. He added, "And I will set thy bounds from the Red Sea even unto the sea of the Philistines, and from the desert unto the river: for I will deliver the inhabitants of the land into your hand; and thou shalt drive them out before thee" (Exodus xxiii, 31).

Once Moses had conveyed all this information to the people an altar was built to the Lord and the blood of slain oxen was sprinkled upon it, then upon the people. In this way the covenant was sealed for all time. Thereafter a tabernacle was constructed, according to the Lord's directions, which the Israelites would be required to carry to Canaan so "that I may dwell among them" (Exodus xxv, 8). And an ark, also to be borne with them, which would contain "the testimony which I shall give thee" (Exodus xxv, 16).

Out of all this emanated the formal religion of the Israelites. Whereas before the One True God had spoken only to Abraham and a handful of his descendants, now he made himself apparent to all the Israelites, demonstrating through displays of fire, smoke, and tremor his awesome power, his capacity for both jealous malevolence and loving benevolence. Struck with a hypnotic sense of their own chosenness and an awareness of their corporate identity, the Israelites set out from Mount Horeb (now Sinai, "Mountain of God") for Canaan, following the cloud that rose up over the tabernacle and drifted northeastward — showing them the way in accordance with God's promise. However, their chosenness did not save them from further troubles. When they reached the southern border of Canaan, Moses sent out scouts from each of the tribes to reconnoiter the land ahead. The scouts returned in forty days with reports of richly fertile valleys and flowing wells — truly a land of milk and honey. But the land was thoroughly inhabited, and the inhabitants were fierce warriors of gigantic size. It would be suicide to attempt to enter — despite God's promises to drive them out.

While the Israelites debated the matter, God made another appearance.

He chastised them for doubting and disobeying him. But instead of destroying or disinheriting them, he sentenced them to a long life of continued existence in the wilderness — until all who doubted him had died. Only then would they be given another chance to enter the Promised Land.

So they wandered again in hardship through the wilderness. By the time forty years had passed they were encamped east of the Jordan River, facing Canaan and the valley of Jericho. Of all the doubters, only Moses still lived. Now he died and was buried in Moab. His military adviser Joshua succeeded him as leader of the Israelites, who were now ready to enter Canaan. When Joshua gave the word to advance and cross the Jordan, the priests bearing the Ark of the Covenant went first. When the feet of the priests bearing the Ark dipped into water at the Jordan's edge, the river divided and all the Israelites walked across on the dry streambed. The Children of Israel had at last arrived in the Promised Land, the land that the One True God had bequeathed to their fathers five centuries before.

They moved inland a short distance and established a new camp, with the Tabernacle and the Ark in the center and the tents of the various tribes around them. They called the place Gilgal. From there they continued on and laid siege to the strong-walled city of Jericho, which they eventually captured and destroyed.

Joshua now moved rapidly, attacking one place after another in quick succession — north, south, westward — until soon the Israelites were settled in the central part of Canaan and the beginnings of the land of Israel began to take form.

There followed a temporary respite from battle while Joshua parceled out the so far conquered part of Canaan among the tribes, according to a plan devised by Moses. The area around Jebus (soon to be Jerusalem) went to the tribe of Judah, with the tribe of Simeon getting the lands to the south. The lands immediately north of Jebus, extending westward from the Jordan, were divided between the tribes of Ephraim, Benjamin and Manasseh. Farther north, and east across the Jordan, the land was apportioned among the other tribes. The community of Israel was now solidly entrenched in the central highlands, but the Canaanites, Philistines and Phoenicians still retained control of the fertile lowlands along the Mediterranean coast.

There was no unity or central authority among the Israelites. It was the time of the Judges, about 1100 B.C. Each tribe was ruled by a "judge" who had won temporary leadership through military prowess in battle. Each tribe fought for itself against the natives in its immediate vicinity, and at times even against its fellow tribes in territorial disputes. It was an era of great lawlessness and turning away from the One True God. The Bible repeatedly tells us: "And the people of Israel again did what was evil in the sight of the Lord" (Judges). In fact, the Book of Judges' final summarizing verse for the entire history of the period is: "In those days *there was* no king in Israel; every man did *that which was* right in his own eyes" (xxi, 25).

In time, though, the constant fear of attack from the natives along the borders forced the tribes of the Israelites to unite. The elders of the tribes asked the prophet Samuel to appoint a king to direct them. After soliciting the advice of God, Samuel chose a young man from the tribe of Benjamin just north of the town of Jebus. His name was Saul.

The Bible here reaches the point at which the Israelites enter the light of secular history. Thus far the account has been a rich compound of fable, legend, miracle and folk history. Up to the point at which they entered Canaan, we have no way of knowing whether any of the events recounted actually occurred.* Indeed, we do not even know with certainty that the Israelites entered by crossing the Jordan in the vast numbers attributed to them.

What we do know from the findings of archeology and the fragmentary records of other cultures in the region is that by about 1000 B.C. the Israelites were established in the central part of Canaan and that they were surrounded by the Canaanites, the Phoenicians, the Hittites, the Aramaeans, the Ammonites, the Moabites and the Edomites. Since these were all probably societies which had evolved from the nomadic tribes that had earlier migrated north from the Arabian peninsula, it is logical to assume that the anthropologists are right: that the Israelites also evolved from an Arabian tribe that spoke a particular variant of the Semitic language called Hebrew; that they were latecomers in the two-thousand-year wave of successive migrations, and that they carved out a space for themselves in the already crowded land between the Mediterranean and the Jordan by force.

Yet concerning the origins of the Hebrews there is still the testimony of the Bible to consider, as farfetched as it might seem to many. Was there ever such a man as Abram (Abraham) who came out of Mesopotamia with his family and servants to found a people that came to be known as the Israelites? It is a question that defies a definitive answer; nevertheless it is a question that is central to the entire development of the Middle East, for the legend of

---

* Again, I defer to the sensibilities of those readers who equate faith or belief with knowledge.

Abraham and his sons was the firmament out of which the dominant culture of the area evolved and on which it rests today. I refer, of course, to the Arab culture.

If we take the story of Abraham to have at least a kernel of factuality and couple it with the theories of the anthropologists, it would not be beyond reasonable hypothesis to assume that he — or more likely his ancestors — was a member of one of the early Arabian tribes that emigrated to Mesopotamia around 2500 B.C. There, in the fertile lands and prosperous Sumerian cities along the Euphrates, the tribe could easily have assimilated itself at least partially into the extant farming and mercantile cultures, retaining much of its nomadic character while at the same time accumulating skills in agriculture and commerce. It could just as easily have become infused with notions about the gods and God — notions that were flowing back and forth across the Middle East along the paths of the caravan routes. Compelled finally to leave Mesopotamia for one or more of any number of possible reasons, Abraham (or a man like him, more likely even a group) might have drifted westward in search of land, commerce, whatever. This would have occurred sometime about 1500 B.C. In their westward wanderings the man and his family (or group or small tribe) might well have encountered another large tribe of Hebrew-speaking nomads drifting north out of Arabia, part of the general migratory wave of the time. The two groups might have joined forces. They might well have wandered around in the desert for several generations, integrating, multiplying, exchanging skills, ideas and knowledge, melding into one people — the worldly Mesopotamian religious ideas imposing themselves on the more primitive ritualism of the Hebrews to produce an entirely new tribal conception of the nature of the world's divinity. Fortified by its own righteous cause, this enlarged people, made up by now of several tribes (which would have been consistent with and very much in the manner of ancient Arabian nomadic societies), might then have set its sights on the promising land of Canaan and said to itself, in effect: "We shall make this land ours."

What occurred thereafter, in this very general panoply, can be reasonably verified by secular history. The Hebrews invaded Canaan, conquered its richest central region, and established themselves there as the "children," or possibly "soldiers," of God — the Israelites. At first they named the land Judah, after the tribe that took possession of its centermost area around the settlement of Jebus, where the Jebusites, an offshoot of the Canaanites, lived.

Whatever the precise geographic origins of the Hebrews-Israelites-Judaeans, it is certain that they were a people indigenous to the region. They were surely biologically heterogeneous, as all the evolving migrating peoples of the region were, and they were certainly Semitic in their culture, language and customs. They most probably had a distant nomadic warrior tribal past that was transformed into a sedentary agrarian and mercantile present over the generations leading up to the time the biblical narratives were written. The only thing that would seem to have distinguished them from the other peoples of the area was their religious beliefs and rituals. And even at that, their beliefs were not that much different from those of the Egyptians or the Babylonians in Mesopotamia; it was their ritualistic expressions that were different.

Saul became the first king of the Israelites.* Under his reign the people renewed their war against the surrounding peoples. He was followed by King David, who continued the Israelite expansion. One of David's first acts as ruler was to capture the stronghold of the Jebusites. He renamed it Jerusalem and made it the capital city of the kingdom. David's armies then drove back and conquered many of the Canaanite tribes still holding out on the borders, and extended the boundaries of Judah until he held sway from the Mediterranean on the west to the deserts beyond the Jordan in the east, from the Red Sea in the south to the Euphrates valley in the north.

The third king was Solomon, David's son. Solomon was a great builder and was apparently obsessed with becoming a glorious ruler whose splendor might rival that of Egypt and Babylonia. First he constructed a series of fortresses to protect his frontiers. Then he turned his efforts to building a magnificent palace for himself, as well as a temple through which he could demonstrate his devotion to the God of Israel.

Solomon's kingdom lasted until about 900 B.C. He had a large standing army which necessitated the building of living quarters for them and roads to move them. To do all this he had to resort to forced labor and even slavery to provide the hundreds of thousands of men needed for the work. The cost of this construction was enormous. It put a tremendous burden on the morale of the people, a burden so great that it brought them to the verge of rebellion. As it was, after Solomon died the great structure of the unified kingdom he thought he had been enlarging and strengthening collapsed.

Solomon's son Rehoboam was crowned in Jerusalem as the new king.

* Since we are now into secular history, I shall relate the balance of this chapter's account of Jewish history in a secular as well as biblical context, leaving out the workings of God.

However, a rebellious spirit continued to burn within the masses. The discontent especially infected the northern tribes, who by now were deeply suspicious of any king from the south, since Solomon had imposed great hardship on the people through his lavish extravagances and his insistence on forced labor. So, in about 850 B.C., the northern tribes called in one of their number — Jeroboam — and crowned him as their king in the regional center of Shechem. Thus did the north, now called the Kingdom of Israel, split off from the south, which remained the adumbrated Kingdom of Judah.

Relations between the two Hebrew kingdoms were not very amicable. They occasionally joined in actions against a common enemy but at other times fought against each other. Against attempts by Judah to recover the north, Israel eventually moved its capital from Shechem to Samaria, high on a hilltop overlooking a broad plain in the center of the kingdom. Here Israel built a stronghold which made a good defense for the protection of its capital — just as Jerusalem, located on the hill of the Jebusites, was impregnable to the foes of the Kingdom of Judah.

Israel and Judah were unable to build a united front against their enemies, since they were too preoccupied with protecting their respective territories from the other. For about a century and a half the northern kingdom of Israel had a series of rulers most of whom ascended the throne after murdering their predecessors. Civil war kept the government in a constant state of upheaval, and the hostile neighboring peoples were always a threat. Moreover, the Middle East had entered the period in which the Egyptians in the west and the succeeding kingdoms of Mesopotamia in the east were beginning to vie with each other over control of the region's riches and trade routes. Thus, in about 722 B.C. the king of Assyria, in northern Mesopotamia, sent his armies westward. Coming upon the demoralized and disorganized Kingdom of Israel, the Assyrians besieged its capital (Samaria), captured it, and carried most of its inhabitants back to Nineveh in Assyria as captives and slaves.*

The Kingdom of Judah survived, but only for a while. After a hundred years the power of the Assyrians waned while that of Babylon, in southern Mesopotamia, increased. The kings of Babylon, one after the other, reached out and conquered Assyria, thereby gaining control over all of Mesopotamia. They then turned their ambitions westward.

King Nebuchadnezzar of Babylon wanted exclusive control over the routes to Egypt so that he one day might send his armies there to conquer it. The

---

* From their Assyrian captivity the Israelites would never return. According to the Bible, their permanent exile was God's punishment for having forsaken him and broken the Covenant.

principal routes crossed the Kingdom of Judah, then ran along the Mediterranean coast of Sinai before fanning out into the Nile valley. So the first order of business would be to capture Judah.

Nebuchadnezzar's Babylonian armies seized Judah and its capital at Jerusalem in 586 B.C. They despoiled the massive Temple of Solomon, tore down the city wall, and carried away the royal family and thousands of ordinary citizens as prisoners of war to Babylon. Only a scattering of Hebrews remained.

From the religious point of view the historical significance of the establishment of the two small Hebrew kingdoms lay in the development of the prophetic and priestly movement which took place between about 850 and 500 B.C. The movement grew out of a fierce concern over the contradictions between, on the one side, the material excesses and preoccupations of the "Children of God," and on the other, the spirit and letter of the Covenant. Those Israelites, originally the majority, who had been indifferent in religious matters, or had even gone so far as to tolerate the practice of heathen religions, lost their influence in the councils of the bipartite Hebrew world upon the fall of the northern kingdom. Thenceforth, using the fall of the Israelites as an object lesson, the elders of the Kingdom of Judah took it upon themselves to reestablish and recodify the religious principles that had come down by way of fragment and folklore through the many generations since the Hebrews crossed into Canaan. Out of this movement developed the establishment, through the writing down and painstaking literary elaboration of these principles — the Bible — of the monotheistic religion that would become the fountainhead of Judaism,* Christianity and Islam.

From the secular point of view, the historical significance of the two Hebrew kingdoms arose from their suppression. For the fall of Israel in 722, and that of Judah in 586, resulted in the establishment and then the enlargement of Hebrew settlements in Babylonia which were the forerunners of similar settlements in every part of the world. With the passage of time the exiled Hebrews found themselves very much at home in Babylonia (some of their descendants have remained there to the present day — in Iraq, in Syria). In prosperous and civilized surroundings, forced exile became willing residence. The Hebrew community increased enormously. They colonized en-

---

* The term "Judaism" derives from the fact that it was the citizens of the Kingdom of Judah — the Judaeans — and their descendants in exile who were largely responsible for giving the religion its form. The term "Jew" derives, of course, from "Judaean."

tire districts, farming the land and engaging freely in every sort of occupation. Individuals rose to high positions in the service of the government.
Nevertheless the Jews (as we shall now call them), although prospering and
well assimilated, did not stop thinking of Jerusalem. Some thought of it only
with sentimental nostalgia. But others, taking part in the ongoing codification
of their relgion's rules, laws and dogmas, thought of it with definite longing
and aspiration. It was their religious center and their homeland. "How," they
lamented, "shall we sing the Lord's song in a strange land?"

About fifty years after the fall of Jerusalem the power of the Babylonian
kings waned and was replaced by the rising might of the Persians in the east.
Under the emperorship of Cyrus, the Persians began to expand westward
with the intention of gaining control of the Fertile Crescent and its riches.
The armies of Cyrus conquered Babylon. Soon Persia had control over all
the land formerly ruled by the Babylonians — including the tiny remnants
of the Kingdoms of Judah and Israel centered around Jerusalem and Samaria.

The Persians were friendly toward the Jews of Babylonia. The militant
keepers of the faith among the exiles from Judah petitioned Cyrus for permission to return to Jerusalem. The Persian emperor agreed. However, when he
issued an edict granting such permission, only a small number responded.
Many of the Jews had married and established homes in exile. Many had
been born in Babylonia; the land of their elders was but a faint memory.
Many enjoyed unprecedented prosperity and security, and few wished to
abandon these advantages. They were more interested in the present than the
past.

Those few who did return to Judah took with them the holy vessels
Nebuchadnezzar had confiscated from the temple at Jerusalem. If, back in
Babylon, the exiles had had glorious dreams of rebuilding their kingdom,
those dreams were rudely shattered by the conditions they faced upon their
return. After the usual difficult journey back across the desert, the outlook in
their homeland was bleak and forlorn. The land of Judah (soon to be Judaea)
was inhabited by a conglomeration of the few poor Jews left over from the
Babylonian conquest, exiled Babylonians, people from surrounding societies
who had moved in to fill the vacuum left by the Jews' departure, and Arabian
nomads who serviced the caravan trade. Jerusalem was a heap of ruins. The
fields about, choked with weeds and rubbish, had to be cleared before they
could be tilled. Clearly, the returning exiles would be in a constant struggle
merely to keep themselves alive.

But they burned with the fury of righteousness and divine redemption. Over a period of time more exiles returned, and soon the rebuilding was underway. After nearly a century a new temple was erected, the walls of the city reconstructed, the fields made arable again, and the Jews had at least a semblance of a community of their own once more.

The new settlement was very limited in area, considerably smaller even than the original Kingdom of Judah. Centered in Jerusalem — by now a cosmopolitan city — it was little more than twenty by thirty miles in size. But as time passed it became the stronghold of a by now strict, highly orthodox religious faith and practice.

Judaea was a nation only in the religious sense. It was by no means exclusively Jewish in population and culture, and politically it was merely a territory or colony of the Persian Empire. Little by little, however, the Jewish influence grew in strength, thanks to the energy and determination of such leader-priests as Ezra and Nehemiah. These figures insisted that the community in Jerusalem should be Jewish from top to bottom — in language, in religion, in culture and biology. They even compelled Jews who had married non-Jews during the laxer days of the exile to abandon their families.

The area around Samaria in the north was in the possession of descendants of the Israelite kingdom who had at least partially assimilated with the descendants of their Assyrian conquerors over several generations. In the beginning these Samaritans (as they were now known) made friendly advances to the Jews of Judaea. But because they did not recognize the religious primacy of Jerusalem their feelings were quickly changed to bitter hostility by the exclusiveness of the leaders there. The same reaction was evoked in the non-Jewish neighbors of other areas adjacent to Judaea — especially in the descendants of the Aramaeans who had mixed with those of some of the original Hebrew tribes in the far north to form the Galileans, in the descendants of the Philistines and Canaanites along the shores of the Mediterranean, and in the still largely nomadic Semites — the Aribi — of the nearby desert areas. The Jews thus formed a cultural as well as religious community. They came to be recognized by Persia as a homogenous group which administered its own internal affairs and was represented in its relations with the imperial central government by its religious chief. Inasmuch as Judaea was not, therefore, a politically independent nation, nor became one during the succeeding centuries (we are now at about 400 B.C.), its development can best be described as that of a religious and cultural Jewish homeland — national in all but political fact.

The expansion of Persia westward in alliance with Egypt brought the Greeks into the Middle East picture, as I earlier noted. About 333 B.C. Alexander the Great invaded the Persian Empire along the eastern Mediterranean coast and cut a swath across the region around Judaea. Occupying the land, Alexander allowed the Jews great liberty in their religion and ways of living. But Judaea now became a colony of Greece, and Greek settlements sprang up throughout the land of Palestine (the Greek name for the entire area, which derived from the fact that its coastal region — the Greeks' first encounter with the land — was inhabited by the Philistines, the nomadic people from the north). The result was that the Jews were constantly in touch with Greek thought and customs and came to feel at home with them. The new Greek culture seemed to many Jews more attractive than their own and they accepted and adopted much of it. This brought about the beginnings of a schism within the Jewish culture and religion, with the orthodoxy becoming polarized against the Greek-influenced liberalizing elements.

After Alexander's death the Greek Empire was divided among the Ptolemaians of Egypt, the Seleucids of Asia Minor and the Macedonians of the Greek world, and the entire Middle East became a battleground of warring interests between East and West. For a century and a half the Jewish homeland of Judaea, in the middle of Palestine, lived a relatively obscure existence while Seleucid-dominated Syria became a strong power in the north and vied with Egypt. Palestine was the bridge between the two, and their armies constantly tramped back and forth across it as each nation alternately surged toward the other. As a result many Jews were swept away on the tides, dispersing to Egypt, to Syria, to Greece, to Persia, to Arabia — either as captives or voluntarily to escape the turmoil. Others assimilated into the forming Hellenized local culture.

Antiochus Epiphanes became king of Syria in 175 B.C. and soon started a movement to forcibly complete the assimilation of the Jews. His designs met with avid resistance on the part of the orthodox Jewish leadership, so Antiochus turned to terrorism and violence with the intention of completely wiping out Judaism. He decreed Jewish laws to be invalid and ordered anyone continuing to practice them, or even possessing copies of them, to be executed. Moreover, he sought to eliminate the worship of the Jewish God — Jehovah — by substituting for it the worship of Zeus.

Many of Jerusalem's cosmopolitan Jews knuckled under to Antiochus' edicts, but outside the city, among the Jewish peasantry of the Judaean hills, insurrection smoldered.

The insurrectionary spirit broke out into armed revolt in 167 B.C. when an obscure farmer named Mattathias killed a Syrian officer after the Syrian tried to enforce heathen worship in the Judaean village of Modin, twenty miles northwest of Jerusalem. Mattathias, his sons and a group of other desperate zealots thereupon took to the mountains and commenced to wage guerrilla warfare against the occupying Syrians. They roamed the land, destroying the hated heathen altars, murdering the apostate Jews who worshiped at them, and drawing pursuing Syrian troops into ambushes in narrow mountain passes.

Mattathias soon died and was succeeded by his son Judas, who was given the additional name Maccabeus, or "the Hammerer." Under Judas the zealot Jews — the Maccabees — recovered and restored the temple in Jerusalem, which had been desecrated by Antiochus.

With the success of this operation in 165 B.C. the rebellion, originally inspired by religious motives, became increasingly political in character. The Seleucids began to loosen their hold on Palestine, and Judas and his expanding band of militants used the opportunity to establish a small independent Jewish community in Judaea. After Judas's death the Maccabees extended the territory of their state by conquest until it included Samaria and Galilee in the north, a good deal of territory south of Judaea, and a portion of the land across the Jordan. The inhabitants of the conquered lands were in many cases forcibly circumcised and in other ways persuaded to hew to orthodox Jewish law and ritual.

Before the new state had a chance to consolidate itself or settle its continuing internal problems, however, it was taken over by the Roman Empire. In 63 B.C. the legions of Rome under Pompey, wresting control of the eastern Mediterranean from the waning Greeks, invaded Syria and then swept down to control the much-coveted bridge to Egypt. Soon Palestine was completely under Roman domination, as was the small, briefly independent Maccabean Jewish nation in its midst.

The new rulers, pending the introduction of direct imperial government, formed out of Judaea a subject state. The nature of its future was highly uncertain. This caused a wave of political intrigue within the land, generously mixed with religious evangelism, as individuals and groups plotted for power and favor. The unsettled state of affairs was heightened in about 43 B.C. when an army of revived Persians suddenly descended upon Palestine and took most of it, including Jerusalem, away from the thinly dispersed Romans. It was heightened still more three years later when the Romans counterinvaded with another strong army and regained Jerusalem. With the army came a young half-Arab from Rome named Herod. Given the title "King of the Jews," he had been commissioned to represent the Roman Empire in Jerusalem.

Two schools of thought developed among the Jews about Herod during his reign. The militant orthodoxists disliked him greatly. In the first place, no non-Jew could legitimately be king of Judaea, king of the Jews. Second, he tended to give privileges to other inhabitants of the land — Phoenicians, Samaritans, Aramaeans, nomads (pagans all) — that should have remained exclusive to the Jews. Third, he was a rank tyrant who imposed crushing taxes on the people to support his mania for building.

The less-strict Jews, on the other hand, saw more in the way of benefits in Herod than vices. True, he taxed heavily, but through his building programs he was elevating Palestine to a degree of material prosperity hitherto undreamed of. He was constructing a magnificent new temple for the Jews. Perhaps he *was* diluting the exclusivity of the religious character of Judaea by putting pagans on a par with the Jews, and perhaps he *did* have a tendency to despotism that often made life difficult. But these drawbacks weighed against the increasing wealth of those Jews who showed a willingness to compromise, to coexist, were tolerable.

Out of the liberal point of view grew an increased cosmopolitanism on the part of the "advanced" Jews — indeed, a good deal of renewed assimilation took place, this time with Roman cultural values and ways. The Jewish population increased enormously in both numbers and wealth, and many of the more prosperous Jews ventured out into the world beyond Palestine to reinforce or establish equally prosperous Jewish communities in Egypt, in Persia, and in all the great cities of the Roman Empire.*

Out of the conservative viewpoint grew both a deepening religious mysticism, based on the idea of a Messiah who might one day come and release the land of Judaea from its continuing servitude to foreign tyrants, and an

---

* The extent of the outpouring from Palestine can be gleaned from St. Paul's account of his missionary journeys through the Empire less than a hundred years later, when he apparently encountered large Jewish colonies in almost every country he passed through.

intense revival of the nationalist spirit that had originally been stirred by the Maccabees a hundred years earlier.

Between the two, disaffection and alienation reigned, political and religious infighting intensified, and renewed insurrectionary tendencies showed themselves. In response, the Romans tightened their controls, which only served to exacerbate matters. Then came the man called Jesus.

# 3.

## JOURNAL: *Cairo, 1974*

ONE COULD FEEL IT coming for weeks before it happened. Encountering highly placed, well-informed Arab acquaintances in New York, in London, in the south of France, on the Costa del Sol in August and September of 1973, one would have to have been a functional idiot not to sense that something was up in the Arab world — something important. An unaccountably new element of pragmatism seemed to filter through the groaning and frustrated bombast of the Arabs with whom one conversed. Gone was the conventional wounded, outraged, suffering-servant tone when the talk turned to the Arab-Israeli situation. Gone was the demeanor of embarrassment usually evinced by Arab friends in the company of Westerners. Gone, somehow, was the shame of 1967 — the humiliation, the resignation, the pitiable and oddly sympathetic sense of impotence that had inhabited the personalities of these Arabs. A Lebanese newspaper tycoon who was on a first-name basis with every Arab head of state, a Saudi prince who had easy access to his uncle's throne room, an economist from Cairo who rubbed shoulders almost daily with the president of Egypt, a Moroccan diplomat closely related by marriage to his king, a deputy Iraqi petroleum minister — each spoke with a strangely new kind of assurance. It was not so much what they said as how they said it that caused one's ears to perk. The transformation in their voices from murmurous apology, even mournfulness, to quiet self-confidence was so sudden and out of character (or what one thought of as Arab character) that at first it seemed just another Arab quirk, symbolic of the sharpness of contradiction that exists in everything having to do with them. But then one realized that there is never any safety in ethnic cliché; one began to wonder if there wasn't something more to the transformation than met the eye. These people knew something that others — you — didn't.

I contacted some equally highly placed Israeli friends, telling of my impressions, warning that something was in the air — something I couldn't quite put my finger on but which had the vague smell of danger. I was not betraying any confidences, not transmitting privileged information, for I had received none. All I had to go on was an impression gleaned from a series of knowing Arab smiles and quiet, surprisingly modest-spoken assertions about the ultimate destiny of Israel. Plus a disturbing new component in the Arab rhetoric: genocide. As hysterical as the Arabs seemed to be able to get about Israel, they had always kept their passions on a political plane. Despite the official rhetorical bombast about driving the Jews into the sea, I had never heard an Arab express his hatred of the Israelis in terms that were other than political; their hatred was for Zionism, not Judaism; Zionists, not Jews. I had perceived little in the Arab approach that coincided with traditional Western attitudes and prejudices toward the Jews. Indeed, they had always acknowledged their common origins, and had often resorted to the "We're all Semites" disclaimer to prove that their intentions toward the Israelis were not racial. Now, however, I detected a change. Emerging was a virulent racial hatred of the Jews. It was new to the Arabs, yet perhaps its very newness made it appealing. "Hitler was right," said one acquaintance, an acquaintance no more. "The Jews cause trouble wherever they go. Most of the major problems of the world would be solved if all the Jews were wiped off the face of the earth."

My warnings to Israeli friends were scoffed at. "So what else is new?" was the consensus of response to my intimations of danger.

A week later the Egyptian army had crossed the Suez Canal and the Israelis were losing planes, tanks and men in numbers undreamt of even in their darkest nightmares.

One graphic way to experience the similarities and differences between Jews and Arabs is to fly from Lod (now called Ben-Gurion) International Airport outside Tel Aviv to Cyprus or Athens, then pick up another flight that takes you back to Cairo International. Identical are the general states of chaos that exist at both terminals when several flights are departing or arriving at the same time. So strong are the similarities that one wonders what Arab and Jew could find in one another to hate — surely the Israelis shove, shout, jostle and seek personal advantage with as much energy as the Egyptians, and with as little attention to human dignity or ethical imperative.

Once out of the airport environment, however, the differences in culture become immediately apparent, although they are not as great as is popularly believed — particularly by the large majority of the Israeli populace. The first sharp difference is reflected in the ambience of the cities you enter in similarly careening taxis. Tel Aviv is a plain, no-nonsense metropolis, a kind of mini–Los Angeles of the Middle East, a compact sprawl whose plastic architectural dullness reflects its late and hurried development and its builders' proletarian orientation. It is a city of glass and linoleum, of bungalows and boulevards as antiseptic as lines and dots on a map, redeemed only by its throbbing, excitable, thoroughly modern commercial and cultural life and its favored position by the sea.

Cairo is dramatically different. Entering it is to be sucked into an uproarious implosion of time, to encounter a people still living in the residual silts of the city's four thousand years of existence. It is a city older than any memory, than any past the Western mind can conceive; it is old beyond one's comprehension. There is a look of worn, casual slovenliness to even its finest neighborhoods — a vague, indelible grime and stain of dinginess accrued simply through the passage of so much time — that at first invariably tends to affront efficient Western sensibilities. Only in a desultory, halfhearted way does the city seem to be hauling itself — with a hectic clashing of truck gears, in a haze of gas fumes and plaster dust, through a cacophony of car horns, streetcars clanging with a dry vicious snapping of sparks under a ganglia of overhead power lines — out of the ponderous inertia of those accumulated centuries of time and custom into the modern age.

For all the din of sound crashing through the blast-furnace air of a summer's day, the people seem dazed, their interminable loud bargainings carried on with a kind of drugged, grieving, slack-jawed moan. The word "Allah," drawn out, never beginning, never ending, hangs in the air over everything like the pulsating background hum of a giant fan. With the wail of desperate, mortal, earthbound loneliness in the sunset cries of the *muezzin* from the minarets of the mosques, the people's celebrations of God are like lingering, brokenhearted howls of longing — abject, wounded, overflowing with some primordial inconsolable woe.

This was the Cairo I had known on the basis of three short visits in the past, and on this visit in the summer of 1974 nothing seemed to have changed — except for one thing: the people. I journeyed to Cairo to interview several government leaders and to get a tour of the Egyptian army's Sinai front in the wake of the 1973 War. The first thing I noticed was a new spring in the step of the average Cairene, a glint of pride and aspiration.

I had come at the time of President Nixon's last foreign hurrah prior to his downfall, a time when the official Egyptian line compelled its citizenry to pour out its simulated love and admiration for Nixon. I stood along the route of the motorcade from the airport to the city in the midst of thousands of cheering, sweltering, sign-wielding Arabs as the open limousine bearing Nixon and his wife, along with Egyptian President Sadat, passed by. The cheers and chants around me seemed hollow, unenthusiastic, the celebrated Arab emotionalism strained. It was apparent the multitudes were there more out of duty than desire — the pro-Nixon signs had been factory mass-produced, a knowing Arab friend in the government told me, the crowds had been compulsorily bused and trucked to the site like regiments of conscripts to a parade ground, and the approving shouts, issued under the direction of conductorlike group leaders, had obviously been carefully memorized and rehearsed. I could understand that it might have seemed like a spontaneous outpouring to Nixon who, as he passed, was responding to it with awkward subathletic gestures and plastic grins that seemed almost to constitute a self-caricature. The staged reality of the spectacle was brought home to me after the caravan of cars had passed. The mob of spectators, the overwhelming majority of whom were factory workers and schoolchildren, became suddenly transformed into dozens of distinct groups by officious, shouting overseers and marched off toward the access roads.

I was with my Egyptian government friend, and to prove his contention that the entire event had been staged he suggested we follow them. We did, and shortly came upon a long line of buses and trucks that had been withdrawn beyond sight of the motorcade. Into them were herded the children and workers, to be driven back to their schools and factories. We mounted a bus of workers — my friend's brother happened to be their foreman — and found their mood one of singular gripery, in the time-honored tradition of those who are forced to do something they have little interest in and no need for. "Nixon, hah!" said one of the workers when my companion posed a question for me. "Do you think we stand for three hours in the sun for Nixon? We do it for Sadat, because he asks us to."

I found out later that it had not been a matter of Sadat asking. In a land where all the industry is nationalized, any order of the nation's government to its factories is carried out without question. "You see," my Arab friend would say to me later, "whatever enthusiasm you heard today was not for Nixon, but Sadat. The people do not especially like to be forced to attend such an event. In that way they are like people all over the world. But since they do attend, they take the opportunity to show their love for Sadat."

"But Sadat was laying back," I said. "He was letting Nixon take all the acclaim."

"Ah, but that is his way. You think Nixon is exploiting this visit to show your people in America how popular he is abroad, how indispensable, so as to discourage his impeachment? If that is the case, then he is using Sadat, no? He is using all us Arabs. But Sadat, you think he doesn't know this? In reality, he is using Nixon more than Nixon uses him. Though Nixon is coming here and getting this warm reception, Sadat knows the reception is really for him. But more important, it gives the world an opportunity to see the *new* Arab — the Arab who has pride and dignity. Perhaps this sudden friendship between Egypt and the United States will frighten the Israelis, make them see the pointlessness of their continuing aggression. So Sadat stages this spectacle. We read your papers, we learn this famous Nixon business about stroking people. People in the government here, the press, we joke about Nixon's visit — we call it the 'Stroke Nixon' visit. 'Stroking' is getting someone to think you feel good about him so that he'll do what you want him to do, no? Sadat is stroking Nixon. Right now Nixon will agree to just about anything. Sadat knows that. The people know that. It is like they are winking at each other behind Nixon's back. That is why the cheers for Nixon. They are really for Sadat, but we must give your Mr. Nixon the illusion they are for him."

"My God," I said, "if Sadat is out-Nixoning Nixon, if Sadat is another Nixon, Egypt is in trouble."

"No," came the humored reply, "Sadat is not another Nixon. This tactic of stroking — it is an Arab custom. Nixon must be another Sadat. Nixon must be an Arab at heart."

I was tempted to say, yes, he must, for the innate inability to distinguish between illusion and reality of which Nixon seemed to be possessed appeared to be a uniquely Arab trait. Instead, I held my tongue.

My friend was not wrong about Arab pride and dignity. It was this that I was seeing in the man in the street throughout Cairo during these blistering

June days of 1974. But was it, again, some function of what had always seemed to me to be the innate manic-depressive nature of the Arab soul? I could understand how their success in crossing the Suez the October before might have instilled in them a new sense of self-worth. Indeed, they could even be said to have deserved some relief from the humiliations they had experienced in the eyes of the world during the past twenty-five years. But at best their foothold in Sinai was a Pyrrhic victory. Were they unable to recognize the real defeat they had suffered for their audacity? Were they up to the usual Arab trick of making reality out of illusion and in the bargain exaggerating that false reality into something that was not only illusory but totally imaginary? Certainly whatever rebirth of pride they might have been justified in evincing as a result of their army's initial rout of the token Israeli force across the canal had been blown out of all proportion six months later into a kind of hubris that was almost animal in its expression. The Arabs, I felt, were riding the peak of the manic cycle, and as deep as their depression had been for so long, their mania would ride as high for just as long. Which would mean — because the long-building problems in the Middle East are fraught with a deep-seated religioethnic emotionalism that often seems beyond any rational tempering — that the world was in for a particularly hazardous time.

# 4.

# HISTORY: *From Jesus to Jihad*

THE STORY OF JESUS is too well known to require telling here. Again, however, as in the Jews' recordings of *their* history, we are required to rely solely on "divinely" inspired literature for our "knowledge" of the origins, life and lifework of this singular figure of the ancient Middle East. And as with the stories of Abraham, Isaac, Jacob, Moses and Joshua, so too is the story of Jesus — as set down in one language and then translated, refined and codified in others several generations after the fact — replete with the kind of legend, fable and miracular event earlier found in the Old Testament literature.*

If we are to judge by the secular histories of the time, the life of Jesus (if indeed there was such a person) had little or no impact on the social, political and cultural events in Palestine. His rather startling career, as related in the New Testament, receives no mention in the secular Greek, Roman or Jewish journalistic and historical accounts of the day. In fact there is not a single mention of his name to be found anywhere in the surviving literature, of which there is a good deal, except for a fleeting reference in a lengthy

* Most biblical scholars agree that the first four books of the New Testament — those which tell the story of Jesus — were originally written in Aramaic, the common language of the time in Palestine (by then the Jews reserved Hebrew for their religious rituals), about two generations after Jesus lived. The Aramaic versions then went through almost three hundred years of embroidery, editing and translation until they were "set" in Greek in the early fourth century A.D. by the followers of the Emperor Constantine when he made Christianity the official religion of the Greco-Roman Empire.

history attributed to the Greco-Jewish historian Philo. And even this is suspect.*

The most likely explanation for this lack of notice (again, if the man did in fact exist) is that Jesus lived and toiled and preached his message in the relative obscurity of the large Jewish community of Judaea. It was a time of religious as well as political intrigue. The staunch upholders of the Jewish laws were battling not only their Roman-Herodian oppressors but also those many liberalized Jews who had learned to put commerce and profit before God. A messianic obsession filled the minds and imaginations of the highly orthodox, as did the spirit of political insurrection. The governing Romans would have cared little for what went on within the Jewish community except insofar as it might have affected their autonomy — the planning of an armed rebellion, for instance. The arts of the police and counterespionage were not as highly advanced as they are today; thus counterspies and planted informers were not used to any great extent. The Roman occupiers simply dealt with potential rebellions as they surfaced. Otherwise they were content to allow the various factions within the orthodox Jewish population — some agitating for purely religious reform, others advocating political overthrow, still others championing combinations of both — to argue among themselves.

Thus Jesus came and went. A religious reformer, a political revolutionary, a divine incarnation — who, really, can know? What we do know with some certitude is that Jesus was probably one of many discontented Jews of the time who infused their "teachings" with the rising messianic fervor;† that he and his message were rejected by the orthodoxy for being too revisionist; that his handful of followers kept his message alive after he had passed from the scene; that the message was passed down through a generation or two of these Jewish sectists until, in the hands of a man named Saul — a Syrian Jew — it was transformed into an increasingly influential offshoot of Judaism; and that as a result of Saul's (St. Paul's) evangelizing journeys throughout the Greco-Roman world, along with those of his successors, it became a new religious ideology that was eventually given official legitimacy by way of

---

* It has been long alleged by many scholars that Philo's brief allusion to Jesus was not of his own authorship, but was later inserted by a neo-Christian editor seeking to give historical credence to the story of Jesus.

† We should remember that by now the Jews as a people were governed by a powerful mythical sense of "chosenness," which was in accordance with their religious tradition. It would not be illogical to assume that this sense had translated itself into a mass psychology. Thus, in a time when the messianic spirit was upon the people, individuals among them might well have envisioned themselves as having been "chosen" as messiahs.

an imperial edict of Constantine I in A.D. 325. It was then that the story of Jesus began to have significance for the Middle East.

The appearance of Jesus, however (starting, according to the best guesses, in about 8 B.C.), does have a minor significance in the chronology of the Middle East, for it marked the time when the rebirth of Jewish nationalism was approaching its height. The zealot Jews had had a brief taste of what it was like to possess their own autonomous and exclusive nation during the time of the Maccabees a couple of generations earlier. Now, under the yoke of Herod and the Romans, the impulse to be independent and self-contained had renewed itself. It was to be an impulse that would soon — and radically — change their destiny as a people.

It started largely, as I have suggested, out of religious motives. From the viewpoint of the orthodoxy of Jerusalem the objection to Roman rule was that it seriously compromised the absolute domination of Jewish law. It tended to encourage the populace to entertain revisionary teachings and to indulge in less than holy practices for the sake of expediency. It was also perceived as promoting an undesirable assimilation between the Judaeans and the much more liberal Galileans and Samaritans to the north, thus yielding a further dilution of the holy laws. Absolutely anathema, for instance, was the idea that the ancient promises of God — the very promises that had endowed the Hebrews with their unique singularity and identity — applied not only to the biological descendants of Abraham but to his spiritual heirs as well. This was a radical idea that had come out of the Hellenizing influence of the Greeks and was now reviving itself as a result of Roman rule. It had gained some currency among the Jews of northern Palestine, most notably those in Galilee, and had to be resisted at all costs to preserve the racial and spiritual purity of the true children of God. It was hardly a coincidence that Jesus, the core of whose teachings was supposed to have been that God's grace extended to *all* men of righteousness, came from Galilee.

From the point of view of those who were politically active among the Jews, Roman rule was objected to simply because it had been achieved by force and was alien to the native aspirations of independent Jewish nationhood — aspirations that had been inspired by the Maccabees. Insofar as the more worldly political Jews believed in the biblical promises at all, they interpreted them to mean that the surviving biological descendants of Abraham (excluding the Ishmaelites — the descendants of Ishmael, Abraham's first son, and those descendants of Isaac who, like the Samaritans, rejected the primacy of Jerusalem) were destined to take possession of the Promised Land and achieve in it an exclusively Jewish political autonomy. Palestine would thus become a homogenous and independent Jewish state within the boundaries specified in the Lord's ancient promise: "From the river of Egypt unto the great river, the river Euphrates" (Genesis xv, 18).

The growing intensity of these nationalist aspirations, coupled with the messianic fervor of the religious community, brought Palestine, and especially Jerusalem, to a boil during the period Jesus was said to have lived. The situation provoked great anxiety in the Roman rulers. Not that they feared the Jews or felt incapable of quelling any uprising; they simply wanted no diversions to get in the way of their main business, which was the accumulation of Middle East riches. The extent of their concern is reflected not only in the contemporary Roman historical literature but also in the New Testament accounts of the period. The concern even touches upon Jesus himself: By characterizing Jesus as a possible leader of a political insurrection, Pontius Pilate justified himself in yielding to the demand of the Jewish religious leadership for his death.*

At first the insurrectionary spirit expressed itself in only scattered incidents of terrorism, but each incident provoked Roman reprisals which in turn, as is usually the case in these matters, brought about increased counter-terrorism. The nationalist movement spread as Roman reprisals and infractions of Jewish religious customs were utilized to inflame public feeling. The cycle of incident-reprisal expanded and intensified over a period of decades until the Romans decided to crack down with all their power and ruthlessness. When that happened, in about A.D. 67, a full-scale Jewish revolt broke out.

The Jews managed to expel most of the small Roman garrison from Jerusalem, but it was not long before they faced retribution. Roman armies gathered from throughout the Middle East and for three years laid siege to the city. In A.D. 70 Jerusalem fell, and with it went the remaining rights of the Jewish state. The struggle was revived periodically over the next sixty-five years, not only in Palestine but in Egypt, Cyprus and other parts of the

---

* It is noteworthy that the Gospels also tell us that Pilate, while yielding to the demands of the Jewish leaders, in exchange released from captivity a well-known Jewish insurrectionist by the name of Barabbas. The Gospels' collective indication is that Pilate was probably confused by the "King of the Jews" designation applied to Jesus, and was persuaded by the "multitudes calling" for his death that he represented a greater danger to the Romans' suzerainty than Barabbas. See, for instance, the Gospel of John xix, 12: "And from thenceforth Pilate sought to release him: but the Jews cried out, saying, 'If thou let this man go, thou art not Caesar's friend: whosoever maketh himself a king speaketh against Caesar.' "

Roman Empire where large communities of exiled nationalist Jews had settled. In all cases the Jews were reduced to submission.

One last suicidal uprising, which came to be known as the revolt of Bar Kochba, took place in Jerusalem in A.D. 135. Its quick and brutal suppression was rapidly followed by the official establishment of the Roman religion in the sacked temple area of the city.

These two events marked the final end of the system, introduced by King Cyrus of Persia some seven hundred years earlier, by which the Jews had been given, through human as opposed to divine sanction, an at least partially autonomous national home. After A.D. 135 the remaining Jewish population of Jerusalem and the surrounding areas of Palestine, while retaining a large degree of religious and social autonomy, lost all political significance.

Nor was it only in Palestine that Jewry was in ruins. The largest Jewish settlements throughout the empire — and by now there were more than a few — had been involved in the general disaster, their members persecuted for the insurrectionary sins of their coreligionists in Palestine. Jewish influence had become strong in the Roman world, and the Jews dispersed throughout the empire had been generally treated with favor. No more. Their influence quickly waned, and under the pressures of unfavorable treatment many were forced to resettle in more distant places. The Diaspora moved into high gear.

The adoption of Christianity as the official religion of the Empire in 325 further weakened the Jewish position — particularly, of course, with respect to the assertion that Palestine belonged to the Jews by virtue of God's promise to Abraham. The developing Christians — unlike the earlier pagans who had ignored or scoffed at the idea — accepted the biblical testimony and acknowledged that such a promise had indeed been made. But they claimed that the Jews, by rejecting the True Messiah and causing him to be put to death, had forfeited their privileged position. As the Christian popular myth evolved, the Jews were no longer the people chosen by God to enjoy the fruits of righteousness exclusively. They were now the "chosen people" in a negative sense — that is, specifically disinherited and singularly cursed to a life of misery and eventual extinction. *They* were the heathens. Henceforth God's promises applied not to the biological descendants of Abraham but to the Christians, his true spiritual heirs — the old Hellenistic Galilean idea. Thus, so long as the religious dogmas and beliefs of Christianity were at the forefront of men's minds, it was inconceivable that Christendom should ever agree to Jewish political domination in Palestine. Indeed, for many centuries it appeared that Christendom could not even tolerate Jewish existence, not to mention domination, in Palestine or elsewhere.

With their final conquest of Jerusalem in 135, the Romans consolidated their control of the Middle East and for a while the area quieted. Most of Rome's attention had been centered on Palestine, the crossroads of east-west trade routes. Now, with a relative peace on the land, the Romans set out to stabilize the entire Middle East and exploit all of its wide-ranging potential.

Under this Pax Romana, in which indigenous political distinctions were blurred and different national economies were integrated, the region prospered. With the blurring of political distinctions and the integration of economies, there began as well the largest-scale assimilation among the local populations yet seen in the Middle East. As trade and commerce expanded, so did communication and travel. There was a constant and growing interflow between the still largely Semitic peoples from the eastern regions of the area and those of the western regions, between those of the north and those of the south. Syrians mixed with Palestinians and Arabians, Palestinians and Arabians with Egyptians and Sudanese, Egyptians and Sudanese with Syrians. Berber tribesmen from the distant western reaches of North Africa joined the process, mixing with the nomadic tribes that had moved into the western deserts from Arabia. The more civilized Persians from Asia did likewise in eastern Arabia and Syria, though on a smaller scale, and there was even the beginning of an interchange between the Semitic peoples of northern Syria and the Indo-Europeans of Galatia (today's Turkey).

While the interchanges progressed at a slow rate on the fringes of the Fertile Crescent, they moved rapidly in the heartland of Palestine and its environs. Distinct Semitic cultures had begun merging with and absorbing one another well before the arrival of the Persian, Greek and Roman empires. The area in and around Palestine had once been inhabited by Canaanites, Philistines, Phoenicians, Hittites, Aramaeans, Ammonites, Hebrews (Israelites), Moabites, Jebusites, and Edomites, to name just a few. By the time of Rome many of these diverse smaller cultures had blended into larger, more unified ones through conquest or natural assimilation. Yet still others remained corporately separate — for instance, the Jews.

This is not to say that the Hebrews, from whom the Jews descended, remained intact. On the contrary, the Hebrew culture as such had disappeared much in the way the Canaanite culture did, through foreign conquest and enforced or voluntary assimilation with neighboring Semitic cultures. The Israelites, the descendants of the Hebrews, had developed a newer culture out of the remains, but this too suffered from conquest, dilution and assimilation (as in the religious defection of the Samaritans and the revisionism of the Galileans, who gave birth to Christianity). What remained, then, was only a remnant of the original culture — the Judaeans — who survived into Roman times as the Jews.

The Jews, of course, were not the only culture of any significance to the area around Romanized Palestine. Two other distinct societies were already well established by the time of Rome's arrival — the Nabateans and the Palmyrans. Both had come out of the Arabian peninsula (according to the popular anthropological hypothesis) as distinct tribal cultures, not necessarily nomadic in nature, in about 500 B.C.

I noted earlier that the appearance of the Semitic word for "Arab" disappeared from the tablature and the epigraphic literature of the region at about this time. Probably the last use of the word appeared in an epitaph written in Nabatean Aramaic script. The epitaph, etched in stone, refers to one Imrul Quais, "King of all the Arabs." It is believed that this title designated the leader of a coalition which existed among nomadic tribes who chose to join forces under the banner of the most powerful chieftain in their midst to fight the Nabateans. The designation thus would seem to signify (a) that the Nabateans did not consider themselves nomads, and (b) that the term "Arab" was reserved exclusively for the nomadic tribes of the desert.*

The Nabateans settled in the area east and south of the Dead Sea (today's Jordan, the ancient biblical land of Edom) and established the capital of their kingdom in Petra. They flourished during the centuries the neighboring Israelites were rebuilding Jerusalem after the Babylonian exile, but were culturally subordinate to the earlier Aramaean civilization to the north. When the Aramaeans became Hellenized by the Greeks after 325 B.C., the Hellenistic influence seeped down to infect the Nabateans, as it did the Galileans, Samaritans, and many Judaeans in Palestine. Aramaic became the everyday language of the Nabateans — again, as it did of the Galileans, Samaritans and nonorthodox Judaeans. Indeed, Aramaic became the principal vehicle through which Hellenic ideas were disseminated through the region during the height of the Greek Empire. Most of the cultures in the area abandoned their distinct tribal languages and adopted Aramaic as a

---

* In case you haven't already guessed, the precise meaning of the word "Arab," and perhaps more importantly what it doesn't mean, have had signal significance in the development of the peoples of the Middle East and their attitudes today. This will soon become more evident.

common lauguage as well as its alphabet. This alphabet was to serve as the basis for what we know as the Arabic alphabet.

The Palmyrans established their kingdom in Syria. This society also became strongly Aramaicized, therefore Hellenized. Its strategic location athwart the caravan routes between Mesopotamia and the west gave it effective control of all transport. Aside from this, the kingdom devoted most of its energies to banking and commerce; it became celebrated too for hiring out its legendary archers as mercenaries.

The Nabatean kingdom, like Palestine, came under Roman domination in the first century B.C. and was subsequently absorbed by it completely in A.D. 105. Many Nabateans merged into adjoining societies, while others remigrated south to a kind of permanent exile in northern Arabia, where they eventually faded into the cultural landscape.

The Palmyrans lasted for another century and a half. The kingdom was given special privileges by Rome as a reward for its consistent loyalty. This status lasted until the third century A.D., when one of its leaders attempted to make Palmyra independent. His ambitions were pursued after his death by his widow, Zenobia. In A.D. 273 the Emperor Aurelian put an end to Zenobia's aspirations, after which Palmyra declined rapidly. As with the Nabateans, many of its citizens were absorbed by surrounding cultures, while others gravitated back to northern Arabia.

During the first few centuries of Roman rule, then, in addition to the mixing of cultures in the northern portions of the Middle East, there was also a series of remigrations from north to south.

Prosperous Jews, fleeing the cultural and religious wreckage wrought by the ambitions of the nationalist Judaeans, were among the first to seek sanctuary in the Arabian peninsula. Bringing their Judaic and Hellenist ideas with them, they either melded into existing northern Arabian societies or joined settlements of other Jews who had migrated from the permanently exiled communities of Mesopotamia and Persia in pursuit of trade and commerce.

The Nabateans were among the next settlers, followed by the Palmyrans. With them into northern Arabia went not only Greek influence but Roman as well. And further remigrations of other peoples still later brought a Christian input into the moil of cultural cross-fertilization.

Tracing historical cause and effect can often lead one onto thin ice. However, it is not to excessively flirt with danger to suggest that out of this enforced remigration of values, ideas, mythologies and language developed

Arab culture as it exists today. Although by the first or second century A.D. Arabs were still considered to be exclusively those who lived the nomadic, tribal desert life — both within Arabia and without — one can safely deduce that the people of the various more cultivated and sedentary cultures of the Fertile Crescent were the proto-Arabs of today. These include all those societies that settled the Fertile Crescent — including the Hebrews — and is due to their nomadic Arabian origins (still, admittedly, hypothetical) and to their later reinfusion of European and Oriental ideas into the native nomad, or Arab, or Bedouin,* culture of the northern Arabian peninsula. It was by means of this reinfusion that the worldly foreign influences of the Fertile Crescent percolated down to the still-primitive kingdoms of the southern Arabian peninsula and eventually brought about the cultural and religious explosion there that would forever change the face of the Middle East.

By the third century southern Europe had declined in economic and strategic importance compared to the lands of the eastern Mediterranean. But growing disorders within the Roman Empire, along with the rise in Persia of a new imperial dynasty (the Sassanids), challenged Roman control of the eastern trade routes and threatened to undermine the political security and economic prosperity of the Fertile Crescent.

To meet these threats, Emperor Constantine I decided to move the political and administrative center of the empire eastward. Near the site of the ancient Greek city of Byzantium† he built a new imperial capital which he called New Rome but which later became known as Constantinople. Recognizing the value the emergent followers of Christ would have in helping to stabilize the Middle East, he decreed Christianity to be the official and only religion of the empire (which came to be called the Byzantine Empire).

Constantine and succeeding Christian Byzantine emperors had an increasingly tough time maintaining control over the Fertile Crescent. In addition to the new Persian peril, they had to worry about the burdens and dangers created by invasions of Teutonic, Slavic and Mongolian tribes — the Barbarians — who overran the Balkans, interfered with trade along the river routes

* The term "Bedouin" was long used as a synonym for "Arab" in the early societies of the Arabian peninsula, with the difference that "Bedouin" had a corollary meaning of "raider." Thus all tribal nomads were Arabs ("wanderers," "passers-through"), but some had the additional distinction of being "raiders." "Bedouin" comes from the Arabic "Badawiyin," meaning originally people who appear in open country or in a vast expanse such as the desert.
† On the Bosporos, that sliver of water that divides modern Turkey and provides entry and exit between the Mediterranean and the Black Sea.

of eastern Europe, and threatened to penetrate into the heart of the empire itself.

Also, as a result of the "fall of Rome" in 476, they were faced with a prolonged economic depression in central, southern and western Europe. When Constantine moved to Byzantium, the western sector of the Roman Empire was already in a state of economic decline; indeed, that was the principal reason he made the move — to preserve the empire's economic advantages in the East. But the western sector of the empire continued to decline economically, then disintegrate politically. When it finally collapsed it left in its wake social decay and economic ruin. Commerce came to a standstill, and the markets for the varied commodities that came either from or through the Middle East dried up. The prosperity of the Fertile Crescent began to lessen, and by the sixth century* rumblings of serious native discontent could be heard for the first time in two hundred years.

While the Byzantines were beginning to experience a loosening of their grip on the northern sectors of the Semitic world, in the south the once-powerful but lesser-known Arabian kingdoms arrayed along the lower Red Sea and Indian Ocean were undergoing a similar decline. The problems of Europe and the dissipation of markets for Middle Eastern commodities had a domino effect. Soon this effect was compromising the economic prosperity of the urban southern Arabian societies as well as their camel-breeding counter-parts in the desert, for with European demand down, the caravan trade decreased and the need for camels — the ships of the desert — dwindled.

During the fifth and sixth centuries a shift took place in the relationship between the primitive nomadic societies of the Middle East's interior and the more advanced sedentary cultures on the periphery: the distinctions between them lessened. This was caused, at least conceivably, by the ongoing assim-ilatory tide, by the gradual redistribution of wealth and economic oppor-tunity brought about by the crises in the Byzantine Empire, and especially by the heightening tensions between the established Byzantines and the ambitious, increasingly powerful Persians.† Many of the nomadic tribes of interior northern Arabia and the southern wastes of the Fertile Crescent were warriors. With the diminishment of the camel and caravan trade, they cast

---

* Henceforth I shall no longer use A.D. to distinguish years and centuries from those of B.C., except where there might be a potential for confusion. In referring to years and centuries B.C., however, I shall continue to include the designation.
† The Persians were inhibited from throwing the full might of their armies against the By-zantines by their own anxiety over Barbarian invasions across the northern borders of their own empire.

about for new opportunities. The new opportunities lay in the north, along the fringes of the Byzantine and Persian empires, where war and skirmish had become constant. So, many of these tribes gravitated north. Originally they went in a kind of mercenary capacity, but they were soon coopted by the Byzantine and Persian rulers and formed into small buffer states whose twin missions were to secure the trade routes and to guard the eastern and western perimeters of the respective empires.

The two principal states were those of the Ghassanids, along the Byzantine border, and the Lakhmids, facing them on the Persian frontier. The Ghassanids were maintained by their Byzantine rulers as "phylarchs," i.e., tribal princelings, while the Lakhmids were tributaries of the Persian emperor. The two tiny states lasted until the beginning of the seventh century and together were a further transmitting chamber between the sophisticated values and ideas of the sedentary, northern Middle East and the simpler, less cultivated life of the basically nomadic south. Although they became states, they remained primarily tribal societies, and through continuing contact with cousin Bedouin tribes flowing back and forth between south and north they filtered the relatively advanced civilization of Hellenized western Asia into the still-primitive culture of Arabia. Too, they were Christians, at least technically. So not just social and economic ideas traveled down the pipeline, religious notions went as well. By the fourth century there were a number of important Jewish communities and Judaized Arabian settlements scattered throughout the states and cities of the Arabian peninsula. Many "heathen" Arabians had already become conscious of the Hebrew religious mythology. This awareness was now to become compounded, in fact irresistibly fascinated, by the introduction of Christian mythology and dogma.

As did the Fertile Crescent, by the fourth century the Arabian peninsula already possessed a long history. The cradle of the four thousand years of civilization in the Middle East — according to the anthropologists — it had given away, by way of people and culture, more than it had kept for itself. Primitive kingdoms came and went during the two or three millennia before the Christian era, and only its spice and camel trades kept it economically viable. It had been generally avoided by the Greek, Persian and Roman conquerors and its life and culture therefore developed at a much slower pace than that of the Fertile Crescent. The rigors of climate and the paucity of arable land within its vast forbidding interior doubtless added to the willingness of foreign empires to ignore it.

Arabia might have been considerably less civilized during this time, but it did not lack a civilization. Indeed, its indigenous civilization has lasted longer in its original form than probably any other civilization in the developed world.*

The matrix of Arabian civilization was the prehistoric nomads who wandered, sometimes aimlessly, sometimes with purpose, through the seemingly endless deserts and scrublands of the peninsula. Out of these ancient roamings evolved a rudimentary form of clan society in which instinct for survival was the hallmark. Under the never-ending pressure of nature, whose harsh and often thoroughly confounding realities are the mold of nomadic society, there developed the concept of safety in numbers. As the validity of the concept was borne out by experience, the corresponding clan concept was refined and advanced. The clan rapidly became a highly cohesive entity. The motivating factor behind this cohesiveness was survival; thus the individual member's rights were always subordinate to the good of the group as a whole. The achievement of cohesiveness came through two mechanisms. One was material: the realization that the individual's survival depended on the group's survival, hence the need for joint self-defense against the rigors and perils of the desert. The other was spiritual: the theory of blood kinship, based on a blood tie between all the members of the clan through the male line. The notion of blood kinship was the underlying social bond of the group.

As time went on clans joined together into tribes — greater safety in greater numbers — in which the same principles of cohesiveness obtained. The tribes pursued two basic forms of livelihood — the grazing of their flocks and herds, which they drove from area to area according to the shifting of the seasons; and the raiding of sedentary neighbors and, as the trade routes developed, of the occasional caravan that ventured across the more remote reaches of the desert. It was through this habit of raiding that the nomads came to be called Bedouin (see footnote on page 70). As well, it was the raiding custom that took the Bedouin farther and farther afield to the north in search of new opportunities and so turned them into the conductors for all the various foreign commodities and ideas that penetrated the area at any point and gradually seeped through the whole of the peninsula.

The ownership of land on the part of an individual tribe member was rare. Instead, the tribe simply exercised a kind of communal control over grazing

* This discounts, of course, the small pockets of still-primitive tribal peoples of "undeveloped" Africa, South America, Australasia and the Arctic.

areas, wells, and so on. Apparently, too, the flocks and herds were usually the collective property of the tribe rather than owned privately within the tribe.

The Arabian nomadic tribal system developed forms of leadership and authority that were mild compared to tribal societies in other parts of the world. The tribes were headed by men called *shaykhs* (elders)* or *sayyids* (lords). These were elected leaders, but seem to have generally enjoyed no more than the authority of a first among peers — perhaps either as a result of age or natural leadership qualities or both. These men lacked the authority to assign duties or to dispense punishment; this power remained within the provenance of the individual clans or families which made up the tribe. Instead, the tribal chieftain's main duty was generally to mediate intratribal disputes.

A sheikh or sayyid did not exercise his office alone. He was advised in all matters by a council of family heads (subsheikhs, so to speak) called the *majlis*. The majlis were intended to reflect the "sense" of the tribe on any matter of importance, and when a decision was being contemplated it would go through the crucible of broad tribal opinion as represented by the individual family spokesmen — an Arabian version of the powwow — before it was made.

Many of the practices, customs, institutions and instincts of early Bedouin life have passed down through the centuries to become the warp and woof of the modern collective Arab character. We shall be encountering and tracing these connections in the chapters ahead; we need concern ourselves now with only three important general aspects of the Bedouin nature: language, religion and, if you will, ethnopsychology.

With regard to the last, the desert life bred a fierce independence into Bedouin society; and within the entire society — ranging eventually from the southern reaches of the Arabian peninsula to the northern perimeters of the Fertile Crescent — there developed a strong, indeed governing, sense of superiority. Originally this sense sprang from the male-female relationship. The first families-clans-tribes all developed in the context of the conventional ancient and primitive patriarchal viewpoint. The man was considered — it

---

* This ancient Arabian word has gone through several transmogrifications of meaning and spelling over the centuries. In the American version of English we are accustomed to seeing it as "sheikh," which is how I shall use it. Its modern meaning in Arabic is no longer restricted to "elder." It is commonly used as a term to denote a man deserving of respect or honor, no matter his age, although it still also applies to an elderly, and therefore presumably wise, man.

was a matter of unquestioned dogma — to be far superior to the woman. Within each family the man was the strong chief, the boys the future chiefs; the woman was the weak servant, the girls the future servants. Within each clan the men were all-powerful, the women totally subservient. Within each tribe the men dominated absolutely; the women were ciphers except insofar as they served the men.

Now this is not particularly startling news, to be sure; no primitive society was ever much different. But within Bedouin society, this acute perception of male superiority soon translated itself into a notion of intertribal superiority. Within a clan or tribe men related to one another as men; except that when a man somehow failed to carry out his male role — exacting revenge for some offense to his family, for instance — he was immediately declassed into a status akin to womanhood.

Public law was nonexistent within nomadic society. The sole deterrent to what would otherwise have been the vacuum of anarchy was the ancient *lex talionis*, which we know as: "An eye for an eye, a tooth for a tooth." In practice among the nomads, this meant that the kin of someone murdered or injured, or even insulted, had the duty of exacting vengeance from anyone of the culprit's equivalent kinfolk. Thus if a father were to lose a son at the hands of a father from another clan or tribe, it was his absolute duty to murder the son of the offending father. If he faltered in any way — either refused to exact revenge out of fear, or tried, failed, and lived to tell about it — he immediately lost his status as a man in the eyes of the rest of the tribe. There were no second chances: once he failed, the man was automatically reduced to the category of woman and some other male in the clan appointed to take on his manly duty.

Within this value system, then, not only were men superior to women, but certain men were superior to other men. Certain families, it thus followed, were superior to other families — for if a man disgraced himself, reduced himself to womanhood, then his family was reduced as well.

From this evolved the consecutive ideas that certain clans were superior to other clans, certain tribes within an area superior to other tribes of that area, the tribal society of one area superior to that of another, and so on up the ladder. Eventually these attitudes of superiority hardened into a general Bedouin sense — reinforced by their isolation and self-sufficiency in the physical world and their seclusion in an emotional universe formed by the mystical bond uniting tribespeople — that they were absolutely superior to everyone. By the time of the beginning of the Christian era, Bedouin society was secure in its long-traditional image of itself as the natural aristocracy of the Middle East. It felt itself inherently superior to any and all of the dependent sedentary kingdom-societies that had come and gone during the course of the centuries in the region, and far superior to the imperial foreign peoples who had more recently been conspicuous by their presence in the land. This attitude soon had an important bearing on future developments in the Middle East.

The nomads developed a strong religious tradition as well. Their religions were based on the idea of petty deities and demons inhabiting particular tribal places — trees, wells, stones, etc. — held to be sacred by that particular tribe. What was particularly sacred to one tribe or group of tribes was not necessarily so to another; however, there were also a few higher gods, or goddesses, who transcended tribal boundaries and were more or less feared, loved and worshiped in common.* But these intermediate deities were subordinate to a still higher being or principle who, like the penultimate gods of the Egyptians and the Mesopotamians, was all-powerful, all-knowing and totally unknowable. This supreme God was generally referred to as "Allah" and was believed to have predetermined everyone's life so that no individual had the power to change what had been set forth by his destiny. This fatalism, deeply ingrained in the Bedouin character, was also to play an important role in the events to come in the post-Christian era.

It was a combination of these deeply felt Bedouin attitudes of social superiority and religious fatalism that led to the evolution of the third ingredient in the equation of the future: language — language not just in the technical sense of nouns, verbs, grammar and syntax, but in the sense of its full range of expression.

The eternal wanderings of the tribes against the harsh and unforgiving backdrop of the desert induced a powerful, mystical sense of kinship which, when overlaid with attitudes of natural superiority and deep fatalism, endowed nomadic life with a dimension that was as singularly heroic as it was monotonous. Indeed, it was to combat the monotony that the tribes formed the habit of engaging in deeds and actions that would be dangerous in the extreme. Often these actions were merely gratuitous — attacking another

---

* These deities covered the whole gamut of natural phenomena — sand, wind, mountains, moon, sun, planets, the offshore swells of the sea, and so on. The nomadic religions were akin to animism — the belief in a power which exists in specific aspects of nature. The nomads believed that spirits manifested themselves to man in the form of material things, and that these objects brought man into communication with the hidden powers which influenced his life.

tribe or a caravan merely for the sake of it, driven by some deeply conditioned warrior impulse. At other times they were carried out in pursuit of a specific goal — to prove one tribe's superiority over another, or to wreak vengeance for some intertribal infraction. Whatever the case, excesses in heroism and tribal self-glorification became the custom of the desert, as if to somehow give the desert inhabitant a measure of equality with his grandiose environment.*

The ancient language of Arabia was common to the entire peninsula, but it had many versions and variations among the tribes. The variegated language evolved, of course, along with the tribal society so that the characteristics and qualities that uniquely marked the society were reflected in the language itself. Thus the fatalism, the superiority and the impulse to heroic self-glorification that became early benchmarks of the nomadic character simultaneously found expression in linguistic practices. Not only were deeds done and emotions felt on a grandiose scale, they came to be described and expressed on such a scale. And when for some reason heroic actions could not be accomplished and profound emotions could not be experienced, their expression in language became a substitute. In a sense, the language of the nomads — spoken and written — became a form of action and emotion in itself.

Because the language evolved as a reflection of heroic deed, profound emotion and aristocratic attitude, its basic and all-encompassing expressive impulse was poetic rather than prosaic. It was poetry — a recognition and appreciation of its power — that enabled the Arabian nomads to transcend their varying tribal identities and create a heritage common to them all. Magic is an integral part of all primitive religion, and poetry is an integral part of magic — insofar as that which is abstract and mysterious can only hope to be given some coherence through a form of language that does not demand literalness. Words, it is said, have power. Words strung together in poetic form have magical power. In their abstract shadings they have the power to thrust beyond literal visions and perceptions, to beguile, persuade, transform. Poetry, undoubtedly a primordial impulse of mankind, in the Arabian peninsula flowered as perhaps never before or since in any other part of the world. It was, of course, deeply religious in orientation, reflecting both

---

* The "desert" of Arabia was, and is, not just a hot, sandy wasteland; life there includes coping with stark mountain ranges, violent storms, floods, freezing nights, murderous animals, venomous snakes, and the like.

a simple awe for the inexorable rhythms of life and nature and an elaborate solemnity in regard to the spiritual perceptions that emanated from these physical states.

Bedouin poetry was at once rich and tendentious in imagery, but it was always thematic, never pointless. The poetic form was used both for storytelling and for ordinary conversation. For instance, if one were asked what one thought of the weather (to put it in simple modern terms), one might reply with a dozen or so stanzas of poetic rumination about the nature of the heavens, the will of the gods, the condition of the animals, and so on, before delivering oneself of an opinion. A classic form of expression was the *qasidah*, long established in tribal custom. This might begin with a throbbing regret for vanished bliss in love, followed by an elaborately stoic recitation of the speaker's acceptance of his divinely predetermined status in the tribe. Then, before coming to his central theme — which might be a response to a question about the death of one of his camels — the speaker would pause to delight his listeners with lush and detailed descriptions of nature, centering especially on the boundless desert, and distant mountains, the oases, the various animals encountered, all leading up to the ultimate object of concern, his camel.

Nature, the gods, the desert, the tribe and the camel were the principal topics of conversation of the ancient Bedouin. Their poetry was obsessed with these concerns. But a man's status was measured, among other ways, by the extent of his ability to "metaphysicalize" such themes. Thus, one always strove to invent new ways of saying things, not only to nail down one's reputation as a champion monologist but to beat off pretenders to one's throne. Hence another reason for the extraordinary opulence in the imagery and vocabulary of the evolving language.

And if ordinary conversation lent itself to linguistic excess, the effects of ritualistic storytelling can easily be imagined. Storytelling was the highest expression of the Arabian language. Almost a nightly ritual among the men of a tribe, who would gather in a tent after a day's work, storytelling appears to have had at least three purposes. It was a form — the only form — of entertainment for the adults; it was the primary form of education for the young; and it was a deadly serious superiority competition whereby one's status in the hierarchy of intratribal importance rose and fell according to one's narrative ability — his power to hold the rest of the congregation in a trance of admiring attention. The substance of the tales nightly woven was always the same — great battles, magnificent deeds, supreme achievements in the never-ending battle against nature — all designed to affirm the heroic virtues and glories of one's own tribe. The forms of the stories were always the same, too. The narrator was constrained by custom to tell his story within the traditional two or three highly stylized poetic forms, such as the *qasidah*. Innovation in form was impermissible, and if the storyteller wandered from the accepted form — indeed, if he even deviated slightly — he would receive poor marks. The goal was to display such virtuosity in the handling of the traditional themes — virtuosity in vocabulary and imagery — as to ascend to the pinnacle of respect and superiority within the tribe.

One can logically suppose that along with such a societal tradition of linguistic grandiosity, conceit and exaggeration there evolved in the Bedouin social character an impulse to self-deception and self-delusion. Or perhaps the linguistic excesses, as graceful and convoluted as they were, grew out of preexisting qualities of self-delusiveness brought about by the urge to give some greater ideality to the stark and barren reality of desert life. Whichever the case, there can be little doubt that the ancient linguistic tradition did much to form the early Arabian character.

From a sociological point of view the highly poetic Arabian language was not just an ornament of life. Heroic convention and grandiose expression became a standard for the nomadic society of the peninsula, thus giving the various tribes, above their petty bickerings, a unified tradition and culture that were solidly embedded in the soil and sand of the Middle East well before the advent of Christianity. The poetic dialect, common to all the tribes, understood throughout the peninsula and as far north as the interiors of Egypt and Mesopotamia — in fact the only source of any kind of cultural unity in the peoples spread across the Middle East — gave rise to classical Arabic. This formalized language would in turn produce the vernacular Arabic that was to become the language of the entire Middle East — from the Atlantic Ocean in the west to the Persian Gulf in the east, from the eastern Mediterranean coast in the north deep into East Africa in the south — with incalculable consequences for the world of today.

During all its centuries of pre-Christian-era development, the Arabian peninsula progressed at a much slower rate of civilization than the Fertile Crescent. This was due in part to the fact that its remoteness, climate and unpromising terrain discouraged foreign colonization. It was due also, of course, to the fact that — except for its most southerly region where the

Yemenite kingdoms had established sedentary mercantile societies based on the spice trade — the peninsula was dominated by nomadic culture with its time-resistant ways.

By about the time of the advent of Christianity, however, the central part of the peninsula had experienced a certain amount of semisedentary development, and some important towns had even evolved out of the Bedouin fluctuations. These were strung along a stretch of land running roughly north-south, parallel to but inland from the Red Sea coast, known as the Hejaz. The two most largely populated of these towns were Yathrib and Makkah (Mecca). They had originally sprung up as waystops on the main north-south caravan route, but their positions in the uplands, away from the semifertile coast and on the fringes of the desert, proved an attraction to the inland nomads.

A common feature of all the nomad religions was a veneration of the mammoth rocks the tribes discovered in the desert. These rocks, to which they attributed a great deal of power, were held to be sacred because they contained gods within them. As if to prove their point, the tribes would carve statues of their gods out of these rocks and then would worship the statues as though the rock gods were real.

With Mecca a halfway point on the caravan route, it became the chief stop and therefore the major town on the route. It naturally became, too, a center for camel-trading and other forms of provisioning, such as food, tents and waterbags. All of these were supplied by various Bedouin tribes, so the area around Mecca became a focal point of nomad commercial forays into semi-civilization. As a result of these visits a certain intermingling between various tribes occurred and soon a new tribe evolved, nomadic in biological origin but semisedentary in its development. This tribe, because of its varied other-tribal input and its considerably more urbanized ways, grew to be thought of as superior to the others. As word of this superiority spread throughout the desert the general consensus accepted it, and a movement developed whereby the superior tribe was put in charge of all the sacred statues. Since the superior tribe — which called itself the Quraysh (Korayish) — was centered at Mecca, the statues would be taken there.

It was done, and within a short period Mecca was esteemed as a sacred city by all the tribes of Arabia. In time a holy shrine, known as the Kaaba, was built. The various tribes placed their statues, as well as smaller pieces of sacred stone chipped away during the carvings, at the shrine for certain lengths of time. This, it was believed, would restore the stones to a better state of sacredness.

Before going into battle, tribal chieftains went to Mecca to pay homage to the gods and to seek advice from the religious elders of the Korayish tribe, who were entrusted with the care of the holy idols. Out of this grew a religious custom by which it became mandatory for all nomad worshipers to visit Mecca at least once a year to pay homage to the gods. Mecca thus became a thriving and prosperous city, overflowing with transient members of various tribes. Since hostilities existed between the visiting tribes, the Korayish elders established a universal truce period — one lunar month each year during which no battles could be fought.

By the beginning of the Christian era the only organized religion that existed in the Arabian peninsula was Judaism. Large communities of Jews were centered both in the southernmost area, Yemen, and in the Hejaz, especially in the city of Yathrib.

There is no universal certainty as to how early in antiquity Jews appeared in Arabia. Some scholars suggest that after the exodus from Egypt and during the long sojourn in the desert, one or two of the Israelite tribes parted from Moses's group and wandered south. Others state that the Jews first appeared in numbers in the seventh century B.C. after Samaria was con-quered and most of the populace of the Kingdom of Israel was transported en masse to exile in Assyria. Still others point to the sixth century B.C., Jewish migration to Arabia being the result of an overflow of the Babylonian exile.

Whatever the case (the likelihood is that it was a combination of all three factors, plus perhaps one or two we know nothing about), by the beginning of the Christian era the Jewish settlement of the Arabian peninsula was large and growing larger. The Jews were not proselytizers; they did not seek to impose their religion on the pagan Arabians. But although they kept mostly to themselves, there occurred a certain amount of natural assimilation. Com-munities of Judaized Arabians therefore began to spring up, augmenting the purely Jewish population.

The Jews came to dominate the trade and culture of Yathrib, more than two hundred miles north of Mecca and another waystop along the caravan route. Although they originally had to fight the nomads to gain their foothold in the city, during the succeeding centuries they lived in relative peace with the natives and spread their influence north and south through the Hejaz. Thus, although most of the Arabian population remained polytheistic in its religion, the monotheism of the Jews was known, especially among the tribal intelligentsia of Yathrib and Mecca.

The arrival of Christianity saw the birth of the evangelistic spirit in the Middle East. Missionaries spread throughout the region to convert one and all to the single true faith. Some found their way to the nomadic tribes roaming the northern borders of the Arabian peninsula. Others crossed over from East Africa (modern-day Ethiopia) to proselytize among the tribes of the south. There had already developed within Christianity several schisms centered around differences in technical interpretation about the precise nature of Christ. So these missionaries, representing various persuasions within Christianity, worked with heightened zeal to win not only converts but converts to their particular christological creed.*

By the sixth century Christianity was widespread in the Arabian peninsula, although among the tribal population conversion was usually never much more than superficial — based on the same impulses to magic and superstition that were the foundations of pagan worship. Christianity "took" much more firmly in the Fertile Crescent. There, however, the division between the Monophysites of the west and the Orthodox of the eastern sector deepened, and the region became a battleground, once again, of religious conflict. The Monophysites were persecuted and terrorized by their Orthodox counterparts, and many priests, monks and ordinary believers were forced to flee to places that were beyond the reach of the Byzantines — Persia, Abyssinia, southern Arabia. Thus did the Monophysite brand become the dominant version of Christianity in the peninsula.

In the second half of the sixth century the northern Middle East was in an uproar — fed equally by the internecine religious turmoil, by the continuing decline of western markets and the concomitant economic depression, and by the increasingly battle-punctuated standoff between Persia and Byzantium. The Byzantine emperor Justinian, in addition to trying to fend off the Barbar-

---

* The principal schism occurred between architects of Church doctrine in Egypt. It revolved about the question of whether Jesus had just one nature (as a God-man) or two (as God and as man). Once Christianity was declared the official religion of the Greco-Roman-Byzantine Empire, the one-nature position was rejected and the twin-nature belief adopted as dogma. The followers of the one-nature theory, the Monophysites, thereafter formed their own group of national churches headed by the Coptic church of Egypt. These churches, which also include the Abyssinian church of Ethiopia, the Nestorian church of Assyria, the Apostolic church of Armenia, and the Malabar church of India, are known today as the Lesser Eastern Rites Catholic churches. The Greater Eastern Rites churches are headed by the Greek Orthodox church and its Russian and Rumanian counterparts. These were the churches that began as the official Catholicism of the Byzantine Empire. Later schisms resulted in the Roman Catholic church and other offshoots.

ian hordes from the north and hold the line against the Persians in the east, was making vigorous attempts in the west to regain control of the "fallen" Roman portion of the empire whose markets were so important economically. His successes in the west were partial and proved to be of a temporary nature, for his western policies undermined his power in the Middle East, causing loyalty to the empire to fade there. Developing in both Egypt and Syria were nascent aspirations of nationalism. The main northern trade routes to and from Asia — the only other substantial foreign market for Middle Eastern goods — were in perpetual peril from the Persians. Since Egypt was also in a state of disorganization, it could no longer provide a safe alternative route down along the western coast of the Red Sea to the Indian Ocean ports. Merchants were therefore obliged to fall back on the more difficult, though more peaceful, route leading down through the western Arabian peninsula — the Hejaz, Yathrib and Mecca — to these ports.

The chaos provided a socioeconomic vacuum in the Middle East into which Mecca, by now the central focus of civilization in the Arabian peninsula, was ready to leap. Leap it did — with an energy and fervor that would soon change the entire cultural face of the region.

It is undoubtedly true to the point of banality that the great movements in history are not created by individuals alone, but by a concatenation of time, events and people. The name of Muhammad, regarded by a sixth of all the people of the world to be the initiator of real history, must be considered the likeliest exception to this rule. More than any other individual in the verifiable past, this man single-handedly inaugurated a new era of world history. The question of whether the "truth" he presented was actually true or not is immaterial to any arguments about his effect on mankind. What *is* material is, simply, his effect. For with his emergence as the spiritual and, later, secular organizer of the varied peoples of the Middle East, the Arabs — a vast, rapidly cohering culture — were introduced into the mainstream of world history as such. And this is just the tip of the iceberg of his significance.

By the end of the sixth century the population of Mecca was a mixing bowl of tribal affiliations. Although monotheism had become superficially established in the Hejaz through Jewish and Christian settlement, pagan tribal religion was still by far the predominant practice, and Mecca its center. The Korayish tribe — the custodians of the religious artifacts and the official defenders, so to speak, of the pagan faith — had become the aristocracy of the city. Its members reigned as the final arbiters not only of all religious matters but, with the rise of Mecca as a busy commercial center, of social and business affairs as well.

Nomads, untouched by the cultural and religious influences now pouring down into Arabia, still roamed the greater part of the peninsula in large numbers. But many of the tribes that inhabited the Hejaz and its fringes had become more and more dependent on expanding cities like Mecca and Medina; they had gradually fallen into a semisedentary kind of existence. And the city-dwellers themselves, although nomadic in background, had become thoroughly sedentary.

The city still recalled its nomadic origins. There was a maximum of individual liberty and a minimum of any form of centralized authority. But ideas and values from the north were becoming thoroughly infused in the city's corporate consciousness, and the Arabian peninsula, at least that part along the Red Sea coast, was no longer isolated from the civilized world outside.

It was out of this milieu that, at the very beginning of the seventh century, the figure called Muhammad emerged. At first simply a gentle, pious-seeming man in his early forties, he preached monotheism, describing himself as God's final and foremost messenger — the same God of the Jews and the Christians. But soon, because in pagan Arabia there was no distinction to be made between religion and politics, he transformed himself — or was transformed by both his followers and his enemies — into a political personality. The transformation continued further into the economic and military realms, for again the ancient Arabian tribal tradition demanded that a leader be superior in all vital aspects of life.

Although he never assigned any divine qualities to himself, as did Jesus, Muhammad claimed that he superseded Jesus, that his message took precedence over Jesus', that he was the last true Prophet of Allah (the mysterious, single, incomprehensible God of the pagan tribes). His message was similar in its monotheistic character and ethical imperatives to that of the Judaeo-Christian doctrine, but it was couched in the elaborate linguistic terms that at once appealed to and reflected Arabian sensibility. He called the new movement he was starting Dar al Islam, which roughly translates as "Society of Submission to the Will of God." As it quickly became an organized religion, its name was shortened to Islam.

Muhammad's movement thrived and expanded within the Hejaz throughout his life. But it was not until after his death in 632 that Islam moved beyond Arabia. Then, in a massive and sudden eruption that was in the very best tradition of the Arabian tribal *jihad* (holy war), but on a much grander scale, Islam shot out of the peninsula and spread on the heels of military, economic and political conquest throughout the Middle East — as far west as Spain, as far east as central Asia.

# 5.

# HISTORY: *Muhammad and Islam*

IT IS PROBABLY NO COINCIDENCE that Muhammad made his appearance at a time when the Christian prophetic and evangelistic spirit was building to its zenith in Arabia — just as it was no coincidence that Jesus appeared at the time when the Judaic messianic spirit was rising to its heights in Palestine, and just as it was no coincidence that the Abraham-Isaac-Moses triumvirate appeared at a time when the impulse to monotheism was spreading across the ancient Fertile Crescent.

What differentiates Muhammad from the latter two entities is that he was a completely verifiable historical figure; that is, his words and deeds were witnessed and recorded as they happened, rather than recalled through legend and folklore by later generations. For this reason, perhaps, Muhammad professed no personal divinity, worked no miracles, indulged in no supernatural comings and goings; the modern secular histories of the time would not have supported such ancient practices. Nor would the paganism of the Arabian soul — however superficially Christian it might have become — permit so radical a contradiction of its deeply ingrained conviction that man is merely a vassal of the gods; no man could be a god, or cause to happen what could only be attributed to the gods, in pagan sensibility. To have had a "revelation" from the Ultimate God — Allah — well, that was a concept not so difficult to handle, especially in view of the by now known but still ill-understood mythologies of Abraham, Moses and Christ that had spread over Arabia.

Speaking of ill understanding, the Western world has long clung to a curiously ill-conceived image of Muhammad. Twelve hundred years of prejudice on the part of Christian dogmatists have shaped of Muhammad in the West a figure of odious fantasy — an infamous heretic or vulgar charlatan too contemptible to be worthy of any consideration whatsoever. In modern America this historical image has translated itself into extreme indifference, and I daresay not more than one in several thousand Americans has more than a passing awareness of Muhammad and his works. This is more the pity because not even the barest comprehension of what the Middle East portends for America in the future is possible without at least a general understanding of Muhammad, Islam and their role in the region.

It is quite possible, at least in part, that Western indifference and/or contempt for Muhammad stems precisely from the fact that he claimed no divinity, worked no miracles. In view of the fact that his teachings were nothing more (from the Western point of view) than a reinterpretation of the Judaeo-Christian message, what profit could be gained in giving such a reinterpretation any serious attention, especially when it issued from the mouth and hand of a man who could prove no relation, direct or otherwise, with God? Psychologically, the contempt was probably heightened by this latter fact: the audacity of an ordinary man to suggest that he "spoke" for God. The world had had plenty of false "prophets" before and would have many more thereafter. Muhammad had merely elevated the art, and his success — went, and in many places still goes, the conventional wisdom — was due simply to the fact that he was dealing with a laughably primitive culture.

On this point there can be no doubt that the culture of sixth-century Arabia was indeed primitive as compared to that of the Christian empires of Europe; or that the general culture of the Middle East today, in comparison to that of the industrialized West, is primitive. One cannot help but wonder, though, where primitive leaves off and sophistication begins in a cultural context. For, after all, the very impulses that built, support, and sustain the still-powerful belief in the Mosaic and Christological mythologies in the West are those which are characteristic of primitivism — irrationality, superstition, iconism and the worship of abstractions. It says something for the primitivism of the Arab Middle East, both then and now, that although these characteristics are as part and parcel of Islam as they are of Judaism and Christianity, the central figure of the religion is approached as pragmatically as he is. A dense web of emotion surrounds Muhammad, and of course he has been legendized and fantasized in the extreme. But never has he been endowed with anything more than human dimension — even among a people as emotionally "primitive" as the Arabs are considered by many to be.

Muhammad is generally thought to have been born in 571 of parents who belonged to the aristocratic Korayish tribe of Mecca. Orphaned at an early age, he was put in the care of a tribal wet nurse who kept him in the desert until he was six. Thereafter he was raised by a grandfather and an uncle, and was educated for a career in Meccan commerce.* When Muhammad was about twenty-five he married a wealthy Korayish woman who was fifteen years his senior. Despite his other obligations, he led a rather mystical and solemn life. Perhaps his early childhood in the desert instilled in him an inquiring and speculative sense of the vastness of nature. Perhaps at a tender age he heard stories related by visiting tribesmen or caravaners about the new and different religious ideas circulating in the Middle East. At any rate, he grew up unimpressed by the local tribal religion and spent long periods of time in a cave at Mount Hira, outside Mecca, in meditation. Everyone in his circle held him in high esteem and called him "the Honest One," even though he did not accept their religious beliefs.

There seems to have existed in and around Mecca at that time a group of people known as Hanifs. They were a pious people in search of some religious alternative to conventional Arabian idolatry. The two locally available alternatives were Christianity and Judaism, but after a close study of the traditions and principles of these religions the Hanifs rejected them. Some scholars think that Muhammad, being of a deeply religious nature himself, must have been involved with or exposed to the Hanifs and through them received a kind of rudimentary education in Old and New Testament lore. In any event, one day when he was about forty years old† he was meditating in the cave at Mount Hira. Suddenly, according to his later account, he envisioned the angel Gabriel, who appeared before him and commanded him — in the Korayish dialect Muhammad spoke — to recite certain verses. Muhammad had no idea of what he was supposed to recite and, confused by the apparition, he resisted. Then he experienced an actual physical pressure

---

* Although his later life unfolded in broad daylight, before the eyes of his contemporaries, and was partly recorded in a contemporary book, most of his early life is cloaked in mystery. This brief account of his early days is in no way presented as absolute fact, but is based on the commonly accepted mix of fact and legend.
† Forty is a popular increment of time in ancient religious happenings, from the forty days and forty nights of Noah and the forty years of desert sojourn of Moses et al. to the forty years of age of Muhammad.

which he later claimed forced him to open his mouth and utter verses which were of a more sublime authorship than his own — ominous verses that described the wrath of an all-powerful God determined to exact punishment for the paganism of Arabia.

As seems to happen in most historical revelations, Muhammad underwent an almost convulsive upsurge of emotion, became ill and fell into a trance. When he recovered he found himself transformed. He was convinced that the message he had been driven beyond his resistance to recite was a sign that he had been chosen as the Prophet of Allah, the only God in existence.

When Muhammad reached home he related his experience to his wife. She accepted his tale without the slightest hesitation and soon became a believer, converting her children as well. Then he converted one of his wife's cousins and began to move around Mecca preaching the message that had been revealed to him: that the One God would soon condemn those who clung to pagan practices.

In the beginning his preaching was as simple as that and offered no elaborate doctrinaire alternative to the pagan religion.* It aroused little interest and no opposition from the ordinary townspeople, and in the early days of his ministry not even Muhammad himself seemed to consider his revelation particularly original. Indeed, his teachings did not go beyond the claim that he was doing anything else but repeating, in the language of the Arabians, the original message of the One God that had been revealed to others before him in other languages — the essence of which emphasized the existence of only one God, the perniciousness of idol worship, and the imminence of the final Judgment Day.

Nevertheless, the aristocratic Korayish elders must have looked at him a bit askance. They had a vested interest in maintaining the pagan religion. Their custodianship of the idols and other religious artifacts of the tribes brought them a constant stream of money, gifts and other special considerations; thus their economic well-being depended on the preservation of paganism. So, as Muhammad began to gain converts in Mecca, and as his views took on a clearer outline and he preached them with a growing fervor, he aroused the opposition of the Korayish rulers of the city. This opposition became unyielding, then irreversible, transforming Muhammad from a humble preacher into a vehement proselytizer, and then into a religiopolitical

* The details of Muhammad's early preaching life come from the Quran (the Koran), his autobiography-cum-gospel which, although supposedly illiterate, he composed in his later years. Much as the New Testament did of Christianity, the Koran became the fountainhead of Islam.

warrior who found the old tribal custom of the *jihad* the best means of over-throwing resistance to his vision.

Within a few years in Mecca, Muhammad had gained a sizable following. But they were still a small minority of the population which, goaded by the Korayish elders, hounded and persecuted them. Muhammad therefore cast around for a new arena of activity, eventually drifting north with a hard-core band of adherents to the heavily Jewish city of Yathrib.

The journey — known in Islamic lore as the Hijra (Hegira), which means "flight" or "escape" — provided the first definite date in Muslim history.* The flight took place in the year 622, when Muhammad was about fifty, and marks the beginning of the Muslim calendar. This is certainly in accordance with the importance of the event, for with the Hegira the Islamic movement was no longer a simple extension of Old and New Testament prophecy, but took on a thoroughgoing life of its own.

Prior to the Hegira Muhammad's wife died. He then married Ayisha, the daughter of his early convert and confederate Abu Bakr. Both accompanied him on the flight to Yathrib. Yathrib, a rich city that had originally been developed by the Jews, had also become a magnet for many pagan tribes. By 622 these tribes had come to dominate the Jews in numbers and were posing as well a clear threat to Jewish cultural influence. The city lacked any stable authority and was being kept in a state of explosive division by the clan rivalries of the two largest tribes, with the Jews acting as increasingly feeble counterweights in the fluctuating balance of power.

Muhammad and his group made a quick impression in the city, one that was considerably more favorable than in Mecca. Monotheism was much more firmly grafted into the Yathribian character, thanks to the Jews. And the pagan tribal elders did not have the vested economic interests of the Korayish of Mecca. So, although he did not in any sense immediately convert the city to Islam, Muhammad found a welcome there. His powerful, by now almost mesmerizing, character and temperament impressed the Arabians. His religious message aside, they saw in him a kind of high-sheikhly presence, one that could equitably mediate their constant intertribal disputes. So they gave him free rein to function on any level he wished. As a result of his success as a referee between the quarreling tribes, they tended to look upon the Islam he espoused not so much as a religion but as an effective vehicle for maintaining political and civil law and order. Hence the enlarge-

---

* In Mecca, Muhammad and his followers had begun to call themselves "Muslims," a word which signified "those who submit."

ment of the equation between religion and politics in the Arabian consciousness.

Muhammad further contributed to this enlargement by becoming more or less appointed as governor of the expanding Muslim populace, which in turn elevated his political influence. This transformation of his role was fundamental to his subsequent success, for he moved from the plane of prophecy to that of statesmanship, which enabled him to implement politically and socially his increasingly dogmatic religious principles.

He initiated the social aspects of this implementation in the early days in Yathrib by revising Islam in the tribal mold — exploiting the traditional, mystical notions of blood kinship and tribal superiority to elevate the sense of tribe into a spiritual entity. In this, ironically, he had a great deal of help from the Jews of Yathrib.

Originally he had sought a conciliation with the Jewish elders, even offering to join forces, as it were, to promote a common monotheistic doctrine among the Arabians. The Jews, of course, rejected him. From their viewpoint he was superfluous. If it was their message he was seeking to disseminate, why was he needed? They were quite capable of the task on their own, and had for a long time before the advent of this Arabian "prophet" been doing precisely that.

Muhammad persisted in pushing a compromise with the Jews. He went so far as to incorporate a good deal of Judaic ritual into the schema of Islam, even decreeing that Muslims turn toward Jerusalem when praying. In spite of his efforts, the Jews declined to cooperate; indeed, their rejection turned to scorn. He had modeled his message on that of the Hebrew Scriptures, but was forced to confess that he had never actually read them and had only become acquainted with the mythology through word of mouth. From the scholarly Jews' viewpoint, then, he was seen as wholly untrained in such matters; his audacity in presuming to call himself a prophet of their God was deserving only of contempt.

In the Jewish Scriptures and ritual law, however — or at least in his simplistic adaptations of them — Muhammad had a convenient framework upon which to construct his own theological edifice. Thus, despite his failure to ally with the Jews, he clung to his new version of the Judaic message and swiftly concluded that the error lay not in his own ideas but in the Jewish tradition. He developed and preached the view that the Jews, and later the Christians, had simply corrupted the original and true tradition, and that his "call," back in the cave near Mount Hira, had been designed by the Almighty to invest him with the solemn responsibility, and the power, to reverse the corruption.

Once this idea was thoroughly embedded in his mind Muhammad turned away from the Jews altogether. Reverting to the tribal traditions of his forebears, he organized his followers — the original Meccans and the newly won over Yathribians — into a separatist tribal organism based not only on the old-fashioned mystical bond of blood kinship but also on a new mystique: the brotherhood of the spirit. The pagan natives were highly receptive to the appeal of this approach, derived as it was from deeply ingrained tribal impulses. Muhammad retained the structure of the tribal order of society along with many traditional practices relating to property, marriage and intratribal relations. His fundamental alteration of the social model consisted of substituting the new faith — Islam — for blood kinship as the fundamental element that bound the tribe together. He thus created a new Islamic form of community — the Islamic tribe — which he called the Umma.

This replacement of the blood tie by the bond of a common faith represented a giant step forward in the civilizing process of tribal Arabia. It suppressed the blood feud as the principal medium of inter- and intratribal intercourse and brought to the surface of the Arabian consciousness a new concept of social interaction: political unity and identity through the arbitration of faith — the Islamic faith.

At first, of course, this notion was restricted to Muhammad's relatively small Islamic community, but as Islam spread it became a highly operant force in the further development of Arab psychology. Again, the political leader was identical with the religious leader, but instead of embodying the wills of the various gods, as in pre-Islamic tribal society, he expressed the absolute authority of the One God. Muhammad become a new kind of skeikh of a new kind of tribe, the Umma. This coalition of values would become the ideal model for future Islamic society. Since it subjugated the blood bond to spiritual kinship, anyone could join it merely by professing the faith. Theoretically, then, the Umma could take in the whole of mankind. And not only could it do so; since it was the expression of God's final and ultimate Prophet, it had a clear responsibility to. Thus were sown the seeds of the later Islamic conquest of the Middle East and its spread to other parts of the world.

This manifest destiny soon became part and parcel of the Umma spirit. Continuing to operate out of Yathrib,* expanding his spiritually constituted

* Which was soon to become known as Al Madinah (Medina), "The City of the Prophet."

Umma, Muhammad set his sights on winning over Mecca. He had suppressed the blood feud as the ruling impulse of the tribe, but not the warrior instinct. Indeed, the warrior instinct was one of those ancient tribal traditions he felt it necessary to preserve and exploit: how else to achieve the dominance and superiority of the Umma? Politics and religion were interchangeable. If the Word of the Prophet was the weapon of the religious portion of this unity, then the sword was the political weapon. In short, the Word and the sword were as one.

Based on this, Muhammad turned to war. At first the combat consisted mainly of raids on the caravans passing through Medina to and from Mecca. The raids helped keep Mecca under curb by pressuring its economy until it could be taken over by the Umma; additionally, they vastly increased the wealth, hence the power, of the Umma. Soon, however, the raids took on a *jihad*-ic character. Their underlying philosophy transformed them from scavenger activities to installments in the expanding — though still long-distance — holy struggle against the inimical Korayish rulers of Mecca; and their successes became thought of as "victories" in the struggle. One of the most important victories of this kind took place in March of 624, when a band of Muslims led by Muhammad himself surprised a caravan at Badr, a battle that is mentioned in the Koran as a signal of God's approval of the Islamic cause. The victory had an especially salutary effect on the Umma because it made believers out of many skeptics and led to a sudden influx of converts.

Thenceforth Muhammad could do no wrong in the eyes of his expanded following, and he used the opportunity to consolidate his sectarian as well as religious authority. He also used his new-found popularity — petulantly, perhaps — as a chance to institute a program of agitation against Medina's large Jewish and much smaller Christian populations. Having turned away from the Jews, he was now determined to make Islam an exclusively Arabian religion. The Jews would become as heathen as the pagans were. If they could not be converted, or even coopted, they would have to be persuaded to go. Jerusalem would no longer be the place to turn toward at prayer. Instead Mecca would be the direction of Islamic worship — Mecca with its ancient pagan-sacred Kaaba as the focus of the new cult and the object of all future pilgrimage. It was in this way that Islam, instead of evolving simply as a continuation of Judaeo-Christianity, developed as an extension of the native pagan tribal religions overlaid with the Judaeo-Christian heritage. Once Muhammad was able to come to terms with this, acknowledging the fundamental dominance of the pagan impulse throughout the land he sought to convert, Islam was on its way.

The Umma began to press in on Mecca. In 638, after a series of battles over four years with the larger armies of the Korayish (some of which were won, others lost, and during which several Jewish communities between Medina and Mecca were wiped out), Muhammad negotiated a truce with the Korayish, the main feature of which gave the Muslims the right to make a pilgrimage to Mecca the following spring. When he, along with two hundred fervid followers, made the journey, it was the beginning of the end of Korayish dominance of Mecca. Their faith lustrous with power and prestige, the Muslims won many new converts from the Korayish, including their two leading military strategists. By 630, they had a sufficiently large force of converts and sympathizers in Mecca to conquer the city once and for all. They destroyed the pagan idols, but kept the Kaaba — the holy shrine in which the idols had been arrayed — and transformed it into the central and most sacred place of Islamic worship.

Having secured most of the Hejaz in the faith of Islam in so short a time, Muhammad and his lieutenants in the Umma were anxious to spread the new doctrine throughout the rest of Arabia. They did so, using their now considerable military might to subjugate the tribes to the north, south and east. And as they progressed through Arabia, they grew stronger and stronger as additional tribes were won over. Thereafter the expansion — driven by the new and powerful sense of manifest destiny created by the spiritual bond of the Islamic Umma, and reinforced by traditional tribal notions of superiority and dominance — spilled beyond the borders of Arabia.

Two years after the conquest of Mecca, Muhammad gave his final speech explaining and summarizing the principles of Islam. Shortly afterward he died (June 632). His death came as a shock to the infant Islamic community, for he had never bothered to lay down a code of laws or make any provision for his succession. The problem was solved, after some bickering between the Meccan and Medinese contingents of his highest councils, by the energetic actions of his father-in-law Abu Bakr, who simply appointed himself Khalifah (Caliph) — that is, successor.*

---

* Muhammad had no sons, so succession could not follow in the usual tribal tradition of blood inheritance. A form of sheikhly election was tried and Abu Bakr was named successor. His immediate successors also rose by election, but the process would eventually be thrown over in favor of a restoration of the principle of blood succession. Thereafter the caliphate became the highest office of Islam, with each succeeding caliph the spiritual and administrative leader of the religion.

Abu Bakr, the first caliph of Islam, initiated a solution to the question of a code of laws by collecting all the writings left by Muhammad and organizing them into a book. The book was refined by *his* successor, Omar, and material was added to it by the third caliph, Othman, but since then the book has been handed down through the centuries without change. The book was entitled the Quran (Koran), and was and is considered to be the repository of all the laws God dictated for the people on earth through Muhammad. Since the tribal consciousness of Arabia conceived of no difference between religious and political organization, the Koran automatically became the law of the land as Islam spread throughout the Middle East.

For Islam, the Koran is the Word of God, just as the Holy Scriptures are for Christians and Jews. According to Islamic tradition, Muhammad was subject to ecstatic seizures all through his life after experiencing his first revelation at Mount Hira. During these episodes he received sacred messages from God in the form of verses. On other occasions the messages came to him while he was asleep. When he awoke he related them to persons who were trained to memorize them and who would later recite them so that they could be put down in writing as holy words.*

The Koran is a collection of *surrahs* (chapters) which contain the verses supposedly recited by Muhammad during the periods when he was undergoing his "symptoms of revelation." According to the ninety-sixth chapter, what was revealed to Muhammad is but a copy of what is written upon the Eternal Tablet preserved in heaven. This concept is similar to the beliefs of the ancient Egyptians, Sumerians and the Hebrews.

Indeed, in basic theophilosophical substance, the Koran differs very little from the Bible; it is mainly in matters of interpretation and techniques of worship that substantive differences exist. So it is not in the area of theology that Islam and the Koran interest us here. What is of interest is the way in which they revolutionized Middle Eastern culture and contributed to the Arab character.

The revolution took place in an astonishingly short time for so early a period in human history. It arose mainly out of the expansionary impulse of

---

* I have already noted that Muhammad is believed to have been illiterate. This would seem unlikely when measured against the belief that he was born of the aristocratic Korayish tribe and was raised by relatives for a career in trade and commerce. Nevertheless, Muhammad's supposed illiteracy lent a certain drama to the claim that he received divine revelation. Unable to read or write, he could not possibly have made up the verses he alleged were messages from God. Hence, they must indeed have come from the heavens.

Islam within Arabia during Muhammad's last years and the confusion stem-ming from his death. The tribes around Medina and Mecca had become in-fused with the spirit of the Umma; their conversion had been deep and thoroughgoing. The outlying tribes beyond the Hejaz, on the other hand, had experienced a conversion that was more enforced than voluntary. They lacked the Umma spirit of kinship through faith, and had accepted Islam only superficially through the power of Muhammad. Upon Muhammad's death they believed themselves to have been released from allegiance to Islam and free to return to their pagan ways.

To bring these tribes back into the fold, Abu Bakr was required to launch a military campaign which became known as the Ridda, "The War of the Apostasy." From Medina the armies of Islam, consisting mostly of the con-verted Bedouin tribes from the Hejaz, poured out into Arabia to subjugate and reconvert the apostate tribes in the far reaches. The Ridda could thus be viewed through the twin lenses of Muslim sensibility: It was a measure of enforcing religious solidarity and a campaign to ensure political dominance within Arabia.

However, the nature of the times was such that once Arabia was resecured for Islam the Muslims would automatically look beyond their borders, espe-cially to the north, east and west. What they perceived was a land long subject to the successive political conquests of imperial powers and to the spiritual conquests of religions, the latest being Christianity. The monotheis-tic beliefs of the Christians and Jews had spread throughout the Fertile Crescent and were still expanding under the protection of the Byzantine Empire. The region, from the point of view of the relatively impoverished Islamicized Bedouins of Arabia, was rich, tempting and accessible. So it was, then, that the Ridda, enlarged and reinforced by the reconverted apostate tribes, spilled over the borders of Arabia toward the Fertile Crescent.

# 6.

# JOURNAL: *Saudi Arabia, 1352*

I HAD JUST ARRIVED in Jiddah, Saudi Arabia. The year was 1352. It was Monday, the first of July, a few hours before midnight, although my watch read 3:30 P.M.

These quirks in time are the first of many things to confound the Western visitor to Saudi Arabia. The heat, which lies on this Red Sea port city with steambath density, is the second. The third is the sight of fleets of Cadillac and Mercedes limousines, packed with white-robed men gesticulating to one another, cruising aimlessly through the baking streets, windows shut tight and air conditioners laboring at full power. They are the mobile offices and conference rooms of Jiddah, where beating the heat has become a way of life.

The time idiosyncrasies take a bit of getting used to. The official calendar of Saudi Arabia is the Islamic one, which begins in the year that is our 622 A.D., when Muhammad fled from Mecca to Medina. Thus, 1975 is 1353.

But that's not the end of it. Once, in my youth, I appeared in a play acting the part of an Arab character. One of my props was a newspaper printed in Arabic, which at one point I was supposed to pick up and read from, simultaneously translating into English as I went along. (What I was supposed to be reading I had, of course, memorized.) I performed the part for several nights to the general approval of audiences and was feeling pleased indeed with what I thought was my skill in transforming myself into a believable Arab — my makeup was effective, my accent practiced, my Arab "demeanor" on the mark. Then, one night, I had a visitor backstage — a real Arab. "You were very good," he said, "but you make one mistake. You see, when you start reading from that newspaper, you do so as if you are reading from an English paper, from left to right. You give yourself away, because Arabic goes from right to left."

So too, in a way, does Arab time, at least in Saudi Arabia. The "day" officially begins at sunset. This means that night precedes daylight in the span of one full day. Thus the Saudi Arabian noon (twelve hours after the start of the new day) comes at approximately 6 A.M., depending on the time of the year and on the time at which the sun sets. Correspondingly, midnight occurs around 6 P.M., again, depending on the time the sunset takes place. Throughout the year, then, the benchmarks of the day fluctuate. This is not to say that the Saudis live as though day is night and night is day. Life goes on much in the same manner as it does elsewhere. But time is considerably more fluid in the Saudi way of life, doubtless on account of the resilience of the timekeeping system, which bows to the flux of nature.

The yearly calendar reflects a similar homage to the rhythms of the universe. The Islamic year is based on a division of twelve lunar months. The lunar month contains only twenty-nine and a half days; thus the Islamic year is eleven days shorter than the conventional Western year, which is based on the Christian calendar. Therefore each benchmark in the Islamic year — a religious holiday, for instance, or a national celebration — occurs eleven days earlier than it did the previous year, twenty-two earlier than it did the year before that, and so on.* Signal events revolve around the year, then, completing a cycle every thirty-three years. According to the Islamic calendar, the months have no permanent relation to the seasons.

These temporal idiosyncrasies (to the Western mind) serve to produce a certain grace and resilience in the overall Saudi national life-style that offsets the rather puritan rigidity imposed by the Koranic law of the land. One cannot help but suppose that the curious juxtaposition of languor and energy one perceives in the Arabian character, of poetic idealism and harsh realism, of pacifism and bellicosity, are somehow produced by and at the same time reflected in the compromise that every Arabian makes between religion and nature.

Traveling throughout the Arabian peninsula in the Islamic year 1352 one constantly encounters Westerners, mostly Americans with either Oklahoma twangs (Aramco employees†) or variations of Harvard lockjaw (bankers and

---

* The one exception to this in Saudi Arabia is National Day, which commemorates the unification of the country and is celebrated every September 23. This is for the convenience of foreign diplomats, who take part in the festivities.
† Aramco being the acronym for the Arabian-American Oil Company, about which more later.

investment seekers). One's ears are constantly assaulted in airplanes, hotel bars and restaurants by American "assessments" of the Saudi (or Kuwaiti, or Abu Dhabian, or Bahrainian) character. These expert analyses are usually based on conventional "ugly American" ethnocentric bigotries: "These here Ay-rabs, no wonder they're so backwards — they write backwards, they tell time backwards!"; or "The trouble doing business with an Arab is he's two-faced; he'll tell you one thing today, and something entirely different tomorrow — why, just the other day . . ." Examples of the deficiencies in the collective Arab character abound within what might be called the traveling American circus of the Middle East.

I too had found frustrations and exasperations in my travels, caused usually by broken or forgotten appointments on the part of Arab dignitaries I had arranged to interview, by the bureaucratic entanglements — brought about by a combination of inertia, indifference and officiousness that the Arabs somehow mistake for progress — which attend almost every aspect of life, and by the simple fact that I was an American, thereby (especially in the northern Arab countries) a personification of the hated Phantom jet.

Yet I found no comfort in the hackneyed analyses of the Americans (and other Westerners) I encountered. Granted there might have been a kernel of accuracy in their explanations for this and that Arab trait, but to accept these explanations on their face meant that I would have had to accept the common oversimplified Arab perceptions of the American character — imperialistic, warmongering, selfish, dogmatic, vulgar, insensitive, culturally inferior, without depth, lacking the capacity for insight, and so on. This litany followed me throughout the Middle East with as much tenacity, although articulated more subtly, as the Western listings of Arab failings. The principal difficulty lay, I concluded, in profound cultural differences that made communication and sympathetic comprehension virtually impossible. Experiencing the high emotionalism, expressed and unexpressed, of almost every Arab I met — the capacity for passion at both extremes of the emotional spectrum — I suspected that it was this quality that gave the Arab character its unique and (from the Western viewpoint) unsavory outline. By attempting to plumb this quality, to excavate some comprehensible rationale for it, I hoped to understand, at least for myself, the vital whole of the Arab character which, when set in the context of man as an entirety, might provide a perspective on the future Arab role in all our lives. After all, I thought, twelve million people in the West today follow the teachings of Moses (an ancient Middle Easterner who, if he existed, was ancestrally an Arab); hundreds of millions more follow the teachings of Jesus (another in whom was incorporated an Arab ancestry). Indeed, the entire Judaeo-Christian Western world subscribes to beliefs and practices that are fundamentally Arab in their origins and were promoted by fundamentally Arab mentalities.

Spiritually, as well as in many ways materially, the West is irrevocably tied to Arab culture. Which is both an irony and a paradox — for we who revere, even worship, men of Arab ancestry dismiss Arab culture and ignore Arab history as though they were totally alien to us. When Pope Pius XII made his famous conciliatory comment about the Jews, that "spiritually, we are all Semites," he was stating the case anthropologically. He would have been just as accurate to put it historically: "Spiritually, we are all Arabs" — which is to say we all derive religiously from a common proto-Arab source.

How, then, did the innate Arab nature of Judaeo-Christianity become transformed until it is today virtually invisible? It did so, of course, through its historical evolution from a Middle Eastern spirituality based on emotionalism and superstition into a Western spirituality based on rationalism and superstition. Religion underlies the present-day cultures of both West and Middle East. In the West it's Judaeo-Christianity — a construct of attitudes and values based on ancient superstitions but cultivated, refined and made attractive over the centuries to pragmatic Western sensibilities through the instrument of rationality — the detailed working out of things by the mind. In the Middle East* it's Islam — a construct of similar attitudes and values based likewise on ancient superstitions but cultivated, refined and made palatable to Middle Eastern sensibilities through the instrument of emotionalism — the detailed working out of things through instinct, intuition, faith and wish.

It is here — in the distinction between the rational and emotional substrata of their respective religion-oriented cultures — that the basic difference between Western and Middle Eastern sensibilities in all things lies. Whether the respective religious systems caused the cultures in which they thrived (European and Arab) to develop the way they did (rationalistic as opposed to emotionalistic) or whether the opposite was the case is not really important (common sense suggests that a simultaneous crosscurrent was at work in each religion-culture).† What is important is that as the rationality of

---

* I leave the Far East out of this scenario deliberately, for the religion-based cultures of the Orient that are not Islamic have no historically demonstrable spiritual ties to the Middle East.
† Anthropologists almost universally agree that conditions of climate and geography play a significant role in the trait-predominance of cultures. Thus, goes the theory, the harsh Atlantic climate and varied geography of Europe contributed significantly to the European tendency

Judaeo-Christianity shaped Western culture, and vice versa, rationality itself became the hallmark of the Western character. And as the emotionality of Islam shaped Arab culture, and vice versa, emotionality became the chief means of expression of the Arab character.

Rationality as opposed to emotionalism, then — therein lies the strategic difference between the Judaeo-Christian and the Muslim character, the Western and the Middle Eastern nature. One interesting experiment I tried throughout my Middle East travels was to ask Westerners who assured me they were practicing Christians (a Texas petroleum engineer, a missionary, a New York bank vice-president, a British parts salesman, a German auto mechanic, an Arkansas oil-rig foreman, to name a few) to explain to me why they believed in God. The answers I got were basically mental in nature, involving long and convoluted expressions of logic — some sophisticated, others naïve, but all sharply reflecting a training and instinct for the rational, thought-out explanation. I posed the same question to a number of Arabs representing a similar cross section of intelligence and education. Invariably the response was a simple shrug and a sentence or two that each amounted to the same answer: "I believe God exists because God exists." With the response would usually come a look, as if to say, "How can you ask such a silly question?"

Jiddah was my gateway to the Arabian peninsula. I had flown there to do some interviewing and general poking around with a view to gaining an informed glimpse into what the Saudis (and other peninsula petroleum states) were planning to do with the dizzily spiraling revenues they were accumulating in the wake of the October War. I had been met and hustled through the airport formalities by a functionary of King Faisal — an arrangement that had been made in London — and was deposited at an American-style hotel to await a summons to Taif, eighty miles away, where Faisal and his court were in summer residence.

Geographically and climatically the Arabian peninsula, of which the Kingdom of Saudi Arabia occupies the greatest portion, is exactly as it was four thousand years ago. Extending from the top of the Red Sea (which separates it from Africa) on the west and from the top of the Persian Gulf* (which

---

toward rationality, while the more temperate climate and less varied terrain of the Middle East were responsible for the dominance of emotionalism in the peoples there. (This is oversimplifying the theory somewhat, but it accurately captures its outline.)
* The Persian Gulf is known in Arab countries as the Arabian Gulf.

separates it from Asia) on the east, its great bulk, in the shape of an irregular square, plunges southeasterly into the Indian Ocean. Roughly 1,400 miles long and 1,200 miles wide at its broadest southerly expanse, the peninsula generally corresponds in size to the land mass of the United States east of the Mississippi. Surrounded on three sides by water, it is ringed by a slender strip of semifertile coastal lowland. A narrow range of particularly steep mountains knifes southward parallel to the Red Sea coast from halfway up the peninsula to its corner opposite Africa. The rest of the peninsula rises more or less abruptly to a high, arid plateau that blankets its interior with various forms of desert, from completely sandy waste to rocky moonscape.

It was across this interior — from Jiddah on the western coast to the capital city of Riyadh in the east-central portion of Saudi Arabia — that I was invited to drive while waiting to go to Taif. On my first evening in the hotel in Jiddah I was introduced to an Armenian who had formerly worked for Aramco but was now an independent consultant to the Saudi government. He had just taken delivery of a new Mercedes at Jiddah port and was setting out the next morning for his home in Riyadh, with a stop at Taif, in the mountains near Mecca, to discuss a business deal with one of King Faisal's retainers. Since I was going to Taif, and then on to Riyadh and the east coast, he would, he informed me over a drink, be delighted by my company.

We set out early the next morning, but not early enough to beat the pilgrim traffic to Mecca. Jiddah is the main Saudi port of entry for Muslims who come from all over the world each summer in the tens of thousands to make the pilgrimage (Hajj) to Mecca and its holy shrine, the Kaaba. The pilgrimage is one of the main articles of the Islamic faith, and as my Armenian companion, Basmadjian, maneuvered his new air-conditioned Mercedes up the steep highway from Jiddah we were surrounded by trucks, buses, taxis and private cars, all packed with white-robed men making for Mecca.

Today Mecca lives on the pilgrimage industry. Located in a dry, rocky valley encircled by hills, the city has a population of about two hundred thousand which is constantly swelled to the bursting point by the daily influx of pilgrims. Due to the hot, dry climate of the area, there is little agriculture in its vicinity and, except for the manufacture of religious articles, no local industry to speak of.

The old part of the city is tightly packed with the Arabian version of tenements — four- and five-story stucco-and-stone structures that gleam a dirty white in the blurred sun and are randomly separated by narrow, shaded alleys. At the epicenter of this jumble is the Great Mosque — the original site of the idols of the pre-Islamic pagan tribes, transformed and enlarged since the eighth century into the central focus of Muslim worship.

It is to the Great Mosque that all the traffic on the Jiddah-Mecca road flows. Technically, non-Muslims are forbidden entrance into the Holy City — indeed, the highway to Taif and beyond (Mecca is situated about halfway between Jiddah and Taif) skirts Mecca, with a special access road branching off for pilgrims only. But Basmadjian — himself a Christian — had influence. Anxious to please me (he had relatives in America whom he was sure I must know), he had promised me a look at Mecca and turned the Mercedes into the stream of traffic heading off the main highway.

The Great Mosque of Mecca was not at all what I thought it would be. Approaching it was rather like approaching Yankee Stadium; it was more similar to an arena in its outlines than to a church. Once past its elaborate front facade, you walk briefly through a cool marbled inner chamber and then are outdoors again, caught up in the tide of a thousand murmuring pilgrims and spilled into a vast, low-walled courtyard ringed with graceful minarets. The sudden transition from darkness to light momentarily blinds you, and everything seems to turn a milky white. Then you see it, sitting like some mammoth beached black whale in the middle of nowhere — the Holy Kaaba. The Kaaba is a giant cube draped in a richly embroidered dark velvet and set into a sunken plaza in the middle of the courtyard. Around it at least five thousand barefoot, scantily robed Muslims shove and push for a better view, reaching out to touch the fabric of its drape, while a second, more distant circle of worshipers stands facing the Kaaba in reverential silence. Scattered around the gleaming courtyard hundreds of men lay prostrate, some moaning painfully, others seemingly comatose.

"Is that part of the ritual?" I asked Basmadjian.

"No," he said, "they are all passed out from the heat."

From Mecca we drove toward Taif, with a detour past Mount Arafat. There I was astonished to see a vast encampment of pilgrims, tents spreading across the plain at the foot of the mountain for as far as the eye could see.

"It is the second stage of the Hajj," Basmadjian explained. "After the pilgrims visit the Kaaba and circle it seven times they come here. They rent the tents and wait all day in the sun until sunset. Then a cannon goes off, which is the signal for them to move on to Mina, about five miles from here. At Mina are the three white pillars believed to mark the place where Abraham* was tempted by the Devil as he was about to sacrifice his son to Allah. Each pilgrim is required to hurl seven stones at the pillars, symbolizing the stoning of the Devil. It is all quite primitive, you see."

"As compared to what?" I said.

"As compared to Christianity, of course," he said.

"But Christianity is primitive as compared to atheism," I suggested, misreading his intention. "Where do you draw the line between primitive and advanced?"

"Oh, it is all relative," he conceded. "But I am not talking about beliefs themselves. I am talking about the way they are practiced, expressed. You say you are here trying to have insights into how the Arabs will deal with their new eminence on the world stage. That is why I wished to bring you through here, so that you could see how they practice their religion. It is through this that you can see what they will do. It is the way you tell any culture. The more primitive they are, the more — how do you say? — obsessed they are with their religious rituals, the more responsible and careful they will be. The less primitive a civilization is, the more irresponsible it will be. The further away one gets from God, the less a man feels he has to lose in the hereafter. It is in the relative primitiveness and sophistication of the religious rituals of a society that you can predict how that society will act in regard to other societies. All this Muslim ritual must seem strange to you, foreign, perhaps even silly. But heed it closely. Allah is much more deeply engraved into the soul of the average Arab than God is in the soul of the Christian or Jew. You have probably already seen this. But do not make the mistake of taking it too lightly. For the Arab, Allah is everything: he explains everything, he is the cause of everything. Thus, the Arab rejoices at his prosperity with the same intensity that he bewails his adversity. But the two are as one, you see. Therefore the Arab does not change. With oil, with money, with military victory — all you people coming from the West seem

---

* The Muslims, like the Jews, trace their spiritual and biological ancestry to Abraham. But whereas the Jewish link to Abraham is through his younger, supposedly more favored son Isaac, the Muslim link is through Abraham's elder, exiled son Ishmael. According to the Scriptures, Ishmael was cast out of the fold of Abraham because he was not born to Abraham's Hebrew wife, Sarah, but to her Egyptian servant, Hagar. God, in supporting Sarah's wish that Ishmael be sent away once her own child (Isaac) was born, is supposed to have told Abraham, in effect, "Do not worry about Ishmael, I will also make a nation of him, as I will Isaac." Later in the biblical account, as Hagar and Ishmael are about to perish from lack of water in the wilderness, God appears to Hagar and says, again in effect, "Hagar, do not be afraid. Arise! Lift up the boy and take him by the hand, for you shall both be saved and of him I will make a great nation." With the Jews claiming exclusive descendancy through Isaac, it was inevitable that Muhammad would hold up Ishmael as the source of the Muslim nation, for God had promised a nation of Ishmael.

to expect the Arab to be different from how he was before. But he will not be different."

After two days on separate business in Taif (I did not get to see the king), Basmadjian and I set off in the new but now dusty Mercedes for Riyadh, some five hundred miles northeast across the desert of central Arabia. We began the trip at noon — that is, at six in the morning. The trunk of the car was jammed with jerry cans of gas and water, just in case. The highway was good, and by noon (Western time) we had reached the small roadside oasis village of Afit. Basmadjian was a skillful driver, and he kept up a running commentary about what the mystique of the desert meant to the Arabs.

Enough Westerners have journeyed across the Arabian waste and have eloquently described its effects to make anything I might say superfluous. To me a desert is a desert, whether it lies in Arabia or Arizona. When experienced from within the cool confines of a modern air-conditioned motor car, it represents nothing more than a passing, monotonous panorama. Until something goes wrong, that is. Then one becomes very attentive indeed to it.

We left Afit at about one in the afternoon after a quick lunch and a replenishment of the car's gas tank. Basmadjian wanted to reach Shaqra, about 160 miles away, before five so that he could drop something off for a friend, then complete the last 130 miles into Riyadh in time for dinner at his home, where I would be his guest.

Speeding across the bleak landscape encouraged conversation. This was a pastime Basmadjian thoroughly enjoyed, although he tended to turn discussion into monologue. He especially enjoyed talking about his Armenian heritage. "All you ever hear about are the Jews," he exclaimed at one point. "Now, I have nothing against the Jews, but after all, our history is similar. Our roots are in Armenia,* a land that was almost never allowed to belong to us. We have been massacred and enslaved and chased into exile for over three thousand years. Every empire treated us badly. The Ottomans were terrible. They slaughtered Armenians by the tens of thousands late in the last century. And the Turks — why, in the First World War the Turks killed a million and a half Armenians. There is no limit to the misery and persecution we have endured, simply because we wanted to live in our own land. There are more than six million of us in the world, and still we are without our land. But do you hear anyone saying, 'Those poor Armenians, they have suffered as

* Armenia is sandwiched between the Black Sea and the Caspian Sea, and like Palestine was a crossroads of the European-Asian trade routes.

much as the Jews, let us give them a land?' Of course you don't. Now, you tell me, what makes the Jews any more special than us that they should have their own sovereign nation and we shouldn't?"

He was about to answer his own question when he was interrupted by a thump and a loud grinding noise from the front of the car. Then we were careering wildly, the car tilted to one side, as Basmadjian braked us to a metal-screeching halt. It was more than a flat tire. The front left wheel had come off and was rolling down the empty highway ahead of us. We watched unbelievingly as it wobbled, skipped off the road, and disappeared behind a gravelly mound.

We were, it goes without saying, in the middle of nowhere. But our plight did not go unwitnessed. As we got out of the car to inspect the damage we noticed two things. One was the heat, especially the way it came up off the pavement and burned the bottoms of our feet through our shoes. The other was a group of tents on a rise in the distance off to our right.

All the bolts holding the wheel to the hub had sheared off. "I don't understand this," Basmadjian wailed. "It is a brand-new car — a Mercedes. These things simply do not happen!"

There was obviously no way the spare wheel and tire could be put onto the hub with the retaining bolts gone. "Maybe it was the heat," I said.

"Those goddamned Germans," he said, tearing at his hair. "We, my friend, are stranded."

"What about that?" I said, pointing to the encampment perhaps a mile away. A vehicle had left the cluster of black tents and was approaching us, spewing a roostertail of dust in its wake. The heat shimmering up off the gray sand made the vehicle — a pickup truck — appear like a distorted image in an amusement park mirror.

We were about halfway between Afit and another highway village called Dawadim, Basmadjian was informed by the driver of the truck. He was dressed in a black robe and a black-and-white houndstooth headdress. With him were two other men, all dark, bearded and dressed identically. I tried to follow the Arabic conversation, but couldn't. The men were obviously Bedouin. The two companions of the driver stared at me expressionlessly.

After much elaborate discussion between the driver and Basmadjian, an arrangement was made. One of the men would wait by the road until another car, going in the direction of Shaqra, came by (in the half hour we'd been there not a vehicle had passed). He would hail the car — or truck, as the case might be — and ask the driver to take us to Shaqra, where Basmadjian could make arrangements to have a tow truck sent back to bring the Mercedes in. In the meantime, we were to be the Bedouin driver's guest in the distant encampment. Lookouts would be posted between the highway and the camp to pass the word along when a car had stopped. And once Basmadjian and I were on our way — by sunset at the latest, the driver assured us, when traffic picked up — the Mercedes would be protected from scavengers until the tow truck arrived to take it to Shaqra or Riyadh.

On this last assurance Basmadjian withdrew a wad of riyals, counted off about half of them, and handed them to the driver. The two men next to him shifted their stare from me and gazed interestedly at Basmadjian's hand as he thrust the rest of his money back into his pocket. Uh-oh, I thought, he's asking for it, flashing money around like that. To my surprise, the driver refused to accept the money.

A few minutes later we were crammed into the truck's driving compartment and bouncing across a dusty track toward the black tents. One of the driver's companions had been left at the Mercedes, while the other was consigned to the rear bed of the truck. The heat inside the truck was blistering, but I, the only one shirtless, was the only one sweating. "Shouldn't you be a little wary of showing your money like that?" I said to Basmadjian when I was sure the driver didn't understand English.

"You are seeing an example of famed Bedouin hospitality," he replied. "This chap is the sheikh of a family of the Suhul tribe. The Suhul are basically friendly souls. Money means very little to them. They are still on the primitive side, even for Bedouin. If I had a goat in the back of the Mercedes they would probably have stolen it and left us for dead. But money — money has no value. And since I didn't have a goat, or anything else of value to them, they are constrained by their custom to be good samaritans."

"So what happens now?" I said, impatient with the delay. I had appointments the next day in Riyadh and an offer of a free plane ride to Bahrain the following morning.

"You think you have troubles," Basmadjian said, reading my souring mood. "You have my abject apologies for what happened to the car. But do you know what it is going to cost me to have it towed to Riyadh? Anyway, you should count this as a stroke of good luck. It gives you an opportunity to experience Bedouin life at first hand."

I had thought of that already, but didn't feel very lucky. The driver of the pickup — Rashid, his name turned out to be — smelled godawful. When Basmadjian explained in Arabic who I was, he leaned across and showed me a toothless grin, then greeted me with some effusive Arabic. His breath was redolent of burnt sulfur.

He jounced the truck to a stop at the campsite with a grinding of gears and a squeal of brakes. A half-dozen men appeared from what seemed to me to be the main tent, a sprawling black goatskin affair the size of a small warehouse. They looked sullen as they gathered about to get a look at Basmadjian and me, but on a curt command from Rashid they burst into gap-toothed smiles. After dispersing several of the men back over our route to the Mercedes to act as what we thought was to be a signal system, Rashid invited us into the tent. It was dark and cool inside, but the combined stench of the goatskin and stale human sweat soon killed the pleasure of the transition from sun to shade. We were served coffee — an acrid brew which is a staple of the Bedouin diet — then taken outside again, to the other side of the encampment, to survey a mixed herd of goats and sheep which was the pride of Rashid and his clan. Then we were shown into an empty smaller tent and told, in effect, to relax for a while.

In all there were twenty-four men — including the ones strung out toward the Mercedes — about seventy woman, and innumerable children, all of whom counted themselves members of Rashid's band. Nine of the women were his wives, as I was to discover to my amazement a few hours later.

The most indelible memory I had of the desert was the suddenness with which day becomes night. On this occasion the transition was particularly memorable, for we had been promised some action out on the highway by sunset. We watched the sun fall toward the barren horizon with almost mouthwatering anticipation. Then, suddenly, it was pitch black, and nothing had happened. It grew colder, a few torches were lit, and still nothing happened. Finally, when I noticed that several of the men assigned earlier to the signal system had gathered in a corner of the tent, I prevailed upon Basmadjian to inquire of Rashid just what was going on. The answer shattered all my hopes of getting to Riyadh in time for my next day's interviews.

Evidently there had been a misunderstanding between Rashid and Basmadjian. Rashid thought that all Basmadjian had wanted him to do was ensure that a traveler was stopped, told of our predicament, and asked to pass by a garage in Shaqra to tell the proprietor to send a tow truck back to meet us. Such had been done, Rashid informed us. In the meantime, we would be his guests for the night — indeed, a lamb had just been slaughtered and was at that very moment sizzling over a fire.

Of all the untoward moments in my journeys through the Middle East, this was the most aggravating. I had expected by now to be back on the road to Riyadh. I had little wish to spend the night (and possibly the next day, and the night and day after that, as it was beginning to look) in a Bedouin camp. I'm sorry to say I behaved badly: I railed at Basmadjian for "getting me into this fucked-up situation. Jesus," I said, "I could've stayed down on the road and gotten a ride by now."

"Shh!" he whispered. "You must not abuse Rashid's hospitality. I take the blame. I thought I made myself clear to him. Evidently I did not. But to walk down to the motorway now with the idea of stopping a car yourself would be the grossest of insults. Believe me, friend Thomas, he would interpret such an act as justification to kill you. He might kill both of us."

"You've got to be joking."

"I joke not at all. Believe me, someone like Rashid has probably killed a hundred men in his lifetime. The Suhul are a peaceful tribe, basically, but they kill when they feel they must. For Rashid to be in the position he is in, he has had to have killed many men. He is not used to making distinctions between nationalities, religions, races. If you insult his honor, his manliness, he will be obliged to kill you to keep his face with his underlings. You will not be able to explain that your insult was an innocent mistake. He will not understand you. Nor would he listen to me. There is no justice — what you call judicial process — among the Bedouin. Every transgression of Bedouin custom calls for an automatic penalty, no matter who commits it. Among the Suhul, to scorn a sheikh's hospitality is to die. I am sorry."

"You mean we're prisoners?" I said.

"At least until tomorrow. Until the towing lorry comes."

"How do you know it *will* come?"

Basmadjian shrugged. For the first time I noticed that he was a fat and repulsive little man. "It will come," he said. "You see, Rashid sent his man to fetch it. That is part of the protocol. He is delighted to entertain us for one night. Two nights would be a strain on his hospitality."

I looked at the beat-up old pickup truck standing in the glow of a fire that had been started by some of the Bedouin. "I've got an idea. Why don't we pool our resources and buy that truck from Rashid? You say we're only two hundred miles from Riyadh, eighty or ninety from Shaqra. We could be in Shaqra in two hours. I could drop you off, then go on by myself to Riyadh. I could be there by midnight."

"He would not sell it. That lorry is obviously his most prized possession. It is better even than a herd of first-rate camels because it does not have to be fed. And anyway, like other things, the lorry has no cash value to him. You see, he stole it."

"All right," I said, "since he stole it from somebody else, let's you and I turn into Bedouin and steal it from him."

"Ah, that is not something I would care to do," Basmadjian said.

"Why not? Since the people out here live by the law of theft, we'd just be following the custom."

"There is also another law — the law of retribution. I am afraid you are unaware of the risks. Even if we were to be successful in stealing the lorry, how do we know how much petrol its tank contains? How far would we get? And then, if we were to steal it, it would mean I would have to abandon my car to them. A claptrap old lorry is not a fair exchange for a brand-new Mercedes."

"So we're stuck here."

"I am afraid so. But not to worry. I am sure the towing lorry will be here first thing in the morning. Rashid's messenger will see to that."

Basmadjian and I had been alone for an hour in the smaller tent, but now something was afoot. Several women were tending the sheep that roasted over the large fire in front of the main tent and there was a babble of female voices from elsewhere. Soon one of Rashid's companions entered our tent, followed by a line of women, all veiled and dressed in black caftanlike garments. The Bedouin said something to Basmadjian and the women formed a semicircle around us. In unison the women stooped down and grasped the bottoms of their caftans. Then they stood upright again, raising the garments to their shoulders. Suddenly I was staring at a collection of sagging, dark-nippled breasts, navels and triangles of thick pubic hair amid a sea of flesh — all glowing dark amber in the flickering light of the torch.

"What's this," I said to Basmadjian, "a Bedouin burlesque show?"

"Sheikh Rashid is putting on a feast for us. But first, to show that his hospitality has no limits, he is presenting us his most favored wives to choose from."

I surveyed the immobile bodies. The women's veiled heads were hidden behind their raised skirts. The Bedouin looked at me expectantly, then made what in America would be considered a vulgar gesture with his hand, as if to make sure I knew what the point of all this was. "Tell me," I said to Basmadjian, "When these women have sex, do they remove their veils?"

He chuckled. "Not for us. Which may be just as well."

"Well?" I said.

"Well?" he came back. "Are you going to choose?"

"No thanks."

"But you must," he said.

The sight of the women was about as erotic as watching a herd of Guernseys waiting to be milked. "What do you mean I must? I'd rather not."

"You cannot decline," Basmadjian insisted. "Sheikh Rashid will be highly insulted. One does not refuse such a gift."

"Now listen," I said, "I've heard all about this business of turning down Bedouin hospitality. But I didn't ask for this. The guest has to have some choice in these matters."

"The only choice you have," said Basmadjian, "is which one you choose to pleasure yourself with."

I could see Rashid's retainer frown. He had sensed my reluctance. Suddenly he barked a command at the women. They dropped their skirts and scurried from the tent. I felt a mixture of relief and apprehension. But I had no time to savor it. Within a few seconds another group of females entered the tent and repeated the same procedure. Their bodies were those of younger women, girls — indeed, they were probably teenagers. The Bedouin said something to Basmadjian.

"What is it?" I asked.

"He thinks you might prefer a younger woman. These are some of Rashid's most favored daughters."

"For God's sake," I exclaimed, "they're barely out of the cradle!"

"You had better pick one of these. He's got another group waiting outside, younger yet."

"I can't, Basmadjian. I have no desire."

"You cannot refuse the sheikh."

"Are you going to choose one?"

"Of course." He pointed to one of the bodies — a lithe, tiny-breasted affair — and nodded at the Bedouin man. The man said something to the girl and she stepped out of the semicircle. "Now it is your turn," Basmadjian said.

"I know, tell him I've got a terrible disease — syphilis — that I wouldn't want to inflict it on any of his women."

"It wouldn't make any difference. They do not know what syphilis is."

"Tell him it eats away the brain, turns a girl crazy, eventually kills her. Tell him it will spread to all those who come in contact with her."

"It would make no difference. No matter the reason, you will still be refusing Rashid's gift. That is all that will count with him. He would gladly sacrifice one of his daughters for the sake of your pleasure. That is part of his obligation."

"But I don't expect to have any pleasure."

"You never know."

"What happens if I refuse?"

"Then Bakr here, he will report it to Rashid, who I can assure you is now sitting in his tent eagerly awaiting word. Things will become very unfriendly for us around here. So do me a favor. Choose a girl."

I shrugged and pointed in the general direction of all of them. Bakr crowed approvingly and moved to the side of one of the girls. Yes, I agreed, that one. He nudged the girl out of the group, then herded the rest of them from the tent. Basmadjian and I were alone with two of the daughters of Sheikh Rashid.

Basmadjian let himself be led off to a dark corner of the tent by his girl. Mine coaxed me into another corner, carrying the torch with her. I fondled her for a few moments, but the smells wafting from her clothes numbed my neurosexual circuits. So I gave up and began whispering gibberish into her ear. At one point I tried to lift her veil and — good luck — she uttered a loud cry which I hoped would be taken as a sign by any eavesdroppers, including Basmadjian, that I had done my duty. To embellish the charade I uttered a loud, long moan.

Evidently it worked, for later, after the girls had left, Basmadjian said, "There, you see, it wasn't so bad, was it? You sounded as though you really got into it."

"Oh, yeah," I said. "It wasn't bad at all." I just hoped the girl hadn't gone back to her father and described my behavior. I imagined that I was already the laughingstock of the girls' tent, or wherever it was they were sequestered.

Our sexual repast was followed by a feast of food. We were brought back to the main tent to be greeted by an expansive Rashid and a grinning entourage of twelve men and a few boys. The roasted sheep was brought in on a leather platter by several women and placed on the ground in the middle of the circle of men. It was surrounded on all sides by steaming mounds of rice and flat loaves of hot bread. Basmadjian and I were invited to start. Following his example, I tore a chunk of meat out of the lamb's midsection with my fingers, wrapped it in a bread disk, dipped it in the pool of drippings in which the lamb lay, and shoved it into my mouth. The Bedouin gestured approvingly and joked among themselves, then proceeded to ignore us as they attacked the food.

The meat was tasty but stringy. I had my fill after five minutes, but the Bedouin ate for an hour, talking animatedly among themselves, the grease from the meat glistening on their beards and moustaches. Coffee followed. After everyone had had three cups all conversation ended. The feast was over and it was every man off to his own tent. I was tired, more than a little cold, and feeling depressed about having to spend the night on the ground under a camel's-hair blanket when I should have been in Riyadh preparing for my next day's interviews. I decided, however, not to let the experience go completely to waste. I asked Basmadjian to ask the sheikh if he would submit to a few questions, Basmadjian translating. What follows is a fairly accurate reconstruction of our conversation:

KIERNAN.   Is this a permanent camp?
RASHID.   No. We travel south with the new moon.
K.   Your family, are they all with you? Or have some left?
R.   Some have left. They go to work in the oil fields. You have noticed, we have many more women than men. Did you enjoy the woman I presented to you?
K.   Oh, very much. Living out here, I don't suppose you get to hear much about what is happening in the world.
R.   The world?
K.   I mean, beyond the desert.
R.   (With a shrug.) What do we need to know? Our world is here.
K.   Are you at all aware of what's going on around you? The great disputes between nations over oil? The wars between the Arabs and the Jews?
R.   We hear certain things. But we do not war with the Jews. We are Arabs. We are the only Arabs.
K.   Do you hate the Jews?
R.   Hate the Jews? We hear they are a dirty, evil people. Infidels. But we do not hate them. We wish them Allah's blessings. I have never seen a Jew. What are they like?
K.   Well, they're much like you, as a matter of fact.
R.   They live in the north?
K.   Yes.

R. They are not Arabs.

K. You mean Bedouin?

R. Arabs. We are Arabs. The others — they are what they are, but they are not Arabs.

K. Have you ever heard of Sadat? Nasser? Qadhafi?

R. I hear of Nasser.

K. Well, he said that all people who live here — in Egypt, Iraq, all over this area — all are Arabs.

R. He is stupid.

K. Do you think the Jews should be thrown out of Palestine?

R. (Another shrug.) If Allah wills it.

K. Have you killed men in your life?

R. Of course.

K. How many?

R. Dozens.

K. How have you managed to escape unscathed?

R. Allah has willed it. Allah wills everything.

K. Have you met many Americans?

R. You are the second.

K. What do you think of us?

R. You make good trucks. But you are not Arabs.

K. Tell me, if I had refused the woman you so kindly offered me before, would you have killed me?

R. But why would you refuse her? If you refuse her, I get you another one. My house is your house.

K. But say I had refused all the women. Would you have killed me? (I was eyeing Basmadjian, wondering if he was translating the question accurately.)

R. You Americans — what do you believe, that we are primitive? Of course I would not kill you. I would only have you wounded. When you are a guest, you must know how to act as a guest, just as I must know how to act as a host. If you don't, you must be taught.

I looked for some hint of humor in Rashid's eyes, but found none. My sleep that night was fitful. Lying on the ground it would have been anyway, but it was made more so by my worry that my question might have provoked Rashid into summoning the girl and demanding her description of what had happened between us.

But morning came without any incident. With it, as promised, came a tow truck from Shaqra. By ten in the morning Basmadjian and I were comfortably ensconced in the Mercedes and creeping northeastward behind the truck.

# 7.

# HISTORY: *The Arabs – I*

THE ARABIAN CONQUEST of the Middle East took less than a century. This is all the more surprising in view of the imbalance in number between the invading Muslims and the settled populations. The settled populations were large, well institutionalized and backed up by the militarily advanced legions of Byzantium and Persia. The Muslims were far fewer and, being Bedouin, had little in the way of institutions and sophisticated weaponry. Most of all, they were militarily primitive as compared to the armies of Persia and Byzantium. The only factors that operated in their favor were that they were mobile and improvisatory, and that the Byzantines and Persians were more concerned with each other than with them. Above all, of course, they were favored by their almost blind Islamic passion.

The conquest did not begin as such. It was not a carefully designed policy conceived and worked out beforehand in the caliphate of Abu Bakr. Rather, it was a leftover from the War of the Apostasy. And its key figure was not Abu Bakr, but one of the pagan Korayish military leaders Muhammad had converted upon his entrance into Mecca, a warrior named Khalid. Khalid had led the Ridda against the apostate tribes in the north and successfully subjugated them. Now, in 633, with his Muslim army expanded by the addition of these tribes, he sent expeditions farther north. The expeditions were not aimed at conquest; they were simply extensions of the time-honored Bedouin raiding tradition. But with their success, Khalid and his adjutants began to view the land beyond the borders in a different light. Further incursions met with further successes, and soon the Bedouin were fanning out in several directions toward the Fertile Crescent, always following the lines of least resistance as the weaknesses of the defenders revealed themselves. The conquest had begun before anyone in Islam realized that there was to be a conquest.

One of the great misconceptions of Western history has been that the Muslim conquest of the Middle East, and then of the regions more distant, was primarily a religious phenomenon — that it was inspired by secret fiats issued by Muhammad and then carried out by his immediate successors, the early caliphs. Such a form of religious expansionism — by the sword — is repugnant to most modern sensibilities, and this popular interpretation is perhaps a large part of the reason Muhammad and Islam have been the object of so much Western prejudice.

It was not fundamentally a religious phenomenon precisely because, as I have noted, the Muslim Arabians were incapable of distinguishing between religious and political action. Muhammad's interests in establishing Islam were confined to Arabia. It was not even secondarily a religious conquest, and this for two reasons.

One was due to the fact that as the Bedouin armies penetrated farther north into the Byzantine and Persian empires, the caliphate in Medina* usually had no choice but to acquiesce in the decisions and actions taken by the far-flung army commanders, who were acting independently and were motivated more by the simple Bedouin raiding impulse, and the booty that would be acquired, than by a desire to implant Islamic religious beliefs abroad.

The second reason was rooted in the economics of early Islam. Muslim fiscal policy was formed out of the practice begun by Muhammad once Islam was firmly established in the Hejaz. Its chief feature was that all those who chose not to convert were required to pay monumental taxes to Muhammad and his governing establishment. This had a twofold effect. One, it encouraged conversion on the part of the pagan tribes; two, it ensured a steady flow of money from those communities that were by their very nature clearly inconvertible — those of the Jews and Christians. After his initial persecution of the Jews and his lesser agitation against the Christians of the Hejaz, Muhammad was content to let them remain as second-class citizens, their only penalty being the monetary tribute, which usually amounted to about fifty percent of their wealth. This is not to say that the tribute-paying Jews and other heathen groups thereby enjoyed freedom from further perse-

* Although Mecca remained the holy city, Medina became the administrative capital of Islam.

cution; rather, the harassment they experienced merely took on a milder tone. They became a valuable fiscal resource, and once it was seen that their theological recalcitrance posed no threat to Islam, they were more or less left alone.

The practice of tribute became the hallmark of Muslim fiscal policy as the Islamic armies moved out of Arabia. As first nomadic tribes, then settlements, then entire regions were taken over by the Muslim Bedouin, little effort was made to convert them. Instead, tribute similar to that imposed on Arabia's Jews was levied against the conquered populations. As the still tiny but rapidly growing Medinese Empire found its coffers beginning to fill up, the caliphate saw little advantage in pressing for the conversion of the foreign communities. Its increasing wealth in turn expanded Medina's power; this enabled it to range even farther abroad, which brought still more riches and established an easy cycle of expansionism. Thus, as Islam spread, it did so primarily out of political and economic motivation, not religious. The religious impulse doubtless served as an effective engine of morale for the armies in the field; the Bedouin warriors, once the raiding pattern had escalated into full-scale military confrontations and set-piece battles, could only have been driven to press on out of religious inspiration. But the caliphate, after recognizing that the tide of Islam had gone forth almost in spite of itself, was motivated out of economic concern to gain control of it and to organize it in such a way as to best serve its fiscal interests.

Hence there was little religious proselytizing conducted in the conquered territories, most of which were by now solidly Judaeo-Christianized. Nor were attempts made to impose religion by the sword, for by the law of Muhammad the acceptance of Islam meant a severe reduction in tribute, which would have been contrary to the designs of Medina. The establishment of religious hegemony would come later, when nonwarrior Islamicized tribes would emigrate from Arabia in the wake of the Muslim armies and settle in the conquered lands, and when the native populations would recognize the economic advantages to themselves by espousing Islam. Islam, then, at least as a religion, in this curious way developed a tradition of tolerance for rival beliefs.

The first large-scale Muslim victory was in Mesopotamia, that land comprising the rich Tigris-Euphrates valley which Persia had earlier wrested from the Byzantines in their ongoing battle for control of the Asian trade routes. With Persian military resources spread thin along the perimeters of its empire, Khalid launched a surprise invasion eastward across the Euphrates and surrounded the provincial capital of Hira. There he instituted a tactic that was to become a chief feature of the subsequent conquests. Instead of attempting to capture the city with his relatively small force, Khalid laid siege to it. Since resistance within the city walls would not save the lush lands around it, he offered the city's leaders a chance to avoid further siege in exchange for cash ransom. The leaders accepted, and the Bedouin found themselves not only in control of a large portion of western Mesopotamia, but in possession of a generous monetary reward in the bargain.

Thus happily enriched, Khalid thought to increase his wealth elsewhere. He turned westward toward Syria, Byzantium's chief colony in the eastern sector of the Fertile Crescent, and in April of 634, after picking up more tribal warriors along the way, stood outside the gates of Damascus with his compact and highly unpredictable fighting force.

Syria, and Palestine to the west, were dominated by an Aramaean population that was closer in culture and language to the Arabians than any other people in the Fertile Crescent. At about the time of Khalid's spontaneous march on Damascus, Abu Bakr, Muhammad's first successor, died in Medina. He was succeeded by Omar, a younger man of more worldly and imperial outlook. When Omar learned of Khalid's success in crossing the Syrian desert and threatening Damascus, he saw it as an opportunity to extend the nascent Medinese Empire in a direction that was likely to offer the least resistance and the most long-term reward: that of the prosperous Aramaic culture. So he placed a rein on Khalid's random military improvisations with the intention of providing a plan and a rationale for further Islamic conquest. Damascus was one of the most powerful military strongholds of the Byzantine Empire, and it would not, in Omar's view, serve the emerging cause well to risk a direct attack there. The better part of wisdom, counseled his military strategists in Medina, would be to gain control of the surrounding territories, thereby enticing the forces of Byzantine emperor Heraclius out of the city and making it more vulnerable.

Omar followed the advice, sending up orders to Khalid to disperse his troops south toward Jerusalem and Palestine. Khalid did so and the diversion worked. Not only did his Bedouin troops plunder as far south as Gaza along the Mediterranean coast of Palestine, but they succeeded in drawing the army of Heraclius out of Damascus in pursuit. The subsequent battles in Palestine ended in Bedouin victories, and soon Medina had effective control of Syria and its environs.

By the autumn of 636, after repelling a series of Byzantine counteroffensives, the armies of Medina conquered Damascus and the other major cities of the northern region for good. Now the thrust of Medinese imperialism turned from the military realm to the civil. There had already begun to occur a spontaneous Muslim occupation of the land, first as many of the Bedouin forces of Khalid broke off and scattered through Syria, then as poor, nonfighting Bedouin tribes, tempted and stimulated by the successes in the north, began crowding up from Arabia into Syria in quest of more prosperous living conditions. Caliph Omar immediately saw the necessity of replacing the nomad and raiding traditions — which would only cause continuing chaos as the various Bedouin tribes fought among themselves for the spoils of war instead of directing them to Medina — with a highly systematic occupation based on a stable civil regime representing Medina. He therefore appointed a civilian governor from among his most trusted associates in the caliphate, and Syria quickly became the first colony of the budding Islamic Empire.

The Bedouin conquest of Syria was aided immeasurably by the inherent weaknesses of the Byzantine forces. Because of its many other foreign preoccupations, Byzantine influence in the Fertile Crescent had, a century before, begun to lose its grip. As in most cases in imperial history, when the Byzantine emperors grew aware of this they doubled their resolve to retain their power. Hence they turned from benevolent despotism to ruthless oppression, and in so doing gave birth to a new insurrectionary spirit. The Muslim invaders, then, were confronted not by a unified, highly motivated and loyal Byzantine army, but by a force ridden with dissidence and mutiny.

The subsequent Muslim occupation and settlement were aided similarly. The native Aramaean populace had long suffered under Byzantine tyranny. Especially persecuted were the Monophysite Christians and Jews, who constituted the large majority of the sedentary population, for their refusal to subscribe to the tenets of the Byzantine church. The appearance of the Islamic civil administration, with its religious tolerance, was a form of liberation for the populace.

The Syrians, then, Christians and Jews alike, gratefully and magnanimously cooperated in the occupation of their land by the Arabians. This cooperation sealed the fate of Syria, setting it on the road to the blanket religiocultural Islamicization and linguistic Arabization that has marked it ever since. It also served as a model for the same process in the other culturally various lands of the Middle East. Thus, with the almost accidental but clearly total conquest of Syria within five years of Muhammad's death, did the Arabs of today find their beginnings.

The next step in the Islamic expansion came in 637 when the Persian Empire, like the Byzantine in Syria, launched an offensive to regain control of the westerly portions of their Mesopotamian province seized three years before by Khalid. The attack failed, primarily because there was little sympathy among the native Aramaean population of Mesopotamia — Christians and Jews, civilians and soldiers — for the Persian regime. The Persian army was decimated by a Muslim counterattack from the direction of Syria. With nothing but lush and unprotected farmland now ahead of them, the Muslims responded automatically: They poured eastward from the Euphrates and soon had all of Mesopotamia to themselves.

Caliph Omar fused Syria and Mesopotamia together into a single province under the governorship of successive dignitaries of the Ummaya clan. (The Ummaya had been one of the leading pre-Islamic families of the aristocratic Korayish tribe. It had switched over early to Muhammad's preachings and became the ruling family of the caliphate after Muhammad's death as a result of the maneuvers of Abu Bakr, who was an elder of the family.*) With the vast region from Jerusalem to the Tigris firmly within Medina's grasp, the folk migration of tribes from Arabia intensified. Soon the Arabic-speaking peoples were filling the niches and crevices of Aramaic-speaking Mesopotamian and Syrian society. The primitive nomadic Arabians and the sedentary Hellenized Aramaeans, though culturally more different than alike, were basically cousin-peoples through language. The Aramaic language had evolved over the centuries in the Fertile Crescent, but derived from the same Semitic roots as the language of the migrant Arabians. As the Arabic-speaking southerners settled in the Aramaean territories and as the large portion of the native population commenced voluntarily to convert to Islam in order to escape the taxes levied by the occupying Muslims on nonbelievers, the language of the Arabians began to dominate the province. Moreover, the Koran, which was still in the process of its final codification, was written in the Medinese version of the flowery Arabic language. To make a proper conversion to Islam one would soon have to learn the Koran, which was a further

---

* The Ummayads would dominate the caliphate for several generations. However, disputes over the proper method of succession — whether by election or by biological inheritance — would plague Medina during this time. Eventually the Ummayads would be overthrown as the leading lights of Islam for their refusal to restore the ancient blood-tie principle of succession.

impetus for the establishment of the language of the Arabians in the Aramaic world.

The migration into Syria-Mesopotamia marked the beginning of the last great folk outpouring from the Arabian peninsula. Since the nature of the migration — first to the north, then throughout the Middle East — was primarily Bedouin in character, it reintroduced into the consciousness of the indigenous populations the concept of the Aribi. Theretofore the notion of the Aribi had been confined in the Fertile Crescent to the desert wanderers of earlier migrations, while in Arabia it was applied more widely to include the large portion of the populace, the Bedouin. Now, as the seventh-century Bedouin poured into the heart of the Fertile Crescent and began to intermingle with the native populations, the notion underwent a fundamental transformation. Since the native sedentary populations had to be aware of their position in the geographical scheme of things, they could only have thought of themselves as Syrians and Iraqis. As far as they were concerned the Aribi had to be thought of as foreigners. But with the mass influx of these foreigners after the Muslim conquest, the fabric of Mesopotamian-Syrian society quickly acquired an Aribi — that is to say, an Arabian, or Arab — texture. First, the language of the Aribi — the language of the Hejaz, or northern Arabic* — imposed itself on the native Aramaic tongues of Syria and Mesopotamia. Second, since the Arabian influx was largely Islamic, little distinction could have been made on the part of the natives between Aribi and Muslims. It was precisely the distinction that the inhabitants of the Fertile Crescent had always made between themselves and the Aribi that had previously succeeded in maintaining a separation of identities. Now, with so many native Mesopotamians and Syrians gradually turning to Islam, that separation of identities began to blur. A Muslim was above all an Aribi, an Arab — fiercely proud of it and of the superiority it implied. For a native Mesopotamian or Syrian to become a Muslim, he had to incorporate into his own identity those Arab attitudes and characteristics which were at the very heart of Islam and through which Islam best expressed itself — superiority, fatalism and linguistic virtuosity.

It was with the almost accidental but successful cooptation of Mesopotamia and Syria that Islam gravitated toward the second stage of its expansion. As a result of the growing and relatively peaceful acceptance of Islamic

* Two principal languages had evolved in the Arabian peninsula out of the common Semitic root of prehistory. One was the language of the Hejaz — Muhammad's language — which is known by scholars as northern Arabic. The other was southern Arabic, which was the language of the Yemenite kingdoms at the tip of the peninsula.

belief in the province following its political and economic conquest, the Muslim leadership began to look upon the area not just as a foreign colony to be subjugated to and administered from the homeland, but as a natural extension of Islamic Arabism. Through the prism of Syria-Mesopotamia, Caliph Omar and his chief advisers perceived a potential Pan-Arab community capable of achieving dominion over the entire Middle East, over the entire Byzantine and Persian empires, perhaps over the entire known world of the time. With this perception the future of Islam became less a matter of spontaneous impulse and more a matter of careful design.

The first problem was Persia. In order to secure the permanent safety of Mesopotamia, the adjoining lands of Persia would have to be subjugated. Although it took them close to ten years, the Muslims finally achieved this, conquering the last outposts of resistance in Persia in about 650.

The decade-long struggle was in striking contrast to the rapidity of the Arab takeover of Syria-Mesopotamia. Its length was nevertheless understandable in view of the fact that the Muslim armies were not this time fighting in a disaffected colony but in the very heart of the Persian Empire. The intensity of the Persians' resistance was compounded by the fact that they were not a Semitic people. This resistance was reflected in the subsequent development of Persia, and evidences itself even today in inter-Muslim relations. Although Persia was eventually thoroughly Islamicized, it never gave up its native language entirely. Indeed, the language was eventually restored as a quite independent idiom, though with a considerable admixture of Arabic, and the Arab Muslims never found conditions hospitable enough to settle there in any numbers sufficient to impose an Arab cast on the culture. Moreover, not only did the Arab language never become the common speech, but even in the sphere of religion the Persians retained a distinctive attitude: They originated a version of Islam that was to become the largest single Muslim sect and remains so to this day — the Shiite.

As Medina was engaging in its conquest of Persia with a view to thoroughly dismantling the Persian Empire, it turned its attention to the prospect of finishing off the Byzantines as well. With Syria and Palestine removed from Byzantine control, Egypt was the only large province of Byzantium remaining in the Fertile Crescent. Thus, in December of 639, a Bedouin general named Amr, who had distinguished himself under Khalid during the Syrian and Palestinian campaigns, crossed the eastern frontier of Egypt with a force of four thousand Bedouin cavalry. There he found conditions among the population similar to those that had prevailed in Syria — disaffection with despotic Byzantine rule, nationalist yearnings, and harassment of the Monophysite Christian Copts.

Fighting and plundering their way across eastern Egypt to the Nile valley, then pouring down the Nile into the rich delta, Amr and his troops toppled the Byzantine capital at Alexandria in 642. The Byzantines returned with a large naval force in 645 and recaptured the city, but a Muslim counterattack in 646 drove them out once and for all, and Egypt fell under the complete domination of Medina.

All that remained now was Byzantium itself, and the Muslims produced a twofold strategy for its conquest. With the southeastern Mediterranean coast now in Muslim hands, they would attack the heartland of Byzantium — Anatolia (today's Turkey) — from the sea as well as by land.

By this time, as a result of the Syrian and Egyptian conquests, and as a consequence of the growing Pan-Arabism of the Muslim community, much of the focus of Muslim power had shifted from its original center in Medina to the periphery of the budding empire, particularly to the provincial capitals, where authority was exercised almost absolutely by the civil governors appointed by the caliph. After the conquest of Syria-Mesopotamia in 640, Caliph Omar had appointed a scion of the Ummayad clan, Muawiya, as governor of the province. When the conquest of Egypt seemed assured in 642, he appointed his foster brother, Abdallah, to administer the region of the Nile. The primary functions of these governors were to organize the native societies along Muslim lines and to enforce the Islamic scheme of taxation. In exercising their authority they found themselves becoming rich and powerful beyond all expectations. In Medina, all the while, internecine strife was becoming more rampant as the doctrinal dispute over the correct methods of succession intensified. The Ummayad approach still held sway, but the caliphate grew increasingly preoccupied with threats to its security from dissident tribes. Hence, with vital decisions slow in coming from Medina, much on-the-scene planning and decision-making had to be undertaken. It automatically fell to the civil governors of the conquered lands to do the planning and make the decisions, responsibilities which Abdallah in Egypt and Muawiya in Syria accepted with enthusiasm. If they were growing personally rich through the administration of their own territories, how much richer could they become if they had all of Persia and Byzantium to administer?

Abdallah, in control of the many shipbuilding facilities in Egypt captured from the Byzantines, proceeded to build a fleet of warships and made plans to island-hop northward across the Mediterranean to attack the Anatolian coast near Constantinople. Muawiya, in charge of all the Bedouin troops in Syria and Iraq, put together a new army — the conquest of Persia was now drawing to a close — and planned to attack Anatolia overland from northern Syria (where the two lands shared a common frontier).

The first Muslim naval enterprise took place against Byzantine-held Cyprus.* Although not known as sailors, the Bedouin Arabs who conquered Egypt adapted very readily to sea warfare, and the Cyprus campaign was a great success. Now, with affairs in Persia being successfully wrapped up, Muawiya and Abdallah (Muawiya held the greater authority because of his seniority) carried out their double-pronged assault on Byzantium itself, sending the Arab fleet eastward in 655 from Cyprus toward Constantinople and massing troops along the Syrian-Anatolian frontier.

The Byzantine navy came out to meet the Arabs off the southern coast of Anatolia. Although the details of the battle are somewhat obscure, it ended in a resounding victory for the Arabs; the whole of the Byzantine fleet, reported as some five hundred ships, was destroyed. Before Muawiya could launch his land forces, however, unhappy events in Medina forced him to turn his attention away from Byzantium.

In 644, toward the end of the conquest of Egypt, the caliph Omar had been assassinated in Medina by a Persian slave who was a member of the small but growing opposition to the Ummayad regime that later grew into the Shiite sect. Now, in 655, Omar's elected successor, Othman, was murdered by dissident tribesmen. The ensuing struggle for the caliphate, in which Muawiya and Abdallah were vitally involved, thus spared the Byzantines from having to defend Constantinople from the Arabs — at least for a while. Later the war against Byzantium would be renewed by both land and sea, and although the Muslims enjoyed occasional successes in the outlying areas, they were never able to make a lasting penetration into Anatolia. The northern frontier of the Arab Empire would remain at the ancient line of division between peoples who had always been Semitic-speaking and those who had not. With the eastern frontiers secure beyond Semitic Mesopotamia and the north shut off beyond Syria, the Muslims would turn most of their attention westward beyond Egypt, where there was little in the way of

---

* In many respects the Greek-Turkish conflict over modern Cyprus has its origins in that island's years of Byzantine control. It was here that the ancient schism between the Monophysite and Orthodox Christian churches was particularly virulent. The consequences of that schism are largely accountable for the divisions in culture and attitude that currently dominate the island.

natural or artificial defense. In the meantime, there was the issue of the caliphate to be settled.

The murdered Othman had been the leader of the Ummayad clan. His predecessor Omar's assassination had been designed to loosen the Ummayad's grip on the caliphate, but with Othman's succession it had turned out to have the opposite effect. Othman had appointed family members to every post of any consequence in the Islamic administration. Much of the booty and tribute that were intended for the caliphate's treasury were being siphoned off at their sources by Ummayad clerks and administrators, both at home and in the provinces. All the Ummayads were growing rich and powerful at the expense of other clans. It was principally for this reason that Othman was assassinated, but his murder was also an attempt to release once again the Ummayad grip on the caliphate and restore the tribal principle of biological succession.

The dissidents' goal was, in effect, to begin the caliphate over again (it was only twenty-three years since Muhammad's death) with the person who had the closest blood tie to the Prophet. Muhammad had left no sons, but he had produced a daughter, Fatima. A woman, of course, was out of the question, but that woman's male children would be Muhammad's grandsons, and the principle of the bloodline could in that way be reinstituted. To preserve the caliphate within the Muhammadan biological sphere until the first grandson made his entry into adulthood, then, the dissidents promoted Ali — Muhammad's son-in-law, the husband of his daughter, the father of his grandsons.

Ali, however, was not a member of the Ummayad clan. The choice of him to succeed Othman profoundly offended the still-plentiful Ummayads, who felt that Ali was benefiting from the murder of one of their own. The offense was particularly galling to Muawiya who, as governor of Syria and with Othman dead, was now the most powerful figure in the Ummayad dynasty. Ali would have to fight for the caliphate.

The struggle was joined early in 656. Muawiya diverted his troops from the Anatolian frontier and sent them south toward Medina. Ali raced north from Medina with his army to meet them. The fight raged across northern Arabia and southern Syria and Mesopotamia. For most of the year it remained a stalemate — Muawiya's forces unable to reach Medina, Ali's unable to penetrate Syria. In the end, though, Ali gained a partial victory. In December of 656 he got a grip on southern Mesopotamia by smashing the Ummayad army at Masra, near the confluence of the Tigris and Euphrates, and by 657 he was in control of all of Mesopotamia and the Persian lands to the east.

These events were to prove of long-range historical importance, for their result was that Arabia itself dropped out of the center of the Islamic Empire and became a backwater. The empire was now divided, forming two centers — one in Syria, one in Mesopotamia — that were to hasten the Arabization of the Middle East and at the same time harden what was to become the permanent doctrinal schism of Islam.

Muawiya and the Ummayads were not about to acquiesce in Ali's Mesopotamian caliphate. Muawiya regrouped his Syrian forces and once again sent them — under the leadership of General Amr, the conqueror of Egypt — against Ali's troops. The armies fought to a standstill at the Mesopotamian-Syrian frontier early in 658, and eventually the two sides agreed to a negotiated settlement of their differences.

The settlement, concluded through mediators in the Bedouin style, was on its face equitable; but actually, through ruses on the part of Muawiya's representatives, it favored him. When this became apparent to Ali's supporters, he lost face. As his authority began to wane, several of his tribes deserted him, setting up a community of their own (which caused them to be known as Kharijites, i.e., Secessionists). With Syria, Palestine and Egypt in his hands, Muawiya consolidated his power in the west while Ali struggled to retain his authority in the east.

Within two years Muawiya was so strong that he felt confident enough to proclaim himself, while in Jerusalem, the true caliph of Islam. This impertinence was the final insult to Ali's prestige; six months later, at the beginning of 661, when he had done nothing to challenge Muawiya, he too was assassinated. Ali's son and successor — the grandson of Muhammad in whom so much future hope had been placed by the original supporters of Ali — was simply bought off by the Ummayads. Muawiya reigned alone in Damascus. The dominance of the Ummayads was restored and reinforced. It was now time to resume the expansion of the Arab Empire.

With the east blocked off by the still-loyal followers of the deceased Ali (the Alids, as they were called) and the north barred by the Byzantines in Anatolia, the natural thrust of the Arab impulse to expansion had to go westward. Even during the Ummayad-Ali crisis the Muslims in Egypt had made exploratory forays into the western deserts and along the Mediterranean coast and found the horizons uncluttered. Now they moved out in earnest across North Africa. There they encountered a new people, much like themselves in custom and tradition, but markedly different too — the Berbers.

The Berbers were a people of mysterious origin, and modern-day speculation about them tends to confound the popular anthropological theories concerning the evolution of man in the Middle East. Many of them were tall, blond and blue-eyed, and they all spoke a language similar to that of the earliest Egyptians — Hamitic, as it is called, rather than Semitic. They were a primitive nomadic people, and on this count they most likely appeared as a cousin-people to the Arab tribes carrying Islam westward. Thus a certain amount of natural symbiosis was possible. On the other hand, they were thoroughgoing pagans, as fiercely independent as the Bedouin themselves, speaking a foreign language, and in no need of liberation from imperial oppressors — as had been the case with the Christian and Jewish populations of the Fertile Crescent.* So as much as the potential for a symbiotic coupling of cultures existed, so too did the potential for rejection and resistance.

At first, resistance took precedence. Indeed, it was not the Byzantines who slowed the Arab advance through North Africa, but the resistance of the Berbers who, upon finding themselves being crowded by the oncoming Arabs, joined forces with the Byzantines along the coast to fight off the new danger. In the end, however, their resistance was unavailing and they succumbed to Arab Muslim domination. They eventually became Islamicized under successive Syrian governors of the North African territories, and in turn became the shock troops of the Muslim invasion and conquest of Spain at the beginning of the eighth century.

The Muslim embrace of North Africa extended to the western edge of the continent, to the Atlantic shores of what we know today as Morocco. Following in the wake of the military and political conquest came the extended folk migration of nonwarrior Arab tribes who settled the conquered lands and gradually imposed their Arabism on the indigenous Berber populations. Sociologically, the further Muslim conquest of Spain and penetration into France was more a Berber than an Arab enterprise, and perhaps because it lacked the wholehearted support of the Ummayad caliphate — which by then was plunged again into a crisis of survival — it was destined to fail. The Arab folk migration had found its natural western terminus at the shores of Morocco. Although the Arabized Berbers did occupy the Iberian peninsula for several centuries — indeed, even establishing a thriving culture there — they were never able to fully impose their own language, religious belief and

* The Byzantines covered the North African coast through a string of seaport colonies, but they made few efforts to control inland areas.

psychology on the region. They would eventually be forced to fall back across Gibraltar,* and the Arabization of the western Mediterranean would remain confined to North Africa.

The Ummayad caliphate did much during the second half of the seventh century to complete the expansion of the Islamic Empire in the west. Through its capable and clever governors it was quickly able — once the Berbers were conscripted — to impose the strict Muslim fiscal and social order that greased the skids of the subsequent Arabization of the vast region. But it did not achieve this without bringing injury — injury which would prove fatal — to Ummayad domination itself.

While conquering the west, the Ummayads renewed their attempts to strike into the Anatolian heart of Byzantium. The effort generally, though marked by occasional successes, was a failure, and it drained much of the Syria-based caliphate's energies and resources. Caliph Muawiya also antagonized many of the tribal religious elders of Islam by introducing a hitherto unknown dynastic principle as the basis of the expansion of the Arab Empire. In endeavoring to organize the evolving Arab society of the Fertile Crescent and the lands of North Africa, he placed primary emphasis on obedience to civil law and the rule of his political representatives. In this way he was replacing religious authority with political power, the natural theocracy and tribal autocracy of Islam with the power of the state. For in his eyes that was what Islam had become: a sovereign state covering the whole expanse of the Middle East and North Africa.

Not only did these objectionable maneuvers create problems for him in the Muslim establishment, the followers of the late caliph Ali in Mesopotamia were also increasing their agitation. By now Ali's death had been elevated by the Shia (as the Alids called their movement, whence the term Shiites) into martyrdom. Playing upon this, the Shiite leaders were able to arouse expanding sympathy for their cause.

Muawiya died in 680 and was succeeded by his son Yazid. The event was seized upon by the two principal dissident groups — the Shiites in Mesopotamia and the orthodox Islamic theocracy in Medina — to force a showdown. Both factions, though otherwise disunited, had a common interest in

---

* Gibraltar gets its name from the Arab general Tariq, who in 711 first led the Berbers into Spain through the island. When the island's rocky pinnacle was encountered on the crossing from North Africa, it was named Jebal (Mount) Tariq, thus Gibraltar.

relocating the center of the empire: in one case to Mesopotamia, where it had enjoyed brief glory under Ali's caliphate; in the other to Medina, where it had originated.

The Shiite Alids seized upon Muawiya's death to reject the primacy of his son Yazid and to elect Ali's second son (also a grandson of Muhammad), Husayn, as the true caliph. Husayn's pretendership was brief, for a few months later he was killed in a battle at Kerbela against the Syrian forces of Yazid. The Shiites thus gained another martyr.

Husayn's death further stimulated the Alid opposition to the Syrian caliphate. The conflict was basically political, but grafted onto the Mesopotamian side of it was the expanding religious fervor promoted by the Alid doctrinairists, who now claimed that although Ali had only been the son-in-law of Muhammad, he had been the primary heir of his prophetic spirit, which lived on solely in Ali's sons. Hence, only a member of the house of Ali could become an authentic caliph. This doctrine became the core of the Shiite movement, which was to coalesce into the focal point for all tendencies in Islam having to do with Arab ascendancy and superiority. To this day Kerbela is the holiest shrine and place of pilgrimage for all Shiite Muslims.

By killing Husayn, Yazid had temporarily overcome the Alid threat to his Syrian caliphate, but now the Ummayads faced further internal troubles. The opposition of the old theocratic orthodoxy in Medina to the heterodox secular rule established by Muawiya in Damascus became loud and insistent. Yazid was therefore compelled to undertake a campaign against the holy cities. He took Medina in August of 683 and then continued southward to quell the orthodox opposition in Mecca. Before he could gain control over the city, however, he died, thereby producing a vacuum in the caliphate which the Meccans immediately sought to fill with their own candidate, Abdallah Ibn Zubayr.*

Abdallah had the backing of one of the largest Arab tribes, the Qays, which had migrated to Syria some time before. Another great tribe, the Kalb, which had long since been settled in Syria and was loyal to the Ummayads, supported *their* new candidate, Marwan Ibn Al-Hakam.† The war began, with the two tribes providing the bulk of the manpower. In 684 it ended in a bloody battle at Marj Rahit that gave the Kalb-supported Ummayads a decisive victory and secured the caliphate of Marwan for Damascus.

---

* "Ibn" in Arabic means "son of."
† The "al-" before many Arab names denotes the clan from which an individual derives.

The victory must have been looked upon as an unalloyed triumph for the Ummayads, but in fact it represented the seed of the eventual dissolution of Ummayad power — a dissolution that would bring an end to purely Arabian domination of Islam. The battle had been so bitter, the losses to both sides so great, and the hatred inspired by the contest of the two major tribes so intense that an unprecedented desire for vengeance and a spirit of vendetta spread throughout the Arab world, provoking an increasingly bloody polarization.

Long before the battle of Marj Rahit the Arabians had been split up into contending tribes. The tradition of rivalry — vying for superiority — had, as I have indicated, long been ingrained in the Bedouin character. This tradition had become encapsulated into a kind of institutionalized cultural myth that demarcated the tribes which originated in northern Arabia from those which came from the south. It had long been taken as an article of Bedouin faith by the northern tribes that they were superior to those from southern Arabia, and vice versa. These beliefs were held respectively not on the sort of grounds that might motivate modern-day myths of regional superiority within a nation (as, for instance, the North-South rivalry in America), but in accordance with the ancient Arabian obsession with lineage, in genealogical terms. Only the enthusiastic desire for booty during the initial Muslim expansion served to override traditional interregional tribal enmity and temporarily weld the Arabs together. But after the battle of Marj Rahit, with the great tribes of the Qays and the Kalb set against each other permanently, the long-practiced custom of fratricidal hatred, which had for a time been suppressed, emerged with new energy and ferocity. The Qays were scattered throughout the Arab Empire, and tribes that had been opposed to them for other reasons now found themselves forced into the camp of their principal enemy, the Kalb. This sharpened the polarity within the empire. The polarity in turn expanded as the natives of the newly conquered territories converted to Islam and assimilated with the Arabians; as they did, they were forced to take one or the other of the adversary sides. Soon a spirit of mutual hatred dominated the land. This spirit did as much to undermine the authority of the Ummayads in Islam as did the religious opposition to their preemption of political power. And it was finally to undermine that political power itself, since it proved impossible for the regional Ummayad governors, and ultimately the Syrian caliphs, to withstand the tug of intertribal strife.

The process took time, though, and after the battle of Marj Rahit the

Ummayads once again consolidated their power. Caliph Marwan, then his son and successor Abd-Al-Malik, subjugated the Medinese pretenders and brought Mesopotamia under control, driving the dissident Shiites of the house of Ali toward Persia. Thereafter, over a period of about twenty years, the Ummayad dynasty reigned supreme over the Muslim Empire, completing its expansion in the west and extending it eastward into northern India and through central Asia as far as the borders of China.

The impulse to expansion was not without its perils, however. Under Caliph Abd-Al-Malik and his successors, Walid and Sulayman, Muslim rule turned into tyranny; the more power that accrued to the Ummayads through expansion, the more they exercised that power to expand further. In the farther reaches of the empire they encountered resistance to the convert-or-be-taxed principle that was at the heart of their expansionary rationale. They were thus forced to heighten the oppression of their subjects, which, in turn, along with the inbuilt and intensifying fratricidal tribal conflicts, produced an insurrectionary mood in the Fertile Crescent. Additionally, the Ummayad obsession with the Byzantines in Anatolia deepened. Having expanded as far as Spain and China and gained control of the distant eastern and western markets, it seemed absurd to the Syrian caliphate that it had not yet conquered its most immediate neighbor to the north. It was only by doing so that the Muslims would be able to penetrate into the prosperous lands of central and northern Europe.

In 715, under Sulayman's direction, the Ummayads made their move. The result was not a failure; it was a disaster. The Syrian army, as well as the navy, was totally destroyed outside Constantinople. The Ummayad regime thus lost its primary means of enforcing its power within Islam. Sulayman's successors labored over the next thirty years to retain the Syrian caliphate's dominance, but lacking the powerful vehicle of enforcement — a strong militia — they labored in vain. By 745 the power of the Ummayad dynasty had waned so much that its authority was no longer recognized outside Syria, and even there it was coming into question.

In the meantime the various Shiite tribes which had been driven into Persia from Iraq fifty years and more before had regrouped and rededicated themselves to regaining the caliphate according to the principles of the Alid doctrine of ascendancy. As in all Arab tribal society there were differences in philosophy and approach among the Shiites, but the question of the caliphate transcended their differences and provided them with at least a rudimentary unity. An Arabian named Abu Hashem had been the founder of an extremist

Shiite sect that was ousted from Iraq in about 670. The sect became known as the Hashemites, and while in exile they converted many Persians to the Shiite cause. When Hashem died he was succeeded by a series of men who claimed indirect blood and direct spiritual ties to Muhammad himself. The most important of these was Muhammad Ibn Ali Al-Abbas, a descendant of one of Muhammad's uncles. In about 738 Abbas launched a rebellion against the weakening Syrian regime. It failed, but it focused further favorable Persian public opinion on the Hashemite cause and elevated Abbas to hero status — perhaps because, unlike previous Shiite leaders, he had survived the battle. When Abbas did die a few years later, of natural causes, he was still given the usual martyr's funeral, and the Hashemite sect was renamed and transformed into the Abbasid movement.

Within another year the Abbasids had a new leader, this one a Persian convert who took the name Abu Muslim. Abu managed to form a large coalition between Arabian and Persian Shiites and in 746 launched an all-out assault against the now relatively feeble Ummayads. The Abbasids swept across Mesopotamia, picking up armies of followers along the way among the oppressed Shiites who had remained there and among the various factions of the great Qay tribe. They penetrated Syria and sent the Ummayad rulers, led by Caliph Marwan II, fleeing westward. Still increasing in numbers, and still directed by Abu Muslim, they followed the disorganized Ummayads into Egypt where, in August of 750, they completed the destruction of the Ummayad dynasty by killing Marwan and his retinue.

The Abbasids claimed the caliphate, appointed one of their own to the exalted throne, and opened a radical new chapter in the history of Islam and the Middle East. No longer would the Islamic empire be exclusively Arabian. It would become a fusion of Persian and Arab culture, centered in Mesopotamia instead of Syria. Nor would its rule be based on the secular principles of the Ummayads; rather it would return to the religious principles of the Prophet and the Koran. This in turn would speed up conversion to Islam across the Middle East. Since Islam was purely Arabian in origin, conversion would in turn hasten Arab/non-Arab integration and the natural imposition of Arabic as the common language of the region. As a result of this biological integration and the universal adaptation of Arabic, a new culture would begin to evolve which would be called Arab. The term "Arab" would no longer be restricted to the nomadic tribes from Arabia (although the nonintegrating Bedouin would continue to reserve that appellation exclusively for themselves down to modern times, as we have seen); rather, it would come to embrace all those peoples who spoke Arabic as their mother tongue and who, through their Islamic acculturation, possessed the uniquely Semitic sociological coloration.

Out of all these factors, accordingly, evolved the Arabs of today.

# PART TWO

# 8.

## JOURNAL: *"Proud to Be an Arab . . ."*

"I ALWAYS HATED IT WHEN I WENT TO EUROPE," a young engineer told me over a drink in Cairo early in 1974. "I would go to register at a hotel, hand over my Egyptian passport, and I'd be met by smirks by the hotel clerks. I would go to business conferences, and when I was introduced as an Egyptian people would suddenly become condescending. I despised being an Arab, I was so embarrassed because of the 1967 war. Finally I just refused to travel anymore, it was so humiliating." Then he beamed. "But now I can hold my head high anywhere in the world. Because of last October, I am proud again to say I am an Arab."

"It used to be fashionable around here to play down our so-called Arab-ness," a lawyer told me on another occasion. "After 1967, 'Arab' became a dirty word. We educated Egyptians began to insist that we are Egyptians, not Arabs, that our heritage went back to our noble Pharaohonic and highly civilized ancestors, not to the Muslims. There was even a movement started whereby modernized ancient Egyptian would replace Arabic as our national language. We were fed up, ashamed of being classed as Arabs. Of course, that movement, those sentiments, died a quick death as a result of the Ramadan War. Now we are delighted to call ourselves Arabs. Even I am proud to be an Arab."

Invariably, when a visitor dropped in on Essam, a newspaper columnist in Beirut, the conversation would eventually turn to politics, and Essam would find a spot to insert his oft-repeated contention that "we Lebanese are Phoenicians, we are not Arabs." But that was before the October War. Now he frequently begins sentences with such phrases as "We Arabs . . ." or "Speaking as an Arab . . ."

Antoine is Lebanese, but a Christian, with a fine appreciation for Western tastes in food and clothing. Before 1973 he spent most of his time in London, Paris, the South of France. "Don't call me an Arab," he often demanded. "I am Lebanese, I speak French, I follow Christ, I wear Gucci shoes, Yves Saint Laurent shirts and I drive an English car." Now, meeting him in the lobby of Beirut's St. Georges Hotel, his first words are: "Come, I take you to have a good Arab dinner."

Saeed is a wealthy young Saudi Arabian entrepreneur educated in the United States in the late sixties. "I can't tell you," he tells me, "how humiliating it was to be an Arab in America after 1967. Everybody immediately judged me as some kind of loser as soon as they met me. It didn't matter that I was Saudi and had nothing to do with the war over Palestine. To tell you the truth, I didn't even care about Palestine, it stirred no passions in me whatsoever. But because I was an Arab, simply because I was an Arab, I was automatically considered — what do you say over there, the Jewish word — a *schmuck*. It created so many problems in my head. I began to hate the fact I was an Arab. And I began to hate my father for being an Arab. I began to hate everything Arab. Then I came back here and we hit you Americans with the boycott. Now when I go to New York I walk through your Kennedy Airport like a king. I am curt with your immigration agents, I am rude with your taxi drivers, I am superior with your bankers. And every time I go out of a building I make sure to spit on the sidewalk. I" — and here he taps his chest righteously — "I am an Arab, and I want every person in New York to know it. You Americans have had your day in the sun. We are the wave of the future."

All over the Arab Middle East I encountered such expressions of the rebirth of people's pride in their Arabness. Indeed, so frequent were the manifestations of this rebirth that a psychiatrist might call them, collectively, a cultural obsession. "To use the word 'obsession' would not be to overstate the case," said Dr. Walid Salam, a professor of law and psychology at Cairo's American University, in a carefully measured pedagogic tone. "But its sources are easily understandable. Arab pride, which by its very historical and anthropological nature runs deep, has been smothered and encrusted by centuries of frustration and humiliation. Not since the golden age of Arab culture a thousand years ago has the Arab character had a chance to express itself on the world stage. What is happening now is simply an extension of the individual human need to have an effect on one's surroundings. Every human being wishes to have such an effect, to leave his imprint on his environment. That is what drives us to achieve the things we do. It is how all human beings measure their own self-worth — to see the effect they have on others. It is no different with nations. Just as the books you write give you a sense of pride as a human being, so do the achievements of your culture provide you with your sense of pride in being an American. I ask you, would you want to be anything else but an American?"

"I suppose not."

"Well, an Egyptian would want to be nothing else but an Egyptian. A Saudi nothing else but a Saudi. An Iraqi nothing else but an Iraqi. And crossing all these national boundary lines, an Arab would want to be nothing else but an Arab. Just as you, in addition to being an American, would want to be nothing else but a Western, Judaeo-Christian, English-speaking individual. But an Arab possesses something that you don't. He possesses a thousand years' worth of cultural inferiority. The Arab and his culture have had no voice in the affairs of the world for all that time, and whenever they tried to make themselves heard they were either ignored or interrupted, shut off. Now that they've forced themselves to be heard — and I'm talking not so much about the October War as I am about the oil boycott and the subsequent economic ramifications. Now that this has occurred, the surface of their long-buried pride in being Arabs has been touched. We Arabs are very conscious of our history, and we are most conscious of our golden age, those three or four centuries when we were the light of the world while the rest of the planet was in darkness. We now realize that we can again become the light of the world. We are being reborn, and because we have been buried so long we pursue this rebirth with a passion bordering on obsession. We are like the man who gets out of prison after twenty years. If he has an iota of sense, he will be obsessed with never going to prison again."

"Political obsessions can be dangerous, though," I said.

"Of course," replied the kindly professor. "Look at the Jews. They have been obsessed with Palestine for two thousand years — obsessed first with getting there, then obsessed with keeping themselves there. The Jews' obsession with restoring their former glory, such as it was, has been applauded by the West. But the Arabs' obsession with restoring their former glory — well, that is another thing. You laugh at us. To laugh at an obsession is even more dangerous than to applaud it."

"But, then, what makes one obsession right and another wrong?" I inquired. "What in the Arabs' mind makes their obsession right and the Jews' wrong?"

"Precisely the manner in which it is expressed. But even more importantly, its consequences. On both scores we are on the side of right, the Jews on the side of wrong. Our obsession with the rebirth of our glory and our pride is a threat to no other nation. Neither the way we express it nor its consequences represent a danger to other peoples. The Jews, on the other hand — well, do I have to draw a picture? First, their obsession caused them to falsify history. It is true that they once existed as an ancient society in Palestine. It is untrue that they were ever a sovereign nation. They were merely one of several societies that lived there. They invaded Palestine and drove out the weaker societies there. Then, later, they were in turn driven out. Their obsession with returning to Palestine as a sovereign nation is therefore based on a historical untruth. When they manifested that obsession they became a distinct threat to the local society. The threat then became a reality. They reinvaded Palestine through political chicanery, and once part of it was in their hands they sought to get all of it. In every succeeding expression of their ambition the consequences became more dire, first for the local Arab society, then for the entire Arab world, finally for the world as a whole. I don't have to tell you that the Jewish presence in Palestine is an affront to all Arab sensibility — you must be aware of that by now. But do you know why?"

"I've heard many reasons."

"I am sure. Political reasons, sociological reasons, religious reasons — endless explanations for why Israel is unacceptable. But do you know the real underlying reason?"

"It's what I've been trying to dig out, if there is one."

"Oh, there is one. And it is this. The Jew personifies all that has in the past been inimical to and destructive of Arab cultural pride. It is a visceral reaction, an instinctive one. It is not the Jew himself we object to. Had the Jews remained in the Middle East — dispersed, yes, but dispersed within the Middle East rather than throughout the Western world — and had they then, two thousands years later, regrouped in Palestine to form a nation, there would have been little objection to them. I do not know for sure if such an Israel would have been allowed to develop, but my guess is it would have. However, the present State of Israel was conceived and born in the West, not here. And it was the West that robbed us of our glory a thousand years ago . . ."

"But it wasn't the Jews who did that."

"No, it was the Christian West. The Crusades and so on. I grant you that. But you see, even though the Jews suffered enormously from the same forces that humbled us, and even though they suffered through the succeeding centuries, out of all that suffering they obtained a rich and technologically advanced state of their own. They thrived, even as they suffered. What did we do? We remained abject, rooted in our primitive past, making no progress technologically or socially. Then, all of a sudden, here is Israel in our midst — a state conceived and born in the West, a graphic reminder of our own thousand years of helplessness and indirection, a hurtful kick in the pants to our awareness of our own cultural ineptitude. The establishment of Israel by the West peeled back the last layer of our historical shame at the hands of the West. It was like pouring salt on a festering wound. It was not the Jews we hated, it was the West, which had carried out this final humiliation, this final act of its traditional contempt for us. Forget for a moment the underhanded tactics of the Zionists themselves in settling in Palestine during the past fifty, sixty years. Forget too the expansionism and militancy of the Jews once Israel was established. It was not the Jews we hated back there in 1947. It was what they represented. For in them was embodied the culmination of a thousand years of Western contempt. Not Jewish contempt. But Western Christian contempt. We saw in Israel an unholy alliance between Christians and Jews, the Jews hypocritically uniting with the Christians, their arch-enemies. They would get a state in exchange for assisting the Christian West — the West of the Crusaders, those hordes who had been our downfall — to deliver its final slap to our Islamic face. Actually that event — the unilateral establishment of a state in our midst that symbolized all that was evil about the West — that event was a blessing in disguise. For in peeling back the last layer of our shame it made us confront it, or at least confront the fact that we bore the stigma of this shame. For the past twenty-five years we have been undergoing a kind of mass cultural psychotherapy in an attempt to bring this shame to the surface and rid ourselves of it. You are just now beginning to see the successful effects of the therapy.

"Don't be fooled by all the self-delusion you see in Arab culture," he continued. "Self-delusion is a behavioral aberration. Just as it is an acquired trait in an individual, so is it acquired in a culture. And as it becomes a solidly entrenched habit in an individual's character, so too does it become entrenched in the character of a culture. It is a difficult habit to break, especially when it has had a thousand years to develop and harden. Self-delusion was not originally a trait of Arab character. We were certainly not self-delusive in the seventh, eighth and ninth centuries. It is a habit we developed to assuage or disguise our own shame at our cultural atrophy and impotence in the face of the Western menace. But we are now in the initial stages of exorcising that particular demon. Of course, it is still with us. But we are aware of it, and we are getting a grip on it. This is the reason for the rebirth of our Arab pride. It is our pride in our ancient past, and our recognition that we stand on the verge of restoring our importance, that has triggered that rebirth. People say that our success in the war has been responsible for the rebirth, or our achievement in using the oil weapon, but they are wrong. It was our reawakening pride that enabled us to achieve those successes. Few people realized it, but a cycle was begun in 1948 with the creation of Israel. But a cycle always has to go backward before it goes forward. Before someone moves forward, he must gather his forces, take a step back and then launch himself ahead. Before you mount a horse you dip your knee, you sink down a bit to give yourself the spring to go up. It has been that way with us for the past twenty-five years. We sunk to our lowest in 1967. But that gave us the spring in our legs to go up. Soon — perhaps it will take another twenty-five years — we will be atop the horse and in full control of our destiny."

"What is that destiny?" I asked.

"To be our own people. To feel the same pride in being Arab as, say, you feel in being American, or even as the Israeli feels in being a Jew."

"Well," I said, "you have just given me an elaborate psychohistorical analysis to explain the so-called Arab character. You agree that this character has been formulated out of a thousand years of self-delusion. Yet isn't it possible that your entire analysis is based on the very self-delusive impulse that you say has governed the Arab mentality for so long? I mean, all this talk about renewed Arab pride. What is it based on? A temporary success in the war? A partly successful oil boycott? They seem to me to be pretty fragile grounds on which to base a whole complex rationale for the rebirth of Arab pride."

"Ah, but you don't understand," he said. "What to you was a temporary success in the war was to us a monumental success. When I was in America I used to watch your prizefights — I even participated in a personality study of prizefighters. I saw it over and over again. Fighters who would go out and lose repeatedly had very little sense of their worth as fighters or as people. They would feel intimidated, inferior. But then one day they would go into the ring against a much superior opponent and knock him down. They might eventually lose the fight, get knocked out themselves, but the fact that they knocked down this superior opponent would be like a massive injection of psychological self-worth. They wouldn't remember all the times they were knocked down themselves, but *would* remember unto the tiniest details the time they knocked down so-and-so. To them, such incidents were the evidence of their potentialities as fighters, and ultimately as people. Such incidents gave them pride in themselves."

"But isn't that a kind of false pride? Most of the prizefighters I've ever seen end up on 'queer street' — do you know the expression?"

"I have heard it, but what does it mean?"

"It means that the fighter, usually a fighter who has deluded himself while still in the grip of all his faculties, as a result falls victim to a kind of permanent, functional self-delusion. It is no longer that one of his character or personality traits is an impulse to self-delusion. Instead the entire fabric of his character and personality has become self-delusive. In other words, he is clinically crazy, or retarded, or whatever — because his brain has been permanently damaged."

"Ah," objected the professor, "but you are taking my analogy too far. I am not talking about brains getting fried — I think that's the term . . ."

"Scrambled," I said.

". . . Yes, scrambled. I am not talking about brains getting scrambled by physical blows. I am talking only about the moral or spiritual or emotional qualities of pride and self-worth. You can apply my example of the prizefighter to all walks of life. The unsuccessful banker, the unsuccessful salesman, the unsuccessful writer — anyone who is unsuccessful in the way of life he chooses must feel inferior, it is a fact of human nature. But give him one success after a long string of failures, and it totally revises his situation. Now he knows that he has the potential to succeed. Perhaps other people will attribute his one single success to accident, to fluke. They might call it a temporary success, as you describe our achievement in the war. And well it might be — the next time he tries something he may fail again. But all he needs is that one success to give him a glimpse of his own potentiality. To others it is unimportant. To him it is everything. Through it he not only gains pride in himself, but he can see what he has been doing wrong to bring about his previous failures. In most cases, his tradition of failure is brought about by self-delusion — not functional self-delusion, as you put it, but the yielding to an instinct for self-delusion created by a past that has given him little pride in himself, little sense of his own worth and potential. As his failures continue he uses self-delusion more and more to rationalize them, to explain them away, to help keep him from facing the inadequacies in himself that cause him to fail in the first place. But to anyone with an ounce of brainpower, failure can be a great teacher. A sufficient amount of failure will motivate one to reexamine oneself, at least to recognize that a problem exists and that the problem is not in everyone else, but in oneself. So in his next venture he goes about things a bit differently. He has a small success, a partial success, a temporary success — whichever you want to call it. That is all he needs to know that he *can* enjoy success, that all need not be failure. To him it becomes a monument in his life, for it intimates the potential fruits that lie in store for him if he cultivates this new approach to his attempts to succeed, if he rids himself of all his own habits of inferiority and self-delusion and forms new habits based on self-esteem and realism."

"Usually easier said than done," I offered.

"Of course. And it is not something that happens overnight. But what I am saying is that we Arabs are going through this process. It is why we find so much meaning in our so-called temporary victory in the recent war. To us the war was a monumental success. No matter that the Zionists managed to get across the canal and freeze one of our armies . . ."

"You admit that?"

"Of course I do."

"You are one of the few Arabs I've talked to who will concede such a thing."

"But, again, that is my point. We no longer refuse to recognize reality. It is a hard, slow process — to break this habit. But we are doing it, bit by bit. You see, what Israel does from here on in matters little. It is what we do that is important. No more will the Jews be able to humiliate us. I say this not with bombast, not with passion, as you can see, but with cool deliberation. I will admit, they may still be able to embarrass us now and again, for our liberation from our self-delusion will take time. But they will never be able to humiliate us. Our entire psychology has been reversed. Now, instead of false pride, we have the beginnings of real pride."

"All right," I said, "I'll grant that there has been a revival of pride among the Arabs. But isn't this more or less limited to educated, sophisticated Arabs, who are in the large minority? Even if it is now more real than self-delusory, how is this revived pride among maybe two or three hundred thousand Arabs out of a total of more than a hundred million going to change things?"

"It is not yet more real than self-delusory. It is in the process of becoming so. And as I say, I am not so naïve as to believe the process will complete itself overnight. It will take years, decades perhaps. But, you see, we Arabs are a very conformist people. We are much more conformist than we are independent. Islam has made us that way. I mean, you can see it throughout our history. In spite of the original independence of our Bedouin ancestors, within Bedouin society conformity was the rule. It is in our linguistic and literary traditions. And of course conformity is probably the chief sociological feature of our religious tradition. As a result of all this, it is largely an emotional conformity rather than an intellectual one. The great Arab masses have always taken their cues from the single charismatic leaders who have appeared throughout our history. It is something Westerners can never understand about us — why we respond as we do to the great leaders who emerge among us. The explanation involves a complex web of sociological and religious factors, which I am sure you are aware of. But this responsiveness is a fact of Arab life. So — it is not exactly true that the renewal of our Arab pride is limited to the intelligentsia. Go to the army and talk to unlettered soldiers, go to the factories and talk to ignorant laborers. You will see the beginnings of this pride there too. But insofar as it is true that real pride, justified pride, is most conspicuous among the Arab intelligentsia — well, this will be its means of transmission to the masses. The masses hunger to conform to the dictates of the leadership. It has always been so in Arab society. Therefore, as the leadership — the intelligentsia and especially the brightest stars within it — rids itself of the habits of self-delusion and false pride and acquires the habits of realism and true pride, these qualities will be transmitted down the ladder to the masses. The masses, always receptive to signals from the leadership, will eventually conform to these new values. And as the institution of formal education becomes available to more of the masses, it will enhance and speed up the process of transmittal."

I said, "That's all well and good, but it seems to me you leave one vital item out of your scenario for the rebirth of Arab pride. Israel. I mean, if Israel is the bête noire that caused this resurgence of Arabism, what happens when — according to the Arab wish — Israel is eliminated? It seems to me that you need Israel, and that you're going to need her for a long time to come."

"I see your point," replied the professor a trifle condescendingly, "but it is ill conceived. The final confirmation of our restoration to what was our long-ago Arab glory will be the elimination of Israel. For again, Israel represents not just a foreign cancer on the vital organs of Arab culture, it is the symbol of a thousand years of Arab subjugation to Western and Christian pretensions of superiority. Insofar as Israel is concerned, then, there are two factors operating in the expanding Arab consciousness. One is the Israel that symbolizes the Jews. Now, I think you asked me before, what makes Arab pride right and Jewish pride wrong in this matter? Our pride — which is to say, our reaction to the creation and presence of Israel — is right simply because Israeli pride is wrong. Israeli pride is based on values similar to ours, except here it is based on the *Jews'* reaction to the creation and existence of Israel. I shall not give you any of the conventional Arab rhetoric about Israeli 'aggression' or 'imperialism,' that sort of thing. I will merely state the simple facts of history and international law.

"The Jews claim that they have a historical right to their state. If the claim of historical rights is to be invoked at all, it is we, and we alone, who have any right to do so. On any objective analysis of history there can be no doubt that the land which is now the state of Israel has never been anything but a specifically Arab land — inhabited by a people speaking the same language, united by the same cultural aspirations, nurtured by the same social values and linked by common interests . . ."

"But aren't these historical arguments rather moot by now?" I said. "They invariably lead to the same impasse. The Arabs have their history, or interpretation of it, the Jews theirs."

"Ah, but wait, I am not giving you the Arab interpretation of history. I am giving you a so-called objective interpretation — an interpretation that comes principally from Western scholars. It is, after all, from the West that we learned of our history prior to the sixth century."

"All right," I said, "let's hear it."

"It is all about Palestine, right?" the professor went on. "For four thousand years and more, since the beginnings of known human time, Palestine has been first proto-Arab, and then Arab. Through all that time it has preserved its Arab character, despite the fact that several states or societies have conquered it in the course of history. Can you accept this as objective? That since its very beginnings in recorded history, since as far back as we can know, Palestine was occupied by Semites, therefore by what were for all practical purposes Arabs?"

"You are making a quantum jump over two thousand years from Semites to Arabs," I replied. "That may be your first mistake, I don't know, but go ahead."

"It is a quantum jump, yes, but it is just a convenient way to save some time. It is convenient, not expedient or misleading. Historians agree that it is accurate to make such a jump in the course of argument on this question. There is no question but that the earliest inhabitants of Palestine were the precursors of the people who evolved into Arabs."

"But what of the Berbers in western Africa? They were not Semites, but today you consider their descendants Arabs?"

"They are considered Arabs because they speak the common tongue. Again, your point is ill conceived. For the original people of Palestine came out of Arabia. The Arabians were the template upon which the later Arab culture was formed. The original Egyptians were not Semites either. Nor were the Mesopotamians. But these non-Semitic cultures were engulfed by Arabian culture, were transformed into cultures whose chief characteristics were Semitic, thus proto-Arab, then Arab. Will you agree to that?"

"With the qualification that much of your theory about the original people of Palestine is just that — theory," I said. "With that taken into account, I can go along with you."

"But," said the professor, raising his hands wide in some exasperation, "it is all we have to go on, isn't it? Theory, that is. But it is, after all, theory that was formulated by you Westerners. And in the event, you cannot deny the fact that Palestine was inhabited for close to thirty centuries before the Jews were ever supposed to have made their first appearance."

"That, in all likelihood, is true," I agreed.

Professor Salam sighed heavily. "I do not wish to appear rude, but I would like not to have to quibble over matters that are largely irrelevant to the point at hand, particularly when they are generally accepted as fact."

"Please go ahead," I said.

"Now, it is recognized that, as the Jews' own Bible tells us, Palestine was the place where tribes of Canaanite Semites had settled long before. The geographical origins of these tribes proves them to have been Arab — or, if you insist, proto-Arab. The Hebrew tribes did not enter Palestine until the fourteenth century B.C. at the earliest, when, under the leadership of Joshua, they conquered certain parts of it. They found there a flourishing and prosperous civilization, as the Bible also attests to. The Canaanites — Semites, proto-Arabs — had been established in Palestine since the Neolithic period. As far as we know, they were the original settlers. It was their homeland. It was the birthplace of the Canaanite civilization. Historically, therefore, the ancient Hebrews, who themselves were proto-Arab, were not born in Palestine. And when they did come to Palestine for a relatively brief period of time, they never occupied the whole of what is now Israel. The coastal plain remained in the hands of the Philistines. The basic fact of history that often gets overlooked, then, is that the land of Canaan, which was the homeland of the Canaanites, who were Semites and therefore Arabs, was later conquered by alien Hebrews. Do you agree so far?"

"On the basis of what historians have been able to reconstruct," I said, "yes."

"But this Jewish conquest was not to last too long. Divided into two mutually hostile kingdoms, the Hebrew society was soon overwhelmed from the seventh century onward by successive invasions of Persians, Greeks, Assyrians, Babylonians and Romans. By the time of the Romans, Palestine was inhabited not just by Jews, but by Idumeans, Itureans, Ammonites and a large number of people who could only be called Arabs. Once the Romans crushed the revolt of the Jews and drove them out of Jerusalem, Palestine reverted to its completely Arab character — a character that had been originally diluted by the incursions of the exclusivist Hebrews, but which never lost its identity or presence in the land. Indeed, the land that was known as the Provincia Arabia to the Roman and Byzantine empires was, in fact, Palestine — which, after having become subjected to the influence of Christianity, became Muslim in the seventh century and once again thoroughly Arab. It is clear from these facts that the effective Jewish political presence in Palestine came to an end almost as soon as it began, and that the period during which it did exist was not long enough for it to prevail over nearly thirty centuries of prior Arab — or, again if you insist, proto-Arab — legitimacy."

"What do you say, then, to the Jewish argument that they are the only distinct people out of all the peoples who occupied Palestine to have survived down to the present day, and on that basis have the right to claim it as theirs?"

"It is specious reasoning of the worst sort," answered the professor. "It is a perfect example of how they distort and falsify history to their own ends. In the first place, the Jews are not a distinct surviving people in the sense that they claim they are. The Jews dispersed throughout the world, assimilating with other peoples for two thousand years. Just as the Canaanites, the Philistines and others who lived in Palestine were absorbed into Arab culture, so were the Jews absorbed into both Arab culture and cultures elsewhere . . ."

"But the Jews claim they were not absorbed," I said. "They did not become Muslims or Christians. They remained Jews."

"They remained Jews — or most of them did — in religious terms. But politically and sociologically they became Russians, Poles, Americans, Spaniards, Italians, even Arabs. You don't suppose the Jews who lived here in the Middle East for the last two thousand years — in Morocco, in Egypt, in Syria, in Iraq, in Palestine, in Arabia — you don't suppose they spoke Hebrew as their native tongue, do you? They spoke Arabic. They were Arab in every way but in their religious practices. So, then, the idea that the Jews have a right to Palestine on the basis of the claim that they are the only distinct people of Palestine to have survived is absurd. The claim itself is absurd. Their religion survived. But they as a distinct people have not survived as such, any more than the Canaanites as a distinct people survived. And that is not all that is absurd about their claim of 'historical rights.' "

"Go on."

"Well, it is a fact of international legal and political precedent that 'historical rights,' so called, are closely linked with the effective exercise of sovereignty. This being the case, the Jews are in no position to invoke such rights. In the first place, the ancient Hebrews never exercised any sovereignty over Palestine during their stay there — they always existed at the sufferance of foreign empires. In the second place, if the Jews are allowed to invoke such rights, then the Arabs must be allowed to claim sovereignty over Spain, which we in fact ruled for eight centuries. And by such reasoning it would be proper for Greece or Italy, even Iran, to claim a historical right over Palestine, Egypt, Syria — the entire eastern Mediterranean — simply because each of them at one time or another ruled it."

"Well," I said, "I understand all that, but in 1948 the United Nations made an exception to such legal and historical precedent. In effect, the UN passed a new law, or a special law, to cover the particular case of the Jews, without upsetting the mainstream of international law. Wasn't that exactly what it did?"

"That is in effect what the UN did, yes. And it was wrong, a mistake, and should be rescinded. Take in your country, for example. Your government made a new law making the selling and buying of alcohol a crime. You called it the Prohibition law. Then, some years later, you realized it was a mistake. For various reasons it simply did not work. It aroused the ire of the great mass of people on whom it was imposed. It created dissension, dissatisfaction, rebellion. It could not be enforced. Your government realized that the American people would never accept such a law. So what did you do? You rescinded the law. The parallel is not far-fetched. In 1948 we Arabs had imposed on us a law in the form of a United Nations resolution that was totally unacceptable to us. It will never be acceptable to us. It has caused incredible turmoil and war in the Middle East for twenty-five years and will continue to do so. We will fight and resist this law for as long as it remains on the books. It is a law that was unilaterally imposed on us at the instance of the Zionists, but one which could not have been imposed without the collaboration and will of the West — America, Britain, France and so on, those powers who had come to symbolize to us oppression, exploitation, imperialism. So you see, in resisting the presence of Israel as passionately as we do, we are not only expressing our abhorrence of the Zionist Jews but our hatred for traditional Western oppression."

"If I'm not mistaken," I said, "Russia also gave its imprimatur to the resolution that created Israel."

"I don't except Russia. In their own way the Russians were and are as imperialistic as America and Britain. In that sense Russia is part of the West."

"But the creation of Israel was not only the result of political impulses," I said. "There was a certain humanitarian instinct at work in the UN as well. Wouldn't you agree?"

"Such has long been the party line of the West," said Professor Salam. "But it is a perverted sense of humanitarianism that grants refuge to one people and at the same stroke ruthlessly imposes exile and unremitting hardship on another."

"Are you talking about the Palestinians or all Arabs?"

"In spirit, the two cannot be separated. A sense of brotherhood is a fundamental quality of the Arab character. It is a historial and sociological reality, but it is one the United Nations ignored when it voted Israel into existence. Did they think only the Palestinians would resist? All Arabs would resist. Beyond the national differences between the numerous Arab states, history has made of all Arabs a single nation — a spiritual nation. Neither the Arab nation nor any man who respects the law could possibly consider as 'legal,' not to mention 'humanitarian,' a solution to the World

War Two Jewish problem that involved the expulsion of millions of Arabs from their homeland and their replacement by non-Arabs."

"But here we get into the old arguments about whether the Palestinians fled more because of the Jews or because of the hysteria-provoking actions and assertions of neighboring Arab countries," I said.

"For the purposes of this discussion we should stay away from that. Do you know why? Because such arguments obscure the fundamental issue. It is like in your Prohibition. The question was always: 'Did the policeman actually catch the man selling the bottle of whiskey, or did he entice him into selling it and then arrest him? Did he actually catch the man buying the whiskey, or did he entrap him into buying it?' Such arguments obscured the central issue, and that was that the law was wrong. I know that the Israelis have endless 'documentation' to prove that they did nothing to cause the Palestinians to flee. The Arab nation has a similarly endless list to prove that the Jews were the ones who were primarily responsible — through their deeds and words. It all comes down to whom you're willing to believe. And that is hardly the point. The point is: Was the creation of Israel by the UN right or wrong — whether it was for political reasons, humanitarian reasons, or whatever reasons you want to ascribe it to? The answer is: It was wrong. It was conceived in infamy by the Zionists. It was carried out in infamy by the West. It was done under the guise of humanitarianism, but its true causes were political — to enable the Western nations to rid themselves of the problem of the suffering Jew without being required to absorb all the displaced Jews themselves. And it has been continued in infamy by means of a coalition between the two. Also for political reasons. Those who resist infamy can only be virtuous. In virtue is true pride. And that is the pride I have been talking about. It is the pride that is going to make all of us Arabs whole again."

# 9.

# HISTORY: *The Arabs — II*

THE FINAL DEFEAT of the Ummayads by the Abbasids in 750 constituted the beginning of the end of Arabian domination over Islam. The Arab Empire remained; but for the next three centuries, as it went through its so-called Golden Age,* it gradually lost its exclusive and dominant Arabian cultural character and took on a more variegated hue.

In the Abbasid victory there was no question of a threat to Islam itself. Indeed, it was the very nature of Islam that brought the victory about. Despite the proprietary attitude of the Arabians toward Islam in the beginning, the religion itself contained an expansive force which, coupled with its doctrinal simplicity, ecumenism and tolerance for other beliefs, made its spread beyond its purely Arabian origins inevitable. The largely Persian Abbasids' seizure of the caliphate was primarily an endeavor designed to reform what was felt to be the dereligionizing impulses of the Arabian Ummayads. What it meant in the longer run was a reshuffling of the various elements of the populations of the region as Islam became rooted in the new society that had developed after the Arabian military conquests. The various classes of the conquered populations, slowly working their way up through

---

* Between about 700 and 1100 A.D., Arab culture reached heights that were only achieved much later in Christian Europe. Scholars made pioneering discoveries in mathematics and medicine, others created the basic tools of technology such as the Arabic system of numbers, astronomers accurately plotted the orbits of the planets, architects produced masterpieces such as the Alhambra and the Dome of the Rock, writers and poets composed timeless literature in Arabic. It was through Arabic translations that modern Western culture first gained access to Aristotle and other ancient philosophers, and Arab philosophy itself was much ahead of that of Europe in the extent of its probing into the nature of the world.

the evolving Islamicized society to a footing of equality with the Arabians, came at last to constitute the new society themselves. Throughout the Fertile Crescent this society became thoroughly Arabic (as opposed to merely Arabian). A society was thus born that transcended interboundary differences and — through the instruments of a common language, a common religion and a similarity in biological identity and tribal heritage — became "the Arabs."*

The evolution of the new Arab society, then, meant the dissolution of Arabian hegemony over the Islamic Empire. During the spread of Islam throughout the Middle East, the Arabians had become the aristocrats of the lands they conquered — first the military, then the tribes that settled on the heels of the armies. But once the conquests had been consolidated and the new society of Arabs began growing up and cementing itself within the newly acquired territories, the Arabians as a class became superfluous. The way was opened for the unfettered proliferation of a new class of functionaries, bankers, merchants and landowners, as well as the category of learned persons — scholars, teachers, mathematicians, religious authorities and the like — who were responsible for the Arabs' golden age.

The Arabians themselves facilitated the entire process by failing to grasp its nature, and especially by continuing to wage the internecine squabbles, based on traditional tribal or regional allegiances, that made cohesiveness as a community impossible. Hence, with the Shiite-Persian Abbasids in power, the exclusively Arabian national focus of Islam was replaced by the international society of the Abbasid Empire, of whom the evolving Arabs of the Fertile Crescent were but a component.

After their victory over the Ummayads, the Abbasids shifted the center of the caliphate eastward from Damascus to Baghdad. The heart of the Islamic Empire thus moved from the Mediterranean to Mesopotamia, and with its increasingly strong Persian influence it took on a more Oriental coloration. Not only did it restore religion to its primacy through Shiite reform, it transformed the basically Arab social institutions and practices of Islam into traditional Oriental ones. No longer was the caliph patterned on a tribal sheikh, or peer among peers, whose rule and edicts were based on consultation with the Majlis. Rather he became, under the aegis of the Persian-dominated Abbasids, a self-sufficient monarch — all-powerful, all-wise and,

* The Arabs did not enforce any regulations of language until the Abbasid caliph Mahmoud visited Egypt in 833 and found that he needed an interpreter to converse with the subjugated Egyptians. He then decreed that Arabic would be the only spoken language of the empire so that neither he nor any future ruler would have to employ an interpreter.

if the need arose, all-terrible. He became, in short, an Oriental despot, a successor in the flesh to the ancient kings of Persia.*

To say that as Islam and Arabic became entrenched a new Arab (as opposed to Arabian) society evolved in the Middle East during the Abbasid dynasty is not to say that this society was in any way aware of being such a culturally distinct entity. Just the contrary is true: However Arabized the populations of the Middle East had become, there was little if any self-consciousness of their Arabness. During the golden age, the term "Arab" again came into use to refer only to those people — the Bedouin — who continued to roam the deserts. The sedentary urban and agrarian populaces were more likely to define themselves as Muslims. Indeed, the use of "Arab" as an appellation of mass identity in the Middle East would not come into vogue until well into the nineteenth century.

Today one might expect that to the evolving Islamicized populaces of the Middle East the term "Muslim" would have been akin, for identification purposes, to "Christian." Such was not quite the case, for the meaning of "Muslim" embraced a great deal more than the meaning of "Christian." As I have earlier indicated, the development and spread of Islam was not merely a religious phenomenon; its initial impulses were just as strongly political and economic. The mystique of Muhammad and his Umma remained embodied by the Koran. There was little theology, as such, in the Koran, and in Islam there were few of the trappings of Christianity — there was no priesthood, no sacraments, no saints, no idols, no celebrations of human divinity. The Koran taught simply that every man had a personal nonintermediated relationship to Allah, and it set down the best methods by which all men were most advantageously (to themselves) able to fulfill that relationship. Under the terms of so personal a religion, it was not enough merely to faithfully execute a few religious observances while living an otherwise worldly life; one had to dedicate one's entire being to one's relationship with Allah (the Umma philosophy). This personal dedication, coupled with the lack of any distinction, as it were, between church and state, meant that Islam developed not just as a religion but as a thoroughgoing way of life.

It was a way of life that — in the Middle East and Northwest Africa, at least — quickly came to transcend national or ethnic dissimilarities and to unite all populaces under one sociological and cultural banner. An eleventh-

* The exploits of the Abbasid caliphs have become familiar to the Western world through *The Arabian Nights*.

century man from the Nile delta would have thought of himself only incidentally as an Egyptian. If he encountered a traveler from the valley of the Euphrates, another from the western Sahara and still another from Nablus near the Jordan River, he would relate to them, and they to him, only as fellow Muslims. Their conversation would be in Arabic, and they might even trade elaborate and regal Arab genealogies in the Bedouin style.* They would not see in each other a specifically Arab commonality, however, but a Muslim one. It was Islam that bound them together — an identicality of values, spiritual and worldly, supported of course by a common language, a common outlook (for we "see" things primarily through language), and underlaid by a common set of customs and traditions that derived from Islam's Arabian heritage.

Thus, although sociologically there were no people known as Arabs, as such, in the early Islamic Middle East (except, of course, for the Bedouin), and although it is technically misleading to describe the Islamic world under the Abbasid dynasty as an "Arab" empire (most of the true Arabs had been absorbed into the various ethnic populations), by dint of language, outlook, custom and tradition, all under the force of Muslim belief, a "new" Arab social entity was definitely aborning. I shall therefore henceforth call the emergent Muslim populations of the Middle East Arabs, despite the fact that they did not think of themselves in such terms until many centuries later, and despite the fact that there is some question in the minds of present-day sociologists and anthropologists as to the technical accuracy of the term when so broadly applied to the various national populations of the modern Middle East.

The Arabs of today are, by and large, the direct biological descendants of the mongrelized, multiethnic Arab civilization that emerged in the Middle East during the centuries of Islam's golden age. Under the Abbasid caliphate that joint society flourished as no other individual society in the Middle East had flourished before. Not only were great strides made in scholarly and artistic areas, but singular progress in the more mundane pursuits of trade and commerce was achieved as well. While Europe struggled through the

* Such tales of biological heritage would usually be made up to compensate for the speakers' uncertain biological origins. By the eleventh century there had been such a high degree of miscegenation among various ethnic groups across the Middle East, and such mongrelization of the Arabian bloodline, that almost every Muslim was forced to "create" a family tree, tracing back to Arabian sources, to give himself a legitimate spiritual link to the Prophet. Such "genealogizing" was an accepted form of status-seeking.

flames and shadows of its Dark Ages, the crescent moon of Islamic Arab civilization shone bright over the eastern Mediterranean. The Arabian aristocracy had been replaced by a new ruling class of wealthy educated bankers, merchants and propertyowners. Immense fortunes were accumulated, both in money and in property, but the wealth was spread more widely across the land, was in the hands of many more people, than it had ever been before. This, combined with the ingrained tolerance of Islam for other beliefs, produced a civilization that flowered well beyond what one might today have expected of the tenth and eleventh centuries, especially in view of Europe's sad record and of the despotic potential of the increasingly Persianized caliphate. Ironically, it was these two factors that led to the fading of Arab glory.

The two worldly hallmarks of Islam — prosperity and tolerance — greatly increased its attraction to non-Arab peoples. To the people on its fringes the attraction was one of a desire to join. To more distant peoples it was one of a desire to destroy.

The period of tolerance and prosperity produced a revival of Hellenism in the Middle East. The literature, philosophy and science of the ancient Greeks was translated and studied with monkish devotion, and those ideas that were not inconsistent with the religious doctrines of Islam were assimilated by the Arab mind. The Greeks, of course, had been the inventors of the notion of a body politic, out of which came the first expressions of nationalistic impulses. The Arabian Islamic conquest of the Middle East in the seventh century had effectively wiped out national and quasi-national boundaries between states. Once the Islamic Empire became established there were no partitions between Egypt, Syria, Palestine, and the like. These lands were swallowed whole into the empire; the empire itself, ruled from Baghdad, was considered the only state. What had formerly been states, or pseudostates, were now just provinces of the imperial center in Baghdad.

The very prosperity and religious and ideological tolerance that spread through the empire in the eighth and ninth centuries made possible the entertainment and consideration of ideas from elsewhere. That Greek thought became the system most revered was surely a throwback to the Hellenization of much of the Fertile Crescent a thousand years before. It was perhaps due also to the fact that the theories of Plato, Aristotle and other Greek thinkers were the only theories contained in so large a body of readily available literature; and due as well to the fact that the Arabs perceived in the translated narratives of the Greek historians an opportunity to better learn their own history. In any event, out of the Arab preoccupation with Greek philosophical and historical literature emerged a fascination for political theory which soon began to express itself in terms of nationalistic ideas. Under the traditions and unwritten rules of Islam there could be no such thing as an individual and sovereign Islamic nation set apart from the rest of Islam; all Islam was a single nation. Greek notions of nationhood spoke of distinct national entities, however — self-sufficient, independent, democratic and, most of all, self-identifiable. These notions had a good deal of appeal, particularly to those Muslims of what had formerly been Spain, Egypt and Syria — once independent entities in their own right. Thus was a conflict introduced into the Islamic Empire of the Abbasids: the intellectual attraction of nationalism versus the emotional respect for Islamic traditions that admitted no partition of or distinction between nations within its purview.

The conflict was never resolved; rather, it was exacerbated. Islamic Spain refused to acknowledge the Baghdad caliphate as early as the ninth century, retaining its own nationalist autonomy. Muslim Egypt asserted its national independence in the tenth century and established its own caliphate. Soon after, the Syrians began to take steps toward independent national status, while throughout this period there were repeated attempts made toward independence from Baghdad by Arabia, although these were mostly on religious grounds.

These nationalist aberrations ate away at the power and prestige of the Baghdad caliphate. Early on, in order to maintain control over their empire, the Abbasid caliphs employed mercenary troops recruited from a large nomadic Asian tribe known as the Seljuk Turks. The Turks first appeared in Baghdad in the middle of the ninth century. As the authority of the caliphs waned in the face of expressions of nationalist impulses within the empire, the Seljuks gradually replaced it with their own. Sent out to bring the dissident Muslim provinces into line, they soon moved into nonmilitary positions of importance within the caliphate. Eventually, converted to Islam and expressing their own nationalistic aspirations, they became so powerful that they were able to take over the caliphate itself and gain control of the entire Islamic realm.

By the tenth century the Abbasid caliphs were little more than puppets of the Turks. At first the Turks, though speaking little Arabic, spread their tentacles eastward and northward from Baghdad, sending out armies of trained slaves, known as Mamluks, to establish their dominance in the name of the Abbasid dynasty. This provoked a series of wars between Persians and

Turks in the east and between Byzantines and Turks in the north. Then they poured westward across the Fertile Crescent to subjugate the lands of Syria, Egypt and beyond. By the eleventh century they were arrayed throughout the Middle East, and as they advanced they plowed under three centuries of Arab achievement and prosperity and put an end to the Arab domination of Islam. In their encroachment upon the shrunken and fading Christian Byzantine Empire, they also brought about the advent of the Crusades. And finally, through their presence in the Middle East, they imposed close to a thousand years of stagnation on Arab culture — a stagnation the consequences of which are today still highly evident.

The Turks were able to do what the Arab and Persian Muslims before them could not: introduce Islam into the heart of the Byzantine Empire. In 1071 Turkish tribal armies overwhelmed the Byzantine defenders of eastern and central Anatolia. Soon thereafter the Seljuks organized a Muslim state in the conquered territory and threatened to expand westward to Constantinople itself. In 1094 Byzantine emperor Alexius I appealed to Pope Urban II for military reinforcements to seal off the Turkish encroachments. The pope's response to this appeal precipitated the Crusades.

In early twelfth-century Europe, conditions were favorable for expansion to the east. In Italy, where urban centers of industry and commerce had developed, the rich bankers, merchants and shipowners of Venice and Genoa saw opportunity and profit in the expansion of their economic activities to the eastern Mediterranean. As increasing production and widening commerce forced the ruling classes of these Italian city-states along the road of such expansion, they became determined to acquire naval and commercial bases throughout the Fertile Crescent, as well as in Asia Minor. Meanwhile, in western and central Europe, the political and economic structure of society remained predominantly feudal. The basis of wealth and power lay principally in the ownership of land and serfs. Existing agricultural methods, however, did not provide adequately for increasing populations; moreover, the expanding populations could not be absorbed by the medieval urban centers because their commerce and industry were as yet insufficiently developed. As a result, political unrest and social discontent grew bitter among the European nobles, the serfs and the townspeople. The times favored agrarian as well as commercial expansion at a moment in history when psychological forces, aroused by the rivalry between Christianity and Islam, provided the emotional and ideological drive. Thus, although the Crusades, launched in

1094, began as a Christian holy war against Islam, they soon became transformed into a political and economic war designed not only to eliminate Islam but to gain European control over the riches of the Middle East and Asia Minor.

The Crusades, which lasted two hundred years, were principally a struggle between Christian Europeans and Muslim Seljuk Turks. The Turks had not only spread throughout the Middle East by the twelfth century, they governed, through their control of the Baghdad caliphate, just about all the political and military institutions of the region. Thus, while the indigenous Arab populations pursued trade and commerce, the Turks and their Mamluk armies took up the defense of the Fertile Crescent.

At first the Crusades seemed to bring about a political standoff in the Middle East. The Christian nobles were able to establish footholds in the lands of the eastern Mediterranean, but were never able to achieve any widespread political power. Yet in spite of intermittent warfare between Christians and Muslims in Egypt, Palestine and Syria, a close commerical relationship developed between Christian merchants of the Italian city-states and their Arab counterparts. While the Christians secured control of the Mediterranean shipping routes, the Arabs continued to dominate, under the protection of the Turkish Mamluk armies, the overland transshipment routes to and from India and China. In the Fertile Crescent countries, then, the Crusades initially fostered trade and brought increased prosperity to the mercantile classes, which were still predominantly Arab.

But it was precisely the lengthening military and political standoff that put an end to the Arabs' increased prosperity. As the Crusades extended into their second century, the Seljuk Turks began to weaken, both in their twin Baghdad-Anatolia centers of power and in their control of the Arab provinces. At the same time a new force was rising on the eastern European–western Asian horizon: the Mongol tribes of central Asia. Toward the middle of the thirteenth century the Mongols overran eastern Europe and thus destroyed a lucrative market for Middle Eastern goods. Ten years later they descended on the Seljuk state of central and eastern Anatolia. After driving the Seljuks westward they pressed farther south and east, razing the city of Baghdad, destroying the last vestiges of the Turko-Persian caliphate, and occupying all of Persia.

The Islamic realm was thus thoroughly fragmented. With the vital Oriental trade routes in the hands of the Mongols, the Crusaders more or less gave up their ambitions and withdrew to Europe to defend the continent against the

Mongol threat to its central and western portions. At the opening of the fourteenth century no single political entity was strong enough to give order and security to the Middle East, which lay in a condition of political chaos. Trade with Europe and the Orient had dried up, and so had the fortunes of the sedentary Arab populations. Persia and the Tigris-Euphrates valley were in the hands of the Mongols. The western regions of the Fertile Crescent — Syria, Palestine, Egypt — were under the domination of the Mamluk slave armies and their Turkish leaders, while the Arabian peninsula retained its largely anarchic Bedouin character. The greater part of the northeastern Mediterranean shoreline leading up into central Anatolia was divided into petty Turkish tribal principalities, none of which was able to extend its power over the whole.

As a result of early expressions of nationalistic self-determinism based on European (Greek) ideas, Islam had lost its dominant Persian cast and had assumed a primitive Turkish character — thanks to the Abbasid caliphate's desire to quash such expressions. Now the caliphate was in ruins, but the Turkish complexion remained on Islam throughout the Middle East primarily because the numerically superior, but sedentary and largely impoverished, Arabic culture had no means of reversing the situation. During the Crusades the Seljuks and Mamluks had taken over the religious, military and political (insofar as there were political) establishments of Baghdad's Islamic provinces, leaving the Arabs to function solely in the economic realm. When the economic structure of the provinces collapsed, the Arab populations were left without a political and military base, and were economically impotent to stem the increasing Turkish power within the provinces. The Turkish interpretation of Islam, as is often the case among converts, was even more strict and orthodox than the Persian Shiite version that had stamped the early Abbasid dynasty. In the wake of the dissolution of Seljuk supremacy over Islam, in the face of further threats from the infidel Mongols who held the eastern portions of the Islamic Empire, and against the backdrop of the religiopolitical vacuum that existed in the Middle East at the end of the Crusades, Turkish zeal intensified. Various tribes that had spilled down into Islam from Turkestan on the heels of the Seljuks in the pre-Crusade centuries, and had become dispersed through the Arab Middle East as a result of the destruction of Baghdad, now vied with each other to become the leaders of a renascent Islam. Out of this rivalry emerged a single dominant tribe, the descendants of which would thoroughly dominate Islam and the Middle East for the next five centuries. They came to be known as the Ottomans.

According to Turkish history, the leader of a tribe of nomadic Islamicized Turks named Ertogruhl came to the aid of a Seljuk sultan and helped him win a battle against an army of Mongol tribes descending on Persia in 1251. As a reward for his services, Ertogruhl and his tribe were granted lands in north-central Anatolia, which was sandwiched between the remains of Byzantium to the west and the Mongol armies to the east. Ertogruhl was succeeded by one of his many sons, a man named Osman. During the first quarter of the fourteenth century, while various Turkish tribes were vying with each other across the Middle East and native Arab populations were fading into economic destitution, Osman, overflowing with Islamic zeal, advanced on the last remnants of Byzantine Anatolia and extended his holdings as far as Constantinople. By so doing he completed the introduction of Islam throughout practically all of Anatolia, an achievement that had been beyond the capabilities of the early Arab Ummayad and later Persian Abbasid dynasties. And by so doing, Osman came to general notice throughout Islam and was endowed with legendary qualities along the Muslim grapevine. He was a man to be feared and revered; consequently his tribe, which came to be known as the Osmanlis, rapidly expanded as less prestigious bands rushed to join forces with it.*

In the second quarter of the fourteenth century the Osmanlis were so strong that Osman's son Orkhan was able to consolidate Osmanli (and Islamic) authority in western Anatolia and cross the Dardanelles into Balkan Europe. Orkhan's successors completed the Islamicization of Europe's southeastern corner in the second half of the century, and the Ottoman Empire was on its way.

With the heart of Byzantium now in their control, the Ottoman Turks spent the next century conquering the Arab world, a task that was aided immeasurably by the presence there of the remnant Mamluk and Seljuk populations from the centuries of the Crusades. Their authority eventually extended beyond Egypt to the Berber lands of the western Mediterranean, but their primary control over Arab culture was centered throughout the region of the Fertile Crescent, from the Nile to the Euphrates. For the first time since the collapse of the Roman Empire a thousand years earlier, the Middle East was brought under the dominion of a foreign state — Ottoman Anatolia (later Turkey) — that had the power to maintain political order and security.

* The name Osman was later Anglicized to Othman, thus providing the name for the Ottoman Turks and the Ottoman Empire.

By the beginning of the sixteenth century conditions in the Middle East seemed favorable to the renewal of economic prosperity and the renascence of Arab culture through a revival in fortune of the native mercantile classes, which were still mostly Arab. The Ottomans had restored order and security to the intercontinental trade routes that passed through the Fertile Crescent. They had eliminated most of the internal squabbles between and among the Turks and Mamluks in provincial areas of Egypt, Palestine, Syria and Mesopotamia. They shared a common religious outlook with their Arab subjects. Nevertheless, instead of an era of increasing prosperity and advancing culture, a period of further economic decline, political deterioration and cultural stagnation was to be the Arabs' fate in the centuries to come.

# 10.

# History: *The Ottoman Yoke*

Ironically, the acquisition of dominion over the Middle East by the Ottomans came at a time in history when Europe was emerging from its era of reactionary medievalism. The Turkish cultural and political structure was based on the same kind of autocratic feudalism — albeit eastern in character — of which Europe was in the process of ridding itself. Supported by the strictest and most complex interpretation of Islam yet seen, administered by regal edict, and enforced by military might, Turkish rule brought about a sudden flip-flop in the relationship between the Middle East and Europe. Five hundred years earlier, on the wings of Arab cultural achievement, the Middle East had been a relatively prosperous, warm and well-lighted place compared to Europe's cold, dark, culturally impoverished cellar. But now the tables were turning. Taking advantage of much of what Arab culture had achieved and transmitted in the way of ideas, Europe began to enlighten itself. The Middle East, meanwhile, under feudalistic Turkish domination that in its own way aped the reactionism that produced the cultural stagnation of an earlier Europe, was becoming a byroad on the world scene.

The de-Arabization of Islam had much to do with this, although not everything. The de-Arabization begun by the Persia-oriented Abbasid caliphate in the ninth century was speeded up by the Seljuk Turks and completed by the Ottomans in the fifteenth. The evolving Turkish culture was formed on Oriental — particularly Persian — models and was based on princely privilege and the rule of wealth. In order to secure its hold over

Islam, Turkish culture had necessarily to demonstrate its superiority to the pure Arabic culture from which Islam had emerged and to the mixed Arabic-Persian cultural milieu in which it found Islam when it arrived on the scene. The Turks quickly developed a distinct language and approach of their own which, by virtue of their expression through Islam, left the Arab heritage with nothing to do but fade into the woodwork. Turkish became the cultivated language of Islam, spreading out from Anatolia and forcing Arabic back into the deserts of the south and west where it fell into disuse.

As its language became stagnant, so did Arab culture as a whole. The independence in thought and research that had been the trademark of Arab culture — expressed through the Arabic language — became a thing of the past. Turkish culture imposed a congealed and formal theological overlay on Islam, one that became completely authoritative in support of the Ottomans' theocratic and autocratic rule. This doctrinal corset caused Middle Eastern society to become intellectually static. As conformism became the mode in public life, literature and speech too became passive and dependent on accepted forms.

Although it was the language of the Koran, Arabic did not lend itself to the designs and interests of the Turks. A language ultrarich in imaginative vocabulary and discursive style, it allowed of too much ideological invention in a time when such invention was dangerous to stern Ottoman orthodoxy. The Turks, while not outlawing the speaking of Arabic, discouraged it. By so doing they created a psychology of passivity in the Arab cultural mind that also discouraged Arab reascendancy. Indeed, Arabic — even as a form of everyday speech — gradually sank to such a level of contempt in the Arab centers of population that it was considered a sign of something inherently unworthy to speak it. Since Arab self-consciousness had always been inextricably bound to the language, the decline of the language resulted in the disintegration of Arab self-consciousness. And since it was considered bad form to speak Arabic, no one seeking status in the Ottoman sphere — not even Arabs — would use it. So Arabic became the vernacular of the peasant and the nomad.

The one exception to this was Egypt, and here lay another irony. As the political center of gravity of Islam came under the control of the Ottomans in the fifteenth century and Arabic was replaced by Turkish as the official language of the Islamic Empire, Arabic retreated to the western and southern outposts of the empire — Egypt and Arabia. For the Ottomans, Arabia was not a problem. It was still a largely tribal, nomadic land. Without any large-scale wealth or power, with only vast dessicated wastelands to its credit (plus, of course, Mecca and Medina), it represented neither threat nor treasure. So the Ottomans, like imperial powers of the previous two thousand years, at first left Arabia more or less alone.

Egypt, however, was a different matter. When the Ottomans ascended to the pinnacle of power, Egypt was ruled by the descendants of the earlier Turkish Mamluks who had been sent there by the Seljuk-controlled Abbasid caliphate to put an end to Egyptian gestures of independence. The Mamluks had remained and had been augmented by further influxes of Mamluk troops during the Crusades. As a result of the political vacuum that opened up throughout the Middle East following the Mongol destruction of the Seljuk state and the Abbasid caliphate in the thirteenth century, the Mamluks moved into power in Egypt and its environs. As their Turkish precursors, the Mamluks were hostile to the Ottomans. Thus, as they sought to blot out the influence of Arab culture, the Mamluks gave it a brief lease on life in Egypt, Palestine and Syria.

The irony mentioned above resides in the fact that the Egyptian people had never regarded themselves as Arabs; nor did they until the middle of the twentieth century when Nasser cast his spell on them. Another irony derives from the circumstances that enabled the Ottomans to subjugate Mamluk-Arab Egypt in the first place. It was a situation that reflected the rapidly changing balance in fortunes between the Middle East and Europe and that symbolized, paradoxically, the positive impact of earlier Arab cultural influences on Europe and the dwindling of those influences in the Middle East.

As Ottoman rule took over and medievalized the Middle East, Europe was emerging from its medieval cocoon — principally through the philosophic ideas and scientific aspirations of Hellenism that had been assimilated by the Crusaders from Arab literature, translations, and research and taken back to Europe. Egypt had always been a hub of European-African-Asian trade routes; it depended for its prosperity on its transit trade with Europe. Toward the end of the fifteenth century, its economy strained by attempts to fend off the growing Ottoman threat, the Mamluks resorted to desperate economic measures to squeeze as much profit as possible out of the transit trade. The result was a series of retaliations from Europe that dislocated the whole of the Egyptian economy. These retaliations were made possible —

again ironically — by what the Europeans had learned from the earlier Arabs about physics, astronomy, geography and other sciences. Out of this knowledge came the impulse to exploration. By the mid-fifteenth century Spanish, Portuguese and Italian navigators were leading ocean expeditions in search of sea routes to the Orient that would enable Europe to bypass the overland trade routes through the Middle East. When in the late fifteenth century a way was found around the southern tip of Africa — the Cape of Good Hope — into the Indian Ocean and beyond, Egypt's role in the European-Oriental transit trade was dealt a fatal blow. As its economy disintegrated in the early sixteenth century, the Ottomans were finally able to move in and displace Mamluk rule. With this, whatever brief sanctuary Arab culture had found under the Mamluks in Egypt was effectively destroyed. Arab culture regressed to what it had been in pre-Islamic times — a desert culture borne on the broken wings of Bedouin nomads, who were by now almost completely disenfranchised from the population centers of the Middle East.

To repeat what I said earlier, the tracing of historical causality is often a tenuous pursuit fraught with oversimplification. Nevertheless, there would seem to be a direct cause-and-effect relationship between the Turkish ascendancy to power in the Middle East and the dramatic decline of the region's importance on the evolving world stage. The initial Turkish conquest of Islam through the Abbasid caliphate precipitated the Crusades. The Crusades brought about the rise of the Turkish Mamluks in Egypt and the rest of the western Fertile Crescent. The Mamluks, seeking to defend their sovereignty against the later Ottoman Turks, put the squeeze on Europe to fatten their economy. Their failure led to Europe's success in finding new and alternative trade routes to the Far East, and thus to Egypt's demise as an important trade center. Once Egypt went, the Ottoman provinces to the east lost their importance for the European-Asian trade. Palestine, Syria, Iraq, Arabia — all became byroads. Thus, as the Ottomans rose to dominance over the entire Middle East, the region, for so long such a strategic locality, was bypassed. International trade would go on neglecting it for another four centuries. Similarly, under Ottoman rule Arab identity would recede into the vast and thinly populated wildernesses. The Muslim Middle East would be transformed from a cosmopolitan and international trading center based on a capitalistic money economy to an insular and regressive backwater enveloped in a feudal political structure having its economic roots in subsistence agriculture. The sedentary Arabic-speaking populations would become peasant masses lacking any trace of political independence or self-determination and would remain so under Turkish rule until World War I.

Just as the Ottoman Turks were instrumental in bringing down the Middle East, so too were they instrumental in keeping it down through the imposition of a political and economic system based on feudalism and privilege and enforced by religious authoritarianism and ruthless militarism. Once the Ottomans consolidated their power in the sixteenth century, the time seemed ripe for a recasting of the region into a leading role in the ongoing world drama. At first the Ottomans ruled efficiently and productively. They brought order to an area that had been beset by five hundred years of sociological disorganization. They established secure frontiers and they were highly motivated economically. However, the very religion-overlaid feudalism which marked their approach proved their weakness.

In order to support their medieval politico-economic structure, the Ottomans were forced to develop a series of complex military, governmental and religious institutions that were contrary in spirit not only to Muslim traditions of simplicity but to the emerging theories and practices of European enlightenment as well. Europeans were rapidly freeing themselves from the restrictions of theological dogma and the unsound premises of mysticism and supernaturalism. Revolts against Roman religious orthodoxy were at hand. Education was beginning to be liberated from the dead hand of religion. Science and its empirical methods were at the threshold of human curiosity. A new system of capitalism was bringing about a vast extension of commerce and a dramatic increase in all areas of production and marketing. Under these impulses, the idea of the centralized national state was acquiring growing unity and power. Medieval military organizations based on nomadic slave armies were being replaced by royal and national armies. Europe was in the process of revolutionary change in all aspects of its life — intellectual, economic, political and social.

The Middle East on the other hand, under Ottoman rule, was embarked on a reverse course. Ottoman society, both Muslim and (on a smaller scale) Christian, was dominated by obscurantist religious leaders who molded intellectual life and constructed educational systems along complex religiolegal lines that were utterly stultifying. The Ottoman state, though it brought for the first time a cohesive political system to the Middle East, was, and remained throughout its history, a theocracy. All fundamental laws were based on the Koran, and every aspect of life — public and private — was governed by these laws.* To implement the religiolegal system, a vast bureaucracy was established, known as the Muslim Institution. At the head of this body of learned Muslims — called *ulemas*, trained in the sacred law and steeped in ancient Arab scholasticism — was a religiolegal hierarchy composed of *cadis* and *muftis* (Muslim judges of supposedly superior wisdom). The chief of this numerous and powerful bureaucracy was a grand mufti who, reigning from Ottoman Constantinople, was also known as the Sheikh of Islam. The Turks' Muslim Institution, then, was the successor of the Arabs' earlier caliphate, the grand muftis the procedural descendants of the defunct caliphs. In their range of authority and complex glorification, however, they were more akin to the medieval Roman papacy than to the earlier, simpler caliphate. Since any law or official act of the Ottoman sultans† or their ministers could be declared contrary to the Sharia by the Sheikh of Islam, he and his muftis had a powerful instrument of control over the government. It was an instrument they applied liberally. Bound by a highly orthodox interpretation of a dogmatic body of religious law, Muslim society became profoundly conservative in its social and political institutions and vigorously reactionary in confronting the "enlightened" ideas by then filtering down from Europe.

This was just one way in which sixteenth-century European and Middle Eastern aspirations clashed, bringing about the emergence of a superior European culture that by its very nature could have little patience in dealing with the revanchism of the Middle East. Another way was symbolized by what was known as the millet system, which concerned the non-Muslim communities of the Middle East.

The Ottoman conquest of the Fertile Crescent left a number of Christian communities sprinkled throughout the Middle East, Arab descendants of the early Christians mixed with Euro-Arab descendants of the Crusaders. Also liberally spotted about were large communities of Jews. Islam was basically a tolerant religion, and the Turks, although not known as a tolerant people, generally respected that heritage — despite their experience with the haughty exclusivity of the Jews and the excesses of the Crusaders. Since the indigenous Christians and Jews could not be compelled to submit to the

---

* The Koran-based legal system was called the Sharia. It was an outgrowth of an earlier trend on the part of the Arab-Persian caliphates to derive a system of civil law from the Holy Book — a trend similar to that by which the body of formal Jewish law was developed from the biblical Scriptures.
† "Sultan" was the Turkish designation for "supreme authority" in the administration of all political, economic and religious affairs within the empire. The sultanate replaced the Arab caliphate as the center of power in the Islamic world.

Sharia, the Ottomans devised the millet system to force them into the embrace of Islamic political rule. Under the system, the Ottoman sultans granted Christian and Jewish communities limited autonomy under their religious leaders, who were answerable to the Muslim government. The Ottomans conferred extensive powers on them, which made it possible for them to exert a strong influence over their lay members in the interest of keeping non-Muslim dissidence to a minimum. The retention of a leader's ecclesiastical power in his community, then, depended on how well he kept his subjects quiet and in line. If he failed, he was replaced. If he succeeded, he was rewarded by the Muslims with additional temporal authority.

The leaders of the Christian and Jewish communities, with their vested interests, thus became lackeys of the Ottoman government, discouraging at every turn the expression of unacceptable political and social ideas. And so the firm grip of conservatism and reactionism not only choked Arab Muslim cultural and economic development, but had the same effect on the semi-Arab Christian and Jewish populations as well.

Two other medieval institutions were developed by the Ottomans which also contributed to the stagnation of Middle Eastern culture. One was (as it was later called) the Ruling Institution, the political counterpart of the religious Muslim Institution. The Ruling Institution was a bureaucracy created by the early Ottoman sultans to handle the administrative affairs of the empire. At the beginning, advancement within the bureaucracy was accomplished primarily through merit, skill and experience. This rule of thumb was broken in the mid-sixteenth century by Sultan Suleiman, who began elevating relatives and court favorites with little or no training to high administrative posts. He also permitted these appointees to acquire huge fortunes by the sale of offices and privileges within the Ruling Institution. Suleiman's precedent was expanded by succeeding sultans, and soon the efficiency and integrity of the Ruling Institution were thoroughly undermined, spreading corruption throughout the whole of the empire. Buying offices and favors became a common practice among the privileged. The burden of these corrupt practices was borne principally by the vast Arab peasant and urban populations of the Middle East, Muslim and non-Muslim alike, whose basic needs were totally ignored by the increasingly corrupt Turkish ruling class.

An adjunct of the Muslim Institution was the Janissaries, an elite military corps. Created out of the Turkish tradition of slave armies (e.g., the earlier Mamluks), the Janissaries were converted, highly fanatical Muslims whose function it was to enforce the religiolegal edicts of the grand muftis and the ulemas. Due to their association with the Muslim Institution, they gradually acquired an independent political power of their own, which threatened the power of the increasingly corrupt sultans and Ruling Institution. In an effort to control the Janissaries, the sultans opened their own corruption to them, granting them more privileges and exempting their officers from the burdens of taxation that even members of the ruling class bore. Soon officerships in the Janissaries were being bought and sold, and the more privileged the Janissaries became, the faster grew their impulse to exercise their own power. They eventually infiltrated the Ruling Institution and undermined the authority of the sultanate. The more power they assumed over the already corrupt civil establishment, the more corrupt they themselves became, and the more reactionary became their authority in the interest of preserving their privileged status.

All of these Ottoman cultural institutions converged in the principal underlying social, economic and political system of the Turks — the feudal land system. One major difference between the Ottoman feudal system and the medieval European system was that the Ottoman system did not produce a hereditary landed aristocracy; it was patterned, rather, after the system created by the earlier Seljuk Turks. Instead of being granted land titles as feudal fiefs, Ottoman military and civilian dignitaries were awarded the right to the taxes of given territories within the empire. These grants were made as rewards for services rendered.* In the early Ottoman period these feudal grants were made to men of proven merit. However, the later corruption in the ruling establishment made such grants the choicest of choice acquisitions, with the result that grants were conferred upon relatives, favorites, courtiers, sycophants, eunuchs and court entertainers, and were bought and sold with even more avidity than high government offices. Originally the territorial fiefdoms had brought political stability and security to the Middle East; each feudal chief had his own army and his own minigovernment and tax-collection apparatus. Now, in the eighteenth century, with the fiefdoms in the hands of inexpert and largely absent landlords, political instability and economic chaos became the rule throughout the region. People — mostly Arabs — were literally being bought, sold and traded from one week to the next without any knowledge about to whom they were to direct their

---

* Recall that the Ottomans themselves came into existence as a politico-tribal entity when their founding father, Ertogruhl — the sire, according to legend, of Othman — was granted an Anatolian fiefdom by the Seljuks in reward for his aid in a battle against the Mongols.

loyalties. Corruption, decadence and their demoralizing effects had finally struck at the very heart of Ottoman imperial stability. By the beginning of the nineteenth century the Middle Eastern portion of the Ottoman Empire seemed ripe for revolution. Or conquest.

It was not to be revolution; the Arab Muslim populations of the Middle East were mired in apathy. It was by conquest that the region was to undergo the transformation that would lead it into its present-day form. Those revolutionary impulses that *were* expressed by the Arabs were done so almost exclusively in the religious, rather than political, realm.

As Europe transformed itself from a collection of feudal city-states into large-scale sovereign nation-states, as industrialization increased, and as an admixture of Christian-religious and republican political righteousness took hold, a new and more sophisticated brand of imperialism developed.* By the eighteenth century Spain, Portugal, France, Britain, Holland and Russia had colonized many of the distant reaches of the world and brought these areas within the embrace of their respective empires. Within Europe each imperial nation measured its status by the size and wealth of its empire. With vast, previously unclaimed foreign lands under the control of the various empires, however, the drive to gain control of more territory did not wane; the focus merely changed. Now the lands of other empires became fair game. Since the Middle East was, relatively speaking, only a stone's throw from Europe, and since its growing stagnation as an economic center reflected the internal weakness of the Ottoman Empire, it quickly became the object of the expanding covetousness of Europe.

The French were the first to move. Following the French Revolution in 1789, Napoleon sought to spread his revolutionary vision throughout Europe. He did not stop with Europe, however. In 1798 he sent an expeditionary force into the soft underbelly of the Ottoman Empire, Egypt. From that time on the great nations of Europe, either individually or collectively, expanded their political influence, their economic interests, and their psychological activities — military, cultural, missionary, educational — throughout the Middle East. In all these areas there was intense competition even when a joint or cooperative action was undertaken. Every phase of life in the Middle East was significantly affected over the next hundred and fifty years by the expansion of European imperialism. Consequently, the his-

---

* As compared to the imperialism of the earlier Greek, Roman and Byzantine European empires.

torical development of the Arabs from the nineteenth century onward is incomprehensible without an understanding of the role the West played in their destiny.

Until the founding of the German Empire in 1871, France and Great Britain were the two chief imperial competitors for power in the Ottoman Middle East. Austria and Russia focused their imperialistic attention on the eastern European and western Asian portions of the Ottoman Empire, respectively. Later the Germans and the Italians made their interests felt. All in all, the Ottoman government had its hands full.

The French invasion of Egypt, and their subsequent spread westward along the coast of North Africa and northeastward along the Levantine coast (Palestine, Lebanon and Syria), must have been tinged by a sense of manifest destiny, for the interests and claims of France in the Middle East went back to the era of the Crusades, when French kings and nobles played an important role in the wars between Christians and Muslims. With the Franco-Turkish Treaty of 1535, moreover, negotiated during the reigns of King Francis I and Sultan Suleiman, France acquired special rights in the Ottoman Empire. France had become the leading Catholic nation in Europe during the Bourbon era. Under this and similar treaties, the French were given the role of protector of Roman Catholic clergy and property within the Ottoman world. Out of this religious investment developed other interests — economic, political, cultural — so that by the time of Napoleon's incursion there was already a strong sense of France on the lands and peoples of the Middle East. This made the concentrated introduction of French culture — the consequence of Napoleon's expedition — all the easier. Indeed, during the nineteenth century the French language became the second language (to Turkish) of all educated people in much of the Middle East — Muslim, Christian and Jewish alike. And French culture became the dominant foreign culture throughout most of the Ottoman Empire.

Napoleon's invasion did not succeed. Thus the French did not at first gain a political base in the Fertile Crescent, although within a short time they achieved control over the more primitive Berber-Arab-Muslim regions of Northwest Africa. During much of the nineteenth century French imperialism remained largely cultural and economic insofar as the Arab heart of the Middle East was concerned. British imperialistic interests were, on the other hand, more definitely political.

After the loss of the American colonies, Britain's major imperial possession was India. The security of India and of the sea routes between Britain and the subcontinent therefore played a predominant role in shaping early British policy with respect to the Middle East and the Ottoman Empire. The ocean routes took British ships around the Cape of Good Hope, up the east coast of Africa, then across the Indian Ocean below the Red Sea and Persian Gulf. It would have been quite easy for alien fleets to gather in these sea coves and gain control of the Indian Ocean, thus cutting off Britain's marine access to India. Britain, therefore, through pact and fait accompli settled itself in Iraq, Persia, and along the coasts of the Arabian peninsula in order to prevent such an occurrence. Later, when the Suez Canal was opened in 1869, providing a more direct route, Britain felt compelled to expand its imperialistic power to include the eastern Mediterranean. Initially, all of Britain's Middle Eastern coastal outposts were military and naval in nature. But as inevitably happens in the affairs of empires, exposure to the region brought about interest in it for its own sake; thus, political, economic and cultural investment followed.

The Suez Canal was originally French-inspired. So intense had the competition between France and Britain in the Middle East become, however, that the British gained control of it. This event gave them an irreversible stake in what had hitherto been an area dominated imperially — aside from the Ottomans — by the French. When French influence was incapable of putting down, in 1882, a minor Egyptian insurrection which jeopardized the by then massive British investments in Egypt, British military forces occupied the Ottoman province. From that moment on, Britain became a significant presence throughout the entire Middle East.

# 11.

# Journal: *"A Turning of the Tables"*

By the end of the nineteenth century the competing imperialisms of France and Britain, soon to be joined by those of Germany and Italy, began to shape the foreign policy of the Ottoman government. Moreover, they significantly affected internal affairs within the Ottoman Empire and had important repercussions on the relations between the various ethnic and religious populations in all regions under nominal or real Ottoman control.

The Ottoman regime had passed through several centuries of increasingly corrupt and despotic rule. The interplay of foreign interests in the nineteenth century resulted in further encroachments of Turkish cultural influence within the empire. The conquest of the Middle East by European imperialism hadn't been military or political; rather, it was economic and — even more significant — cultural. The stamp of nineteenth-century European culture was indelibly impressed on the consciousness of the Middle East, or at least on those portions of it that were at all cosmopolitan. As compared with the intensifying Western cultural input, which was sophisticated, technology-oriented and seemingly liberating, Turkish culture and its concomitant rule became increasingly regressive, reactionary, stultifying.

Western ideas and cultural trends were having an impact on the Middle East similar to that which Middle Eastern ideas and cultural trends had had on the West seven hundred years earlier. Up to the beginning of the twentieth century the process had taken roughly seven centuries. It had been stimulated and initiated by a series of historical and religiosociological accidents.

The infusion of European ideas into the Middle East throughout the last half of the nineteenth century produced a myriad of cultural movements among the indigenous populations. Probably the most immediately significant of these was the Ottoman attempt to reform its cultural-cum-governmental structure. The most important movement in the long-range sense, though, was the reemergence of Arab self-consciousness. History is shot through with irony; it is no small irony that this rebirth — or birth, as many anthropologists contend — was inspired almost exclusively by Western cultural influences. Nor is it a minor irony that the impulses to cohesive nationalism that grew out of the Muslim Arab world's expanding self-consciousness in the late nineteenth century were inspired principally by Christian-European persuasions.

But it is not the ironies of the past that are the focus of this book. Over the span of the seventy years since the beginning of the present century, aided by two world wars that involved them indirectly but crucially (from their point of view, accidents of history), the Arabs have reconstructed out of the ruins of the Ottoman Empire (for the Ottoman reform was no match for the tide of events) a totally new sense of themselves — a sense emotionally based on their own heritage and rationally supported by the logic of Western nationalist political philosophy.

It is the potential ironies of future history, then, that we seek to espy here. We also seek to understand — or at least perceive — the Arabs from their own viewpoint. At the present time in their history many educated and influential Arabs — nationalities aside — are overwhelmed by a powerful sense of the future ironies history has in store for the world. Everywhere I went in the Arab realm in 1974 I encountered among the intelligentsia and political leadership a conviction that history is in the process of turning the tables on the West — again, as a result of its accidentality. It is a conviction that is held with particular fierceness by those who have their fingers on the pulse of Arab awareness and who have a sharp perception of Arab history.

This "turning of the tables" theory of future Arab history was first suggested to me in 1967 by an Arab scholar-diplomat, with whom I had been working on the publication in America of some minor works by the Lebanese poet Khalil Gibran. It was just after the Six-Day War, and every Arab I knew was burning with the shame of the Arab debacle — except for this calm and confident gentleman.

"You will see," he told me, more in sadness than glee. "This war, it is the best thing that could have happened to us. It has changed the tide of our history, of all history. History runs in cycles. Once we were the flower of all civilization. Then we gave the West our best ideas, and the West overtook us. We atrophied, lay fallow for eight centuries. But now the cycle is coming our way again. You wait and see. It took Europe two hundred years to eclipse us. The way time is telescoped today, it will take us ten, twenty, at most thirty years to do what Europe did in two hundred. We will take the best ideas of the West, just as the West took ours eight hundred years ago. There was one great event that brought about our downfall, and that was the fact that we gave Europe the know-how and the inspiration to go out into the world. In going out, the Europeans bypassed us. They destroyed the economic basis of our society and left us to fend for ourselves. Well, there is going on right now one great event that is going to work in a reverse way. That is oil, and the technology of oil. The best ideas of the West are technological ideas. You are giving us technological ideas, just as we gave Europe humanistic ideas. You — the West — are in the process of giving us the technology of oil. We will take this technology, we will take all your technology, and will leave you behind. Just as you left us behind in the fourteenth century. Mark my words — in five years, ten at the most, we will be in a position to do the equivalent of what the West did to us. We will be in a position to destroy the economic basis of your society. And we in fact probably will do exactly that. It will be a turning of the tables of history. Arab civilization will reascend, Western civilization will decline and atrophy. Europe, America, will turn into the same cultural wasteland, relatively speaking, that the Arab world turned into after you surpassed us. The ascendancy of every civilization in history has been based on money, economics. It is wealth that gives societies their power and influence. Well, the wealth of the world is coming our way again. Once we have it, and the modern ideas we will acquire with it, it will be our turn to rule the world for a while. We will become the imperialists, and you the provincials."

"If I didn't know you better," I said to him, "I'd think you were indulging in the kind of self-delusion your people are noted for over here." It was, after all, 1967; the phrase "energy crisis" had not yet entered our lexicon. In retrospect I was probably being on the smug side. "Look," I added, "even if you do have the majority of oil in the world, it's not a bottomless well. The kind of ascendancy you're talking about — even if it came true — could only last as long as you had oil."

"Not so," he said. "History is not only cyclical, it is also process. It is not just one thing leading to another, it is many, many things leading to many, many other things. Oil will simply be the major factor in the turnaround. It will initiate the process, just as our ideas about astronomy and navigation initiated European expansionism in the fourteenth and fifteenth centuries. It is a complex process. With the economic wealth we gain from oil we will acquire the other things — the technological ideas — that will enable us to sustain and expand our wealth. We will end up exploiting the West as the West has exploited us, though in a more sophisticated, modern way. Already there is talk of this in the Arab world. So far it is hushed talk, for at this point we do not want to be overheard. But it is not an empty dream — a self-delusion, as you call it. It is a reality dictated by the flow of history. Of course it is to our advantage that you in the West continue to think that we indulge in Arab self-delusion. It will make our ascendancy and your decline all the more easy."

I gave his words little thought over the next few years. Then, in 1971, I heard the idea reiterated in a slightly different form during a casual conversation with a Cambridge-educated Kuwaiti banker in London. "There are two kinds of people involved in our oil industry," he said. "There are the economic technocrats, mostly Western-educated, who can see what is coming in regard to the economic balance of power in the world. It is on their minds at all times, and they are fully cognizant of the havoc they could wreak by nationalizing the Arab oil industry and raising prices. In five years we could utterly destroy the economies of the West and be standing on top of the world."

"With no one to sell oil to," I said.

"We would no longer need to 'sell' oil, you see?" he replied. "We would be in control of all the oil-consuming industry of the West, and thus would merely need to supply oil to those industries which we required to satisfy the product demands of our society."

"But doesn't the law of diminishing returns take over?" I suggested. "I mean, once your society's demands are satisfied, what happens to these industries? And what happens to your oil? It seems to me that your economic power would be short-lived."

"Exactly. That is why the Arab technocrats seek to proceed slowly. It is inevitable that we will become the economic masters of the West over the next decade or two. How fast this happens depends on the approach we take.

The technocrats, who have been exposed to Western economic history, wish to proceed slowly to ensure long-run development. They say — quite rightly, I believe — that the changeover in the balance of economic power must be gradual. This is not only to lull the West into thinking it's not happening, but also to ensure that the capitalistic system remains intact. For if capitalism dies while we become rich, the entire effect of our becoming economically dominant is lost."

"In other words," I said, "you will not only become the rich of the world, you will remain so by taking over the capitalist system."

"Precisely. Of course, we will bring our own refinements to it. But it is not our success in becoming economically dominant which is the key to sustaining our wealth and power over the world. It is our success in adapting Western capitalism to our own objectives. This is what will take time, and it is this time our economic technocrats are trying to buy by counseling a go-slow approach."

"And the others?"

"Yes, the others. These are the political zealots among us. For every Arab economic technocrat in our oil industry, there are three political zealots. They are pushing for the immediate nationalization of all foreign oil interests in the Arab countries. Why? So that they can immediately increase the price of oil to the industrialized world. They too see the inevitability of our coming economic dominance. But they want it to happen now. It is a shortsighted and, in the long term, a destructive approach. But, alas, I am afraid they are beginning to wield more and more influence. They want all that wealth immediately for the power they believe it will put into their possession — power they think will enable them once and for all to solve the Zionist problem and force the hated West to crawl at their feet."

"I take it you don't object to the West."

"I think the West has behaved abominably toward the Arab world. But I realize that no one is perfect. If it weren't for the West, we would not have suffered so many centuries of decay as a society. Mind you, I do not blame it all on the West, for as I say, no one is perfect. We — our Arab ancestors — must bear much of the blame ourselves. Just as the Jews, I might add, must bear much of the blame for their unfortunate history themselves. However, if it also wasn't for the West, we would not be in the very favorable position we are in today. We are today witnessing the dawning of a renewed Arab civilization. It will turn out, I am sure, that Israel was merely a brief unpleasant episode in our rebirth. As Arab culture comes again to dominate the world, Israel will disappear — either through the force of our economic power, or through attrition. That is, if our economic technocrats have their way."

"And if they don't?"

"Ah," sighed the banker, "that is a constant source of worry to me. If the political zealots hold sway — well, as surely as my sense of history tells me that the Arab world is about to reascend to the pinnacle of world influence, so does it tell me — Allah preserve us all, but it is true, isn't it?"

"What?"

"History has always been made by zealots, not by technocrats."

Over the next two years I encountered the contention that the Arabs were in the process of turning the tables of history with more and more frequency. Some expressed it with greater vehemence than others — usually those in positions of government and those in official economic and political advisory positions spoke it in a more circumscribed way than those with no official attachments. But all in one way or another gave vent to it. The idea was that the Arabs were sooner or later going to acquire most of the industrialized world's economic wealth through ballooning oil prices; they would then turn around and use that wealth to gain control or ownership of the industrialized world's production resources, turning Europe, Japan, the Americas into manufacturing provinces of the new Arab economic empire and the societies of these regions into subservient labor forces. The scenario was not so much a matter of conscious Arab strategy as it was a pure and simple matter of fateful historical inevitability. "It is Allah's will," as one Saudi Arabian acquaintance put it, reverting to that instinctive Islamic explanation for all things beyond the machinations of mere men. "But this time we shall grasp his will and let it carry us to the summit of prosperity."

Then came the Arab-Israeli war of 1973 and the Arab oil embargo. The real effectiveness of the embargo was the sparking of the realization in the Arab mind of what had hitherto only been an idea — that they, through their vast natural petroleum resources, possessed the power to realize the even larger dream implicit in the "turning of the tables" theory that had been surfacing with increasing regularity among the Arab intelligentsia prior to October 1973. It was almost as if the joint Egyptian-Syrian pincer movement against Israel, ostensibly launched to regain territory and build bargaining power vis-à-vis Israel, had in fact been attempted to put the idea to the test.

Whatever the case, once the October combat was brought to a mediated end, the theory of future Arab destiny no longer retained its soft-spoken nature in the civil and political leadership circles of the Arab world. The Arab intelligentsia suddenly came to the conclusion that the reacquisition of Palestine was no longer their primary challenge. Surely, bickering and bartering over Israel would continue for a while. But the land of the Zionists no longer represented an end in itself; henceforth it would be but a means to an indescribably higher end — eventual economic (and consequently political) dominion over the Western world.

I found the notion reflected everywhere I traveled in the Arab Middle East during 1974. Despite the still-frequent squabbles between and among various Arab governments and their representatives, between one national Arab group and the next, between one profession of Islamic faith and another — between and among even Arab Christian, Arab Muslim, Arab Druze* and Arab heathen — I discovered a larger solidarity united behind the still vague outlines of the idea of Arab reascendancy over the West.

With the hope of measuring the pulse of the idea, of learning how deeply it had penetrated the general Arab consciousness, I one day organized an informal symposium of informed Arabs from various countries. All were in Beirut on one form of business or another, and when I explained my purpose they were all eager to participate. The group consisted of

an Egyptian commercial attaché in the United Arab Republic's embassy in Beirut;
a Syrian journalist;
a Lebanese ex–prime minister;
a Kuwaiti who was deputy minister of finance and petroleum in Kuwait;
a Palestinian economist working for the Saudi Arabian government on that country's hundred percent takeover of Aramco;
a Jordanian deputy minister of information;
an Iraqi banker.

All were articulate and independent-minded individuals. We met on a hot summer's afternoon in the air-conditioned conference room of a leading Beirut newspaper. The discussion lasted three hours, and although it was often lively, it was mostly free of the conventional Arab political rhetoric. I started the discussion by asking each of the group to comment in turn on the ques-

* The Druzes are a small, heretical Arab Muslim sect scattered throughout Lebanon, Syria and Israel.

tion of whether or not the idea about the reascendancy of Arab society according to the general scenario I had been receiving was in fact a widely held one within the Arab world; and if so, whether in their opinions it was a realistic one. What follows is an abridgment of the tape-recorded discussion, including some of my own questions and comments.

SYRIAN: It is no secret that many people in the Arab world feel this way. Why just the other night I was having dinner with an uncle of my wife. He runs a large agricultural cooperative near Latakia. He is an administrator by vocation, but at heart he is still a peasant. But that is all he talked about. How in ten years we will be sending food to America to help the starving population there. How we will be sending foreign aid to France. He is convinced it is going to happen . . .

K: Are you?

SYRIAN: Not in ten years, no. But perhaps twenty . . .

K: You're serious?

SYRIAN: Let me put it this way. We have been down so long, there is no place to go but up.

K: But how far up?

SYRIAN: The way in which events have come together in the last forty or fifty years . . . well, I am convinced that we have been witnessing — though we haven't until recently possessed the perspective to comprehend it — a turnabout in the tide of fate. The great events in the flow of history — or should I say their meaning? — never make themselves known to the people they most directly affect until many years later. It is like a change in the electromagnetic field around the earth. Such a change brings rain to areas that have long been ravaged by drought, and turns what were fertile areas into deserts. But a fertile area does not become a desert overnight. Nor does a drought-stricken area become fertile overnight. It takes years, it is a natural process. That is what has been happening in the human realm. Our fate changed some years ago. It is only today that we are beginning to feel its effects.

K: You put it all on fate. Isn't that a bit too mystical an explanation to support the kind of idea I'm talking about? I mean, hasn't that always been a central problem in the Arab world — making political decisions based on some mystical adherence to fate?

SYRIAN: I don't mean fate in the religious sense. No, we have progressed beyond clinging to notions of fate. I agree, it *has* been a problem for us. It is why we accepted our degradation as a people for so many centuries under the Turks. But I am talking about a different kind of fate. The fate of history. The sway of events. You can not deny that even your country was started on a sense of historical fate. Look at your Declaration of Independence. It is like a secular prayer. It is filled with fatefulness, with the belief that the time had come for there to be a United States of America. "We, the people . . ." Do you see what I mean? All great societies are born out of a sense of fate, an awakening sense that the events of their past have conspired favorably, have gestated healthily, until — boom! — you have a people who believe it is their fate to rise to the pinnacle of prosperity and culture. We went through that experience once before, though then it was based on a religious sense of fate. The Prophet. Having experienced it, we can sense it coming again. And this is the sense *you've* been getting. Forget the scenario, as you call it. Forget for the moment the strategy, the tactics, the consequences of the Arab rebirth. Whether we end up ruling the world or not — at this point that is only a dream. What the people are caring about now is the reality they sense down to their bones. Which is, that the Arab world is again going to become preeminent.

K: It seems to me that it's more than that — that there's an actual deep-seated conviction that you *are* going to rule the world.

SYRIAN: Well, I am a journalist. I have trained myself to be skeptical of all great visions, even Arab ones. I have had too much experience in writing about shattered hopes. Perhaps one of the other gentlemen can be more articulate about the scenario you speak of. We must rise first before we can rule the world. The idea of rising — and I do believe that this is the process we are now undergoing — the idea of rising is exciting enough for now. I don't dare look beyond that . . .

EGYPTIAN: I agree that fate as it flows through the world has altered. I would venture to say that, not being an Arab, you are constitutionally unable to perceive this fact.

K: Yes, but you see, I'm a skeptic, too. All this talk about the Arabs reemerging and turning into the effective powers of the world — I'm trying to determine in my own way if it is wishful thinking or in fact has a chance of happening.

EGYPTIAN: It has a very good chance of happening. Indeed, barring some nuclear disaster in this part of the world, I am convinced it will happen.

K: Why?

EGYPTIAN: Fate.

K: Here we go again.

Egyptian: You see, not being an Arab, you do not understand our notions of fate.

K: Okay, I'll go along with that. But my understanding of your notions of fate is not the question. The question is: Can your notions of fate — this fated destiny you all believe in — can they actually make it happen?

Egyptian: No, our notions do not make things happen. That is the whole idea about fate. Fate is what makes things happen, not our notions. But it is our notions that allow us to grasp the happenings of fate and turn them to our own benefit. That is the scenario you mention. The phenomenon of our Arab reascendancy has already started. It started, as our Syrian brother said, years ago. We have just recently become aware of it. Now that we are aware of it, our sixth sense of fate causes us to give it organization, to direct it in the ways that will be to our best advantage. It is to our ultimate advantage to regain our stature in the world. Which means, in Arab terms, in Muslim terms, to dominate the world. That is why you hear so many people now talking like the gentleman's uncle. Once the fact of our reemergence is established — as it has been — the next logical question is: How high do we go? We see that fate has decreed that we are to go high. So why not go to the highest? It is a dream, yes. But what great achievements have not been impelled by dreams? As time has passed, the dream has taken on greater urgency, for now we sense that we have the means to realize the dream.

K: But what is it in the stream of historical fate that made your fate change?

Syrian: It was a combination of things. It was the great advanced powers of the West falling into the beginning of moral and cultural decadence by waging imperialistic wars among themselves. It was their trying to force Israel down our throats. It was . . .

Palestinian: . . .Oil. Pure and simple.

Syrian: That, too.

Palestinian: More than "too." Political events, yes. The political events in the West for the past forty or fifty years did play a role in reawakening our awareness of ourselves as Arabs. But all that awareness wouldn't be worth a piastre if it hadn't been for oil. The discovery of oil is what has put us in the position we're in to carry out what our American friend is talking about. The fact that we have all this oil is what changed our fate. The oil was there all the time. As long as it went undiscovered, our fate bubbled along as it always had. But once it was discovered, our fate changed. At a

crucial time in our history Allah gave us the Prophet and he made us great
We conquered and controlled the civilized world in the name of the
Prophet. But even then we were fated to decline. Fate — either divine fate
or historical fate — does not run a level course. If it did, there would be no
such thing as the rises and falls of civilizations. We were fated to fall just as
surely as we were fated to rise. Now Allah has given us oil, and with it we
are fated to rise again. We will again conquer and control the civilized
world. Not through arms and the Koran, as we did before. Through
money and the Koran.

K:   You think this is inevitable, then?

KUWAITI:   If I may interrupt, I would say very definitely yes, it is inevitable. . .

PALESTINIAN:   But we will not stay on top forever. We will fall again.

KUWAITI:   Of course, but that is not our concern at the moment. Let us get
to the top first before we worry about falling. Being in the position I am in,
I see our rise already well on its way.

K:   You expect Arab society to dominate the world?

KUWAITI:   Absolutely. And it will come about sooner than most imagine.

K:   But there's the question — do you have the motivation to do it? I mean,
some societies have set out with the goal in mind of dominating the world.
Others have come to their domination in a kind of accidental way. Do you
think the Arabs really want deep down to dominate the world?

LEBANESE:   That is your scenario theory again, is it not?

K:   Yes. In other words, are the Arabs — if only unconsciously — are you
secretly plotting such a scenario?

LEBANESE:   I wouldn't put it that way. It has the odor of conspiracy about
it. No, I would say that if any scenario is being written, it is being written
by the West. It is not our intention to dominate the world. We would be
content simply to dominate our own region. But if my estimate is correct,
the West has been in the process of forcing us to move beyond that simple
proposition.

K:   Well, you all seem to confirm that this idea of eventual Arab domination
is very much a part of everyday thinking here. But, really, does it have
even the remotest possibility of becoming a reality?

IRAQI:   If I may say, I think you will find that this idea will become more
and more a part of long-range Arab planning. What is the phrase you
people use — "It is an idea whose time has come"? I believe that is what

my colleagues mean with their talk of fate. The likelihood that we will rise to rule over the West is an idea that ten years ago might have seemed the epitome of lunacy. Now it is entertained very seriously in all official circles. When the leaders of the various Arab nations meet, they very earnestly discuss the prospects of having the power of the world thrust into their laps. This is precisely why you hear so much talk of Arab unity. They are supremely aware that in order to assume world dominance the Arab nations must do it together.

K: Well, that's my point. Forgetting everything else — forgetting the fact that the West is not likely to let it happen — isn't there a built-in prohibition against it happening in the very nature of the Arab world? By that I mean, doesn't the fact that the political differences that exist between the various Arab nations militate against the Arab world as a whole rising to such a position of power?

IRAQI: That is precisely the point I am making. You will see more and more cooperation between the Arab nations as the idea, the prospect, becomes likelier. Look at Europe. We speak of the European rise to world domination in the seventeenth century. But Europe was not one nation. It was a group of nations, each with its own interests, each constantly vying with the others. Yet the Europeans transcended national differences. All the countries had a share in the European ascendancy. Unofficially, Europe was always a union of independent states. Then America. Or Russia. Both civilizations were made up of polyglot peoples. But both rose to power when these peoples united. America is called the "United States" — states that are united. Russia is called the "Union of Soviet Socialist Republics." They are a union. Thus far we have had no "Union of Arab Republics," socialist or otherwise. But history is forcing us into that position — a union of sovereign Arab states. Iraq, Saudi Arabia, Egypt, Jordan, Libya — all will overcome their differences sufficiently to achieve such a union. Even if, say, the Iraqi form of government is incompatible with the Saudi, and vice versa, a compromise will be reached. All the Arab nations will unite under the pressure of world power passing into our hands. Individual differences will still remain, but a union will eventually come about. It will be a natural process. The momentum of contemporary history will force us to unite. I don't think there is an Arab leader who is not exquisitely aware of that.

K: But that is all still theory. How do governments like Iraq or Syria or

Algeria, which are committed to revolutionary political philosophies, reconcile themselves with Saudi Arabia, Kuwait or Jordan, which are highly conservative, even reactionary, regimes?

JORDANIAN: The way I see it, there will be a leveling process. The union we are speaking of — well, I agree that it is being forced on us by events. We are coming to the acute awareness that it is our destiny as a people to rise again, but this time the stakes are infinitely higher. The union of Europe was really an unconscious thing. Europe united almost in spite of itself. Through all their centuries of internal strife, the Europeans emerged as an inadvertently united people. That is, despite the differences in their petty goals — the extension of borders, the acquisition of lands or resources held by someone else — their higher goals were identical. Their higher goals were prosperity, power, influence and so on. These goals were centered around an ingrained sociological ethic that was based on a common ideal — the religious ideal, the Christian ideal. It is not much different with us today. Indeed, the conditions for union are even better for us, for our religious ideal is so much more a part of our lives than the Christian ideal was a part of Europe's or America's lives. The Christian religious ideal produced a leveling of European society. The Christian ethic eventually overrode everything else to produce an unwritten union of European peoples. You might even say the Christian ethic is precisely what propelled European culture into its position of dominance. So it will be with us. The Islamic ethic is the glue that holds us together. Remember, Islam came six hundred years after Christianity. It is only now, six hundred years after the Christian ethic started Europe on its ascendancy, that the Islamic ethic is beginning to have its impact on Arab society. As the forces of today's history are shifting onto us, the Islamic ethic ignites us to bring these forces into harness and direct them to our own higher good. Whether one is a socialist or a monarchist is only incidental. These things will work themselves out in the natural process of our ascendancy.

EGYPTIAN: I agree. All this talk about national difference is old-fashioned, out of date. There is already an instinctive understanding among Arab nations toward union. All that remains is the working out of the details. And many of the details will work themselves out as we are projected into our position of power. Fundamentally, we have always been united in spirit. That is the effect of Islam. We are all the same, despite our separate national political identities. All that needs to be worked out are our material differences. And since the power that is coming to us is based on material things, these material differences *will* be solved.

K: Your anticipated Arab rise to domination takes on a religious tinge, then. Is this some sort of holy-war psychology at work?

Lebanese: We are not talking about a war.

K: Well, maybe not in the military sense. But it seems to me that the ascendancy you're talking about is based on a kind of economic warfare.

Lebanese: Ah, to be sure, it is economic. I wouldn't call it warfare, however. Unless the West chooses to turn it into that.

K: What would you call it?

Palestinian: I would call it cornering the world market on money. (Laughter all around.)

Kuwaiti: Let us be realistic. It *will* be economic warfare. Why should it not be? The West has waged economic warfare on us for centuries. Why should we not be entitled to return the compliment?

K: Do I detect a note of vindictiveness in all this? Is the so-called Arab dream of ascendancy based on a desire for vengeance?

Kuwaiti: Not vengeance. It is a simple reality. For centuries we have been the have-nots of the world, while the West was the haves. It is a matter of it being our turn now to be the haves.

K: Can't the West continue to be the haves while you acquire your piece of the loaf?

Kuwaiti: Of course not. There is only so much of the loaf, as you call it. The loaf does not expand infinitely. That is the first rule of economic imperialism, and it is a rule we have learned well from the West. In order for us to become the haves, someone else must become the have-nots.

K: So — you are all convinced that the Arab world is destined to more or less take over the major share of power in the world. None of you disagree with that?

Syrian: I think we are all agreed.

K: And it's going to happen through the acquisition of most of the world's economic resources?

Syrian: And through those, the materials we will need to maintain our power.

K: And you say that this idea now plays a central role in all Arab political planning.

PALESTINIAN: I would not say that the leaders are yet sitting around saying to each other: "Aha, we are going to rule the world. Now, let us see, how should we exercise our rule?" I would say it is merely an unspoken assumption that permeates all thought and discussion of the future.

K: Okay, but what in your view will be the mechanics of the takeover?

IRAQI: Don't call it a takeover. We will not be "taking over" power. We will be "assuming" power as it drains out of the West.

K: All right, assuming. What do you see as the mechanics of this assumption of power? How is it going to happen?

EGYPTIAN: Your scenario again?

K: Yes.

EGYPTIAN: I believe it will come about this way — indeed, it has already begun. We will manipulate the production and price of oil in such a way as to bring the West to the brink of economic depression and hold it there for a long period. The West cannot function without our oil — at least not for thirty years, no matter what your politicians say about independence from Arab oil by 1980. Think of it — twenty-five years of existence on the brink of depression. Out of the vast portion of the Western world's treasury that comes into ours, we will send just enough back in the way of trade to keep the West viable. And just enough in the way of hidden investment to acquire ownership of most of the West's industrial resources . . .

K: Well, before you go on, let me say this. There are people who say that will never happen. The West — America, Britain and the rest — will take measures to foil such attempts. They will pass laws forbidding more than a certain percent of foreign ownership of their industries. Or they will nationalize their industries . . .

SYRIAN: Then we would refuse to sell them oil. Or we would elevate prices to the point where they would go bankrupt.

K: But wouldn't that be defeating your purpose? I thought the whole point was to keep the West viable.

SYRIAN: It is just another way of achieving our purpose. If they went bankrupt, they would have to come to us for the money to start them up again. Where else could they go, if we have all the money?

IRAQI: And then we go in with our money and run the economies on our terms.

K: Would the effect not be — assuming this scenario worked — to destroy capitalism?

IRAQI:   Not destroy it. Revise it.

K:   And you actually believe this is going to come about?

PALESTINIAN:   Perhaps not exactly in that fashion. The precise scenario no one really can predict. But the simple fact is that it's going to happen. Increasingly the West is going to become economically dependent on the Arab world. Our leaders will orchestrate this dependence in such a way as to maximize the benefits to us without destroying the West's technological resources.

K:   But what about the other alternative the West has to prevent this?

EGYPTIAN:   Which is?

K:   War.

EGYPTIAN:   That is always a possibility.

K:   It seems to me a certainty. I mean, if this economic conquest of the West is really the Arab design, it seems to me the West will recognize it and use its military resources to prevent it.

EGYPTIAN:   Ah, but the West knows that to make such an attempt would be to cause the destruction of our oil resources.

KUWAITI:   We are prepared to blow up every oil-producing facility in the Arab world in the event of Western military intervention. The West would be defeating its own purpose in invading us and trying to seize our oil resources. Besides, the United Nations would not stand for it.

K:   The UN wouldn't have much choice in the matter. I mean, what could it do if, say, many of its most powerful member nations decided to band together to seize your oil industry? And anyway, even if you blew up every one of your producing facilities, the oil would still be there in the ground.

IRAQI:   Wrong on both counts. In the first place, invading the Arab countries to seize our oil would bring about a nuclear war. Do you think the Russians would permit the West to annex the Middle East? Such a move on the part of the West would be suicidal. I believe Western people would still rather be poor than dead. Secondly, even if they did — even if, say, the U.S. sent its armies here — we would not only destroy our facilities, we would destroy the oil fields themselves. So it would not be simply a matter of them coming in and building new production facilities, if that is what you are getting at. There would be no oil left for them to produce. So you see, such a move would be fruitless. They might destroy us, but they would destroy themselves at the same time. And they know this. So they know it is better to negotiate with us.

K: Negotiate? But what would there be to negotiate if you have all the chips?

IRAQI: Oh, a great deal. The West will negotiate its survival.

EGYPTIAN: That is correct. We do not want the West to die. If it does, then we have much to lose, too. We will simply put the West to work for us.

K: But then, what about the Russians? If you take over control of the West, won't they then be inclined to aim their missiles at you?

PALESTINIAN: I think not. We will come to an accommodation with Russia.

K: How, for heaven's sake?

PALESTINIAN: There will be a merging of economic and political systems. We Arabs are primarily socialistic. We will do away with free-enterprise capitalism. There will be no substantial ideological differences between the Russians and us. We will divide the world between us. They can have the East. We will take the West. We will be compatible systems.

K: No ideological differences? What about the difference between the antireligious beliefs of the Russians and the Islamic beliefs of the Arabs?

PALESTINIAN: Not significant. The struggle between Russia and the West has never been over religious differences. It has been based on political and economic ideology.

K: Well, most of the oil that's going to be used to engineer this hypothetical economic takeover by the Arabs is in the Arabian peninsula. How can you be so sure that the Arab oil states won't go about this whole thing uni-laterally, leaving the Arab non-oil nations out in the cold.

KUWAITI: It is simple. The oil that sits under our territories we do not consider our oil. Kuwait does not think of her oil reserves as Kuwaiti oil. It is Arab oil. The same feeling exists in Saudi Arabia.

PALESTINIAN: He is right. I have been in Saudi Arabia for eighteen years now, and I can tell you that every Saudi believes this. Their oil is not just a Saudi resource, it is an Arab resource. It was merely Allah's will that its custody be with the Saudis. As Muslims and Arabs, the Saudis have an almost mystical commitment to their stewardship. The riches their oil brings will go to all Arabs.

IRAQI: And this goes back to your scenario. Many Arabs believe that the placement of vast oil deposits beneath their territories was an act of Allah, a divine act to ensure that the Arab world would again rise. This is why so many Arabs are convinced that the time has come for us to reascend. Such a belief is becoming an article of faith — even among our intellectuals, who are most inclined to separate the practical world from the religious. Believe me, it is an article of faith stronger even than the fanatical faith that drove the Crusaders.

K: Aren't the results likely to be the same, then? The Crusaders sought to conquer the Arab world. They failed.

IRAQI: They failed because their faith was unsupported by realistic ideas. It fed on fanaticism alone. We have two things they didn't have. Our fanaticism is tempered by our pragmatism, one. And two, we have ideas — I mean to say, knowledge. We don't yet have complete knowledge about technology. But we have the knowledge and the practical resources that will enable us to acquire that knowledge.

LEBANESE: I have one advice for the West.

K: What is that?

LEBANESE: Capitulate.

K: Capitulate to the coming Arab assumption of its power?

LEBANESE: Correct. I know, it is natural to resist. But to resist is to provoke self-ruin. There are too many lessons about this in history. I have been to America many times, and I have seen what a sensible and practical people you are. I hope you are sensible and practical enough to read the situation realistically.

K: But practicality works in other ways, too. A lot of people said it was impractical to resist Hitler. Others said it was impractical not to. We resisted, and it turned out that it *was* practical.

LEBANESE: Yes, but Nazism was an aberration of history. You were right to resist it, for no one nationality has a right to seek power over the world. History teaches us that. But an entire people does have the right. History teaches us that, also. What is coming will not be an aberration of history. It will be history fulfilling itself. It is practical to resist an aberration of history. For after all, look at us — Israel is as much an aberration of history for us as Nazi Germany was for the West. Don't misunderstand me. I know it is fashionable to equate the Israelis with the Nazis these days in Arab circles. I don't mean it in that sense. I simply mean that Israel poses the same kind of threat to us by its existence as Germany did to its neighbors. You found it practical to wipe out Germany. Why should not the same logic apply to us regarding Israel? However, I regress. My point is, your resistance to the coming — what shall we call it, Arabism? — your resistance to the coming tide of Arabism would be foolhardy. It would be resisting the natural logic and flow of history, not a historical aberration. So, my advice — do not resist. You will only make it doubly hard on yourselves.

The discussion continued in that vein. In the interest of devil's advocacy I threw up many more theoretical obstacles intended to preclude the likelihood of the scenario carrying itself out. But for each obstacle there was an answer which, in their minds, at least, smoothly flattened it out.

Were these Arabs, as the saying goes, putting me on? I could hardly think so. Except for two, all were strangers to one another and had had no opportunity to confer beforehand on a unified line to take. Moreover, they were deadly serious in their convictions — not pulsatingly fanatical, but rather like a group of stock analysts calmly forecasting an upturn in the market.

These were educated men, sophisticated, cosmopolitan. Had the legendary Arab trait of self-delusion become so refined that it could be disguised behind a calmly measured mien and an even voice? Or was there something of substance to this idea of the inevitability of Arab ascendancy over the West? I resolved to explore the matter further.

# 12.

# History: *The Arab Reawakening*

UNDER MORE THAN FIVE HUNDRED YEARS of Turkish rule the large Arab populations of the Middle East accrued little in the way of political, economic and social awareness. Arab society was rooted in nonpolitical, nongovernmental, pre-Islamic values. Since the time of Muhammad it had assumed a certain organizational character, but that character was almost exclusively religious in nature — the religious leaders were perforce the political leaders, religious organizations the social ones, religious law the civil law. The Turks merely refined matters to the point where religious institutions became the hard and fast political fabric of Arab life.

Thus it was, then, that the first stirrings of Arab independence from the Ottoman grip, the first impulses to Arab self-identity, were largely religious in motivation.

What we know today as the major Arab nations — Egypt, Syria, Iraq, Saudi Arabia, for instance — were at the beginning of the nineteenth century simply provinces of the Ottoman Empire.* By now the Ottomans had combined the sultanate with the caliphate so that the reigning sultans were not only the political rulers but the absolute religious authorities as well.

---

* The Arab lands of Northwest Africa — today's Morocco, Algeria, Tunisia, and Libya — except for their purely religious allegiance to Constantinople, were generally outside the political orbit of the Turks. Administered from Egypt, they remained relatively backward territories, more Berber than Arab in ethnic character, more nomadic than sedentary in social makeup. It was because these lands were neglected that Europe found it so easy to gain political control over them after Napoleon tried to establish France politically in Egypt, Palestine and Syria at the very beginning of the nineteenth century.

With the complex overlay of strict theological laws, dogmas and institutions which the Turks grafted onto Islam, the religion assumed an elaborate orthodoxy that became more or less the official form of worship, and thereby the official form of life. This orthodoxy was given the name *sunna*, the approximate English translation of which is "the right path." Those who committed themselves to the official version of Islam therefore came to be known as *sunni*, or Sunnite Muslims.

There remained throughout the Muslim world, however, a large body of believers who refused to accept the Ottoman interpretation of Islam. They instead clung to the precepts of the early Shiites, who had been responsible for starting the Baghdad caliphate. When the Abbasid dynasty was taken over by the Seljuk Turks, then later destroyed, the Shiites persevered. Many retreated to Persia, the birthplace of the Shia movement, but others scattered throughout the Arab lands where they continued to agitate for the resurrection of their fundamental principle — that only the direct descendants of Muhammad, through his son-in-law Ali, were legally and morally capable of assuming the caliphate.

With its establishment of the Sunnite interpretation of Islam, which officially negated this principle, the Ottomans tried to put an effective end to such Shiite aspirations. The Shiite movement was too religiously impassioned and widespread to accede to the Sunnite view, however. It never abandoned its militancy. It thus evolved throughout the centuries as the primary doctrinal opposition to the Sunnite orthodoxy. Today the Shiites remain second only to the Sunnites as the principal sect of Islam in the Arab world, while in Iran the Shiite interpretation is the dominant religion.

The ideological struggle between the Sunnites and the Shiites brought the insulated Arab world into the nineteenth century heavily weighted down by the complexities of religious observance. The attempts by the Ottoman sultans to stem the influence of Shiite ideology, thereby sustaining their own non-Muhammad-descended rights to the caliphate, resulted in the creation of a suffocating Islamic theology which featured, among other things, the veneration of saints, the celebration of miracles, the accumulation of riches and the construction of gilded edifices designed to glorify Islam's ecclesiastical leaders. Such ornamentation of the simple original precepts of Islam was obviously influenced by the Ottomans' exposure to the Christian Byzantine institutions they had conquered. It had considerable appeal to the sedentary Arab populations of the Fertile Crescent, which had been exposed first to the Christian Crusades, then indirectly to sixteenth-century French Catholic influences that seeped into the eastern Mediterranean as a result of France's special link with the Ottomans, and then directly to the cultural glories of Christian Europe that were borne by the Napoleonic expedition into Egypt, Palestine and Syria at the beginning of the nineteenth century. But to the nonurban Arab populations — populations which had had little exposure to Christian European ideals — it had no appeal at all. Indeed, the Turkish version of Islam soon provoked Arab reaction.

It was inevitable that this reaction would emanate from the birthplace of Islam, the Arabian peninsula. Arabia had long been nominally part of the Ottoman realm, but the Ottomans exercised little control over Arabia other than to ensure a certain amount of tribute and to make the holy places safe for pilgrimage. The Hejaz was about as far as Ottoman rule extended at the beginning of the nineteenth century — that relatively narrow strip of Arabian coast that extended from the top of the Red Sea down to about its midpoint and contained the cities of Mecca and Medina. The rest of the vast peninsula was divided up among tribal Bedouin sheikhdoms which, if they observed religion at all, practiced a brand of Islam that was as simple, harsh and unforgiving as the desert itself.

The vast arid region of central Arabia was known as the Nejd. It was populated by both nomadic and semisedentary tribes that had come down through dozens of generations with scarcely any change in life-style. Although nominally under Turkish rule, they were responsible to no government and existed autonomously. Their only allegiance was to the Koran, the Koran of seventh-century Islam.

Out of this tribal society, at the end of the eighteenth century, emerged a man named Abd Al-Wahhab. As a privileged son of the Wahhabi tribe, he had been sent to Baghdad for religious studies. Repelled there by the Turkish theological perversions of Islam, he returned to the Nejd inflamed by a passion for reform. He preached a return to Muslim purity and a revival of the simplicity of Islam. He denounced the assumption of religious authority by Turkish political rulers and declared that the Koran was the only source of authority. He inveighed against the worship of Muslim saints and against the decoration of their tombs by pilgrims to Mecca and Medina. He assailed beliefs in superstitions and miracles which had, like barnacles, attached themselves to the pure and unadorned monotheism of early Islam. Finally, he insisted on a mass Arab return to the plain, penurious life of the early Muslim leaders.

Wahhab's puritan preaching found a receptive audience in the Nejd, for, after all, the desert tribes were long used to a life of deprivation and utter simplicity. He won many converts among the tribes, one of whom was an important local warrior sheikh by the name of Muhammad Ibn Saud. With the help of Ibn Saud, the Wahhabi reform movement spread quickly, naturally and fiercely through Arabia during the first decade of the nineteenth century. But when Ibn Saud began to lead tribal armies into Syria and Iraq to forcibly impose Wahhabism on the Arab strongholds of the Ottoman Sunnite realm, the conflict became more than religious; it became political, as well. And when Ibn Saud and his Wahhabi forces took over the Hejaz and closed off the annual pilgrimages to Mecca and Medina, thereby compromising the authority of the Ottoman sultanate throughout the Islamic world, they touched off a series of political and military events that would, a hundred years later, bring the entire Arab world out from under the yoke of Ottomanism and produce the Arab political awakening.

The Turkish sultan at the time of the Wahhabi revolt was Mahmoud II. He had set out to make reforms in the Ottoman institutions so as to strengthen the empire sufficiently to meet the threat of the increasingly apparent European imperialist designs on the eastern Mediterranean. (France had already attempted its invasion of Egypt and the Levant; although the invasion was unsuccessful, it was surely not the end of things.) Mahmoud had inherited an empire shot through with corrupt political practices and institutions. He made a vigorous beginning at reform, but he was totally unprepared for the Wahhabi challenge to his authority. As caliph, he was responsible for the safety of pilgrims traveling to the shrines of Islam. The Wahhabi occupation of the Hejaz, followed by the interruption of the pilgrimage, brought protests from Muslims in all parts of the Islamic world. Action by Sultan Mahmoud was imperative. But the Ottoman government was still so enfeebled by corruption that it could not put together enough forces to attack Ibn Saud and his armies nor could it compel the pashas (governors) of Syria and Iraq to carry out imperial orders to destroy the Wahhabis.

Another revolt had occurred in the Arab portion of the Ottoman Empire, although it was not, properly speaking, an Arab revolt. Long before, the Ottomans had taken over Egypt by deposing its Mamluk leadership — the leadership that had evolved out of the Turkish slave armies sent to Egypt by the earlier Seljuk Abbasids to quell Egyptian stirrings of independence and to defend Egypt from the Crusaders. The Ottomans then ruled Egypt through a series of provincial governors. In the latter part of the eighteenth century, at about the time Abd Al-Wahhab was getting his exposure to Turkish Islam in Baghdad, Ali Bey, the leader of the large but subservient Egyptian Mamluk community, overthrew the Ottoman administration in Egypt, expelled the Turks, and set himself up as an independent ruler. The resulting confusion — for the Mamluks were neither Egyptians nor Arabs, but were of Asian origin — threw Egypt into a state of extreme disorganization that made it seem a fruitful target for invasion by expansionist Napoleonic France.

The French invasion in 1798 in turn compromised the authority of the Mamluks, who were now led by Ali Bey's successor, Ibrahim. When the French broke out of Egypt and entered Palestine, the Ottoman government appealed to England for help in stemming what seemed to be shaping up as a Napoleonic tide that could overrun the Turks' Arab domain. It was, of course — given the rivalry between the British and French empires — supremely in England's interest to prevent a unilateral French takeover of the Middle East; thus the English responded to the Ottoman appeal with a force of military advisers. Using British strategy, Turkish armies from all over the empire quickly threw the poorly supplied Napoleonic forces back into the Nile delta. Then the Turks decided that if they could chase the French out of Egypt altogether, they would be in a good position to recover their former province from the Mamluks.

Toward this end an Anglo-Turkish force invaded the delta in 1801 and defeated the remaining French troops. A ranking officer in this force was a man of Turkish and Persian ancestry whose father was an official in the Ottomans' European province of Albania. His name was Muhammad Ali, and through a succession of events after the defeat of the French he was appointed by the Turks to be the new ruler of Egypt — the personal viceroy of the Ottoman sultan.

Muhammad Ali's first assignment was to erase all vestiges of Mamluk power. This he did with dispatch by means of a roundup and public massacre of the Mamluk leadership. Thereafter he instituted reforms in the provincial government. He set out to restore Egypt's economic prosperity by encouraging agriculture, industry and commerce. He started a printing enterprise to increase literacy and spread education, and built a modern, disciplined army and navy. By 1810 he was the most powerful and influential man in the Arab part of the Ottoman Empire, and it was to him that Sultan Mahmoud finally appealed to put an end to the Wahhabi revolt in Arabia.

Muhammad Ali responded by sending an expedition to the peninsula in 1812. After six years of intermittent warfare the forces of Ali, led by his son Ibrahim, captured Dariyah, Ibn Saud's capital in the Nejd, and snuffed out the power of the Wahhabis in Arabia.

This feat gave Muhammad Ali singular stature in the Ottoman world. When, three years later, the sultanate was faced with another revolt — this time in Greece — Mahmoud again turned to his Egyptian viceroy for help, promising him dominion over Palestine and Syria in return. Envisioning the makings of his own miniempire within the Ottoman sphere, Ali sent his army and navy to Greece in 1825. After two years of fighting, the Egyptians were on the verge of crushing the Greek revolt when Britain, France and Russia jointly intervened out of their respective self-interests. The Egyptian forces were destroyed and the Ottoman Empire further weakened.

Despite the defeat, Muhammad Ali called Sultan Mahmoud on his promise of Syria. When Mahmoud refused, Ali promptly decided to seize Syria by force and in 1831 launched an attack across Palestine. His conquest of Syria was rapid and caused profound consternation in the sultanate. Muhammad Ali had made his intentions clear. He was now intent on wresting the sultanate away from Mahmoud and taking it for himself. Mahmoud went to the British for help, but Ali had already convinced them that his drive to Constantinople was directed at strengthening the Ottoman Empire so that it could resist growing Russian imperialistic designs in Ottoman Europe; if Ottoman Europe fell to Russia, the Russians would only be a short remove from central and western Europe.

The British supported Ali's rationale. Sultan Mahmoud then turned to Russia for assistance. Nineteenth-century European great-power political competition was at its height, and the Russians, perceiving an opportunity to gain an easy foothold in the Ottoman Empire, promptly came to Mahmoud's aid. This in turn brought British and French threats against the Ottomans and resulted in what in modern political parlance would be called a "grave international crisis." After a good deal of saber-rattling between Britain, France, Russia and the Turks the crisis was resolved, but not before Muhammad Ali was granted Syria (along with four more Muslim territories) and the Russian presence was firmly established by treaty at the very gates of Constantinople.

The rivalry between Ali and Mahmoud continued unabated. While the two jousted over the limping empire, the European nations sharpened their attention. If the Ottoman Empire were to disintegrate through its own internecine strife, each of the European imperial powers was intent on picking up the pieces for itself, or at least preventing its rivals from gaining control of the Turkish domains.

Particularly intense was the rivalry between Britain and France. France had failed in its earlier attempt to gain colonial control in Egypt. But due to distractions in Constantinople, it had managed to gain a foothold in Arab-Berber northwestern Africa. Now France supported Muhammad Ali against Sultan Mahmoud with a view to earning further concessions in the Arab world — perhaps special economic and political privileges throughout the entire Fertile Crescent, privileges that would eventually enable France to transform the region into its own.

Foreseeing this possibility, Britain transferred its support to Sultan Mahmoud. The British desired to maintain the status quo of the Ottoman government, at least for the time being, so as to thwart French designs. In 1838 Ali announced his intention to remove all Ottoman lands from Syria westward from the control of the sultanate and to incorporate them under his own independent Egyptian rule. This brought an attack of forces from Constantinople. The Ottoman forces were completely routed by Ali's armies in Syria in June of 1839. Shortly thereafter Sultan Mahmoud died, and the disorganized Ottoman leadership had no choice but to accede to the victorious Ali's demands.

It looked now as though the sultanate and the center of Ottoman power were about to shift from Anatolia to Egypt, where the French would enjoy special status. Britian could not permit this to happen. The British persuaded three of the other four great European powers — Russia, Austria and Prussia — to join it in putting a stop to the transfer. The four then put pressure on France. In 1840 France was forced, under the threat of war with British and Russia, to acquiesce in a British attack on Muhammad Ali's forces in Syria and Palestine.

The British won, thereby shoring up the sultanate and forcing Ali to abandon his dream of ruling the Ottoman Empire. The Europeans permitted Ali to retain independent control over Egypt, at the insistence of France; in so doing they guaranteed Ali's autonomy except in religious matters and thereby dictated Constantinople's loss of Egypt. From this date on, the flow of events in the Middle East was no longer dependent upon the Turkish or Egyptian rulers, but upon the European powers.

The interplay of imperial rivalries and interests in Europe subsequently brought about the Crimean War (1854–1855), which pitted Russia against the

Ottomans, in alliance with Britain and France. Although the Ottomans won because they had enlisted the aid of Britain and France, their empire came irrevocably under the economic and political tutelage of these two countries.

Thereafter, the Ottoman government fell into a steady state of decline. Constant inter-Arab warfare in the Fertile Crescent — usually religious combat by Muslims against Christians incited by reactionary Ottoman rulers trying to shore up their influence — brought repeated European interventions.

Another cause of intervention was money. Britain and France had loaned the Ottomans vast sums to fight Russia. As well, once the Ottomans defeated the Russians, further vast sums of private and public money poured into the Ottoman world from western Europe in the form of investment and development funds. But in 1877 the Turks waged another war with Russia — this one unsuccessful — and fell into functional bankruptcy. In order to protect their investments, the British and French stepped up their intervention in Ottoman affairs.

The first massive intervention came in 1882 when the British occupied Egypt in order to protect their Suez Canal and other economic interests during an uprising of nationalist Arabs against the Turkish ruling-class descendants of Muhammad Ali. The occupation only served to fortify the native population's resentment against foreign presence and influence. This marked the first installment in the Arab political awakening.

By 1882 the idea of revolutionary nationalism, forged out of the French Revolution, was a well-established ideology throughout Europe. Indeed, it had for some time been at the heart of the Ottoman Empire's troubles as first Greece, then other Ottoman provinces in southeastern Europe, struggled to free themselves from Turkish control and establish, by revolution, their own sovereign states.

The sultan in 1882 was Abdul Hamid II, and behind him were arrayed the forces of Ottoman reactionism. Hamid was a fanatical Muslim who promulgated a policy of Pan-Islam, a policy that envisioned the entire Ottoman world free of any other religious influences. He despised the growing influences of Christian Britain and France in his realm — despite, or perhaps because of, the fact that they were his support — and dreamed of one day restoring Ottoman power sufficiently to wage a holy war against the European interlopers. In the meantime, to consolidate his own power within Islam, he played on Muslim fanaticism and incited Muslim populations within the Middle East against Christian and Jewish communities — both native and foreign.

The exclusivist religious impulses generated by the Hamid sultanate had political, economic and cultural ramifications that would soon backfire on the Ottomans. As agitation against the Christian communities of the Fertile Crescent increased, France established missionary schools in its domains of influence, especially in Syria, to counter Muslim exclusivism. In Egypt, Britain took over many of the schools begun by Muhammad Ali earlier in the century as part of his reform. Through these Christian-oriented but Arabic schools there began to ferment among educated Muslims certain European political and economic notions that were utterly contrary to Ottoman dogma. As Sultan Hamid's rule became more repressive in his efforts to reconstitute Ottoman power, and as French and British colonial aspirations began to make themselves felt, these notions gained currency among the Arab populations, Muslim and Christian alike. Foremost among them were the ideas of national identity and political sovereignty, ideas that had been at the heart of Europe's rise to world prominence and which at that very time, embroidered by a new, revolutionary humanist-socialist-Marxist overlay, were on the rise again.

By the 1890s small but vocal secret Arabic societies had sprung up in Syria, Iraq and Egypt devoted to the struggle for local political independence from Ottoman rule. Simultaneously, in Europe, a small movement called Zionism — based on the Jews' dream of restoring their original homeland — was gathering adherents and momentum.

Initially the impulse of Arab political self-identity manifested itself most powerfully in Syria. The rising Egyptian consciousness had to do less with a specifically Arab identity than it did with an Egyptian one. Although the large majority of the Egyptian populace was Arab-blooded, Egyptian dissidents were busy chiseling out a mythology of pure "Egyptian-ness" — one that emphasized a noble Pharaohonic heritage and relegated Arabness to the nomads of the Sahara. In Syria, on the other hand, and to a lesser extent in Iraq, the conception of a distinct people, all speaking a common vernacular — Arabic — began to emerge in the form of a specifically Arab identity. This was doubtless due to the French academic custom of identifying a people by the language it spoke. The ordinary Ottoman subjects of Syria spoke Arabic; therefore, despite any protests that might have come from the Arabian peninsula, the Syrians were Arabs.

The idea of a specific Arab identity in the heart of the Fertile Crescent caught on among anti-Turkish Syrian dissidents. At the beginning of the twentieth century it was still barely more than a parochial idea, but by 1905 it had gained some notice. In that year a book appeared in Paris called *The Awakening of the Arab Nation*, published under the imprint of the League of the Arab Fatherland. It propounded the notion of an independent Arabic-language nation extending from the Tigris-Euphrates area across Syria and Palestine to the Suez Canal. The state would have an Arab "sultan" to exercise political rule and a caliph to administer religious affairs. By 1905, then, Arab nationalism — however much the concept depended on a religious structure that contradicted truly nationalistic impulses — was in its first stages of birth.

This nationalistic expression, though still feeble, aroused the suspicions of the Ottoman government. In response, Sultan Hamid instituted corrective measures. He sent agents roving through the Arabic-speaking world disguised as Muslim preachers; their job was to exacerbate tensions between Muslims and Christians, intensify traditional rivalries between tribes, clans and families, and sow discord and distrust among the educated classes — all to keep the Arabs sufficiently fragmented to preclude the possibility of any concerted Arab dissidence. In addition to promoting disorganization, the sultan also instituted a practice of "inviting" potential influential Arab enemies to Constantinople, where they could be kept under close watch while living in the lap of cosmopolitan luxury.

Perhaps the most notable of these compulsory guests was one Hussein Ibn Ali, leader of a regal Hejazian family that traced its descent back to Muhammad through his daughter and the Alid-Hashemite line, and that for generations provided the holy city of Mecca with its grand sharifs. Hussein, in his late thirties, though never noted for intelligence, had a reputation for entertaining dangerous (read Arab-nationalist) ideas. He also had four young sons — Ali, Feisal, Abdullah and Zaid — in whom he was said to have invested his ideas. Thus his sons were invited to Constantinople with him in 1893, and there they lived for fifteen years under virtual house arrest.

The stresses and strains to which the Arabs were subjected during Sultan Hamid's harsh regime were alleviated somewhat, if only temporarily, by a palace revolution in Constantinople in July 1908. A group of young Turks (whence the contemporary expression), exasperated with Hamid's rampant despotism, ousted him in a coup d'état and set out under the banner of their Committee of Union and Progress to institute real reform within the empire and restore it to its former glory.

However, the Young Turk movement soon became riddled by internal strife. At the same time, Europe stepped up its colonial activities in Arab North Africa. France already had control of the former Ottoman provinces of Algeria and Tunisia and was moving on Morocco. Britain was firmly ensconced in Egypt and along the Arabian peninsula. Now the relatively new nation of Italy wanted a piece of the pie. The Italians selected the Ottoman provinces of Tripoli and Cyrenaica on the North African coast west of Egypt, which came to be known collectively as Libya. Big-power European politics was at work again. In consideration of various alliances, the European powers granted Italy a stake in Libya. The resulting Italian invasion in 1911 touched off a local war between Italy and Turkey that eventually led to the Balkan Wars of 1912–1913, to World War I in 1914, and to the ultimate dissolution of the Ottoman Empire at the end of the war in 1918.

By the time the First World War broke out, manifestations of Arab self-expression were percolating throughout the Middle East. In Arabia, the descendants of the original Wahhabi leader Muhammad Ibn Saud — who a hundred years earlier had revolted against the Ottomans and gained control of the Hejaz, only to be deposed by the Egyptian forces of Muhammad Ali — had again risen and won control of the central and eastern regions of the peninsula. This revolt, launched in 1902 by the original leader's namesake, Abdul Aziz Ibn Saud, was again primarily religious in nature, directed at the corrupting influences of the ruthless sultanate in Constantinople.

After Sultan Hamid was overthrown by the Young Turks, the new Ottoman government sent Hussein Ibn Ali — the Hejazian nationalist who had been living in loose captivity with his four sons in Constantinople — to be grand sharif of Mecca.* There existed up until the First World War, then, an uneasy truce in Arabia between the political chauvinist Hussein Ibn Ali and the religious chauvinist Ibn Saud.

At the time of the Young Turk coup in Constantinople, those agitating for Arab self-identity expected that the advent of the new, avowedly liberal and reformist regime in Constantinople would lead to a large measure of autonomy and local government for the Arab provinces. They were soon disappointed, though. Nationalist revolutionary movements were proliferating in the eastern European and western Asian territories of the Ottoman Em-

---

* Although, after Muhammad Ali's victory over the original Wahhabis, the Ottomans had maintained a provincial governor in Mecca to oversee their interests, the real figure of authority in Arabia had always been the grand sharif, a kind of provincial Muslim subcaliph. Hussein Ibn Ali, due to his family lineage, was a natural choice for the position.

pire, threatening to shrink the empire despite the reforms of the new regime. The Young Turks, through their Committee of Union and Progress, had themselves successfully organized a revolutionary movement and effectively carried out its objectives in 1905. They showed no capacity, however, to deal with non-Turkish revolutionary groups, such as Armenian and Balkan activists who were seeking national independence. Their response was repression and subjection. And when they got wind of Arab aspirations for national separatism, their response was the same.

Until 1909 preachers of Arab autonomy within the Ottoman realm were looked on with a certain amount of tolerance by the regime of the Young Turks, and Arabs were even permitted to form societies and committees to work out long-range plans in this direction. But in 1909 conservative elements in the Young Turk leadership overthrew the ruling liberals. One of their first acts was to put the clamps on Arab aspirations, ordering all such committees and societies disbanded and banning any further such activities.

Arab reaction was swift. Secret underground societies dedicated to revolution and national self-determinism were formed in all the major Arab cities of the Fertile Crescent. Inciting long-suppressed Arab passions by pointing to the glory days of earlier Arab civilization, the movement spread like wildfire over the next two years, even penetrating Europe where Syrian, Lebanese and Egyptian political exiles lobbied among governments for support.

In June 1913, an Arab Congress composed of all nationalist groups and parties was convened in Paris to hammer out a consensus scheme for an autonomous Arab state, to be presented to the Ottomans. The Turkish government nominally agreed to accede to Arab demands, but it soon became apparent that their agreement was merely a device to gain time; they had no intention of carrying it out. When this became evident there was a renewed flurry of nationalist activity. Then, in August of 1914, the war erupted.

As a result of a series of big-power maneuvers in Europe, the Ottomans found themselves allied with Germany at the outbreak of the war. The First World War had many significant long-range effects on the Middle East, not the least of which were the complete destruction of Ottoman imperial rule over the Arab populations and the apportionment of political dominance of the region between the victorious French and British. A more immediate effect, however, derived from the fact that the competing European powers sent so many military and civilian support elements to the area. This brought the Arabs into contact with the Europeans on a scale unprecedented since the Crusades. The waging of modern war in the Middle East introduced to the indigenous populations, on a wholesale basis, new weapons, new means of transportation and communication, and new political and social ideas. Just as the Arabs' effect on the Christian Europeans during the Crusades had hastened the destruction of medievalism in Europe, now the Europeans' effect on the Arabs helped bring about the end of the medieval stagnation of the Arabs. In doing so, however, it introduced into the Middle East complexities and perplexities which have not, even today, revealed their full ramifications.

The war brought Arab nationalist aspirations into full bloom. By now the Turks were well hated in the Arab world. The fact that they were enemies of Britain and France made it seemly for the Arabs — and especially Arab nationalists — to side with the British and French. Such sympathy was a turn on the old Bedouin saying: "The enemy of my enemy is my friend."

It was not as simple as all that, though. The Arab leaders were not so naïve as to believe that unalloyed support of the Allies would result in any special rewards to them. They had almost as little reason to trust Britain and France as they did the Turks, for the British and French had long expressed their own imperialistic ambitions in the Arab world. Nevertheless, the Arabs perceived them as being the lesser of two evils for the moment.

For their part Britain and France cultivated Arab sympathy, at least implying the reward of an autonomous Arab state at the conclusion of the war, a state that would take in just about all of the predominantly Arab Fertile Crescent and the desert lands contained within and south of its horns. Such a state would exclude Egypt, of course, since this former Ottoman territory was already a British protectorate. It would exclude also the Arab Berber lands west of Egypt, for these were already under solid French control.

Because British Egypt was closest to the Ottoman war zone, it was British armed forces that spearheaded the Allies' military drive against the Turkish armies in the Middle East. And it was British civilian and paramilitary support elements that prosecuted the political and diplomatic war. An integral part of British strategy in overcoming the Turks became the policy to exploit Arab hatreds and foment Arab revolts with the idea of distracting and diverting Turkish forces, thereby facilitating British military operations. The British recognized that the most propitious place for such efforts was the Arabian peninsula, where Ottoman military presence was minimal. An Arab revolt there would require a large Turkish army traveling a thousand and more miles to quash it.

Early in 1915 Britain made secret approaches to Hussein Ibn Ali who, before he became grand sharif of Mecca and therefore the spiritual ruler of most of Arabia, had been the long-time "guest" of the despotic Hamid in Constantinople. The British proposal: Lead a revolt against the Turks and we will back you up with arms and advisers. Hussein's reply, in effect: I would be happy to lead a revolt, but your offer of support is hardly the recompense I am interested in. What are you interested in? came the disingenuous British response. A sovereign Arab state, said the grand sharif, with myself as ruler.

Secret negotiations followed. On October 15, 1915, Sir Henry McMahon, British high commissioner of Egypt, wrote Hussein that he had been authorized by London to pledge that Britain was prepared "to recognize and uphold the independence of the Arabs" in all regions lying within the frontiers proposed by Hussein.

The frontiers that had been proposed by Hussein, in consultation with secret Arab nationalist groups in Baghdad and Damascus, embraced all of the Fertile Crescent, less Egypt, and extended southward into the far reaches of the Arabian peninsula and northward into southern Anatolia. Hussein was using an ancient bargaining tactic: Ask for more than you can reasonably expect to receive. In his letter, McMahon made the reservation that southern Anatolia and a piece of coastline extending down from it "cannot be said to be purely Arab, and must on that account be excepted from the proposed delimitation."

Hussein and his followers accepted the British commitment with a mixture of glee and caution, then set about their revolt against the Turks. Their caution derived from the deeply ingrained Arab distrust of foreigners and their promises. As it turned out their caution was hardly ill considered. Unbeknownst to them, Britain was attending to other obligations that were contradictory to its commitment to the Arabs.

France, Britain's partner against the Turko-Italo-German Axis, had already begun to propose a division of the Ottoman Empire between the Allies at the successful conclusion of the war; as had Russia, another ally, although a barely functioning one due to internal civil discontent being orchestrated by Marxist revolutionaries. Britain, in order to maintain France and Russia's full-fledged cooperation on the European battlefields, was forced to acknowledge its allies' postwar expectations. Thus the three entered into a secret agreement — which came to be known as the Sykes-Picot Agreement — in the spring of 1916 which totally ignored McMahon's agreement with Sharif Hussein. Moreover, the Jewish-nationalist Zionist movement had spread its influence into the innermost councils of the British government, and serious consideration was being given to the proposition of setting aside part of the territory committed to the Arabs by McMahon — namely Palestine — for the Jews as a "homeland."

In the meantime Hussein and his sons had embarked on their revolt. Despite their caution over the nebulousness of the British promises, they were by now in such deep trouble with the Turks for conspiring with the British that they had no choice. Under the military tutelage of a minor British officer named T. E. Lawrence, the celebrated Lawrence of Arabia, Hussein and his sons successfully carried out their action and by 1917 had destroyed the last remnants of Ottoman rule in the Hejaz.

But then came the bad news. The Russian communists had successfully overthrown the Tsarist regime, and one of the first things they found in the Kremlin archives was a copy of the secret Sykes-Picot Agreement. When they published its contents, Britain's treachery became clear to the Arabs. Shortly thereafter the British released for publication a copy of the Balfour Declaration* which, although it took pains to state that "nothing shall be done which may prejudice the civil and religious rights of existing non-Jewish communities," viewed "with favor the establishment in Palestine of a national home for the Jewish people" and pledged Britain's best efforts "to facilitate the achievement of this objective . . ."

In the ensuing confusion Britain and France issued a statement assuring the Arabs that their goal was the complete and final liberation of the peoples who had for so long been oppressed by the Turks. "In pursuit of those intentions," continued the statement, "France and Great Britain agree to further and assist the setting up of indigenous governments and adminis-trations in Syria and Mesopotamia. . . ."

This sop, even if it was not just another piece of imperial European expedi-ency, was clearly insufficient to the Arab nationalists. They felt they had been doubly double-crossed. So indignant were they that they even put out feelers to see if a reconciliation with the Turks was possible. The Turko-Arab contacts came to nought, however; Arab hatred and distrust were too great. The Arabs, their nationalism still in its infant stage, and without the military might or intra-Arab unity to go it alone, were thus left at the direct mercy of the British and French and, at the conclusion of the war, the indirect mercy of the United States.

* Named after the British prime minister at the time, Sir Arthur Balfour.

# 13.

## JOURNAL: *The Road to Damascus*

THE CONTRAST BETWEEN BEIRUT AND DAMASCUS, the capital of Syria, is striking. Beirut is an interminably noisy and frenetic city, a wild-eyed confusion of traffic jams, buildings, costumes, faces, with an atmosphere that borders on anarchy. Damascus on the other hand is tranquil — even with the muffled thump of distant cannon constantly in the air and the whine of patrolling Migs slicing the silence overhead. Except for the bazaar district the city, only sixty miles over the mountains from Beirut, is solemn and subdued. Beirutians are explosive, Damascenes phlegmatic. I wondered where they got the energy to be so feverish in their hatred of Israel.

I made the trip from Beirut in the car of a Lebanese government official who was to meet with Syrian president Hafez Al-Assad to discuss recent Israeli raids on Lebanon's Palestinian refugee camps. I had been promised an interview with Assad. Also in the car was the wife of another Lebanese dignitary, herself a well-known political writer and an ardent supporter of the Palestine liberation movement.

The 1973 Arab-Israeli war had been over for some months, although the Syrians and the Israelis were still dueling by cannon and rocket across the Golan Heights, south of Damascus. One of the pressing Israeli concerns at the time was the fate of a hundred or so Jewish soldiers who had been captured by the Syrian forces during the war. Rumor was rife that the Syrians had massacred them, rumor based on the fact that the bodies of several Israeli troops had been discovered bound, shot and castrated when the Israeli army regained the ground it had lost on the first day of the war. Syria, of course, denied allegations that it had murdered prisoners-of-war. At the same time it refused to display the Israeli prisoners, heightening fears in Israel and the West.

The day before my journey to Damascus I mentioned the matter to the writer who was to go along in the same car. "It is not true," she said. "It is just another example of Zionist propaganda to enlist the sympathy of the world and make the Arabs appear bestial. I have seen these prisoners with my own eyes. They are being well treated."

"Do you think I could see them?" I said, knowing that she had influence in Syria.

"We shall see," she replied. "Tomorrow, when we arrive in Damascus, I will try to arrange it."

Driving up in the car the next day the woman — as politically ardent and militant an Arab as I had met, and highly articulate as well — was off on one of her usual anti-Israel diatribes. (So ardent was she that she often boasted that she was raising her sons to be Palestinian guerrillas.) We were arguing the Arab pros and cons of the recent Israeli air raids when suddenly she announced, in rebutting one of my arguments, "You know, of course, that the Zionists, when they send their planes to attack the camps, they chain their pilots to their seats."

"They what?"

"There, you see!" she exclaimed. "It is a surprise to you. Do you doubt what I say?"

"I find it hard to believe."

"It is true. They chain them to their seats so they cannot bail out when they get hit. You see, the Jews are basically cowards. The people in their government, they found out that their pilots were telling us everything we wanted to know when they bailed out and were captured. So now, they have ordered them chained in so they cannot bail out. They lock them in before they take off, then they take the key."

"Come on," I said. The idea that the Israelis would resort to such measures boggled my mind.

"I know," she said. "You think what I say is just another Arab exaggeration. Well, I will prove it to you. I received a call this morning. A Zionist plane was shot down last night. They found the pilot chained in the wreckage. They have brought the body to Damascus. I am going to see it, and you may come with me."

Upon arriving in Damascus we were driven to an army compound and ushered into a large stucco barracks. At the center of the barracks a group of uniformed men — Syrian officers — and photographers stood in a circle around a large square shallow box draped in white sheeting. In the middle of the box lay a charred naked body, arms stiffly upthrust in rigor mortis, one leg severed at the knee. Heavy chains were wrapped around the upper torso, meeting at a lock on the corpse's chest, then traveling down through the groin and attaching behind to what appeared to be the tubular remains of a seat frame. The chain attached likewise behind the shoulders.

The woman gazed stonefaced at the corpse for several moments while the officers stepped back in embarrassment. Then she looked up at me. "Do you believe now?"

I shrugged. "How do I know he's an Israeli?"

She turned and said something to one of the officers. He nodded, disappeared, and returned a moment later with a sack containing the corpse's missing leg. It must have torn off on impact and flown free of the fire, for it still had shards of fabric clinging to it, unburned, and a boot on its foot. The officer lay the leg in the box, butting it up against the corpse's stump to prove that it matched. Then he presented it to me, boot-end first, and said something to the woman. "Look at the sole of the boot," she said.

I did, and saw that a trademark — in Hebrew — was stamped into the rubber where the sole met the heel.

"Now do you believe?"

My first impulse was to argue that for all I knew it could be a Syrian pilot, with the boot thrown on at the last minute to give the impression he was an Israeli. But no matter how closely I examined the boot I could find nothing to indicate that such was the case; there was no evidence of tampering. I looked at the woman.

"It is not a pretty sight, is it?" she said.

"No."

"But you should see the women and children pilots like him are killing every day," she said bitterly.

"But that's war, isn't it? I mean, women and children get killed on both sides. Atrocities are not new."

"Ah, but the Zionists — they are always saying we are the only ones who commit atrocities. They are pure, they are the victims. And the world believes them. And then they deny they chain their own pilots to their planes. Now you see that the Zionists do not tell the truth. Look at the atrocities they commit on their own pilots."

"Maybe it's just this one pilot. Maybe he decided he'd rather die than face torture if he was shot down."

"No, it is policy. We have seen dozens of dead pilots in these chains. You hear how the Jews have such great reverence for human life, and how the Arabs have no reverence. Does this look as if the Jews have such reverence, when they do this to their own?"

"Is that the point you wanted to prove?" I said.

"I have nothing I want to prove to you," she said, her anger rising. "You can make your own judgments. But I will tell you this. We will never give up our struggle — never! Not so long as we have swine like this in our midst."

With that she leaned over the box and spat into the charred, featureless face of the corpse. Then she wrenched the leg from the sack, held it in her two hands by the ankle like a pick, and with the stump clumsily traced a large Star of David in the sandy floor of the barracks. The men around her looked at each other in astonishment.

When she was finished she tossed the leg into the middle of the star, then looked up at me. Her cheeks were wet with tears. "I hate myself for doing that," she said. "That is what the Jews have done to my people. They have made us hate ourselves."

# 14.

# HISTORY: *Zionism and Arabism*

THE EVOLUTION OF ZIONISM and its culmination in the establishment of Israel is well enough known to require no detailed retelling here.
Suffice it to say that the Zionist movement was the creation of a handful of
European Jewish activist-thinkers who aspired in the late nineteenth and
early twentieth centuries to give the long and variously oppressed Jewish
peoples of the world — especially those of eastern Europe — a sovereign
nation of their own, preferably in the land of their spiritual ancestors.

But the evolution of Arabism is hardly known in the West at all. Since this
book seeks to capture an accurate perception of the Arab point of view in the
ongoing Middle East struggle, we should have a closer look at the nature,
character and history of Arabism. By Arabism I mean, of course, the movement through which strivings among Arab activist-thinkers toward a sovereign nation for their own long and variously oppressed peoples were created
and expressed.

It has long been fashionable in the Western world to belittle Arabism as
being nothing more than a reaction to Zionism. Had it not been for the rise
and presence of Zionism in the Middle East, runs the theory, the Arabs
would have felt no need to develop their own sociopolitical aspirations. Such
a view makes it easy for its numerous proponents to dismiss or demean Arab
strivings. But at the same time it has reduced our perception of the Arab
world to the level of conventional wisdom and stereotype, and has thus raised
more problems than it has solved. It may be true that certain elements within
the general Arabist movement developed in reaction to Zionism. But Arab-

ism was not in itself a reactionary outgrowth of Zionism any more than the Zionist movement was a reaction to Tsarism or Nazism, although certain elements within it were.

It has also been fashionable in the West to condemn the Arabs for not accepting the creation of the state of Israel in 1948. What, goes the question, was the point of Arab intransigence in this matter? Why couldn't the Arabs simply have accepted Israel in the tiny sliver of land apportioned to it and let it go at that? Their irrational stubbornness has resulted in nothing but woe and grief for themselves and others!

Such an oversimplified expectation, so commonly held, reflects more the shortcomings of Western thinking than it does those of Arab behavior. For by the time Israel came into existence, the ideology of Arabism was solidly rooted in the Arab world.

Sociopolitical ideologies come and go, but the nature of ideology remains the same. Ideology serves many purposes. It provides an interpretation of reality that is consonant with the self-image of those who subscribe to it. It supports those who subscribe to it by giving them a set of defenses for the things they value, the things they would like to attain, the people they would like to be. It is most often impermeable because it lies beyond the realm of logic, if not dispute. One cannot meaningfully ask whether an ideology is true or false, good or bad. As a mixture of the interpretation of one reality and the passion to create a different one, an ideology transcends such sober categories. It changes, becomes more fruitful or less, through experience rather than rational argument; loses or adds elements in accordance with their usefulness or relevance rather than through their accuracy as descriptions of the past or through their reasonableness in anticipating the future.

The holders of one ideology tend to judge other ideologies according to the extent of the similarities and differences between them. It happened that Zionist ideology, based on democratic socialist ideals, was a good deal closer in outline to Western values than was the ideology of Arabism, which in its beginnings seemed nothing more than an extension of Turkish autocratic values. Zionism — in addition to satisfying the West's psychological need for exculpation of its guilt over its centuries-old maltreatment of Western Jewry — was a correlative of Western ideology, whereas Arabism was thoroughly alien to Western sensibility. Thus Zionism secured Western approval, while Arabism was ignored or rejected.

Nevertheless ideology is ideology, and according to the rules of the game of ideologies, Arabism had every bit as much right to express itself as Zionism. Since ideologies express themselves not according to the expectations of other ideologies but according to their own, and since by their very nature they defy the logic of other ideologies, the Arabs could react to Zionism, and then to the creation of the state of Israel, in no other way but the way in which they did.

On the face of things, Arabism made a good deal more sense than Zionism when both began to gain momentum toward the end of the nineteenth century. Zionism, which sought the creation, or the re-creation, of a sovereign and exclusive Jewish state in the original land of Zion, could only have been judged a pathologically delusive dream as compared to Arabism, which addressed itself to a much more logical and probable prospect — first the autonomy, then the sovereignty in national terms, of the Arabic-speaking peoples of the Middle East. The liberation from imperial rule and the self-determination of peoples indigenous to a geographical area were concepts that had already stood the test of history. The idea of bringing together a scattered people unified only by religious belief, and using them to carve out a sovereign nation in a land inhabited by another people unified by language and culture, had failed every test of history; not only that, it smacked of a reversion to the colonialism and imperialism against which the new nationalism had arisen. Hence, even before these two ideologies got off the ground, the seeds of contradiction between them were well rooted.

The roots were then nourished by the fact that neither ideology was what it pretended to be. The Zionists, led first by their founder, Theodore Herzl, and then by Chaim Weizmann, publicly pretended to want only a "homeland" for world Jewry while privately they planned on a sovereign state. The Arabists, led by the Arabian Sharif Hussein and his sons, publicly pretended to want an independent democratic Arab nation while privately they planned on an absolute monarchy that would clearly have been despotic and highly disruptive of European economic interests in the region. (How, for instance, would citizens of Beirut or Damascus, exposed for more than a century to French culture and all its concomitants, react to being ruled by an Arabian tribal monarch — no matter that he was Arab rather than Turk.)

As between Zionism and Arabism, the British and French were caught in the middle when World War I came to an end and were snared in the crosscurrents of their own conflicting interests as well. There had already been several waves of Jewish migration to Palestine from eastern Europe, making the Jewish "homeland" a theoretical possibility, so the British gave the idea their official sanction in the Balfour Declaration. But as far as the Arabists were concerned there was no such thing as Palestine. What had once been known as Palestine had long been part of the Ottoman province of Syria, and in the minds of the Arab nationalists Palestine was merely a southern extension of Syria and an integral part of the large Pan-Arab nation they envisaged. Southern Syria (Palestine) was as Arab as northern Syria, Iraq, even the Hejaz, although perhaps a bit more cosmopolitan. There could be no question in the Arabist mind of a separate geographical entity called Palestine, or of a separate cultural entity called Palestinian. A Jewish "homeland" within the independent Arab nation — well, that was a feasibility, for Jews had lived throughout the Arab world more or less peaceably since Roman times. But it could only be a homeland with the sovereign Arab government closely regulating Jewish immigration and citizenship, just as it would the immigration and citizenship of any other foreigners. Such was the prerogative of a sovereign nation.

Zionism and Arabism, then, worked at cross purposes from the very beginning, and their inherent incompatibility was intensified by British and French diplomatic maneuvers. Ironically enough, the Zionists and Arabists at first cooperated with one another in anticipation of the British commitments to them. At the end of the war Zionist leader Weizmann and Sharif Hussein's son Feisal — his father's chief spokesman and negotiator on matters concerning the future Pan-Arab state — issued a statement that recalled "the racial affinity and the bonds existing of old between the Arab and the Hebrew peoples" and declared that any dispute that might arise between Jew and Arab in the establishment of a Jewish cultural and religious homeland on Arab soil would be negotiated between them — provided that the state promised to the Arabs became a reality.

It might be conjectured that had the European powers allowed the Arab nation — as planned by Hussein and his sons — to come into being, the entire course of Zionist-Arab relations would well have been more productive. Perhaps the Zionists would have been content to live as a well-functioning citizen minority in the national Arab world. It is doubtful, however, for the ultimate aim of the Zionists was not a cultural and religious homeland but a sovereign Jewish state.

In any event an independent Arab state was not to be, for Britain, influenced by strong Zionist pressure and propaganda and supported by the increasingly Zionist-inspired United States, finally withdrew its commitments to the Hussein-led Arabists. The prospective Arab state was cut up between Britain and France into various territories, protectorates and mandates — nonexistent (from the Arab point of view) Palestine among them.

To the Arabs it was the grossest of injustices, not so much because it was perceived as giving the Zionist any advantages but because it was another example of European, and now American — in sum, Western — treachery.

In anticipation of the postwar formation of Sharif Hussein's Pan-Arab state under British sponsorship, the Arabists set up, in 1918, a provisional Muslim government in Syria with Hussein's son Feisal at its head. France objected to this, fearing the repercussions it would have on the Muslim territories it controlled in northwestern Africa. Moreover, France had decided to respond favorably to pleas from leaders in Syria's Mediterranean coast — known as The Lebanon — to set up a semiautonomous Christian state under French protection. This region had been the center of French missionary activity for more than a century and had been widely Christianized. The Christians, although proud of their Arabic language and culture, nevertheless wished their homeland to be independent of the Muslim world. When France declared its intentions, the new provisional Arab government of Syria protested, for The Lebanon, like Palestine, was part of Greater Syria. France dealt summarily with the objections, sending its troops into Damascus and ousting Feisal's provisional regime.

This caused a profound split in the Arabist movement. Arab nationalists who had gone along with the Hussein-Feisal conciliatory approach to the European powers were disillusioned by Feisal's unwillingness to resist the French takeover of Syria. They further interpreted British acquiescence in the French action to be indicative of Britain's intention of carrying out its commitment to the Zionists but not to the Arabs. In short, went the suspicion, the British had made a secret deal with the French: You can do what you want with northern Syria if you leave us alone in southern Syria. These events, plus the aggressive land-acquiring activities of the Zionists in Palestine, made it clear to the more radical Arabists that the Arabs were going to end up with nothing.

With northern Syria under the control of a French military administration and southern Syria under British military control, pending final disposition of the defeated Ottoman Empire's Arab provinces, the Arabs in the south found themselves, for the first time in almost two thousand years, a distinct political entity, cut off from the rest of Syria. It was within this territory, the Palestine of Roman times, that the more militant and radical elements of the Arabist movement settled.

In order to maintain his credibility as leader of the Arabist movement, and because the British were obviously reneging on their promises, Feisal dropped his pledge of cooperation with the Zionists and encouraged active Arab resistance against their British-sponsored incursions into the land now known again as Palestine. With this, the focus of the Arab nationalist struggle shifted from Damascus to Jerusalem.

Living in Palestine at the time (1919–1920) were about 650,000 Arabs and about 60,000 Jews, most of them recent immigrants from eastern Europe. The great proportion of the Arab population were *fellahin* — peasants, farmers and craftspeople who had lived in the land for centuries. They were basically lethargic, in some ways backwards, in others sophisticated, content with life as it was and little interested in ideas of Pan-Arab nationalism.

Above the peasantry was a small aristocracy of landowners, many of them of the absentee variety, administering their holdings from the luxury of Beirut, Cairo, even Paris. Nevertheless, their roots in the land went back for centuries, and they were as instinctively bound to it as the *fellahin* themselves. Unlike the peasantry, though, the landowning aristocracy was an educated class and was familiar with the nationalist aspirations of the greater Arab world. Indeed, many of them had taken part in the Arabist movement during the later stages of Ottoman rule and had suffered for it.

In the Palestine of the Ottoman Empire nearly all administrative officials were Arabs. There was also a middle class of merchants, shopkeepers, teachers and the like. These also were essentially "Palestinians," but at the same time sympathized in greater or lesser degree with Arab strivings in general.

Within the Arab population there existed a vigorous Christian minority. The Christian Arabs were centered in the major towns and cities of New Testament lore, such as Jerusalem, Nazareth, Ramallah and Bethlehem. For the most part they were descendants either of families that had been Christianized in the centuries before the advent of Islam, or of Crusader groups long since assimilated into the local environment. In any case, except for religious outlook, they were thoroughly Arab in culture. The Christians were also conspicuous in administrative posts, in the professions and in commerce. They maintained close relations with Christians throughout Syria, with whom they intermarried freely.

As for the small Jewish portion of the populace, up until the first immigration from Poland and Russia late in the nineteenth century there were no such people as Zionists, merely a minuscule native Jewish minority that devoted itself mostly to religious matters. Unlike Jewish communities in the rest of the Arab world, the indigenous Jews of Palestine were largely unworldly, pious and secluded. They were for the most part poor, uneducated (except in religious matters) and indifferent to the political turmoil around them.

The initial immigrations from Europe changed that somewhat, but it was not until the end of World War I that the nature of the Jewish presence in Palestine changed. When it did so it changed radically. With the blessing (supposed or real) of Britain's Balfour Declaration and the increased backing (both official and unofficial) of the United States, which was beginning to play a crucial mediatory role in the final disposition of the Ottoman Empire, European Jewish immigration into Palestine accelerated rapidly. With it came an influx of ethnic attitudes, behaviors, bigotries and values which, when concentrated in a tiny land that was, culturally and ethnically, markedly different, produced acute mutual interpersonal antagonisms far beyond political and ideological concerns.

To put it more plainly, the Arabs found much in the behaviors and attitudes the Jews brought with them repugnant and detestable.

There were certainly individual Jews who were highly sensitive to the feelings of the Arabs as the latter were confronted with the sudden Jewish incursion into their lives and institutions, and who humanistically strove to soften the impact of this increasingly abrasive foreign presence. But the majority of Jewish immigrants, heady with the Zionist dream and convinced that the land was already theirs, were blatantly indifferent to Arab sensibilities. This fact has not been given much circulation in the Western world, due primarily to fears on the part of those who might broadcast it of being accused of anti-Semitism. Nevertheless it is a fact, at least from the Arab point of view, as well as from that of a handful of Zionists who were unwilling to ignore the negative effects and pitfalls of their movement.

The attitude and behavior of many of those who were part of the first large-scale Jewish migration to Palestine after World War I probably did as much to harden Arab feelings against Zionism as Arab nationalist propaganda against the failed promises of the European powers did. Yet the Jews cannot be held alone to account, for as wealthy Palestinian landowners were joining in denunciations of the Zionists on the one hand, they were beginning to sell large blocks of their land to them on the other, at greatly inflated prices. Thus early Jewish-Arab feelings of contempt were justifiably mutual.

Late in 1919 Feisal was still trying to come to an accommodation with the British and French over a Pan-Arab state. He was also still trying to work out a secret arrangement with Weizmann and the Zionists whereby the Arabs would guarantee the Jewish homeland in return for the Zionists' help in persuading the British to back the Arabs. But the Zionists wanted no part of such an intrigue. They felt their cause would proceed better under the auspices of Britain than of the Arabs. The British had already permitted them to establish a provisional government of their own; called the Zionist Commission, it was able to operate and administer Jewish immigration under British military rule. They wished not to endanger such de jure national status while they worked toward the fulfillment of their dream of a de facto nation.

When Weizmann turned Feisal down, and it became increasingly evident that the British were pressing for a Jewish entity in Palestine at the expense of Arab nationalist aspirations, Feisal abandoned any further pretense at cooperation with the Zionist leadership. There followed an outbreak of Arab hostility against the Jews in Palestine which was put down only with great difficulty by the British military administration. In its aftermath came a memorandum from General Louis Bols, commander of the military administration, to British General Headquarters in Cairo, in which he recommended the dissolution of the Zionist provisional government. Bols, reflecting frustration over the Palestine problem as it has existed from that day to this, wrote:

I cannot allocate the blame to any section of the community, or to individuals, while their case is still *sub judice,* but I can definitely state that when the strain came the Zionist Commission did not loyally accept the orders of the Administration, but from the commencement adopted a hostile, critical and abusive attitude. It is a regrettable fact that, with one or two exceptions, it appears impossible to convince a Zionist of British good faith and ordinary honesty.

They seek, not justice from the military occupant, but that in every question in which a Jew is interested discrimination in his favour shall be shown. They are exceedingly difficult to deal with. In Jerusalem, being in the majority, they are not satisfied with military protection, but demand to take the law into their own hands; in other places where they are in a minority they clamour for military protection. . . .

It is unnecessary to press my difficulty . . . in controlling any situation that may arise in the future, if I have to deal with a representative of the Jewish community who threatens me with mob law and refuses to accept the constituted forces of law and order. . . .

It will be recognized from the foregoing that my own authority and that of every department of my Administration is claimed or impinged upon by the Zionist Commission, and I am definitely of opinion that this state of affairs cannot continue without grave danger to the public peace and to the prejudice of my Administration.

It is no use saying to the Moslem and Christian elements of the population that our declaration as to the maintenance of the status quo made on our entry into Jerusalem has been observed. Facts witness otherwise: the introduction of the Hebrew tongue as an official language; the setting up of a Jewish judicature; the whole fabric of government of the Zionist Commission of which they are well aware; the special travelling privileges to members of the Zionist Commission; this has firmly and absolutely convinced the non-Jewish elements of our partiality. On the other hand, the Zionist Commission accuse my officers and me of anti-Zionism. The situation is intolerable, and in justice to my officers and myself must be firmly faced.

This Administration has loyally carried out the wishes of His Majesty's Government, and has succeeded in so doing by strict adherence to the laws governing the conduct of the Military Occupant of Enemy Territory, but this has not satisfied the Zionists, who appear bent on committing the temporary military administration to a partialist policy before the issue of the Mandate. It is manifestly impossible to please partisans who officially claim nothing more than a "National Home," but in reality will be satisfied with nothing less than a "Jewish state" and all that it politically implies.

I recommend, therefore, in the interests of peace, of development, of the Zionists themselves, that the Zionist Commission in Palestine be abolished.*

By this time, however, the British Cabinet had other ideas. Britain immediately reaffirmed its commitment to the Balfour Declaration and, instead of disbanding the Zionist Commission, abolished General Bols's military administration. In its place it established a civil administration, headed by a Jewish high commissioner, Sir Herbert Samuel. Samuel had a reputation as an experienced, fair-minded and liberal administrator, but he was a man whom the British colonial secretary himself, Winston Churchill, had called an "ardent Zionist" and who, in fact, had been one of the chief champions of the Zionist movement in the British War Cabinet.

The British inaugurated the new civil administration on July 7, 1920, with a message from their king, George V, "to the People of Palestine." The message began: "The Allied Powers, whose Arms were victorious in the late War, have entrusted to My Country a mandate to watch over the interests of Palestine and to ensure your Country that peaceful and prosperous development that has been so long denied to you." The text, couched in vague

---

* As reproduced in Boustany, *The Palestine Mandate*, p. 136. It appears that this report was never officially published by Great Britain.

diplomatic language, went on to reassure the "general population" of the "country" the British had so recently freed from Turkish rule that the "gradual" establishment of a Jewish national home would in no way infringe upon their civil or religious rights.

About ninety percent of the "general population" of the country the message called Palestine was Arab, although no such precise characterization was made. Nevertheless it is noteworthy, in the light of later claims, that the text of the message, addressed to the "general population," referred to Palestine as "your country." Not only, then, was there a basic built-in conflict between Zionism and Arabism; this conflict was given a specific focus and then exacerbated by the British efforts to satisfy both parties while at the same time securing their own interests in the area.

The subsequent history of the conflict was tied directly into active British — and later American — support of the Zionist movement and to the lip service paid to Arabist aspirations. The mandate mentioned in the opening paragraph of King George's message referred to negotiations then under way in Europe — in accordance with American president Wilson's Fourteen Point Program — concerning the future of territories liberated from Turkish rule. A system of mandates had been devised under Article 22 of the Covenant of the League of Nations whereby territories that had previously had no experience in self-government would be administered as "Mandatories on behalf of the League" by "advanced nations" (namely, the victorious Allies) "until such time as they are able to stand alone." Article 22 went on to state: "The wishes of these communities must be a principal consideration in the selection of the Mandatory."

By the time of the king's message it had become clear that the territories of the Fertile Crescent under former Turkish rule would be mandated rather than given self-rule as a collective Arab state according to the Arabists' expectations. The ongoing negotiations at the League had partitioned these territories into three arbitrary regions: Iraq, Syria (including the coastal Lebanon area), and Palestine (including the land east of the Jordan River, which was given the name Transjordan). Frontiers were drawn between the three; France chose Syria and Lebanon, and Britain took Iraq and Palestine-Transjordan.

Although negotiations on the mandates had not been concluded, it was on the basis of these generally accepted distributions that Britain instituted its civil administration in Palestine. Since the arrangements had still to be submitted for the approval of the League of Nations, and since no peace treaty had yet been concluded with Turkey, the British action had no legal validity and was, in fact, in violation of international conventions.

More pressing than the question of the British civil administration's legality was the fact of the increasing hostility of the Arabs of Palestine and its environs toward both the British and the Zionists. The king's message was the straw that broke the back of any lingering Arab hope that Britain might still keep its promise of an Arab state. Prince Feisal's conciliatory influence over the Arabist movement dwindled further, and the radical, militant elements of the cause took it over. Arab activists feverishly declared that the land now called Palestine was their country; even if the British had reneged on their promise, it was still theirs by national right. It was becoming rapidly clear to them that, despite "reassurances," British policy showed special favoritism to the Zionists and ignored Arab rights. Zionist policy was becoming more apparent, as well. By their very words and deeds the immigrating Jews, and the Zionist leaders, were making clear their intention of eventually establishing an independent state.

No one listened with any seriousness to the Arabists' claims. Frustrated, betrayed, powerless to hurt Britain, they struck back at the nearest and most convenient target — the Jews. An American investigative commission (the King-Crane Commission), dispatched to Palestine to look into previous disturbances there, had reported that "the fundamental cause of the Jaffa riots and the subsequent acts of violence was a feeling among the Arabs of discontent with, and hostility to, the Jews, due to political and economic causes and connected with Jewish immigration, and with their conception of Zionist policy as derived from Jewish exponents."

In spite of these warning signs, the British government and the Zionist organization, sure that the Arabist movement had collapsed, at least for the time being, continued their discussions in London on the future of Palestine without any further consultation with Arab opinion in general or with Palestinian wishes in particular. And it was true — the Arabist movement, if not collapsed, had at least lost much of its momentum. Prince Feisal, as a sop to his and his father's failed expectations, would later be installed by the British in their Iraq mandate as king. His brother Abdullah would be placed at the head of the new mandate state of Transjordan, while still another brother was readying to succeed their father, the British-supported Hussein Ibn Ali, grand sharif of Mecca, as ruler of the Hejaz. Iraq, Transjordan and northern Arabia together would constitute the beginning of a collective Arab state, argued the British, or at least a tripartite Arab kingdom ruled by the ancient

Hashemite family. That should have been enough to soothe the Arabist passions of Feisal and his brothers. For a while it was, and the Arabist movement waned.

But the diminution of kingly Arabism only fanned the fires of the Palestinian Arab cause. New riots between Arabs and Jews broke out in Palestine in 1921 and required British martial law to put them down. These disturbances were not the haphazard affairs of the previous two years that had been reported on by the King-Crane Commission. They were disciplined expressions of resistance organized by the new leadership of the Arabist — a specifically Palestinian Arabist — movement.

Most notable among the new leaders were Amin Al-Husseini, a Palestinian Arab who had been an officer in the Turkish army, and Aref Al-Aref, also a Palestinian who had served with the Ottoman forces. Both had originally supported Feisal, but soon became convinced that the prince had not so much Arab nationalist as his own and his family's interests at heart in his dealings with the British and Zionists in securing Hashemite dominion over the Arab world.

Husseini and Aref broke with Feisal and founded the Arab Defense Committee, which instigated the anti-Jewish riots of 1919 and 1920. The two fled Palestine to avoid arrest by the British, but were amnestied early in 1921 and quickly returned to Jerusalem. They immediately formed the Supreme Muslim Council, an Arab provisional-governmental counterpart of the Zionist organization, with Husseini as head. The council propagandized the Arab population of Palestine, turning anti-Zionist feelings into patriotic virtues. Husseini sent the British government a memorandum which set the guidelines for Arab resistance to Zionism that every Palestinian would be required to subscribe to and, if necessary, die for. His intentions were sophisticated, designed not only to awaken Palestinian Arab identity and patriotism, but also to turn British public opinion against support for Zionist aspirations.

In the 1919–1920 riots, Arab demonstrators had denounced the British as intensively as the Zionists, inadvertently driving the two closer. With Husseini now in complete control of the movement, however, a clear tactic was developed to drive a wedge between the two. Thus, as the 1921 riots began, in May, the demonstrating Arab masses linked their anti-Zionist slogans with declarations of faith in the British administration — headed by, of all people, the "ardent Zionist" Herbert Samuel!

The Arabs marched, shouting "Death to the Jews!" and "We Believe in the British!" It was an effective tactic by Husseini. It showed the Zionists that in the Supreme Muslim Council they were faced with a worthy adversary. But far more damaging was the calculated forethought of Husseini's policy as set out in his memorandum to the British. It demanded the dismantling of the entire Zionist superstructure in Palestine, including the very concept of a Jewish national home. It demanded the formation of an Arab national government and the reintegration of Palestine and Transjordan into Syria as a single Arab state.

Husseini knew that such demands would not even be considered by the British. But he also knew what this show of militancy would mean to the Arabs. There was to be no recognition of the Zionists, no acceptance of their presence, and no direct negotiations with them. The only dealings with them would be through the British, and then only for the purpose of accepting the Jews as citizens of Arab states; in no other way would they be accepted.

Husseini's strategy resulted in a total breakdown in discussions between the Zionists and the Arabs and succeeded in stemming, if only temporarily, the tide of Jewish immigration. It also set the tone and pattern of all future Arab policy vis-à-vis the Jews, making it impossible for any Arab politician to publicly propose a settlement with the Zionists on terms that would be acceptable to them.

In doing so, however, Husseini overreached himself. Evidently failing to take into account the sympathy the Zionist cause was able to elicit in the West, failing to acknowledge the lack of any meaningful Western empathy for the Arab world, and naturally unable to anticipate the Second World War and the bestiality to be visited upon European Jewry by the Germans, his strategy merely served to stiffen Zionist resolve. He forced the Zionist leadership to abandon the Weizmann policy of negotiation and accommodation and go all out to prepare the conditions for complete statehood and control over Palestine.

# 15.

## JOURNAL: *The Arab "Mentality"*

DURING MY JOURNEYS I was almost daily confronted with ill-humored exclamations on the part of non-Arabs I encountered having to do with the Arab "mentality." Is there such a thing as a distinct and identifiable Arab mentality — "mentality" being a way of perceiving and thinking about things, and valuing and responding to them to produce a mass pattern of behavior — that sets them apart from other peoples?

One Arab acquaintance said to me, "Great myths, usually condescending, have been created in the West about our so-called mentality. Yet there is a kernel of truth to these legends. Every people in the world suffers from contradictoriness in values and behavior. It is just that we Arabs have been cursed to suffer most from this dualism. Perhaps it is because we are the oldest of peoples."

Most of our traditional impressions of Arab behavior and the Arab mentality come to us through the lens of the Western perspective, which has always tended to be at once self-righteous and romantic. It is as though our fascination with the pristine simplicity of the desert aroused in us an expectation of behavior on the part of its inhabitants that had to be equally uncluttered by diversity. Many early Western firsthand observers brought back to us descriptions of the Arab mentality that reflected disappointment, at times even indignation, with it. From very early on the Arab character and personality have been presented to us as some kind of tightly uniform entity which, while it explained everything about the Arabs, explained nothing.

T. E. Lawrence, for instance, from whom the Western world received many of its impressions about the Arabs, wrote: "Semites have no half-tones in their register of vision. . . . They exclude compromise, and pursue the logic of their ideas to its absurd ends, without seeing incongruity in their opposed conclusions. . . . Their convictions are by instinct, their activities intuitional."*

There is no doubt in my mind that, generally speaking, Lawrence's cryptic assessment is true. But it is also misleading, for the art of compromise is very much a feature of Arab life. Indeed, negotiation and mediation, the very point of which is the achievement of compromise, are as central to the Arab character as intransigence and fanaticism.

There have been hundreds of books and scholarly theses written which seek to delineate the Arab mentality in a more scientific way. All agree that it is not the simple and basically animalistic engine of behavior that early witnesses described. All agree, too, to a greater or lesser extent, that it is a highly contradictory one, ascribing its dualistic nature to a whole host of contrary inputs dating back to earliest times: tribalism vs. individualism, religious unity vs. sociological diversity, superiority vs. inferiority, linguistic fancy vs. the barren starkness of real life — the list is endless.

It is helpful to study these books before venturing into the Arab world because they provide a certain amount of understanding concerning types of behavior one may not encounter elsewhere. It is helpful in very much the same way that it would be helpful for an Arab, venturing into the West, to study carefully researched books on the Western mentality† — if, again, there is such a thing. Yet such books only scratch the surface of any comprehension of another culture's traits. And if not approached with skepticism, they can lead more easily to misunderstanding than understanding, for they tend to raise more questions than they answer while at the same time beguiling the reader into generalities which might apply in one situation, yet would be totally inapplicable in another.

Rather than give my own impressions of the Arab mentality, character, psyche (whatever one might want to call it) — which would after all be simply another perception of the Arabs as seen through Western eyes (and expectations) — I shall record here some self-appraisals given to me in inter-

* T. E. Lawrence in his introduction to Charles M. Doughty, *Travels in Arabia*, 3rd ed., New York, Random House, 1936.
† For instance, it is considerably more difficult for an American to comprehensibly explain to an Arab why there is so much wanton killing in the streets of New York than it is for an Arab to explain to an American the whys and wherefores of instances of Arab cruelty and bestiality.

views with several Arab educators, psychologists and social scientists who have devoted much of their research to analyzing Arab culture.

"In the first place, is there such a thing as an Arab mentality?" I asked Dr. François Gemayel of the American University of Beirut.

"Oh, of course," he replied. "First, understand that as between Arabs from different regions of the Arab world there are differences in character and personality. Most of these differences depend on extent of exposure to Europe, class position within the specific society, degree of literacy, religion, and so on. In other words, the Saudi Arab is very much different from the Lebanese, the Lebanese very much different from, say, the Moroccan, the Moroccan from the Egyptian, the Egyptian from the Saudi — depending on which two individuals you are talking about, and the circumstances that have gone into forming their specific characters. However, these are more differences in degree than in kind."

"In kind. You mean there is a quality that cuts across all lines, that makes an Arab an Arab, psychologically and behaviorally, no matter where he is?"

"I believe this is true."

"Okay, but what is this quality?"

"Oh, it is a collection of things. Language, for one. Religion. The Bedouin influence. Many others. These are the cornerstones of our tradition. They embody all our faults and all our virtues."

"You put that in a way that indicates you subscribe to the theory that the Arab character is one of conflicting extremes, which has always been the Western view," I said.

"But it is true," he replied. "The Arab personality is a split personality, if I may employ your Freudian terms. You see, there are two things fundamental here. First, the conflict between our Bedouin heritage and our Islamic one. The values we have ingrained in us are the values of the Bedouin. The values we are then taught to follow are those of the Koran. There is a fundamental difference between the two."

"Which is?"

"Well, it is the difference between God and man."

"I don't understand."

"You are acquainted with our famous ideas about self-respect, self-esteem, are you not?"

"Yes."

"Well, the Koran teaches us to strive for self-respect so that we may be worthy before God. The Bedouin tradition, on the other hand, demands self-respect so that we may be worthy before other men. Do you see the difference?"

I nodded uncertainly.

"It is simply a matter of two conflicting paths. Koranic self-respect implies humility, acquiescence, kindness, gentleness. Bedouin self-esteem demands the opposite — bluster, fierceness, aggressiveness. It is this dichotomy that pulls us from both sides and gives us our tendency to extreme forms of behavior. And then there is the other. But that is more an external influence."

"What is it?"

"It is tied into what I've just said. We — all Arabs — are conditioned culturally — no, make that biologically, or bioculturally — we are conditioned to a sense of superiority. Our language, our traditions, our religion — all imprint their superiorness on our souls. But at the same time we look around us and what do we see? We see ourselves in a position of inferiority. We are subservient to this people, that people, the next people who come to rule and live among us. We do not like it, but for centuries we have been unable to do anything about it. This contradiction — it carves a deep cleavage in our innermost mind, our soul, if you want to call it that. This also contributes to our uncertain behavior."

I put Dr. Gemayel's views to Kamal Hassan, who teaches Arab cultural history at the University of Cairo.

"As a theory it is probably accurate in its general outlines," he said. "The second part I would not be sure about, though. I would say that there it depends on exactly who the Arab is. The Saudi, for instance, is much less affected by external factors than, say, the Syrian. Yet the Saudi is just as extreme in his values and behavior, perhaps even more so."

"But you agree that this element of contradiction is a primary mark of the Arab character."

"Yes, but for different reasons, really. I would put it down more than anything else to language. Religion — well, I know hundreds of Christian Arabs, and basically they are no different than a Muslim. As for the Bedouin tradition — well, here you get into something very secondary. The Bedouin tradition is basically on the way out. It is the language of the Bedouin in which this tradition has lived on — Arabic. Language is a living, dynamic vehicle. Remember, one cannot think without language. Without words one can only visualize, but not define. Our language, as you know, is one of great verbal and literary scope. It compels us to think and imagine the kind of things that match it. With highly educated people, the pretensions of the language are tempered by the realism, the pragmatism, that comes through education. With uneducated people, or undereducated ones, the language has no brakes applied to it. So what happens? Since they think, and in a stronger sense feel, through this extreme language, they tend to become extreme themselves. This is why Arabs have a reputation for exaggeration. Most Arabs, all they have in the way of thinking process is their language. You do not speak Arabic?"

"A few words," I said.

"Well, then, you really cannot know what I mean. But I will give you something to look for. I am sure in the work you are doing you are in communication with many Egyptians of all educational levels, are you not?"

"Yes."

"Well, look for this. Many Egyptians speak English, even uneducated ones. Listen to how they speak in English. The more exaggerations and superlatives and elaborate praises and denunciations you hear from a man, the less educated you can be sure he is."

"I've already noticed something like that."

"Unfortunately, the great masses of Arabs are uneducated. Because of the hold the language has over them, they are constitutionally incapable of speaking, therefore thinking, therefore behaving in any other way than the way they do. And, of course, because they speak, think and behave with such extreme intensity, the other side of their behavior must be equally extreme. An ordinary Englishman — he will chuckle and will frown. In England, someone given to great extremes of expression — howling laughter, bellowing anger — he is looked upon with disapproval. Here it is the opposite. Someone who shows little variation in emotion is thought to be — how would you say — retarded? It is our language."

"No," said Dr. Adnan Butros, a French-educated Lebanese sociologist teaching in Damascus. "I would not call it language. It is strictly a matter of acculturation. It is not language, it is not Bedouin influence. Look at the difference between the Saudis and the Egyptians, the Syrians, the Iraqis. Arabic is the language of the Bedouin. Saudi Arabia and the other states of the peninsula — they are still closest of all Arab societies to the Bedouin influence. Yet see the differences between the way *they* speak and act, and the way in which the northern Arabs speak and act. When Faisal says he is going to do something, it is wise to listen. He may put it in arcane language, but it will be by and large understated and you know — you know! — what he says he is going to do, he *will* do. Until recently it has not been so in the north. Nasser was the perfect example. Threats, bluster, always saying more than he could possibly fulfill. That is another reason why Saudi Arabia has become so important. To you in the West it is important because of oil. To us it is important because they have shown the Arab a new way to act. That has been the trouble, really. The Saudis have always been secure in their power and authority. Also in their means. They were never colonized the way the Arabs in the north were."

"You mean," I asked, "because the northern Arabs were always under foreign rule they developed this extremism of behavior and personality?"

"Exactly. The Arabs had to submit or be punished. They were required for dozens of generations to be obeisant to alien influences and at the same time sustain their own traditions. This produced a kind of cultural schizo-phrenia that burst out in all its glory once the foreigners left. But now they are reverting to the true Arab character, and they are taking the lead from those who are the truest of Arabs — the Arabians. That was Nasser's greatness. He had many faults, but his greatness was in centering the focus of the Arab people on their true nature, their true identity. 'We are all Arabs,' he said. Only he was blocked in his own instincts from being a true Arab. He was a child of the old order, the days of Arab subjugation. So he could not act like a true Arab, he could only aspire to this state. His death was a fabulous turning point in Arab history. He symbolized the Arab struggle to free the Arab soul from the bonds of foreign influence. His death was like a purging of this influence. Arabs could truly be Arabs again. Take Sadat, for example. Or Assad. Or Boumedienne. They have become like Faisal, like true Arabs. They say, and they do. It is truly a cultural revolution."

"Well," I said, "perhaps Sadat, Assad and other leaders are speaking with less bluster these days, but it seems to me that the people are still subject to the same kind of wishful thinking as before."

"Oh, it does not happen overnight. But it *is* happening. Arabs revere their leaders, accept them with no qualifications, copy them. Once the Sadats and Assads of the Arab world take hold, and their successors, then you will see a totally new Arab people. Quiet, determined, confident — a people of action, not a people deluded into believing that words and rhetoric are the same thing as action. It will take time, but it is coming. As education spreads, as habits change — oh, we have many, many bad habits to change — but it will come. I am not saying we will be like any other people. We will be Arabs. Our good habits will remain."

When I put Professor Butros's ideas to Dr. Hamid Hilal, an Egyptian political scientist, he replied, shaking his head, "Oh, poor Butros. He is the kind of idealist whose very ideas betray his possession of the bad habits he is talking about. No, the Arab will be very slow to change. The Saudis Butros cites are merely showing one face to the world. That is very much a part of the Arab character."

"Then what do you see as the central component of this character?" I said.

"The Arab character — mentality, if you wish — revolves around several interlocking syndromes, each of which is composed of a polarity that goes back deep into the evolution of Arab culture. A good example is the polarity of honesty and dishonesty coexisting with the polarity of honor and dishonor. Now, honor has always been the highest of all Arab strivings, and of course dishonor has been the thing to be avoided at all costs. That is our tribal heritage. And honesty is the highest of virtues according to our religious heritage. So now we come to a situation: Say a man learns that his wife has been with another man. In the old days, even if no one else knew about it, he would have rushed out and killed the other man. He would have exposed the dishonor visited upon him, but by so doing would have retrieved his honor. That still happens in the desert. But you are not going to be dealing with desert Arabs, you are interested in the ordinary Arab. The ordinary Arab, with his exposure to more modern ideas, deals with this differently. Suppose no one knows for sure that his wife has been with the other man, but suppose some suspect. They ask, and of course he says no. In other words, he lies to protect his honor. And even if the others know that his wife has indeed been with the other man, as long as the cuckold is convinced that his lie is believed, then his honor is safe. And of course the others, although they know differently, will then pretend that they believe him — they will respond to his lie with a dishonesty of their own so that the man may feel secure in the myth that his honor is preserved. Therefore it is honorable to be dishonest when circumstances dictate. And this is how things work in the Arab mind. It all comes down to the fact that all behavior is constantly directed and controlled by the dual endeavor of trying to avoid what is dishonorable and trying to do what is honorable. Within this tribal instinct operate numerous religious polarities, such as honesty-dishonesty, aggression and submission, pride and humility — I can name dozens — which work at cross purposes and pull the Arab in two opposite directions. The divisions between extremes break down, and it is often found that what is bad in one situation can be good in another. There is inherently no consistency in the logic of the value system. Thus the Arab frequently seems, to the outsider, illogical and inconsistent in his behavior. Which leads to all these mystified foreign interpretations of the Arab character. To the Arabs, though, it is all perfectly logical, consistent and acceptable."

There is doubtless a bit of truth in each of these assessments, as there was in dozens of other opinions I solicited during my travels. Truth always comes in bits and pieces, and there is little I can add of my own that would more than barely scratch the surface of the Arab character and mentality.

Nevertheless I should append this short exchange I had during the course of a talk with President Anwar Sadat of Egypt.

"It seems to me," I had said to him, "that going back to the very beginnings in World War I, the Arab-Jewish conflict was always, as far as the Arabs were concerned, a clash between absolute right and absolute wrong, with the Arabs, of course, the representatives of absolute right. Many analysts have said that this is because the Arab mind tends to view everything that confronts it in an absolute way, in terms of black and white. Yet sitting here talking to you, I get a sense of a man who has a distinct appreciation for the subtleties of life. Are you an absolutist?"

"Only in certain matters," Sadat replied, after giving my question a moment's thought.

"On Israel?"

"It is true," he said. "We Arabs unfortunately tend to see things in extremes only. This comes out of our history. Remember, there was a time when we did almost all the thinking for the world. We were the inventors, the idea men, the innovators. Those were the great centuries of Islam, and I assure you we did not then think in such simple ways. How could we, and achieve what we did? How could we think merely yes or no, right or wrong? No, we also thought maybe, perhaps, possibly. But while we were busy doing all that thinking and exploring in the mind, others came and took us over. It was not the Arabs who turned themselves into such rigid absolutists, it was the peoples who conquered us, took over our religion — an Arab religion, mind you — and turned it into theirs. The Turks. So, this way of thinking we have had, it is really something we learned from the Turks, or was forced on us, because in their hands Islamic thinking became frozen and very authoritative. The Turks believed everything was black and white, nothing gray, and the Arab learned to believe that too. He had no choice."

"But as regards Israel," I said, "how does that work in with the famous Islamic submission to the forces of fate? On the one hand, the Arab tends to accept diversity, he simply shrugs it off as God's — Allah's — will. On the other he has fought tooth and nail against Israel. Why didn't the Arabs simply shrug off Israel and say, 'Well, it is Allah's will, we must learn to live with it'?"

"Ah, but the Arab does not accept such diversity. It was a matter of land. One Arab does not yield his patch of land to another. If a storm comes from the skies and wipes it out, floods it and washes it all away, he says it is Allah's will. But not when another tries to take it away from him. Then it is a dishonor, and he will fight to retain it. And particularly if he is a Muslim. A Muslim does not give up an inch of his land to an infidel. It is a double dishonor. If the Zionists had come to us and asked us to share a piece of Arab land, then it might have been different. We would have given them a home-land, if that was all they wished. A refuge. We gave the Jews refuge once before, remember. But they did not ask. They came and they took. And they took. And they took. Under the protection of the British. They did not come and ask if they could have a room in our house. They came and said we are taking over your house — you can live in the rest of it, but we will live in this room. Now I ask you, what would you do if a man came into your house and took it over, then said, if you want to stay you can, but you cannot use this room?"

"A good question. But was it as simple as that?"

"I don't understand," Sadat said.

"I mean, there were a lot of other factors involved, too. Arabs sold land to the Jews."

"Some Arabs, yes. But that was before their real intentions became clear. I would have sold land to a Jew then. What if a German came to you in America and asked to buy a piece of land from you, offered you a very good price. Would you refuse to sell it to him simply because he was a German?"

"Probably not."

"But what if you then learned that other Germans were buying other land, and that their secret intention was to take over your country. You would then be sorry, no?"

"I suppose so. But even after the Zionist intention became clear, Arabs continued to sell their lands."

"Only a few," replied Sadat. "Greedy Arabs, Arabs who put money before the wishes of their people. Is there any society in the world without its handful of people without principles?"

"No."

"Do you think there are not Jews who would sell out other Jews to make a profit, Americans who would not sell out other Americans?"

"No."

"So? Who said the Arabs are perfect? But it was only a handful. Most of the land of the Jews today was gotten not by buying it from Arabs but through other means. Expropriation, annexation, military occupation."

"You mean that if the Zionists had used a more polite approach to you back in the early days, things would have been different?"

"Oh, I definitely think it is true."

"It wasn't their goals that mattered, it was their method."

"Their goals — if their goals had been sincere rather than ones of trickery, if they could have been content with a sanctuary within the Arab world, and if they had approached us with respect instead of with disrespect and hostility, there would have been no problem. Indeed, we would have welcomed them among us, for they could have made a great contribution to our society."

"But the Jews were a bit desperate," I said. "The whole point of Zionism was to get them away from being the guests of other nations and giving them a nation of their own."

"They were only desperate as a result of the Nazis. Before that they were not desperate, they were just ambitious."

"You acknowledge how desperate they were after the war?"

"Of course. And I understand it. But you must remember, we Arabs have a history also. We had suffered many, many centuries of oppression and exploitation. We respond to the traumas of our own history just as the Jews do to theirs. However, there has been too much obsession with the past, on both sides. It is the past that makes absolutes. We are looking now to the future. We are willing to accept Israel. It is still a historical injustice to us, but we are realistic. We will accept the Israel that was created by the United Nations . . ."

Sadat chuckled to himself. I asked him why. "It is curious, is it not? Everybody is saying, 'Ah, the Arabs are becoming like the Israelis, they copy their tactics to beat them in the war.' But what is the fact? The fact is, the Israelis are becoming like us. For so long we refused to recognize the Jews as a legitimate nation. Now we are willing to do so. And now the Jews are unwilling to recognize the Palestinians as a legitimate nation. Absolutely unwilling! They won't even discuss it. While we emerge from the absolutism of the past, they sink further into their own absolutism."

"They refuse to grant a Palestinian state because they fear it's just an Arab ploy to make their own state more vulnerable."

"I know that," Sadat said. "Yet all the reasons they used to justify their attitude toward the Palestinians, they condemned us for using to justify our attitude toward them. Don't you see it? The Jews have just become Arabs of a different faith. That is why I am confident of the future. With Jews we never knew how to deal. But Arabs . . ."

# 16.

# HISTORY: *The Western Factor*

ASIDE FROM THE POLITICAL OBJECTIONS to Zionism articulated by Amin Al-Husseini, Aref Al-Aref and other newly emerged "Palestinian" activists after the close of World War I, objections were raised on other grounds. These were mostly voiced by anthropologists and historians, Arab and otherwise, who contended that the entire concept of a Jewish "people" was a myth. Although these claims were generally ignored, they had, as it turned out, some validity.

Anthropologists concluded, after reconstructing the histories of the various bloodlines that formed the Jewish "people," that the eastern European Jewish inventors of Zionism had little or no biological connection to Palestine. The great mass of early-twentieth-century European Jewry was descended from a seminomadic Turko-Finnish people, probably related to the Bulgars of the Volga River basin, who first appeared in what is now southern Russia in the second century A.D. They came to be known as the Khazars, and by the eighth century they had established a powerful pagan kingdom that touched upon the northern frontiers of the Byzantine Empire (the Kingdom of Khazaria).

As if to counterbalance the Christian and Islamic conversions that were taking place among other peoples of the region, the Khazars made a mass conversion to the Jewish faith in the seventh century. Three centuries later they were conquered by the Russians and the Byzantines and were scattered throughout what is today Russia, Hungary, Rumania and Poland. They kept their faith nevertheless, and their numbers were swelled by Jews who fled central and western Europe at the time of the Crusades and during the Great Plague (which the Christian populations often blamed on the Jews because of their so-called accursedness under Christian mythology).

That the Khazars were the lineal ancestors of the great mass of eastern European Jewry — the progenitors of political Zionism — was a historical fact. The Khazars and their descendants had little if any biological connection to ancient Israel-Palestine. Their kinship was purely religious — a fact readily acknowledged by some Jewish historians and religious textbooks. Nevertheless the founders of Zionism chose to overlook it, dismiss the Khazar connection, and claim that religious kinship was sufficient justification for the creation of a Jewish national home in Palestine.

No matter the arguments marshaled by the Arabs against the establishment of a large-scale European Jewish presence in a land overwhelming Arab in culture and Islamic in religion, their objections went generally unheeded. There followed in the 1920s a period of intermittent civil strife directed on the Arab side by Amin Al-Husseini* and his expanding following and on the Jewish side by a hardening Zionist leadership. Generally speaking, although much Jewish blood was shed, the Jews got the better of the exchange as the British mandatory authorities, as well as the London government, invariably supported Zionist claims and ignored those of the native Arabs.

Jewish achievement during the two stormy decades prior to World War II was on a scale unprecedented in nation-building. With the help of about a quarter of a billion dollars in foreign (mostly Jewish) capital investment and the stepped-up immigration of technologically skilled Jews from Europe and the Americas, the Jewish homeland became a prosperous shadow-state. The Zionists created a well-entrenched and constantly enlarging society on the European model, based on socialist-capitalist economic practices. Industry, land reclamation and agriculture, construction, education, health care — all flourished as the European Jewish culture settled in and expanded. Zionists added a new justification for their expanding presence in Palestine: "Look what we are managing to do with this barren land. What are the Arabs crying about? With them alone here, the land has always been unproductive, the society fallow and impoverished. Look what we are doing."

True, what the Jews were doing constituted an economic and social miracle — for the Jews. Despite the fact that a few Arabs prospered from the

* Husseini had been named mufti of Jerusalem, and thus had acquired a religious legitimacy that added to his political influence among Palestinians.

Jewish accomplishments, for the general Arab population it was a miracle in reverse. The Jewish economic success brought an influx of poor Arabs from lands around Palestine hoping to find jobs in the hyperactive economy. What they, along with the local Arabs, found was poverty, for Zionist labor policy for the most part excluded, or otherwise discriminated against, Arab labor.

The ordinary Arab in Palestine in these years was faced with a steeply escalating increase in his cost of living which was brought about by the economic transformation of the area by the Jews. His feelings were intensified by the spectacle of the handsome new boulevards built in the more desirable parts of the towns and cities by and for the immigrant population, and by the vast tracts of Jewish workingmen's quarters erected by Jewish building societies. Sometimes, too, he had the experience of being driven away from work sites by Jewish pickets, and he resented the fact that when he was allowed to work, the government paid the Jewish workman double the rate it paid him.

It was in the less populous middle and upper classes of Palestinian Arab society that the transformation had the most profound effect, however. It is true that many Arabs in these classes, especially landowners and merchants, prospered as a result of the Jewish influx. Many families acquired considerable wealth from land sales to the Jews. Others found their shops and businesses increasingly patronized by the immigrants, all to their monetary advantage. Many used the capital so acquired to plant citrus and banana groves. They also used it to educate their sons and daughters. In the course of fifteen years there grew up a generation of young men and, to a lesser extent, young women who had received at least the rudiments of a modern education. Hundreds of them had been sent abroad and had spent a number of years in European schools and universities. This younger generation was brought up on the ideals of the vigorous postwar Arab nationalism that emanated from the broken promises of the European powers, and they could not be kept quiet, as the older generation had been, by half-hearted Jewish attempts at conciliation or by such British backing-and-filling maneuvers as the proposal that Palestine be partitioned between Arabs and Jews — with the Jews getting the rich northern coastal plain and the Arabs the dry southern desert region.* There thus came about a complete transformation in the

---

* This proposal was contained in a 1937 report by the Royal Commission, one of a countless number of investigatory bodies assigned by the British to look into the causes of civil disturbances in Palestine. The Zionists were no more enthusiastic about the proposal than the Arabs. In the words of Vladimir Jabotinsky, a particularly hard-line Zionist leader who sought all of Palestine for the Jews, "A corner of Palestine, a canton — how can we promise to be

nature and intensity of the Arab opposition to the Judaization of the country.

By the mid-thirties the Arab population was altogether better educated and more articulate than it had been in 1920. The commonly perceived danger of total Jewish control, moreover, was bringing the various sections of the population together. Christian and Muslim Arabs, the large peasant populace and the smaller elite, were acquiring together a stronger sense of Palestinian identity and a new sense of solidarity. The formation of Palestine into a political entity, symbolized by the passport and customs barriers by which it was now separated from the rest of Syria, served to additionally accentuate a sense of Palestinian identity while at the same time, through protests over this artificial separation, heightening the notion of Palestinian nationalism.

Moreover, the Arab world around Palestine was bestirring itself. In Arabia the kingly nationalism of Sharif Hussein had been displaced by the powerful reemergence of the reactionary and isolationist Wahhabi religious movement. Iraq was busy consolidating its position as an independent Arab state under Hussein's son Feisal and the tutelage of Britain. French Syria was a hotbed of secret Arab nationalist fervor. The Kingdom of Transjordan had been established by the British and, although not yet independent, was harboring such notions. And Egypt was full of activity — the final negotiation of its independence from Britain might be expected at any moment.

While all this was occurring, another series of events was taking place that at the time seemed to have little to do with the Arabs but in retrospect was central to their evolving fortunes. In a word, these events were spelled o-i-l.

By the late nineteenth century John D. Rockefeller's America-based Standard Oil Company had all but cornered the market for oil — its production, refining, transportation and sale — in the Western Hemisphere. In those days the greatest primary source of industrial energy was coal; the internal combustion engine had not yet been perfected, the horseless carriage (except for a few random experimental prototypes) was still a dream, and Western householders still banked the fires of their coal furnaces or wood stoves before retiring on wintry nights. Oil was largely refined into kerosene for lighting and other purposes.

By the beginning of the twentieth century Great Britain had by far the largest navy and merchant marine in the world. Once it became a matter of

---

satisfied with that? We cannot. We never can. Should we swear to you that we should be satisfied, it would be a lie" (*The Jewish Chronicle*, May 13, 1938).

practical fact that ships could be driven economically by oil, influential elements in the British admiralty began to propose that the navy be converted from coal to oil; the benefits in terms of the weight, space and mobility of its ships would be enormous. After oil was discovered in the Caucasus region of Russia, just north of Persia, in the early 1870s, Britain realized it had two choices in the conversion of its fleet to oil: either become customers of the American or Russian oil monopolies and pay premium prices, or develop its own petroleum resources. It chose the latter course.

A private British-Australian financier named William Knox D'Arcy had, on the advice of some Persian friends, become interested in the oil prospects there. In the spring of 1901 he obtained a concession for the production of oil in Persia. Although a company was organized in 1903 to operate the D'Arcy concessions, little was accomplished. Soon D'Arcy and his associates were in financial difficulties. But it was at this time that the British admiralty decided to switch over to oil; thus the British government lent D'Arcy its financial support. In May 1908, after several more years of unproductive exploration, a gusher was finally struck, proving the existence of large quantities of oil beneath Persia. The very next year the Anglo-Persian Oil Company was incorporated, and once all negotiations were concluded the British government owned a controlling share. Britain, in effect, had its own seemingly unlimited access to oil.

At about the same time, Britain was maneuvering on the European big-power scene to prevent Germany from gaining oil concessions in the Ottoman Empire. Oil had been discovered in northern Mesopotamia (Iraq), and the British, the Dutch (who had developed oil resources of their own in Southeast Asia) and the Germans were all vying for the rights to it, along with an American offshoot of Rockefeller's Standard Oil Company — the Standard Oil Company of New York, or Socony. The British teamed up with the Dutch in 1914 to control seventy-five percent of the newly formed Turkish Petroleum Company, while the Germans were left with twenty-five percent and the Americans out in the cold.

Before Turkish Petroleum could get any effective drilling underway in Mesopotamia, the First World War broke out. With the exception of the Persian oil field being exploited by the Anglo-Persian Oil Company, the development of petroleum resources did not begin until the end of the first war. Actual drilling operations were preceded by diplomatic maneuverings in 1919 during the period of the Paris Peace Conference, at which time Socony lobbyists urged upon the American delegation the necessity of assuring American oil companies of an equal opportunity to obtain oil concessions in what was clearly seen as the bottomless well of the Middle East.

The real competition among Western powers to gain oil concessions in the Arab world* did not begin until after World War I. The war had inadvertently served as a climax of the Industrial Revolution that had begun in the West a century before. The enormous increase in productive capacity in the Western world and the vast expansion in the manufacture of motor vehicles stimulated several of the great oil companies to secure control of the Arab world's petroleum deposits.

During the late twenties and thirties, despite Anglo-French efforts to minimize American access to Arab oil riches, several large American companies secured concessions† and the oil-production race was on. Most of the concessions obtained — American and European — were done so through negotiations between the government-backed oil companies and individual leaders of the Arab lands, who usually leased the concessions with only immediate monetary rewards in mind. There was little in the way of formal government in the Arab lands at the time, particularly along the eastern shore of the Arabian peninsula where oil was most abundant; hence concessions were private affairs, and the income from them invariably went into the personal treasuries of the sheikhs and emirs who granted them.

The eastern shore of Arabia, the southern shore of Mesopotamia and the western shore of Persia marked the boundaries of the Persian Gulf — that • alcove of the Indian Ocean that had long been the preserve of Great Britain. The various Arabian tribal sheikhdoms strung out along the eastern shore of Arabia and at the head of the gulf were, by virtue of a series of treaties, under exclusive British protection. And of course Britain was well established in Mesopotamia and along the Persian shore. It would have seemed that the entire Persian Gulf area, as far as oil concessions were concerned, was securely in the hands of the British. Once the war was over and the Arab world was divided up between Britain and France, the British government was sure it would have no "foreigners" to worry about as it set about preparing the region for exploitation.

Such was not the case, for the British did not figure on the Arabs themselves. The brisk and businesslike parceling up of the Middle East by the victorious European powers failed to take into account the fact that the lands

* Persia (Iran), of course, although a Muslim country, is not Arab.
† A concession was basically a contracted promise to pay the host country a certain amount of money in advance, plus a specified royalty on future production, in exchange for the exclusive right to drill for oil in a given region of the country.

wrested from the Turks were, in fact, Arab lands. The Arabs had fought on the side of the British and French on the understanding that, once the war was over, they would be rewarded with an independent Pan-Arab state. Smarting under what they considered British duplicity, various chieftains of the Arabian peninsula quietly let it be known that they were open to all offers regarding oil concessions. There followed a decade of furious plotting and backbiting on the part of the various international oil companies to gain control of the oil on the Arabian side of the Persian Gulf. In the end the United States was the winner, although Britain managed a good showing in finishing second. By the beginning of World War II America had the oil resources of the island sheikhdom of Bahrain, off the Arabian coast, under its leasehold and was sitting on the vast oil deposits of Arabia itself (now the independent Wahhabi Kingdom of Saudi Arabia). Britain, of course, still had Persia, and in addition had gotten the Sheikhdom of Qatar, a peninsula jutting into the Persian Gulf, and half of the small Sheikhdom of Kuwait. The oil fields of Mesopotamia (Iraq) were controlled by a consortium of British, Dutch, French and American companies.

There would be further rivals by the end of World War II, and further oil fields to conquer — in the deserts of North Africa, in the exotic sheikhdoms farther south along the coastline of the Arabian peninsula and beneath the waters of the Persian Gulf itself. But for the time being all the productive regions, as well as those territories that had shown a potential for future exploitation, had been partitioned among the major Western powers.

The Arab rulers of the concessionary territories had little say in how the concessions were to be operated, and their people none. There was not much they could have said anyway — the concessionaires had powerful governments behind them to enforce the terms of their tenancy. In any event the Arabs had no technical knowledge or skills to exploit their riches themselves and little if any appreciation of the far-reaching international meaning their petroleum resources possessed. It was a time to take the money (in the case of the rulers), the construction and maintenance jobs that opened up (in the case of the people), and to abide by the old Bedouin saying: "The hand you cannot bite, kiss it."

The long-term future of the Middle East as a primary focus of international tensions was formed largely by World War I and its immediate aftermath. But it was the Second World War, and *its* aftermath, that provided the form with its substance.

By the start of the war the strife in Palestine between Arabs and Jews had reached a dangerous peak. Arab resentment against Zionist colonization was no longer centered exclusively in Palestine but had spread throughout the Arab world. Amin Al-Husseini, still a leading spokesman for the Palestinian Arab cause, turned to the virulent anti-Jewish racism of Nazi Germany, thus injecting a new element into Arab anti-Zionist feeling. In Europe, meanwhile, Jews were being persecuted and slaughtered and were desperately looking for a haven. The natural sanctuary for many was Zionist Palestine; it was precisely to prevent further pogroms against world Jewry that the Zionist movement had originally come into existence.

But in 1939 Britain, in response to another wave of riots and Arab insurrections, abruptly reversed its mandatory policy that had for so long favored the Jews. The English, now desperate to appease the Arabs as war threatened and Germany sought to curry Arab favor, released a White Paper which stated in no uncertain terms that it was not the policy of the British government "that Palestine should become a Jewish state." It placed a limitation on Jewish immigration during the following five years to a total of 75,000 and provided that thereafter Jewish immigration would be permitted only if the Arabs of Palestine were "prepared to acquiesce in it." The document also provided for very definite limitations on the acquisition of further land by Jews.

The 1939 White Paper was of the utmost significance in shaping future developments in Palestine. It immediately turned a cautious friend, the Zionists, into an implacable enemy, and transformed a bitter enemy, the Arabs, into an at least tractable friend. What the White Paper reflected most of all, however, was Britain's inability to impose its will on the Middle East.

Arab political leaders in Palestine and other Arab countries — except for those now solidly committed to the support of Nazi designs — received the White Paper with tentative approval and a sense of relief; after twenty years their voices, and their actions, were being heeded. The Zionists, on the contrary, reacted to it with profound indignation, unremittingly opposing it until the day Great Britain finally gave up its mandate ten years later. It aroused such bitter feeling against Britain that a dangerous Zionist underground movement developed against the British, one that culminated in a Jewish insurrection at the end of the Second World War over Britain's refusal to revise its 1939 ban on immigration so as to accommodate the hundreds of thousands of Jewish refugees from Nazi Europe.

Except for the fighting in Arab North Africa, the war left the Middle East virtually untouched. A pro-Axis government set itself up in Iraq in April of 1941, with Palestinian leader Husseini serving as a liaison between the Iraqis and the Germans. Within a month and a half it was bounced out of power by the British.

Syria and Lebanon for a short time became the stage for a brief but sharp military campaign of British and Gaullist Free French forces against those of wartime France's Vichy mandatory regime.

Saudi Arabia remained neutral until early 1945, then made a pro forma declaration of war on the Axis powers, as did Syria and Lebanon, in order to obtain an invitation to join the then-forming United Nations.

There was an additional reason for Saudi Arabia's sudden belligerency, however. Earlier during the war, oil production in that land came to a virtual standstill due to difficulties in transportation across the U-boat-infested high seas. As a result, the American oil companies' royalty payments to King Ibn Saud's treasury dried up. Saud became desperate for money to keep his reign afloat; his only other significant source of revenue came from the pilgrimage trade to the Hejaz, and that too had dwindled to a trickle because of the war. Saud and his finance minister, Abdullah Sulaiman, began demanding large-scale advance payments against future royalties from Aramco, the consortium of American oil companies that held the concessions in Saudi Arabia. Implied in these demands was the threat that if the money was not forthcoming, King Saud's regime might topple, and with it would go the validity of the concessions.

The oil companies prevailed on President Roosevelt. He, through a series of irregular dealings involving the Lend-Lease Program, saw to it that Saud got his money. Later, in February of 1945, as Roosevelt was returning from the Yalta Conference, he met King Saud abroad the cruiser *Quincy* in the Suez Canal. The two discussed U.S.-Saudi cooperation in the future exploitation of Saud's oil resources. But that was not all they talked about. Arab concern over the postwar outcome of the Zionist-Palestinian conflict had spread to Saud's domain. As leader of the Wahhabi sect, thereby the self-appointed conscience of the Arab world, Saud sought Roosevelt's assurances on the question. Roosevelt promised, first orally, then by letter, that as President he would take no action which might prove hostile to the Arab people and would make no changes in America's Palestine policy — a policy which generally supported the British White Paper position — without consulting the Arabs beforehand.

With a commitment such as this, and with Germany on the verge of surrender, Saud was delighted to declare war on the Axis and become an official ally of the United States.

At the end of the war the oil consortiums — American, British, French and Dutch — were busily back at work in the lands surrounding the Persian Gulf and were starting to tap the rich deposits arrayed along the Mediterranean coast of North Africa. A tremendous international petroleum boom was in the making, but quietly so. In the meantime, the focus of concern and anxiety returned to Palestine.

Palestine had been relatively quiet at the beginning of the war. Although the Zionists were stunned by the White Paper, they officially supported the British cause against Germany and its virulent anti-Jewish program. Once the German policy of mass extermination of European Jews became known, however, the Jews of Palestine were stirred to their depths. This powerful emotional reaction reached a state bordering on frenzy when the British government, using the White Paper as its authority, resorted to violence in order to prevent the immigration of refugees who had managed to escape the Nazi concentration camps and crematoria. A Jewish militia was organized to counteract the British military blockade of Jewish immigrants. Out of this evolved several fanatical underground terrorist groups that viewed British policy in the same light as that of Germany — bestial and inhumane. Thus, while Britain fought the Axis powers in Europe and North Africa, it was, toward the end of the war, involved in combat against the very Jews it had encouraged to settle in Palestine during the two prior decades.

During the war years four principal groups were making plans for the future of Palestine, each according to its own exclusive design. Of these only one achieved its goals, and then only partially. With the holocaust in Europe, the Zionists received a monumental injection of moral support and money from Western Jewish populations — especially those in America, which had the largest concentration of Jews of any country in the world. In 1942, at a conference of American Zionists held at the Biltmore Hotel in New York and addressed by Zionist leaders from Palestine — most notably, David Ben-Gurion — a resolution was adopted that demanded unlimited Jewish immigration into Palestine and the establishment of a Jewish "commonwealth" there. These demands subsequently became the irreducible minimum of all Zionists and most Jews. Abandoned were any further questions concerning the moral or legal justification of such demands vis-à-vis the Arabs; European Jewry was in desperate straits, and survival took precedence over the niceties of morality and legality.

The Arabs of Palestine were no less intransigent. What was happening in Europe was not of their making. They had been deceived once before by Western appeals to humanitarianism; they would not be deceived again. To counteract the Zionist movement, the governments of the seven principal Arab nations — Lebanon, Syria, Iraq, Transjordan, Saudi Arabia, Yemen and Egypt — with British encouragement, created the League of Arab States (subsequently known as the Arab League). Its primary purpose was to promote — through propaganda, concerted action and others means — Palestine as an Arab state under Arab control. Termination of the British mandate, cessation of illegal Jewish immigration,* and Palestinian Arab independence became the militant and nonnegotiable demands of the Arab League.

The British, for their part, hoped to retain Palestine despite the inherent difficulties posed by the Jewish-Arab deadlock. To resecure the support of the Jews and still hold on to the goodwill of the Arabs was a totally unrealizable goal, as was its obverse. The fruitlessness of the British hopes quickly made itself evident at the war's end as Palestine fell into a state of anarchy. British public opinion soon grew frustrated with England's residual, unappreciated imperialism, and the government in London began to make plans to terminate its mandate over Palestine.

The United States under Roosevelt had trod the middle road. Profoundly cognizant of its expanding petroleum interests, it desired stability on the Arab side. Equally aware of the electoral weight of the American Jewish populace — a populace that had begun to assert itself — it recognized that the placation of Zionist aspirations was also vital. The United States therefore produced a compromise plan which called for a national communal Jewish government and a national communal Arab government within Palestine, for continued Jewish immigration, and for large-scale development of the water, land and mineral resources of the country, development the fruits of which would be shared equally by the Jewish and Arab populations. The plan was naïve and unrealistic, for it failed to take into account what was by then the Zionist obsession with the establishment of a sovereign Jewish

---

* According to the White Paper, Jewish immigration after 1943 was illegal without Arab "acquiescence." The Zionists were by then smuggling immigrants into Palestine, or attempting to do so. Many immigrants were being intercepted by the British and shunted off into detention camps in such places as Cyprus and elsewhere.

state — an obsession that had been hardened by the events in Europe and was widely supported by a host of politically influential American Jews — and the Arab mistrust of Western "solutions."

What happened thereafter is well known. At the conclusion of the war in Europe a Labour government was elected in Britain, with an avowed socialist, Aneurin Bevin, as foreign secretary. Since Zionism had loosely based its political and economic principles on the nineteenth-century revolutionary Marxist socialism that had germinated in eastern Europe and had given birth to the British Labour movement, the Zionists expected the Bevin foreign office, as a gesture of socialist solidarity, to relax the 1939 White Paper restrictions against Jewish immigration and land transfers in Palestine. But they did not anticipate Bevin's intractable Britishness. The Zionist militia and underground terrorist groups had recently been killing British troops and civil administrators in Palestine as the English sought to enforce the White Paper regulations. Such behavior was an affront to British sensibility. Besides that, there was little concern within British Labour over Jewish survival; Jewish financiers, bankers and merchant-kings had long been accused, along with non-Jewish English capitalists, of exploiting the common workingman, and a general anti-Jewish sentiment had deeply etched itself into the fabric of the Labour movement. Bevin, then, refused to open the gates of Palestine to the wretched, dispossessed survivors of Hitler's death camps.

The Zionists reacted, in Palestine by intensifying their terrorist activities against the local British authority, and abroad by mounting a vast propaganda campaign to win over Western public opinion. The member states of the Arab League watched all this activity with a mounting sense of foreboding. Their cause — that of Arab sovereignty over Palestine — dated back to the breakup of the Ottoman Empire. Just when they thought they were going to get a hearing before the world, along with some positive action, they watched their cause get lost in the shuffle of the Zionist-British conflict and the political maneuvers that attended it throughout the West.

Their foreboding was transformed into outrage when President Harry Truman, who had succeeded the deceased Roosevelt, abandoned Roosevelt's 1945 promise to King Saud that as President he "would take no action which might prove hostile to the Arab people" and would make no American commitments regarding Palestine without first consulting the Arabs.

The Arabs, accustomed to hundreds of years of autocratic government, had little understanding of how the American system worked. A foreign commitment of one president, even one that was written down, had no binding effect on the country so long as it was not incorporated in treaty form and ratified by Congress. A succeeding president could easily abrogate such a commitment when political exigencies, domestic or foreign, so required.

This is precisely what Truman did. Whether this profane and acerbic Missourian had any feelings one way or the other about the Jews of the world is unknown, but he was a consummate politician. Pressured on all sides by the American Jewish electorate, most of which had theretofore subscribed to the philosophy and goals of the Democratic party — of which, of course, Truman as President was head — he publically advocated the immediate admittance of 100,000 Jews into Palestine, thus causing a break with England over its mandatory policies. Britain refused, but in so doing intimated that it was ready to wash its hands of the entire affair and renounce its mandate.

The Arabs saw the writing on the wall. If Britain abandoned Palestine, the United States — with its large Jewish population and its susceptibility to sophisticated Zionist propaganda — would automatically fill the vacuum. The Arab League made an effort to mount a propaganda campaign of its own, but it was doomed from the start. The Zionists, Westerners in culture and habit, mixed hard pragmatism with the ideals of humanitarianism in their pleas to American and European public opinion, adding a strong dose of suggestion and innuendo designed to appeal to Christian notions of guilt. It was highly effective. The Arabs, on the other hand, built their propaganda on an entirely different appeal — one that revealed little understanding of the Western mind. It was rooted in the values of the Arab language, filled with grandiose expressions of despair mixed with elaborately veiled threats, and packaged in prolixity. It was aimed not at a real sense of Western guilt but at an imagined sense of Western shame. A shared subliminal feeling of guilt the West may well have had over the long-tragic fortunes of European Jewry. But shame over the many centuries of Arab disenfranchisement in the Middle East? Never.

The Arab campaign, aside from lacking sophistication, was disorganized and, in Western terms, linguistically laughable to the point of pitiability. Rather than advance the Arab cause, it discredited it, for it confirmed many of the negative Arab stereotypes that had long been endemic in the Western mind.

Britain made one final effort to work out a solution to the problem of the

Palestine mandate in September 1946, by convening what was called the Palestine Roundtable Conference in London. Both Arab and Zionist leaders flatly rejected the proposals that came out of the conference, and thereafter the train of events telescoped. Britain referred the Palestine issue to the United Nations in February 1947. The UN appointed a Special Committee on Palestine to study the problem and make recommendations. In September the Special Committee recommended partition of the land into separate Arab and Jewish states.

The idea of partition was not new; the British had proposed it as early as 1937. This time the Jews were not disinclined to agree to it. By now a Jewish state — any Jewish state, however small — was imperative.

The Arabs had not changed their attitude, however. The militant precepts of the first notable Palestinian leader, Amin Al-Husseini, remained in force, even if he himself had lost some of his influence in the Arab world due to his collaboration with the Nazis.* They were: the absolute refusal to recognize the Zionists, or accept their presence, or negotiate with them; and the establishment of a national Arab government over all of Palestine. Because Palestinian Arab aspirations — the priority of which went without saying — were well into their third decade of profound neglect at the hands of the West, these precepts had expanded and hardened into irrevocable Pan-Arab policy. They had become, in the Arab mind, as much of an *idée fixe* as the creation of a Jewish state had become an obsession in the Zionist mind.

Strongly influenced by what many objective observers felt was improper American and Zionist pressure, the United Nations General Assembly endorsed the partition of Palestine in November 1947, after the British announced their decision to terminate their mandate and withdraw their troops. In March of 1948 a provisional Jewish government, headed by David Ben-Gurion, established itself in Tel Aviv, the seaside capital city the Zionists had built next to the old Arab port of Jaffa during the preceding decades. In mid-May of that year the British high commissioner left Palestine and Britain began the wholesale withdrawal of its troops and civil administrators. On the same day the Jewish provisional government proclaimed that the area of Palestine provided the Jews by the UN partition was, from that moment on, the sovereign independent State of Israel.

* After the fall of the pro-German Iraqi regime in 1941, Husseini went to Berlin, where he broadcast anti-Jewish German propaganda to the Arab world. After the war he was captured and imprisoned in France, but escaped in 1946. He was given sanctuary in Cairo, where he resumed his anti-Zionist activities, this time as part of the Arab League.

At the very moment the proclamation was being read, Arab armies from Egypt, Lebanon, Iraq, Syria and Transjordan were advancing on the frontiers of the small state. The Arabs had refused to accept partition. Israel was about to be plunged into its first war. And the Middle East was about to move to center stage in the affairs of the world.

# PART THREE

# 17.

# HISTORY: *The Arabs — III*

ALTHOUGH THEY CALLED IT THE WAR OF INDEPENDENCE, to the Jews it was a war of survival — if not as a people, at least as a state — against a vastly more numerous force of Arabs. Nevertheless the Israelis possessed a clear superiority in morale, in training, in organization and, most of all, in motivation. Funded and armed largely by private interests in the United States, they not only prevailed over the Arabs, but occupied considerably more territory than had been allotted to them under the UN Partition Resolution.

The Arabs perceived it as a war of justice and self-determination. Their ideological objections to partition had their roots, of course, in three decades of subservience to Western expediency and in their own frustrated nationalist strivings. On the more practical level their objections were territorial and demographic. Up to the time of partition, the Jewish population of Palestine possessed just over 5.5 percent of the land, while the Arabs owned almost 95 percent. The partition plan adopted by the UN expanded the territory to be held by the Jews to 56.5 percent, while shrinking Arab territory to 43 percent — this in spite of the fact that in 1947 there were more than twice as many Arabs living in Palestine (1,327,000) than there were Jews (608,000). Even had the Arabs given some consideration to the acceptance of the idea of the partitioning of Palestine into separate Jewish and Arab states — and some moderates among the leadership did in fact propose that such consideration be given — the division of land under the UN partition was in their view balanced grossly in favor of the Jews. To accept such a partition would have been simply another knuckling under to unfair and unjust Western dictates.

In addition to territorial considerations, the Arabs viewed partition as illegal under international law. One of the fundamental tenets of the United Nations Charter was the defense of the right of a people to seek and obtain self-determination. The Arabs had been seeking such self-determination in the form of an independent Pan-Arab state since the First World War. Their aspirations had been shunted aside by the European powers under the League of Nations; instead, the groundwork had been laid for a conglomerate of separate Arab nations whose respective boundaries were to be drawn by big-power fiat.

There had, for instance, been no Lebanese "people"; The Lebanon had been part of Syria; the Lebanese people, a distinctly Arab people, had been created by the post–World War I parceling up of the Arab world by the Allies. Once created, the Lebanese eventually achieved national self-determination. Moreover, in religious coloration, Lebanon was approximately half-Christian and half-Muslim, with a Druze minority. Yet Lebanon had not been partitioned into two separate states, Christian and Muslim. Or into three, Christian, Muslim and Druze. It was allowed to develop instead into a unified Christian-Muslim-Druze federation. This was a case of Arab self-determination under the letter and spirit of the United Nations Charter, which representatives from Lebanon had helped write.

Why shouldn't the same principles apply to Palestine? the Arabs argued. Palestine, too, although part of Greater Syria for centuries, had been created as a separate entity by the Allies after World War I. At the time of its creation the population was much more overwhelmingly Arab than Jewish — about 644,000 Arabs to about 56,000 Jews. Lebanon, Syria, Iraq — all had been artificially carved out of the prospective Pan-Arab state, but all the Arabs of these territories had eventually achieved self-determination, if only after long struggles against European covetousness. Why not the Palestinians?

Because of the Jews, was the obvious reply. The Jews had a claim on the land.

But the Jewish claim was a religious one. The Jews — the Zionists, to be more precise — had no legal claim. The Zionists were Europeans. Their cultural and anthropological roots went back to strictly European and western Asian origins. There was absolutely no biological or anthropological connection between the progenitors of European Jewry — the Khazars —

and the ancient Hebrew tribes that had invaded the land of Canaan. The Jewish claim was in reality no different than claims European Christians might make, yet Christians were not demanding an independent nation in Palestine (except, of course, Arab Christians, who were seeking an Arab, not a Christian, nation). The Jews of Europe had no more legal or rightful national claim to an inch of Palestinian soil than they had to soil in Uganda or Argentina — other places where it had earlier been proposed that a Jewish national home be established.

If the Jews wished to live as a religious minority in a Palestinian Arab state — much as the Druzes did in Lebanon and Syria and as the Copts did in Egypt — well, all right, such was in the realm of Arab acceptability. But the United Nations' establishment of a Zionist Jewish nation on Arab soil and in the midst of an overwhelming majority of Arab people — Muslims, Christians and Jews alike, for the indigenous Jews of the Arab world were in language and culture Arab — was a clear violation of the UN's principles on the self-determination of peoples indigenous to specific lands. The UN had acted, again, out of Western expediency, correcting one injustice (the persecution of European Jewry) by inflicting another (the further disenfranchisement of Arabs and the thwarting of Arab self-determination).

Although the arguments advanced by both sides were based on moral and legal questions, the conflict itself was carried out principally in the political and military realms. And although the Arabs, morally and legally, seemed to have the advantage, politically and militarily they were destined to be the losers.

Two things militated against them. One was that on the world political stage they were neophytes. Having evolved out of a culture which had for so long made no distinction between political and religious institutions and ideas, there was little in the way of an experienced political infrastructure within the Arab alliance that could plan, execute, and sustain a united political program to counter the maneuverings of Israel, which was steeped in Western political sophistication, and its big-power sponsors. Despite the fact that the Arabs were ideologically united, they lacked the political machinery and organization needed to integrate and advance the political goals of the various Arab states that had committed themselves to the fight. Still in a relatively primitive state of religion-as-politics, they conducted their side of the war against the new Israeli intruder as a *jihad*, the psychology of which was that it was unthinkable for Muslims to surrender their land to infidels.

But this psychology had been diluted during the centuries of Ottoman rule, and further so by the splitting up of the Arab Muslim world into separate national units. There no longer existed the overpowering psychological fealty to Palestinian land on the part of those Arabs who had national identities of their own — Syrian, Egyptian, Iraqi and the like. Holy-war psychology, in other words, no longer worked in a world in which wars were political, not religious. Zionism was a political nationalism in the guise of a religious movement; but Arab nationalism was still a religious movement in the guise of a political one.

Thus, despite their superiority of numbers, the Arabs were no match for the Israelis. They had on their side only moral righteousness and religious fervor. These may have been the very qualities that had enabled their forebears to conquer the Middle East in the seventh and eighth centuries; but in a world where political necessity rather than moral righteousness and religious belief defined the nature of temporal events, they were useless.

The second force that militated against them derived from the first. The qualities that had glorified virgin Arab Islam — its flexible, nondoctrinaire principles — had been perverted by seven centuries of Turkish domination into a rigid theology that permeated every area of Arab life and hindered the evolution of modern social and political forms. Rather than progressing with the passage of time out of the tribal values of their ancestors, as other societies had done, the Arabs remained mired in them. Thus they not only had no access to modern political sophistication, they also were instinctively forced to conduct their intranational lives — one Arab state with another — on terms that were much closer to pre-Islamic tribal models than to modern geopolitical ones. This led to a continued pattern of internecine tension and bickering among various Arab leaderships that made practical and effective unity in the Pan-Arab nationalist movement an impossibility. The establishment, finally, of a group of independent Arab nations did not mean that these nations stepped with parity into the world of advanced, politically experienced nations. Rather, they became microcosms of the earlier Arab tribal world, with each nation-tribe vying with the others for superiority and honor, struggling to become the "peer among peers."

Waving the banner of Pan-Arab unity and crying "Into the sea with the Zionist infidels" on the one hand, while on the other distrustfully jockeying among themselves for position and power, the leaders of the various Arab states arrayed against Israel were working at extreme cross purposes. They would continue in this pattern over the next two decades, thereby securing Israel's sovereignty in a way that no outside force possibly could. The failure of the Arabs against the Jews in 1948, so dramatic when compared to their bombastic and extravagantly bloodthirsty propaganda at the time, left a permanent residue of embitterment in the Middle East — not only between the Arabs and the Israelis, but among the Arabs themselves.

By 1949 it became obvious to the Arabs that the war was too costly and unprofitable to continue. The rivalries between the Arab states made it possible for Israel to reach separate armistice agreements with them through UN intermediation. In the truce negotiations of 1949 Israel was in a stronger position than on the day of its creation, not only because of its military victories, and not only because of its territorial enlargement,* but because in March of that year the Security Council of the United Nations voted 9 to 1 to admit Israel as a member of the UN. The dream of the fathers of Zionism had finally been realized. The Zionists had produced a sovereign and independent Jewish nation in Palestine. Now they were formally recognized as such before the bar of world opinion. All Arab arguments about the legality or morality of Israel had become, at least from the Jewish point of view, moot.

That, in many people's view, should have ended it. But of course it didn't. The world was unfamiliar with the Arab ethic. No wrong could ever be allowed to go unrighted. The Arabs retired behind their own frontiers to lick their wounds and stew in the sour juices of collective shame.

* During the war Israel annexed a considerable portion of the land that had been apportioned to the Palestinian Arabs under the UN partition. At war's end there was still no Palestinian state. Most of the remaining UN-assigned Palestinian territory along the Jordan River was kept by Transjordan, whose British-led army had occupied it and whose king, Abdullah, eventually incorporated it into his own domain and renamed the whole the Hashemite Kingdom of Jordan.

# 18.

# HISTORY: *Egypt*

EGYPT HAS FOR MORE THAN A CENTURY been the bellwether of Arab attitudes, the symbol of Arab values, the embodiment of Arab polarities. The irony of this resides in the fact that Egypt is anthropologically the least Arab of all the Arabic-speaking nations of the Middle East. This traditional position of leadership is due not so much to Egypt's Arabness, then, as it is to its geographical placement at the heart of Arabdom, to its early and extensive linkage to the world beyond the Middle East, to the size of its population, and more recently to its relatively worldly political and economic institutions.

The long period between the end of Islam's golden age and the beginning of the nineteenth century was for Egypt an era of progressive decline. Bypassed by European trade, neglected by the Ottoman Empire and corrupted by the Mamluk dynasties, it had become, culturally and economically, a stagnant backwater.

The history of modern Egypt began in 1805 with the rule of Muhammad Ali, the Turko-Albanian officer who had helped the Ottomans repel the Napoleonic invasion and who later crushed the first Wahhabi takeover of Arabia. In destroying Egypt's Mamluk dynasty, Ali established a dynasty of his own, one which committed itself to the reform and modernization of Egypt's medieval social institutions within an Islamic context and without Western influence.

Under this dynasty an intellectual awakening occurred. Autocracy was seen as contrary to Islamic doctrines of equality and humility. Ali and his successors fostered the communication of ideas through print and education by establishing a network of elementary and secondary schools in which children were indoctrinated in the application of pure Islamic ideals to Egyptian life. Intellectual life was further stimulated by Egyptians who were sent to Europe to study and by foreign schools, mostly missionary in nature, that were opened in Egypt. Cairo gradually became the intellectual center of the nineteenth-century Arabic-speaking world. Out of all the renewed mental activity that took place, there emerged a revival of the Arab language (which the Turks and Mamluks had devitalized) and a strong Egyptian nationalist fervor based on liberal and humanistic ideas.

However, although enlightened for its time, the Ali dynasty was not without its faults. The repression of ideas that came into serious conflict with Islam was usually brutal, and in order to retain its power in the face of some of the more impatient revolutionary movements that sprang up, the dynastic rulers often reverted to the most fundamental forms of Ottoman oppression. Islam was still the central organizing factor of all life, and any breaches of Islamic laws or traditions were dealt with summarily. Nevertheless, once begun, the combination of education and intellectual activity soon outstripped efforts to keep a clamp on nonorthodox ideas, and Egypt became the center of revolutionary economic and political impulses within Arabdom.

The Ali dynasty also brought considerable material progress to Egypt. The wide-scale cultivation and export of cotton, which revolutionized the Egyptian agrarian economy, was introduced. A modern irrigation system was developed which extended the fertility of the Nile valley. Foreign capital investment was encouraged, making possible the building of the Suez Canal, the development of up-to-date shipping ports, the laying of railroads, and the introduction of modern municipal facilities — waterworks, sewer systems, lighting and mass transit facilities. European banking methods and institutions began replacing antiquated commercial practices. Cotton-spinning and cigarette-making enterprises became the models for the establishment of other industries.

The very achievements of the Ali dynasty contributed to its downfall. First, after destroying the corrupt ruling class of Mamluk feudal landowners, Ali and his successor-sons merely replaced it with another. They created a new privileged class of landowning gentry that took over the political and economic life of Egypt and ran it with not much less financial corruption, exploitation and oppression of the Egyptian masses than had the Mamluks. With the powerful influx of Western political ideas into the native Egyptian consciousness, conditions grew ripe for internal resentment. The Ali dynasty was, after all, a Turkish one still, and although the standard of life was improving for some Egyptians, especially those who were able to ease their way into the khedival* bureaucracy, the majority still suffered from the effects of feudal government. Thus, by 1870, under the reign of Muhammad Ali's grandson Khedive Ismael, Egypt was aboil with conflicting impulses symbolized by Egyptian peasant resentment against increasingly harsh and oppressive Turko-Egyptian rule.

Second, modernization had opened Egypt to Western economic exploitation well before the Egyptian people were able to acquire the means with which to protect themselves from the economic and social ills that were the concomitants of European penetration. Early nineteenth-century Europe itself had been the center of ruthless economic exploitation of the masses by the capitalist elite, but by the latter part of the century humanitarian movements had ameliorated their plight to some degree through social legislation, trade unions and other progressive institutions. Such social and economic ideas had not yet developed in Egypt. Hence European exploitation had a free rein; it was dependent only on the cooperation of the Egyptian ruling class, which of course found an expedient source for its own further enrichment through such cooperation. The situation created further conditions conducive to the development of an insurrectionary mood among the general populace.

Events came to a head at the beginning of the 1880s. The Turko-Egyptian ruling class itself had been maneuvered and exploited by sophisticated European financiers to the point where much of the Egyptian economy was under Europe's direct control and the government of Khedive Ismael was on the verge of financial disaster. At the same time a crisis was brewing within the khedival army, where a group of lower-ranking Egyptian officers was expressing discontent with the discrimination directed at them by higher-ranking Turkish and Albanian officers who were members of the ruling caste and who had achieved their positions through privilege rather than merit.

The leader of the disgruntled officers was Ahmed Arabi, the son of a local sheikh and a man who personified the whole of the Arabic-speaking Egyptian peasantry. Arabi and his group were originally concerned merely with mili-

---

* In 1867 the Ottoman sultan bestowed the title of *khedive* — a Turko-Persian word meaning Prince — on the rulers of Egypt. This replaced the title *pasha*, which had been used to indicate the governing representative of the Ottoman sultanate. Thereafter, pasha became an honorary title bestowed by the khedives on those wealthy landowners who ruled various Egyptian territories on behalf of the khedivate.

tary discrimination, but they soon expanded their focus to take in the entire structure of inequity between the corrupt minority ruling class and the Egyptian majority. Impelled by socialist and nationalist currents that had seeped down from Europe, the dissident spirit of the Egyptian officers was quickly transformed into a social and political revolutionary movement designed to overthrow the khedivate and replace it with a purely Egyptian government that would, theoretically, institute some form of democratic order.

The revolution failed, but it served as the template for all future attempts by the Egyptians to throw off non-Egyptian rule. Fighting broke out in 1881. When Britain, the heaviest European investor in Egypt, recognized that if successful the revolt of Arabi would seriously compromise its economic interests (especially the Suez Canal), it sent an army into the country in 1882 to put it down. Thereafter Britain remained in Egypt as an occupying power, administering the government under a series of British viceroys, for the next fifty-four years.

The long-term British occupation had two major contrasting effects. First, British rule brought order and efficiency to Egypt and at the same time eliminated much of the oppressive practices of the khedivate (which remained intact as a puppet government). Governmental finances were put on a sound basis, disciplinary practices were modernized, health and sanitation were greatly improved. Business flourished, the influx of foreign capital resumed, and agricultural and industrial enterprise expanded greatly.

Superficially, then, Egypt prospered. But its prosperity was largely confined to the ruling-class survivors of Arabi's brief revolt. The British were not concerned with bringing about revolutionary changes in the social order. They were merely interested in maintaining it while purging it of its worst abuses, so that revolutionary movements would have as little as possible to feed on and their own economic interests would remain secure.

Although social conditions improved, the balance of power and wealth in Egypt remained in the hands of the traditional upper merchant and land-owning classes. It has always been the nature of advanced colonial governments to support and sustain the native ruling classes of less advanced societies under their domination, for it is through these classes that the colonial regimes exercise their control over the people. However, it is likewise true that colonial rule invariably introduces advanced social and political ideas into the colonized societies. These ideas are contradictory to the more archaic ideas that produced the social philosophy and structure through which the existing native ruling classes emerged and sought to sustain their position and power. This has always been the inherent contradiction of imperialism and colonialism, and it is the fundamental seed of revolution and nationalism.

The process had already taken hold in Egypt under the semicolonial rule of the Turks. Its first manifestation was the Arabi revolt of 1881. With the British in control, it merely accelerated and expanded. By 1900 a new Egyptian nationalist movement under the leadership of Mustafa Kemal was well established.* Kemal organized a nationalist party whose slogan became "Egypt for the Egyptians" and whose goal was the absolute independence of Egypt (and the Sudan to the south, which was also under British colonial rule).

By the time World War I broke out in 1914, the Egyptian nationalist movement had spread throughout rural and urban Egypt and had produced an articulate and popular new leader, Saad Zaghlul, who, although of peasant origin, had become a high official in the Ministry of Education.

Egypt was, theoretically at least, still subject to Ottoman control at the outbreak of the war. But practically speaking it was under British colonial rule, and since the Ottomans were allied with Germany, Britain unilaterally proclaimed a wartime protectorate over Egypt to ensure the security of the Suez Canal.

Egypt remained relatively quiet during the war years, but the Egyptians themselves, chafing under stricter British military occupation, didn't. They grew restive and more deeply responsive to Zaghlul and his nationalist movement. The determination and ardor of the nationalists were in turn intensified by proclamations made by the Allies about guaranteeing the rights of small nations and pursuing the ideals of self-determination for all peoples once victory over the Axis powers was achieved. The Egyptian nationalists became aware toward the end of the war of British commitments to the Arabs of the Hejaz concerning an independent Pan-Arab state. As soon as the war was over Zaghlul and his followers established an organization called "Wafd al-Misri," or the Egyptian Delegation, to present demands regarding

---

* A distinction should be made here between Egyptian nationalism and Arab nationalism. The latter had not yet taken any form except for the idea, still in its germination stage, of Hussein Ibn Ali and his four sons living as "guests" of Sultan Hamid in Constantinople. Their notion of Arab nationalism — of a Pan-Arab nation — was considerably more religious and kingly than the idea of Egyptian nationalism, which was largely political in nature. Indeed, at this time Egyptians in no way considered themselves Arabs. The neophyte Arab nationalists doubtless received much of their inspiration from the Egyptians, whom they too recognized as a separate people; when the Pan-Arab state was later being planned, Egypt was not included as a part of it.

Egyptian independence to the British government and the Paris Peace Conference.

The British were not going to give up Egypt so easily, however; their stake in the land was more enormous than ever and they had little trust in the Egyptian ability to independently protect it. They refused to allow the Wafd al-Misri mission to leave the country. When this refusal was met with widespread and violent protest demonstrations, the British detained Zaghlul and three other leading nationalists in Malta. Later, when the United States government assured Britain that it would not support the claims of the Egyptians, Zaghlul and his group were allowed to go to Paris. There the moderators of the peace conference denied them recognition. These events made national heroes out of Zaghlul and his collaborators. In many Arab quarters, resentment toward England turned into intense hatred.

Agitation increased until finally the British, in 1922, agreed to terminate their protectorate and to recognize Egypt as an independent sovereign state. However, the terms of the proposed recognition were such that Egypt would have ended up as nothing but a satellite of Britain. When the nationalist leaders protested, they were seized and once again exiled. The British then declared the protectorate at an end and took the existing sultan, Fuad, and made him king.

These temporary expediencies failed to solve the Egyptian problem, for British troops remained in Egypt to shore up the new monarchy and guarantee the security of British investment. In 1924, after more nationalist demonstrations, Britain's puppet Egyptian government adopted a constitution under which, in the first countrywide election guaranteed by it, the nationalist Wafd party won a large majority. In 1924 Saad Zaghlul became the first prime minister in a parliamentary government modeled on the English system. But still the problem of Egypt was not over, for differences between the British and the new Egyptian government over the Sudan, and the continuing presence of British troops on Egyptian soil, continued to keep matters at an impasse. But at least Egypt had a measure of independence and self-determination. It was the first Arabic-speaking land to achieve them. It was a beginning.

It was, at best, a murky and uncertain beginning. During the many centuries of Turkish-Mamluk-Albanian rule over Egypt, the Egyptian character had become thoroughly infused by two fundamental values that should have been contradictory in nature but which in fact often complemented one another: spiritual (Islamic) authoritarianism and material corruption. In this the Egyptians — or any other Arab society, for that matter — were not substantially different from most societies that had evolved elsewhere under other religious banners. The impulse to corruption and authoritarianism is certainly not unique to any one society of the world; it is merely the manner in and degree to which they are pursued that distinguishes them.

As Egypt gained a kind of semi-independence in the 1920s all sorts of internal struggles were born, most of which were generated not so much from a concern for social reform and democratization as from the specifically Egyptian instincts of authoritarianism and corruptibility. Wealth still meant privilege in Egypt, and the customary road to wealth had always been through corruption. Authority meant power as well, and the route to authority had always been through Islam. The nationalist movement that had culminated in Egyptian independence, then, was not a revolution; it was merely a transfer of wealth and power from one group to another, with the means by which both were attained and sustained remaining more or less the same.

After the death of Zaghlul in 1927, Mustafa Nahas, his successor as leader of the Wafd party, became premier. The Wafdists consolidated their political power under Nahas and became representatives of the traditional Egyptian establishment as the old corrupt economic and authoritarian religious ruling classes began to back them. Nahas compromised with the British, negotiating in 1936 a twenty-year treaty that enabled Egypt to become a member of the League of Nations in exchange for the British right to maintain a naval base at Alexandria and a military force of ten thousand in the Suez Canal Zone. Otherwise, British military occupation of Egypt was ended. On the surface, it seemed that the Anglo-Egyptian treaty would leave Egypt free to concentrate on the solution of its internal social problems, but by this time the Wafdists had become so preoccupied with extending their authority and lining their pockets that the needs of the Egyptian masses were generally ignored.

The situation prior to World War II was exacerbated by two further elements. One was the succession to the Egyptian throne* of the sixteen-year-old King Farouk upon the death of the British-appointed Fuad. At first

* The office of king in Egypt was, as I've already indicated, a creation of the British colonial government, but it was not abolished once Egypt gained its independence. Rather, since it was an extension of the earlier sultanate and therefore had important religious meaning for Egyptians, it was continued.

broadly popular, the adolescent king early on demonstrated a taste for decidedly non-Islamic pursuits.

But even more politically unsettling was the growing strife to the northeast between Arabs and Jews in the Palestine of the British mandate. Again, Egyptians did not yet identify themselves as Arabs. But they were increasingly cognizant of their Arab heritage. *And* they were Muslims. This sense of religious brotherhood was buttressed by the appeals of a large core of Arab nationalists who had exiled themselves from the British Palestinian and French Syrian mandates in the wake of their failed dream of a post–World War I Pan-Arab nation and who constantly reminded the Egyptian masses of their common Arab inheritance. It did not take long for Egyptian emotions to become aroused with regard to the Zionization of Palestine. These feelings were even more aroused by the fact that it was under British sponsorship that the Zionists were making their inroads. The Egyptians were thus easily persuaded that Palestine was another Muslim land in danger of falling victim to Western Christian (therefore infidel) imperialism and being handed over to infidel Jews.

It should not have been surprising, in view of all this, that Egypt displayed little enthusiasm for the British cause at the outbreak of World War II. Even when Egypt was invaded by the Italians and Germans, the Egyptians did not look upon the Axis powers as their enemies. Egypt, like Saudi Arabia, remained neutral until victory for the Allies became certain and an invitation to the then-forming United Nations hinged upon a declaration of war against the Axis.

World War II, however, broke the back of the two institutions within Egypt that had come to mean the most to the Egyptian masses: the Wafd party and the monarchy. The youthful King Farouk's flirtations with the Axis powers brought a force of British troops into Cairo in 1942. In surrounding the Royal Palace and forcing Farouk to publicly disclaim his Fascist sympathies, the British proved that they still had the last word in Egypt's affairs. Britain's intervention was a violation of Egypt's neutrality, and Farouk's capitulation was a profound humiliation to those avid Egyptian nationalists who had been living under the myth of Egyptian self-determination. During the war, moreover, Farouk's scandalous personal behavior — public drinking, gambling, wenching — deeply offended Egypt's pious Muslims. The enthusiastic acclaim he had received upon his accession was replaced by contemptuous unpopularity.

The esteem in which the Wafd party had been held was shattered when one of its leaders, disgusted with the corruption and graft that permeated its upper ranks, published a documented exposé of Wafdist financial wrongdoing.

The war shut down most of Egypt's foreign trade, and by its end the Egyptian economy was in a shambles. Whatever economic gains and social reforms had been achieved in the thirties were dissipated; the country was back at the point it had been decades earlier, with the small avaricious upper classes running things and the large peasant and petit bourgeois classes enduring deprivation and bitterness.

By 1945, then, Egypt was a political vacuum, with the monarchy powerless, the Wafdist establishment severely discredited, and civil discontent widespread. Into this vacuum stepped an organization that had been evolving within the religious-reactionary fabric of Egyptian society. Called in Arabic "el-Ikhwan el-Muslimin," it came to be known in English as the Muslim Brotherhood. Devoted to throwing off the evil effects of Western culture upon Islam and remolding the Egyptian way of life according to strict Islamic precepts, the Muslim Brotherhood had been founded by Hassan Banna, a scholarly and dynamic Muslim schoolteacher, in 1928. Like many another charismatic political leader, Banna was the product of a profoundly maladjusted society seething with social, economic and ideological discord. Driven by an extreme religious zeal and a love for power, he had managed by 1945 to transform his religious society into a powerful political movement with a broad base among the discontented and somewhat bewildered Egyptian masses.

Once the war was over the Brotherhood made its move. It had developed a well-armed clandestine paramilitary organization which it used to assassinate establishment political leaders, terrorize the ruling class, and whip up mass sympathy during the immediate postwar years. So powerful did the Brotherhood become that Banna and his followers came very close to taking over the country in the aftermath of the humiliating rout of Egyptian forces by the newly created State of Israel in 1948. Only internal differences within the Brotherhood prevented it. Thereafter the Brotherhood's influence waned. But it had exacerbated tensions within Egypt and fostered an atmosphere of intense revolutionary discontent.

Also contributing to the discontent was the postwar reaction to Zionism. Zionism was no direct threat to Egypt, but there was already an in-built abhorrence to it as a consequence of native Muslim brotherly empathy and increasing Egyptian Anglophobia. The Egyptian political machine found it an easy matter indeed to inflame mass emotions against Israel. Such a strategy tended to unite public opinion and to mask the political establishment's own failings.

The strategy backfired, however, when the well-equipped Egyptian army was repelled by the comparatively ill-equipped Israelis. As a result of this defeat, which was directly attributable to the inherent corruption of the military establishment — where privilege, as in the old days, went before merit — and to the ineptness and indirection of the political leadership, all public faith in Egypt's governmental institutions was shattered.

After the Muslim Brotherhood's bid for power was short-circuited in 1949, Egypt slipped into a state of near-anarchy. Unable to take the rage of their humiliation out on Israel, the Egyptians turned it on the British forces that had remained under the terms of the 1936 Anglo-Egyptian Treaty. Armed clashes between bands of Egyptian nationalists and British troops took place along the Suez Canal and escalated into steady guerrilla warfare. Demonstrations and violence in Cairo and Alexandria continued sporadically throughout 1951 as a coalition of nationalists, the Muslim Brotherhood, socialists and communists agitated against the continuing British presence on Egyptian soil.

Finally, in October of 1951, in order to placate the populace, the Egyptian government unilaterally proclaimed the Anglo-Egyptian Treaty to be over and ordered all British military forces out of Egypt. It was a desperate and daring move, for the British might well have responded by sending in more troops to enforce the treaty, which had five years to run. But after their dismal experiences in Palestine, they were utterly tired of the Middle East. They went quietly, entrusting the Suez Canal to international administration.

If the Egyptian government expected this to end matters, however, it was wrong. Still Wafdist in its majority, and still suffering from the deep stain of corruption, its ouster of Britain unleashed an orgy of celebration that was quickly turned upon the government itself by dissident groups seeking its overthrow. In riots in Cairo in January 1952, over seventy-five people were killed and much British property was destroyed. Anti-Wafd feeling intensified during the months that followed while martial law ruled the land. Finally, on the night of July 23, a group of dissident army officers who had quietly been plotting for some time to restore Egyptian dignity and balance staged a coup d'état. Included among them was an impassioned colonel who, as a junior officer, had been witness to the Israeli rout of the Egyptian army four years before. His name was Gamal Abdel Nasser.

The group of army men called themselves the Officers' Revolutionary Council. Their coup was successful, but their reign over Egypt was at first tenuous as other aspirants to power schemed against them. In order to retain their foothold in the government they quickly assumed dictatorial powers, abolishing all political parties, scrapping the constitution of 1923, dissolving the Muslim Brotherhood, and ruling, often brutally, by military fiat.

At the head of the junta was another colonel, Muhammad Naguib, who became president and prime minister when the Revolutionary Council terminated the monarchy and proclaimed Egypt a republic in June of 1953. Named deputy prime minister and minister of the interior was Colonel Nasser.

In 1954 dissension arose within the ranks of the junta between supporters of Naguib and Nasser. The Naguibites were advocates of a moderate and only gradual reform of Egypt, while Nasser and his disciples were intent on carrying out immediate and extreme reforms. The differences were temporarily solved by Nasser's becoming head of the Revolutionary Council and prime minister, while Naguib retained the presidency, though with only nominal power.

Since that time, of course, Nasser rose to become a worldwide symbol of the Arab way of doing things in the international community of nations. At once a cautious tyrant and a daring politician, he early on evinced an ambition to become the leader of a united Pan-Arab nation stretching across the entire Middle East. Toward this end he uttered the rallying cry: "I am an Arab." It was a cry that transformed the Egyptian nationalism of the previous decades into a broadened Arab nationalism, and one that — much in the way John F. Kennedy's rhetorical *"Ich bin ein Berliner"* committed the United States to the defense of western Europe against "communist imperialism" — committed Egypt to the defense of all Arab lands against the assaults of "Western imperialism." Nasser's "I am an Arab" had the same emotional effect on the Arab masses as Kennedy's later *"Berliner"* utterance had on Europe, and his popularity throughout the Arab world zoomed.

Nasser's career has been recounted so often elsewhere that there is little need to devote space to it here. Suffice it to say that his sixteen years of dictatorial but popular rule left Egypt in much the same condition as when he started. The lot of the people improved somewhat, to be sure. And much of the corruption associated with earlier regimes disappeared. But Nasser created more problems than he solved, for Egypt and for the Arab world in general. It was only after his death in 1970, which brought an end to government by charisma, that Egypt took a pragmatic turn.

# 19.

# JOURNAL: *Anwar Al-Sadat*

IF POLITICS IS THE ART of the impossible, then Egyptian president Anwar Al-Sadat, assuming he's still in business when this book appears, must rank as one of the most accomplished political artists on the world stage. When Sadat succeeded Nasser upon the latter's death, few observers of the Middle East scene predicted a long political life expectancy. A supporter of Nasser during the 1954 split in the Officers' Revolutionary Council and a faithful but hardly influential functionary of the long Nasser regime, he had, it was believed, neither sufficient political experience nor personal acumen to survive the vagaries of Egyptian politics. Rising to power in the shadow of Nasser's legacy and personal charisma, he faced what seemed an insurmountable task.

Yet he succeeded. And as I traveled through the Middle East in 1974 I discovered that even the most politically sophisticated Arabs found it hard to believe; it was as if they didn't know what to make of an Arab leader who actually accomplished something in deed, not just in word.

Sadat's great accomplishment, of course, was the 1973 war against Israel. Although from a military point of view it proved to be far less than a victory, from a political perspective it was a triumph, for it extricated the Arabs from the political and diplomatic impasse created by the Six-Day War of 1967 and the subsequent war of attrition along the Suez Canal.

I wanted to ask Sadat about the 1973 war and what implications he thought it had for the future of the Middle East when I was ushered into his presence in the presidential summer residence at Alexandria shortly after he had entertained President Nixon. I had been granted a ten-minute interview, but happily the discussion went on for almost an hour.

Sadat is an urbane man with a taste for British tailoring. He has a slight but athletic physique, and his face is an interesting one, much more so than Nasser's. It is extremely dark-hued, with a sharply receding brow that merges into a smooth, balding scalp which bears the mark of the *sabiba*, a coin-shaped indentation acquired by regular contact with the Muslim prayer mat. His brown eyes are wide-set but small, slightly feline and limpid. Prominent, high cheekbones accentuate his Oriental look. In repose his face reflects a certain prim and weary sadness, but when he smiles it comes alive, the generous gleam of blindingly white teeth beneath his British-officer moustache bathing his interlocutor in warmth. His voice, slightly hoarse and accented, is sincere. He is altogether a handsome man with an excess of natural charm (I almost said charisma). I wondered why he had remained in Nasser's shadow for so long — was that his only strong suit, charm?

One tends to be awed by the trappings of power. Certainly one can easily be overimpressed upon meeting Sadat in the rich damasks and satins of his surroundings, with squads of retainers bowing and scraping about. Yet I was determined to ask questions, hard questions. Constant telephone interruptions, with Sadat switching to Arabic, punctuated the interview. He seemed very capable at shifting his attention back and forth. He had, of course, been briefed on the purpose of my visit by people whom he trusted and who had helped me to obtain the interview. After a few brief amenities, I said that I hoped he did not mind being asked what might appear to him to be some rude questions.

"Such as?" he said with a sly look.

"Well, you are not well known in the West. We now read a great deal about how you functioned under President Nasser. About the strong-arm methods of the Nasser regime — the jailings of political enemies, the tortures, the executions." Sadat's expression did not change. "Were you part of that?" I concluded.

He laughed heartily. "That is what always amuses me about you Americans. You expect us to act all the time like Americans. I see no need to explain or defend what we did or did not do. We are Egyptians, and we do what is necessary for Egypt."

There was no rancor in his answer, yet he had evaded the question. I was about to rephrase it when he held up a finger. "Why is it so important for

Americans to know these things?" he said, still good-naturedly. "You have your ways and we have our ways."

He had recently extracted a promise from President Nixon for a quarter of a billion dollars in immediate financial aid and the construction of a nuclear energy facility in Egypt. I turned my answer on this. "I think Americans want to know these things because of the recent aid commitments you have received. There are, as you probably know, rumblings in Washington about giving aid to a government that may indulge in, well, practices that seem to Americans to be a bit on the despotic side."

He nodded, showing now a hint of anger. "Don't tell me about that," he said. "Americans do not care a bit where their government sends their money. The proof is that your country has given billions in aid to governments that are far more tyrannical than you are hinting us to be." He waved a finger. "National hypocrisy is an essential part of diplomacy. Let us not have a discussion about who, about which peoples are more virtuous, or more righteous, than others. We all know about your famous American idealism here. The trouble is, you are idealistic only when it suits you. When it suits you to be realistic, even if it means violating this idealism, you are realistic. But we are the same. If we have trouble getting this money, it will not be because of what we are as Egyptians, but because we are enemies of Israel."

"Speaking of realism," I said, "are you a realistic man?"

"How do you mean that?"

"Well, I think this is another thing that concerns the West. Many Westerners have come to see Egypt, perhaps the Arab world in general, as unrealistic. The constant war against Israel. The seeming inability — in the past, at least — to carry out your threats, your ambitions. You might say that this has all been bad for your image . . ."

"Ah, yes. Image."

"But the events of last October seem to have changed that image somewhat. What I want to know is, were the events of last fall a kind of accident, or do they really mean that the Arabs have found a new way to go about things, a more realistic way?"

"I should be insulted by your question, for I suspect it is based on the old Western condescension of us," he said. "But I shall not be, for I think you mean well. My answer is that in Arab terms we have never been unrealistic. From the Western viewpoint perhaps we have, but then, from our viewpoint, you are the unrealistic ones. Why? Because for all these years you have supported the existence of this foreign Zionist state in our midst. It is not only unrealistic. When you stop to think about it, it is insane."

Sadat narrowed his eyes at me. "I am told that this book you write will try to present the Arab case fairly."

"That's correct," I said.

"But I am sure you are a sympathizer of Israel, are you not?"

"I can't say I sympathize with Zionism, if that's what you mean. But I had nothing to do with the creation of Israel. Forgetting for the moment whether the establishment of Israel was legally right or wrong, the fact is, well, it is there. It seems to me that, legally, even morally, once a state has been given existence by international sanction, that existence cannot be taken away. I realize there are many fine lines of argument on this question, from all sides, but I think the ultimate moral and legal imperative is that Israel cannot now be denied her existence. Which seems to be what the Arab case is ultimately all about."

"Ah, but I think you will find that the Arab world is no longer concerned about the existence of Israel. We only object to the way in which it chooses to exist. That is what we fight for. To make Israel observe the international laws of territorial sovereignty."

"You mean the Sinai, the Golan, Jerusalem," I said.

"That is correct."

"Well look, Mr. President, that's really what I meant by realism. I mean, the two sides in this conflict each seem to have painted themselves into an ideological corner . . ."

"Painted . . ."

"It's an expression, sorry. They, you — the Arabs on the one hand, the Israelis on the other — have so hardened your views of each other that there seems no room for compromise. Now, the Israelis are utterly convinced that it is your ultimate intention to destroy them completely. Thus, from their point of view, any concession they make is tantamount to cooperating with you in achieving that intention. From all the polemics that have come from the Arab side over the last twenty-five years, one can hardly blame them. Can you?"

"Their fears cannot be my concern."

"All right, I understand that. And your fears cannot be their concern. But look, I really think we should avoid this kind of discussion. I didn't come here to defend the Israeli cause. Nor do I expect you to defend the Arab cause. I know that in your view it needs no defense. What I'm trying to learn is . . ."

"You said something there," he interjected. "You said our fears cannot be their concern. But that is precisely what is at the center of this whole struggle of ours. You must remember, the Arabs did nothing to the Jews in the beginning. What was done to the Jews was done by others. And then the Jews came here among us with the cry of Zionism on their lips. I have studied Zionism very thoroughly, and there can be no doubt that their intention was to rid this so-called biblical land of theirs of all its Arab inhabitants and make it their own. And in many respects this is what they did — at least to part of the land. Zionism will not rest until it has all of the land. Their ambitions are no secret. We see it every day. What they could not get with the help of the United Nations they try to get by conquest. Then they send their Jewish settlers into the annexed land to make it their own. This expansionism is the basic principle of Zionism. It is the Jews who started this business. It is the Jews who made the Arabs afraid, originally, by their tactics, by their Zionist manifestos. You should not say Arab fears cannot be their concern. Every fear that we have had about them, going back to the time they first began coming here, has come true . . ."

From there we spent about ten minutes raking over the past as Sadat divested himself of his views on Israel. (I have reproduced the substance of that part of our discussion earlier.) When he finally likened the Jews to Arabs and on that basis expressed his confidence in the future, I asked him what he thought the future held.

"You mean Israel?" he said.

"Israel, yes. But beyond that, what is Egypt's future? And what is the future of the entire Arab world?"

"Well, it is a very complex question. As for Israel, there can be no future until she decides to sit down and talk on a reasonable basis and renounce her expansionist ambitions . . ."

Here we go again, I thought. "But, sir, can we get away from these debating points? Can we talk in the language of people rather than in the language of governments. For instance, suppose some settlement is worked out. Is Egypt going to be willing to let it go at that?"

"I don't understand . . ."

"Will Egypt be prepared to allow Israel to exist? If a settlement is arrived at, even if it doesn't fulfill all the parties' demands, even if there is plenty of residual hatred and resentment left over, will Egypt accept the existence of Israel and stop collaborating in efforts to wipe her off the map?"

"As I said," he replied, "it is not our intention to wipe Israel off the map. It has been a difficult idea for Arabs to accept, but we are willing now to accept Israel and to coexist with her in peace — provided that certain conditions are fulfilled. This is something that I, as president of Egypt, want. This is something that I as an Arab want. I recognize that Israel is a reality. The damage has been done. We must learn to stop crying — how does the phrase go? — over spilled milk. We must clean up the table and put another glass of milk there. Do you understand me?"

I nodded.

"This is what I as an Arab want. However, I will not yield one more inch of Arab soil. We have seen what this mistake has caused us, and we will never make it again. And of course there can be no peace until the Palestinians have a nation of their own. These are the conditions of Arab acceptance of Israel."

"Yes, but you must admit," I said, "that there are dozens of different Arab spokesmen saying dozens of different things about Israel. How can Israel be sure that what you say is not just a smokescreen?"

"A smokescreen?"

"A disguise. A trap. What guarantees would they have that you — I don't particularly mean you personally, but the Arab world in general — will not then try to force them into further —"

"They will have international guarantees. You must remember, what happens here in the Middle East does not happen in an empty space. What happens here happens within a larger frame. We do not wish the big powers to go to war over us. That is why what I say is not a smokescreen. Also . . ." He held up a finger again. "Also, it is a well-known fact of history — the Jews . . ." And here he struggled for the right words, as if trying to ensure that I wouldn't misunderstand his meaning. ". . . the Jews, the Jewish people, they are . . . they are inevitably . . . a self-destructive people. Every few centuries they go through a form of . . . mass suicide!"

Was this the old European anti-Semitism in Arab garb? I shook my head. "I'm sorry, I don't know what you mean."

"It is true. We hear all this talk about Arab fanaticism, Arab pride, and we laugh. The real fanatics, the true victims of pride, have always been the Jews. Look at their history. Look at all the mass slaughters they have submitted themselves to. Rather than compromise with the Romans, they sat up there in Masada and signed a suicide pact. Through the centuries in Europe they brought about their destruction time and time again because they refused to fit into the landscape. What the Germans did to them — I don't say the Germans are not accountable, but the Jews did not exactly resist, did they?"

"I'm afraid that's a view of their history quite different from their view."

"It may be different," said Sadat, "but it is not wrong. And this gets back to your question about guarantees. We know that the Jews will go to the very end to preserve this state of theirs. You asked if I was a realist? Well, I will tell you this. When a state has an arsenal of nuclear bombs, and when its people have a history of committing mass suicide to defend a religious principle, then I am a realist."

"You're saying that the Israelis, if everything else was lost, would use nuclear weapons?"

"I am. Even if we were able to put them in a position where we could wipe them off the map, we know what would happen. They would not go down without trying to wipe us out with them. So you see, we do not wish to wipe them off the map. We only wish to make them respect our territorial rights and the territorial and civil rights of the Palestinians. And to restore the Palestinian refugees to their rightful place on the land."

My temptation was to say that all these problems about rights — territorial, national and otherwise — had been initiated in the first place not by the Israelis but by the Arabs. That in 1948, when Palestine was partitioned, Israel was the only country in the Middle East to recognize the Arab part as a Palestinian Arab state; it was the Arabs who refused to do so. And to say that when Israel was created, there was no such thing as a Palestinian refugee; the refugees were the consequence of Arab intransigence. But that, I knew, would produce only additional hairsplitting. I wasn't there to argue. And my time with Sadat had already gone well over the allotted ten minutes. I decided to get on to something else.

"Your praises are being sung quite loudly throughout the Arab world as a result of what you engineered last October. Even people in the West were impressed with the way you carried off the war, as I'm sure you know. In terms of the future, what do you think the war accomplished, aside from bolstering Arab confidence?"

"The war was necessary for one simple reason — to show the Israelis, and the West, that the Middle East is no longer subject to the myths of the past. I notice that there is this great agony in the West over all the Zionist soldiers who were killed, three thousand or so. Our people in New York tell us that every night there were displayed on American television these scenes of Israeli women screeching and fainting over the loss of their sons and husbands. Nothing about Egypt, though, eh? Again, we are pictured as the barbarians who care nothing about human life, while the Jews are pictured as the victims. This is one thing we fought the war for. To destroy those myths. To destroy the arrogance of the Jews, and destroy the support of that arrogance in America. For as long as that arrogance continues, there will never be peace here."

"Perhaps," I said, "the inattention paid to the Egyptian side is due to your censorship, and to the exaggerated claims you have made in past wars."

"Ah, but that is just the point. Do you think there is no censorship in Israel? Of course there is. They only let the world see what they want it to see. Very clever. We would like to do the same. But it is a hard struggle in the face of all the prejudice against us. So I have abolished our old censorship. Now, in the future we shall see if the American press reports *our* casualties honestly. If it shows our women and children in mourning. I myself lost my brother in the war. Do you think I celebrate? Do you think his wife celebrates? What makes the death of an Israeli soldier more tragic than the death of an Egyptian? 'Ah,' they tell us, 'the Israeli, he is a vital part of their tiny population, he is educated, he is a skilled worker, cultured, it is such a waste. But the Arab,' they say, 'the Arab soldier is illiterate, a grain of sand in a desert of people, unskilled, uneducated, a peasant, he is no loss to Egypt.' It is attitudes like this that we fight against. It is time for the Jews to stop trading off on their history. I find it disgusting the way they do this to enlist the sympathy of the West. They dishonor the memory of all those Jews who died in Europe. They must face the fact that they *are* a state, and not a dispossessed people. They must stop living in the past in this morbid way they do. They must realize that as a state they are not wandering, persecuted Jews, but a nation of Israelis. And as such, they are subject to the same risks as any other nation of people that engages in war. They are not Jews who get killed, they are Israelis — just as it is not Muslims or Copts or Druzes who get killed, but Egyptians, Syrians and Moroccans."

"May I ask you a somewhat personal question?" I said.

For the first time in our conversation Sadat looked at his watch. The hard edge of his intensity softened. He nodded.

"Do you feel any personal animosity toward the Jews?"

He thought for a moment, twirling the end-hairs of his moustache with his dark, graceful fingers. "I have no animosity against Jews as such," he finally said. "But Zionists, Israelis . . ." He shrugged. "I have heard how in America one is considered anti-Jewish — as you people say, anti-Semitic — if one is not sympathetic to Israel. I have never been able to understand this. That is what I like about your Secretary Kissinger. He apologizes for this. He knows how idiotic it is. He is a Jew. But he is not a man who is ashamed to be a Jew. I am sure that most American Jews are ashamed to be Jews, and this is why they succumb to the Zionist line. They cover their shame by trying to become more Jewish than the Israelis. No, I have no bad feelings toward the Jewish religion. Only the people. They kill my people."

"But that brings us back to point zero again," I said. "You kill their people."

"We kill Israelis and Zionists because they are Israelis and Zionists, not because they are Jews."

We were interrupted by an aide, who entered the room and spoke in Arabic to Sadat. He looked at his watch again. "One more question?" I said.

"I must meet a delegation from Beirut," he replied, shifting in his seat. "But go ahead, last question."

"Is there anything you would care to predict on the basis of your discussions with Mr. Kissinger and with other Arab leaders concerning how this entire matter is going to turn out? Do you anticipate another war, for instance?"

"Look, my friend, I am only one man. I must respond first and foremost to the wishes of my people. At this point, my people do not want or need another war. They are quite satisfied with what we have achieved — for now. We have used war to obtain a diplomatic breakthrough. When you stop to think about it, it was a cheap price to pay in order to get the issue resolved. But we can only be patient for a certain time. It is now the Israelis who must take action. Even for them, with three thousand* dead, it was cheap, because they now have the opportunity to live in peace. The war, you see, not only proved to them that they are no longer in a position to dictate the terms of their existence among us. It also got rid of their reactionary government and put in a more realistic leadership. And it brought the Palestinians around to the idea of a separate state of their own, rather than the old obsession of regaining Israel. So you see, the war achieved a great deal, at a very low cost. But the Israelis must move soon toward taking advantage of the door that has been opened. If they don't, then there will be more war. We are prepared to

* The actual figure was lower, according to official Israeli sources.

fight, and fight, and fight again. We do not want to, but we are prepared to. The next war will be even harder on Israel. This is not boasting. It will be harder on us as well. But we can go along much, much longer than Israel. It will be one of the great ironies of history. If we do wipe them out, it will be because they invited us to do so. The traditional situation has turned itself about. It is now Israeli pride and self-delusion against Arab realism . . ."

"Above all else, though, you are in a conciliatory mood?"

"I am for conciliation, yes. But, again, I caution you, I am only one man. And I am not a superman. I have given everything I could without being shot as a traitor to Egypt. I can make no more concessions, and to be frank, my friends in other Arab countries are growing bored with my pleas. They say, 'Eh, Sadat, you made this a good war, but you see, the Zionists did not learn from it. We must give them more war.' And I say, 'No, wait, a little more time.' And they answer, 'What time? They have had enough time.'"

Sadat rose and ushered me to the door of the large room. "One final item," I said. "I've heard much talk about how the Arab-Israeli conflict has become just one component of a larger Arab design to assume control of the industrialized world. Do you see this happening?"

"It is already happening."

"Well, I mean is there such a grand design, a secret one?"

"I don't know what is secret about it. If it is secret, it is because you in this industrialized world you talk about refuse to take your head out of the sand. Just as you have in the past, eh?"

"May I assume, then, that Egypt is part of it?"

"How can we be part of it? We have no oil to sell."

"In other ways."

"I expect that Egypt will be included in any blessings that come to the Arab world."

"As a reward?" I asked.

"As a reward?" Sadat repeated quizzically.

"For keeping tensions high?" I suggested, feeling a bit reluctant. "For justifying the economic maneuvers of the oil states."

Sadat took my impertinence in good form. "Ah, my friend," he said, "you give us Arabs too much credit now. When it comes to principles, we will unite in a common cause. But when it comes to money — well, that is another matter altogether."

# 20.

# HISTORY: *Syria*

EVEN MORE THAN EGYPT, Syria has been the most consistently belligerent and implacable of Israel's foes. The reasons for Syria's hostility are both similar to and markedly different from Egypt's. Egypt's opposition has been basically political and intellectual, with the emotions of the Egyptian people carefully incited by the Cairo regimes primarily for the purpose of sustaining and extending the power of those regimes. Syrian opposition has been basically sociological and visceral, and accounts — in part, at least — for the fact that since it gained its independence in 1946, Syria has been a rapidly unfolding kaleidoscope of many successive regimes.

Today's government, headed by General Hafez Al-Assad, is probably the most stable Syria has had in its nearly thirty years of sovereign existence. Its stability derives from its utterly contradictory character. It is at once a military dictatorship, a socialist party, an esoteric religious sect, a Pan-Arab movement, a family fief, a police state and a liberal political coalition. These contradictions to a very great extent have been produced by, and at the same time reflect, the diversity of Syrian society and the contrasts and conflicts that have for so long existed within it.

The Syria of today has existed in various forms since prebiblical times. Originally a desert buffer zone and battleground between empires along the western and eastern horns of the Fertile Crescent, its only distinctive asset was the town of Damascus (originally known as Esh Sham), which became during biblical times an important hub of caravan routes between East and West. Set in an oasis on the northern boundary of the great Arabian desert, it communicated naturally with the habitat of all the old Arab tribes in the heart of the peninsula. By the time of Islam, it was a well-settled commercial center with a predominantly Bedouin cultural coloration.

With the present-day claim of being the oldest continuously inhabited city in the world, Damascus became the center of Islamic (and Arab) power in the seventh century under Muawiya and his Ummayad successors. It was from here that the Islamic conquest of the Middle East and southern Europe was for the most part administered. With the spread of Islam, Damascus and its surrounding areas grew opulently rich from the vast sums which flowed into the Ummayad treasury from all parts of the Arab Empire, a fact that is reflected today in the remains of the splendid Ummayad architecture of the city. The reign of the Ummayads brought about a reintegration of all Syria, including the Palestine of Roman times, into the Arab world, and a loosening of most cultural connections with the West. Jerusalem became an important Islamic religious center and Palestine nothing more than a Syrian Arab sub-province.

Once the Ummayad dynasty was overthrown by the Abbasids, however, and the caliphate was shifted from Damacus to Baghdad, Syria was no longer the center of the empire; it reverted to what it had been earlier under the ancient Egyptians, Persians, Romans and Byzantines — a province of other empires. First the Seljuks, then the European Crusaders, then the Ottomans, and finally the French, dominated Syria. In the process the land lost its uniquely Arab singularity and became a hotbed of cultural, sociological and ideological crosscurrents.

It was the French who had the most profound effect. During the nineteenth century, following the Napoleonic invasion, French culture spread up along the Levantine shore and across the mountains of The Lebanon to Damascus. French-Christian schools were established and French investment began to filter into the region, all with the tacit approval of the Ottoman sultanate, which recognized the special relationship France had with the large Christian population dating back to the Crusades. France was one of the principal European philosophical centers of revolutionary nationalism, and it was not long before French nationalist ideas began to graft themselves onto the consciousness of Syria's Christian Arabs.

During the centuries after the fall of the Ummayad dynasty, Syria had become the center of warring Islamic tribal sects. The Ummayads represented what had become the established expression of Islam — the Islam of the Arab conquests. The Abbasids, who succeeded them, represented the

Shiite interpretation of Islam, and even though the caliphate was moved to Baghdad, many Syrians were converted to the Shiite persuasion. Thus the basic schism in Islam became anchored in Syria.

The schism was compounded in the eleventh century by the evolution of the Druzes. When the Abbasids overthrew the House of Ummaya in the eighth century, the surviving Ummayad religious leaders fled to Egypt, where their descendants eventually joined with the Egyptians in establishing a countercaliphate. The sixth Egyptian caliph was Hakim, and around him developed a mixed cult of Copts, Muslims and pagans who believed him to be the final incarnation of Allah. This belief spread to various tribes of the Syrian-Arabian desert that were centered around a mountain south of Damascus known as Jebel Druz. As the belief took hold, these tribes consolidated themselves into a single group of Arabs who became known as the Druzes. By the time the Ottomans took over Syria, the Druzes were a third ingredient in the schismatic patchwork of Syrian Islam.

Religious tensions were further sharpened by the Crusades. There had been an indigenous Arab Christian population in Greater Syria that dated back to the first century A.D. Large segments of the pagan population of Syria had converted to Christianity prior to the seventh century, only to be in turn converted to Islam by the Ummayad dynasty. Christianity thereafter kept a low profile in the area until the arrival of the Crusaders, when it underwent a renascence and became once again an influential religious component of Syrian Arabdom. Yet it always remained a minority within the larger and often warring factions of Islam, and was frequently drawn into Islamic disputes against its will. Thus, during the Ottoman centuries, the Christian Arab minority tended to remain apart from the Muslim population as much as possible in order to preserve its integrity and security. When the French began to take a colonial interest in Syria, they were welcomed and encouraged by Syrian Christians, who saw in them an instrument of protection from the always-hovering threat of Islam.

Indeed, it was the Arab Christians of Syria who first, among all Arabs, responded to European ideas of nationalism in the nineteenth century. And it was through this medium that notions of nationalism began to be funneled into the Muslim Arab world. The Christians of Syria initially perceived in nationalism an opportunity to separate themselves from the great mass of Islamic culture and secure themselves behind the frontiers of an independent Christian Arab state. The notion rapidly became an organized movement within Christian Syria at about the same time a similar idea —

Zionism — was taking hold in Europe. It was never able to gain the backing of the Ottoman regime, however; thus it died aborning. Yet it did not go unnoticed, for soon it was coopted by Muslim Arabs frustrated by Ottoman rule. By the beginning of the twentieth century it was well on its way to becoming the ideology of Pan-Arab nationalism.

Like its Arab Christian origins, the Arab Muslim nationalist movement began principally as the expression of a religious impulse and was understandably greeted with disfavor by the Ottomans — remember the enforced residence in Constantinople of Hussein Ibn Ali, one of its leading exponents, and his four sons during the last decade of the nineteenth century and the first five years of the twentieth. By the start of the First World War, however, the Ottomans were distracted by other matters and within Syria the idea of an eventual Pan-Arab state, centered there and radiating in all directions to embrace the entire Arabic-speaking world east of Egypt, began to look like a reality.

What happened thereafter we have already seen. France wanted no part of a Muslim state in heavily Christianized Syria. Nor was it interested in permitting Arab nationalism to realize itself at all in the Fertile Crescent, for such notions were likely to spread to its Arab colonies in Northwest Africa. France demanded instead that the Fertile Crescent be divided up between itself and Britain, with France retaining hegemony over Greater Syria — minus the southern part straddling the Jordan River, which Britain could have, along with Mesopotamia.

Britain preferred this plan to its earlier commitments to the Arabs guaranteeing a Pan-Arab state. Much of the immediate aftermath of the war in the region consequently consisted of an expanding wrangle between the Arab nationalists and the Anglo-French colonialists. As the dispute became increasingly violent, it succeeded in stripping the infant nationalist ambition of the Arabs of its mostly religious nature and instilling it with a strongly political character.

Prince Feisal, one of the sons of Grand Sharif Hussein Ibn Ali, the nominal leader of the nationalist movement, was installed by the British as king of a provisional government of Syria while Britain and France negotiated the final parceling up of the Arab world. This was a sop to Feisal and his father in exchange for Britain's lopping off the Syrian territories of Palestine and Transjordan, which the Arabs had envisioned as being integral components of their Pan-Arab state.

Feisal was hopeful still of negotiating the future of Syria with the British, so he spent much time immediately after the war in London. But the hardcore Syrian nationalists, feeling betrayed and bitter, were not so inclined (these included, of course, the newly declared body of Arabs living in what was now known as Palestine). While Feisal traveled and negotiated (invariably to his disadvantage), the home corps of nationalists, centered in Damascus and Jerusalem, grew more restive.

When it became clear in 1920 that Britain would turn over Syria to the French, Feisal switched the locus of his negotiations to Paris. When he returned to Damascus he had come to no accommodation with France. But what was worse, he found a mood of insurrection building against his provisional rule among the nationalist cadres. Feisal was a scion of the ancient royal Arab Hashemite family, but Syrians and Palestinians owed no allegiance to the Hashemites. Furthermore, by his waffling with the British and his sporadic cooperation with the Zionists, he was suspected of making concessions intolerable to the ideal of Arab nationalism merely to ensure future foreign support of his kingdom. And, of course, he had allowed himself to be tricked by the British in the first place, for it was he who had traveled the Arab world a few years earlier announcing that the British had promised an independent Pan-Arab state in exchange for a wartime Arab revolt against the Ottomans.

When British troops were withdrawn from Syria in the summer of 1920 and replaced by French forces, fighting developed in many parts of the country between Arab nationalist guerrilla elements and the French. France was to be given a mandate over Syria, and when Feisal was unable to control the guerrillas the French summarily ousted him from his throne, dissolved the provisional nationalist government, and installed their own puppet regime.

One important consequence of these events was the split that developed between the nationalists of French Syria and those of British Palestine. During the immediate postwar period the two groups had acted as one in their determination to resist both the fragmentation of Syria and the dissolution of their ambition to achieve an independent Pan-Arab state. But once it became known that Britain and France were going to go ahead with their split of Syria despite the protests of Feisal, the resisting nationalists became divided. Now the activists of what had been southern Syria turned their attention to the British and the Zionists, while those in central Syria focused on the impending French occupation.

When Arab riots broke out in Jerusalem in April 1920 against the Zionists, one of their most striking features was that they evoked no reaction from Syrian nationalists in Damascus. This was because the nationalist cadres in Damascus were still, if only tenuously, obeying Feisal; he had told them to remain aloof from the struggle in Palestine in the hope that the British, out of gratitude, would reconsider their intention of giving Syria over to France.

It was, of course, an empty hope, and when, that summer, the impending French mandate was revealed and French troops replaced the British in central Syria, any lingering Arab trust in Feisal's ability to lead the nationalist cause was demolished. He had on the one hand forced the Syrian nationalist movement to abandon southern Syria to the Zionists. On the other he had turned the nationalist Arabs of southern Syria against those of Syria proper. And, finally, he had turned the wrath of all Arab nationalists, but especially those of Palestine, against himself and the traditionally respected Hashemite family.

These developments, which occurred more than fifty years ago, still figure importantly in the interplay of nationalist ambitions in the Arab world. Indeed, they are at the root of much of the argumentation that goes on today between the militant Palestinian movement and the Kingdom of Jordan over the ultimate status of the Palestinians, for the king of Jordan is a Hashemite and therefore deeply resented by many Palestinians.

They account too for the particularly deep hatred that Syria harbors for Israel, a hatred that goes well beyond standard Arab anti-Israeli feelings. Burned into the Syrian consciousness is a deep sense of humiliation over its abandonment of the Palestinian resistance to Zionism in 1920. Prodded by the Arab custom of face-saving and by constant reminders of its Arab shame on the part of the Palestinians, Syria has ever since been forced to construct an elaborate matrix of hatred for the Jews by way of compensation.

Syria submitted most unwillingly to French domination after 1920. Although the country was outwardly calm for several years, nationalist revolutionary groups — each representing different religious blocs: some highly conservative, others rabidly radical — plotted against the French mandatory government and fought among themselves. Much of Syria's Christian population crowded itself into the coastal province of The Lebanon, where the French presence was most conspicuous and where it could expect protection from the warring Muslim and Druze factions. In 1925 a Druze uprising was followed by a Muslim rebellion, and although they were quickly overcome by the French (actually, the Druze revolt continued sporadically for two years), they set the stage for even more intense resistance. In 1926 France, acceding to Christian demands, prised The Lebanon from the rest of Syria and proclaimed it a separate republic. This further aggravated Syrian sensibilities, and revolutionary resistance heightened into the 1930s. The only trouble was that with all the religious divisions in Syria, the nationalist movement was never able to sustain itself as a united force. The will to independence was there; the way was not.

It had not been until the late thirties that a movement was born which had a clear political orientation, one that transcended the various religious ideologies. The movement started, ironically enough, not in Syria but in Paris, where two young Syrians had gone to study at the Sorbonne. One was Michel Aflaq, a Christian Arab taking courses in European literature. The other was Salah Bitar, a Muslim enrolled in legal studies. Both had grown up in Syria and were exposed to the conflicting liberation and independence movements. From their distance in Paris, where they were deeply immersed in the ideological socialist literature of European nationalism, they saw the deficiencies that were at the heart of the failure of the independence struggle at home. The impulse to national independence could not be based on religious tenets, but must have a cultural-sociological-ethnic base.

By virtue of the fact that Syria was a discordant agglomeration of religious sects, the basing of the nationalist movement on religious tenets would inevitably produce disunity and failure. Revolutionary socialism on the European model had gained its successes through encouraging political unity by means of appeals to ethnic and cultural identity, appeals that overrode religious differences. The application of this principle, concluded Aflaq and Bitar, would be the key to the success of Syrian self-determination. And the key to Syrian political identity was not the diverse religious character of the people, but their communal Arabness. The Syrian nationalist movement would have to be transformed from a congeries of religious impulses into a unity of ethnic identity — Arab identity. From this sense of unity would flow a powerful political entity that would nourish itself on the belief in Arab political rather than Muslim religious destiny, and would be able thereby to work out its goals of nationhood.

Upon their return to Syria in 1940, Aflaq and Bitar taught for a short time in Damascus, but then shifted their activities to the American University in Beirut, a gathering place of Arab intellectuals that had developed into a seedbed of Arab nationalist ideas.* There they indoctrinated Arab students in their ideas, and while World War II went on around them the new and infant nationalist movement evolved into an organized party.

The party appealed mainly to intellectuals frustrated with the capitalistic imperialism of France and Britain and attracted to what seemed to be the effective counterimperialistic socialist principles of Marx and his Russian disciples. Structured on the basis of party cells of seven men each, according to the communist model, the organization was called the "Baath," or Arab Resurrection Party, and during the war it spread its semiclandestine cellular network across the Arab world.

Syria spent the war still under French domination, although this time, at least at the beginning, it was the France of the Vichy government, collaborators with the Axis powers. As a result of the brief appearance of a pro-Axis government in neighboring Iraq, which had been released from British mandatory control nine years earlier, British and Free French troops occupied Syria in 1941 to curtail the spread of German influence there. In so doing, the British, in exchange for Syrian cooperation, committed themselves to guaranteeing Syria's independence and the removal of all French forces as soon as practicable.

Once the war appeared to be won in Europe and the security of the Allies' Middle East oil holdings was certain, the Syrians called the British on their promise. At first the French objected, but in view of the fact that France as a nation had performed badly in the war, their insistence on retaining control of Syria held little weight. In June 1945, after an ultimatum from Britain, they finally withdrew their troops and civil administration from Syria and Lebanon. Syria proclaimed its independence.

Independence found Syria with severe economic and social problems and with no political direction. Geographically it had been shrunk by Britain and France to a territory with artificial frontiers, and its long history of subjugation to foreign rulers had left it with little in the way of tested political institutions. Its approximately four million people were largely agrarian and pastoral by occupation, living at a subsistence level, suffering a high rate of illiteracy, and torn still between tribal and religious rivalries. As invariably

---

* Beirut's American University was founded late in 1866 primarily as a Protestant educational and missionary school by American religious philanthropy. Today only about five percent of the student body is American, mostly offspring of members of the American diplomatic service. The rest is made up largely of Arabs, Christian and Muslim, from throughout the Arab world. The faculty, too, is mostly Arab.

occurs in such situations, the government of newly independent Syria was not so much formed as seized by dictatorial elements in the nationalist movement led by — what else? — an army officer by the name of Husni Zaim.

Prolonged military rule was almost preordained for Syria, for the only group with any knowledge of the outside world and any experience in administrative matters, aside from the small professional and merchant class of the cities, was the military. During the twenty years of the mandate the Syrian military had been the French civil administration's contact with the people. As a result, the military establishment had built up a network of quasi-political centers throughout the country. And it was almost exclusively Muslim. The merchant and professional class embraced all religious facets of Syrian life and reflected the great variety of intra-Syrian discontent. There had developed little unity of purpose or nationalist method within this class. Thus it fell to the military, with its French-instilled sense of organization and unity, to assume the role of government.

The military government under strongman Zaim was immediately faced with a highly contradictory situation. On the one hand there was the phenomenon of Zionism on its way to statehood in Palestine — still considered an integral part of Syria. On the other was the intense religious and tribal factionalism within Syria that went back to the early days of Islam. The solution of both problems had equal priority, but neither could be dealt with simultaneously. The consequence was that neither got solved, a result that has plagued Syria to this day.

Thoroughly imbued with a purple hatred of the Zionists as a result of Syria's shame at having abandoned the Palestinian segment of its population twenty-five years earlier, General Zaim made forestalling the creation of Israel Syria's first task. Although he could not have done less in view of Pan-Arab sentiment, the defeat of the Syrian army by the freshly minted Israelis in 1948 opened the worm can of Syrian factionalism and eventually brought about the increasingly ruthless Zaim's downfall. Nationalist civilian and religious groups thereafter vied for power. With little experience in the political and administrative realm, however, they invariably turned to Syrian army officers to carry out their ideas for a stable Syria. Consequently the country was ruled through the early and mid-fifties by a succession of military dictators, each representative of a competing civilian faction and all, together, transmitting the factionalism of the civilian world into the military establishment. To complicate matters, the native Syrian factionalism was compounded by the influx of many thousands of Palestinian refugees from Israel in the wake of the 1948 war.

Shortly after the 1948 debacle Michel Aflaq, the theoretician and co-founder of the Baath socialist movement, was called in by Zaim for consultation. The Baath philosophy, an idealistic mix of Arab unity and social justice, had gained the sympathy of Syria's restive intelligentsia, and Zaim was hoping to gain Aflaq's endorsement in order to stem the rampant discontent that was spreading on the heels of the Israeli victory. When Aflaq hesitated, Zaim had him arrested and tortured until he signed a declaration supporting the regime. Deeply humiliated, Aflaq exiled himself to Brazil.

During the fifties the parade of Syrian strongmen who followed Zaim at the helm turned the country into a fertile ground for wide-scale revolt. Anti-Israeli sentiment had become an obsession, but little was being accomplished to improve the fortunes of the great mass of Syrian people. A communist movement surfaced, financed and supported by Russia, which saw, in the most intense period of its Cold War with the West, an opportunity to establish a long-coveted outpost in the Arab Middle East and thereby compromise the exclusivity of Western influence there. The Russians' cause was given an immense boost in 1956 when they rattled their sabers on behalf of the Arabs against the combined British-French-Israeli assault on Egypt over the Suez affair (Nasser had just nationalized the Suez Canal).

Aflaq, from his sanctuary in Brazil, watched these developments with a grave sense of foreboding. His ideas of Arab Syrian nationalism were socialist, true, but they did not call for a communist methodology. Communism was atheistic, and such a political system would be contradictory to the deeply felt Muslim and Christian religious beliefs of the Syrians. Consequently he left Brazil in 1957 and returned to Egypt to enlist Nasser's help in forestalling a communist takeover of Syria.

Nasser had his own ideas about Syria. Having successfully abolished big-power control of the Suez Canal the year before, his star had risen throughout the Arab world. He was fast on the way to becoming the personification of the new Pan-Arabism, and few were the Arabs who did not bask in the glow of his achievements in dealing with the old imperial powers. Nasser responded to this adulation with oratorical cries of a new Arab nation — if not a geopolitical one, at least a single nation in spirit — and proposed himself as the man to lead it. His reputation became particularly lofty in Syria, which had ages-old ties to Egypt, which was passionately allied with Egypt in the fight against Israel, and whose military regime was similar to Egypt's.

Moreover, Nasser and his associates were in the process of developing a political and economic system they liked to call Arab socialism, one that was not substantially different from the Baathism of Aflaq and his following.

Nasser agreed to help the Baathists, but his larger design in so doing was to persuade the Syrian military regime of the moment to join Egypt in a union of the two countries, with Nasser the overall leader. He was successful; in 1958, the Syrian government, fearful of the growing Baathist movement, elected to join with Egypt in what the two renamed the United Arab Republic. With his initial goal achieved and his power over Syria consolidated, Nasser had no further need of the Baath party.

When it became clear that Nasser had merely used Aflaq and his Baathists, a split developed in the party. Aflaq and Bitar retained leadership over part of it, while a dissident Syrian colleague named Salah Jedid branched out with his own faction.

In the meantime Nasser sent groups of political emissaries into Syria to organize the government along the lines of his Egyptian model for Arab socialism. These groups built up a native Nasserite political following within Syria, and on the basis of this, plus the fact that the Egyptians began to act more like imperial proconsuls than advisers, the Syrian regime grew anxious about Nasser's real intentions. Nasser constantly reassured the Syrians he wanted only coequal union, but the actions of his emissaries reflected the likelihood that Syria would end up on the bottom of the equality scale.

Finally, in 1961, Syria seceded from the union and expelled the Egyptian missions. But the damage had been done, for the growing enthusiasm of the Syrian Nasserites, now a distinct political party, could not be quelled. The unexpected slap in the face provoked Nasser himself into renewing his interest in the Baathist exiles living in Egypt, for now, he realized, the only way of reacquiring control over Syria would be by supporting a Baathist takeover.

Here the normally Byzantine course of Arab politics took several more-convoluted-than-usual twists. In March of 1963, the Baathists, with the approval of Nasser and the help of the Syrian Nasserites, staged a successful coup in Damascus which put Aflaq and Bitar, the cofounders of the movement, in power. Once at the helm, their first task was to cut off Nasser's influence; thus, within a few months they abolished the Nasserite party.

As Aflaq and Bitar sought to expand their grip they quickly realized that the army was still all-powerful in Syria and that they could not protect Baathist rule without the support of the military establishment. So they installed important army officers in key posts, and once again the Syrian government took on the look of a military dictatorship.

Aflaq was a Christian, Bitar a Sunnite Muslim. But Salah Jedid, the man who had earlier split the party into two factions, was descended from the Alawites, an esoteric subsect of the Shiites centered in northern Syria. The Alawites, like the Druzes, had long suffered under Sunnite rule in Syria. Jedid had taken part in the Baathist coup and had been included in the new government. But soon the native religious antagonisms began to surface and Jedid was shunted off to the sidelines. There he seethed, all the while recruiting Alawite officers into his branch of the party.

Under Aflaq and Bitar and their mostly Sunnite military functionaries, Syria's economy shriveled further and the government grew less and less efficient. The country's raison d'être seemed to be simply to eliminate Israel, and while this kept the military establishment happy — for it provided them with increasing influence — the rest of the nation stagnated. Then, in 1966, Jedid, backed by a corps of Alawite officers, ousted Aflaq and Bitar and assumed sole power.*

Jedid followed Aflaq's course, but this time it was Alawite officers who were appointed to head most of the ministries. In Syria it was a case of "the more things change, the more they remain the same." The country was still a military dictatorship hiding behind such Baathist slogans as "Collective Leadership," "Dictatorship of the People," and "Our Holy Mission: Death to the Jews!"

Each of these mottos, and the elaborate political rationales behind them, proved merely to be masks for the Alawite junta's own failures, including its defeat in the 1967 war against Israel. The regime had no popular base and was supported only by Syria's Alawite minority. The country was losing its educated people and its private capital; since 1957 close to sixty percent of its university graduates had left the country. Its inability to get along with Nasser left it with no allies in the Arab world and contributed directly to the rapidity of the wholesale Arab defeat in 1967.

The original Baathist takeover in 1963 had been designed to prevent the ascendancy of communist rule and to provide Syria instead with a form of secular socialism amenable to Islamic beliefs. But the country's increasing isolation under Aflaq, due mainly to his fear of Nasser's Syrian ambitions, and its obsession with Israel forced it to become more and more dependent

* Aflaq fled to Iraq, which had also experienced a short-lived Baathist takeover in 1963.

on the Soviet Union for economic, military and diplomatic assistance. Russia saw a strategic advantage for itself in the ports of the Syrian coastline between Lebanon and Turkey; a large naval base there would give it an unprecedented foothold in the eastern Mediterranean, one that would enable its fleet to begin to act as a counterbalance to the considerable United States and NATO military presence in the area. Russia therefore pledged its support to Syria. When Syria accepted the pledge and saw it translated into arms, money, military advice and diplomatic support, it became in the late sixties a full-fledged client state of the Soviet Union, much as Israel was of the United States, and another component in the strategic chess game between America and Russia.

Salah Jedid's ouster of the Aflaq regime in 1966 was basically the result of the quarrel within the Baath party rooted in ancient Alawite-Sunnite sectarian differences. But it also derived from Aflaq's hesitancy in overcommitting Syria to Russian influence. The fervor with which Syrian leaders railed against Israel was usually a measure of their popular support. But rhetorical fervor was not enough; eventually there would have to be action (Syria had not fought a formal war against Israel for almost twenty years, and the continual stream of bellicose declarations were no longer sufficient to rally the people). Jedid's program was therefore to further curry favor with Russia so as to receive sufficient material to turn Syrian diplomatic rhetoric into military action.

As is well known, the 1967 war was not fought on Arab terms. Indeed, Syria was not yet ready to go to war, for although it by then possessed a large measure of relatively modern Russian arms, its military had not yet been sufficiently trained in their use. Nasser, however, decided to indulge himself again in one of his daring power plays against the West in order to revive his sagging popularity and divert the Arab world's attention from the imperial-type war he had Egypt fighting in Yemen. He summarily ordered United Nations peace-keeping forces to leave Egyptian soil, where they had been stationed as a result of the 1956 Suez crisis. When the UN obeyed, and when Nasser, perhaps a bit surprised, followed its withdrawal by closing the Straits of Tiran and massing divisions of troops and tanks in the Sinai, facing Israel, the Israelis interpreted his moves as an intention to go to war and struck first.

Although Egypt and Syria had entered into a loose military confederation (along with Jordan), there was never any effective coordination among the three. Nassar exercised the initiative, but the Syrians were largely uninformed with regard to his ultimate intentions. The Syrian army was receiving its orders from Egyptian generals and Russian military advisers, at least in the days immediately prior to the start of the war, and when the Israelis launched their sudden and surprise attack the Syrians had no choice but to fight.

Unlike the situation in Egypt, where Nasser's position was actually strengthened by the Arab failure, in Syria the loss seriously damaged the prestige of the Jedid regime. And when, in 1970, a bloody civil war broke out in Jordan between the Palestine Liberation Organization, supported by Syrian troops, and the forces of the Hashemite King Hussein, Jedid's days were numbered.

In 1970 Syrian politics became a Byzantine variation on a Byzantine theme. Although the Jedid regime was composed almost exclusively of Alawite officers and civilians, within the Alawite sect there were individual tribal and family rivalries that went back for hundreds of years. The Alawites had taken over the government from the Sunnite majority, but now representatives of rival families began to maneuver for power.

Jedid's defense minister was General Hafez Al-Assad, an air force officer by training and therefore a member of the most elite and modern part of the Syrian armed forces. An Alawite, he was also a member of a clan that was traditionally a rival to that of Premier Jedid. He had been sorely humiliated by the role Syria played in the 1967 debacle and had been particularly incensed when Jedid kept his best-trained troops in Damascus to defend his regime rather than sending them against Israel. During the civil war in Jordan, Assad refused to send his air force in support of the Syrian troops Jedid had sent to support the Palestinians — he could not bring himself, he says today, to wage war against another Arab country. When Jedid attempted to oust him because of this, Assad, who had quietly been organizing a loyal following among the air force hierarchy, retaliated with a coup of his own. Jedid was bloodlessly removed from power and Assad ascended to the leadership of the Syrian junta.

Since his takeover and installation as president of Syria, Assad has introduced a level of stability into the country that it had previously and profoundly lacked. To be sure, the Syrian government has remained a military dictatorship, with the most important posts held by generals who are also top functionaries in the so-called Regional Command of the Baath party. But it is a dictatorship with a difference, for it has craftily attuned itself to the conflicting interest groups within the Syrian body politic. By retaining its military nature and giving the generals a say in political decisions, it has soothed the army. By retaining its socialist Baath orientation and bringing differing socialist (even communist) points of view into the ruling councils, it has blunted the popular appeal of dissident political groups. By filling many administrative posts with members of Assad's Alawite clan, while at the same time not excluding representatives of other Muslim sects, it has calmed much of the internecine conflict that had been a distinctive and destructive feature of Syrian life. By ending Syria's isolation and renewing its ties with the rest of the Arab world, it has appealed to the Pan-Arab nationalist sentiment left over from the post–World War I era. By conducting itself still as a police state, it has managed to keep social restiveness to a minimum and thus reassure the old middle-class merchant and professional group, which constantly feared a wide-scale revolt of Syria's unlettered peasantry. And by introducing a few liberalizing reforms, it has managed to appease those Christians who, inimical to Communism and the Russian presence, have been calling for a turn to the West.

To achieve all this Assad has had to walk a thread-thin tightrope of belligerency and conciliation. That he has so far been successful is a telling reflection of the split personality of Syrian society, a society that, of all the Arab nations, most closely mirrors the Arab character as a whole.

# 21.

## JOURNAL: *Hafez Al-Assad*

EVERYWHERE ONE GOES IN DAMASCUS one sees pictures of Hafez Al-Assad, a moustached, rather baleful-looking man, somewhat portly in a plain dark civilian suit. The ubiquitousness of the photo reminds one of Cairo in the 1950s, when Nasser's visage peered from every wall.

There is one difference between the Cairo of then and the Damascus of now, however, and that is the preponderance of signs in Russian. They are leftovers from the years prior to the 1973 war, when thousands of Soviet technicians and military advisers wandered the streets of the city in their off-time. The Syrians had left the signs up. Although I saw few Russians on my two separate visits in 1974, they were obviously expected to return en masse. What I did see were plenty of brand-new Russian tanks and cannons being transported through the city south toward the Golan Heights.

Through its succession of military regimes during the fifties and sixties (some observers have counted as many as twenty transfers of power), the Syrian government, despite its slogan of "collective leadership," seemed to most Syrians nothing more than a faceless dictatorship. Assad has changed that. Now the dictatorship has a face. And as is usual when Arabs choose to make a shift in style, in Syria they swung to the opposite extreme. It is likely that much of the approval of Assad derived primarily from the fact that Syrians could now see who was making their decisions for them.

My first thought on observing all the portraits came as a question: Did Assad aspire to be the new Nasser of the Arab world? The conditions seemed ripe for such an ascendancy. President Sadat had told me that his own greatest ambition was to retire from the active leadership of Egypt within the next year or two — whether or not some sort of peace was worked out with Israel. Sadat was a fairly modest man; he did not throb with a drive for power and adulation, and he seemed extremely worn down by the 1973 war and its frenzied diplomatic aftermath.

There seemed to be no particularly charismatic leader on the Egyptian horizon. Egyptian leadership would doubtless pass to bureaucratic politicians from Egypt's ruling Arab Socialist Union, its only political party. The recently surfaced Libyan strongman Colonel Muammar Al-Qadhafi (always there are colonels) was certainly charismatic, but his Islamic fanaticism was as anachronistic as transporting oil by camel. There was no one in Lebanon, a necessarily fence-straddling Arab nation and a relatively democratic one at that, who could assume Nasser's mantle. In violent Iraq, leaders had a tendency to appear and disappear as fast as a rifle could be reloaded. In Jordan King Hussein's life was constantly in peril; anyway, he was a Hashemite and therefore a political unworthy. The Arabian kingdoms, sheikhdoms and emirates, despite their oil riches, were still too rooted in either tribalism or personal profligacy to produce a political magnet. And on the fringes of the Arab world — the Yemens, Sudan, the three nations of Northwest Africa — well, they were simply too far away from the center of things.

But Syria — here was a country that cried out for a Nasser of its own. Perhaps his style would not be the same as Nasser's. But Assad's immediate predecessors had already set Syria on a Nasser-like course — instituting agrarian reform, controlling the banks, nationalizing key industry (or what there was of it), exporting Arab socialism according to the Baathist model, inciting anti-Israeli sentiment. Assad refined this course when he took over, adapting it to his own quiet but tough personality.

Assad's popularity among Syria's masses was cemented by his conduct during — and perhaps even more after — the 1973 war. After the initial successes resulting from their massive surprise attack on the Israeli-occupied Golan Heights, the Syrians were hurled back, losing even more territory than had been lost in the 1967 war. Furthermore, Damascus itself was bombed and a large chunk of Syria's heavy industry was destroyed by Israeli aircraft. Nevertheless, the initial Syrian military success, coupled with Assad's later diplomatic triumph in forcing the Israelis to withdraw from the newly captured territory, resulted in almost universal approval in Syria. While the equally victorious (at least in the psychological sense) Sadat in Egypt was putting out conciliatory feelers, however, Assad remained hard and firm in his attitude toward an ultimate settlement, and his star thus shone brighter. Now, in the summer of 1974, rearming Syria's forces with fresh and plentiful supplies of sophisticated Russian weaponry, and quietly — not hys- terically — promising a new and even more bloody war if the Israelis didn't begin to spit up the territories they had captured in 1967, the ball of hard-line Arab leadership appeared to have been passed from Egypt's court into his own.

The adulation I observed for Assad in Syria was a lot calmer than the Egyptian worship I had seen for Nasser in the 1950s. But at the same time it seemed more genuine, rooted deeper in mind than emotion. Assad was cer- tainly far from being an oratorical wizard, and though his picture was proudly displayed everywhere, he himself was not personally conspicuous; there were few public appearances, no political rallies, no whizzing through the streets of Damascus in siren-wailing motorcades. Perhaps a man who has mastered the technical intricacies of flying Mig-21s, as Assad has, tends to take a more deliberate approach to life. In any event, his style was low-key and determined, and it had obviously, from all the laudatory talk I heard from a broad cross section of Syrians, struck a responsive chord in the Syrian character — indeed, in the Arab character, for I heard enthusiastic approval of Assad expressed elsewhere as well.

It will take another war, I was told by a high Egyptian diplomat in Da- mascus who knew him well, to truly gauge Assad's staying power as the emerging symbol of Arab pride and potential, or else the immediate capitula- tion of Israel to Syrian demands. Since the latter was thoroughly unlikely, the minister went on, another war was inevitable. For as with Nasser, Assad was deeply aware of the hopes and expectations Arabs throughout the Middle East were now investing in him vis-à-vis Israel. This investment would soon force him to decide whether or not to rise to the challenge. He is not a power-hungry man, but he is deeply Arab and is heavily weighted with a sense of Pan-Arab responsibility. He would likely rise to the challenge, the Egyptian concluded. He can look around and see that there is no one else. He will become the Nasser of the seventies, the eighties. But only if he can carry through on the promise most Arabs perceive in him — to put Israel in its place. "Diplomacy is a tedious process. In order to secure his influence he will have to start another war. Even if it is unsuccessful militarily, so long as it speeds up the diplomatic process it will be enough. We Arabs — we don't really expect to win our wars with Israel on the battlefield. But we have seen what effects these wars can have on Israel on the diplomatic front, particularly now when it is a matter of life and death to the big powers. So long as Assad can bring further pressure on Israel, he will be the winner. And he is not a man who is afraid to make a decision."

It was with this question — whether his ultimate aim as president of Syria was to assume Nasser's mantle as the inspirational leader of all Arabdom — that I decided to open my interview with Assad.

Meeting him, I was surprised at how much larger he was in stature than I expected from the pictures I had seen. He was tall and thick-set, yet there was about his physique a certain squat softness, almost flabbiness, rather than muscularity. Forty-five years old, he had plain brown hair, tightly clipped and sprinkled with gray, and a matching moustache. His eyes were brown and his skin, in contrast with that of most Arabs, was smooth and pinkish. His barrel neck supported a large head, the most conspicuous features of which were two prominent ears whose thick ligatures and massive lobes made them seem cauliflowered. His expression in repose was kindly and phlegmatic, almost meek.

Throughout our talk he spoke slowly and deliberately, his voice occasionally fading into a guttural murmur as he reached the end of a thought. He sat on a plain couch in a plain office whose drapes were drawn against the summer afternoon's sun. As he answered my questions — our exchange was conducted in English and Arabic through an interpreter — he kept the fingers of both his heavy, fleshy hands tightly intertwined. He listened expressionlessly, gazing at the floor, as the interpreter relayed my questions to him, and when he answered his only change of expression was a narrowing of his eyes. I, of course, understood very little of what he was saying as he talked, but I could detect no animation in his words. There was no gesturing, no rises and falls in emphasis, no flashes of anger, no humor, just a low monotone. When he didn't want to answer a question he simply shook his head at the interpreter. He did not look at me once.

"Mr. President," I began, "it has been suggested to me by many of the people I have spoken to that you are the new hope of the Arab world, that you are in a position to assume the influence and impact that President Nasser had before his death. Can you tell me if this is part of your thinking?"

"President Nasser was a great man," came the translated answer. "It would be presumptuous of me to think in such a way. Nasser was a man of great words and deeds. I am not a man of great words. Besides, it is not our way here in Syria to conduct government in the Egyptian style. We do not encourage the glorification of the personality. We seek simply to do what is right in a collective way."

"But would you accept the responsibility of being acclaimed the new leader of the Arab world if it was thrust upon you? Even if you did not agree with it?"

"This will not happen," replied Assad. "The Arab world has passed through the stage when it needed one great single leader. Remember, when Nasser arrived, the Arab world was in a state of disorganization. He brought Arabs together into a common purpose. He brought unity to the Arab world. Now that we have this unity, it is the task of the individual leaders to refine and strengthen it."

"You speak of unity," I said, "but there seems to me — to many in the West — that there is as much disunity as unity in the Arab world. We have seen the various countries arguing with each other, Libya with Egypt, for example, Syria with Jordan. How do you explain this contradiction?"

Assad mused for a moment, in a schoolteacher's way. "I speak of unity in the moral sense," he finally said. "We Arabs are like a large family. It is only natural for there to be quarrels in a family. But when someone comes from outside the family and threatens its security, its existence, to take away its property, the family unites to repel this threat. We quarrel, yes. But these are merely quarrels between brothers. 'Do we do it this way or that way?' — that sort of quarrel. We still remain a family. What happens within our family is our business. It has nothing to do with Arab unity in the international sense."

"What exactly is meant by the term 'Arab unity'?" I asked. "We hear it when Arabs talk about Israel. But does it have any other applications?"

"It is far more than Israel," he replied. "Arab unity is the struggle of the entire Arab people to achieve equality with the other peoples of the world. To be able to control our own portion of the world just as Americans control theirs, Europeans control theirs, Chinese control theirs, and so on. That is the meaning of Arab unity."

"And you expect that this will happen?"

"Yes."

"When?"

"I beg your pardon?"

"When do you envision the Arab people gaining complete sovereignty over this part of the world?"

"It has already happened to a great extent."

"Yes, but don't you think it's more of an illusive sovereignty than a real one? I mean, there is now a significant Russian presence here. And an American one. Doesn't it seem to you that instead of the Arabs being forced to live under the influence of earlier foreign powers, such as the Turks, the French, the British, they are now required to live and operate under American and Russian influence?"

"That is only because of Israel. We know that the United States and the Soviet Union are here only because of Israel. When we get rid of Israel, we will no longer have them here."

"Well," I said, "that raises an interesting question. Israel depends on the United States. Your country, and other Arab countries, depend on the Soviet Union. Do you suppose America and Russia are giving their respective support purely for altruistic reasons?"

"Of course not," he answered. "America has supported Israel in the interests of its own imperialism, to keep a sphere of influence here."

"And the Russians are not doing the same thing?"

"I concede the Soviet Union helps us with its own interest in mind — that is, to combat the expansion of American power. But, you see, Soviet interest coincides with ours. We do not wish the American presence here. We have had enough with the imperialism of the West. Before it was military imperialism. Now it is economic imperialism. America has supported Israel for all these years knowing completely in its mind that we could not tolerate Israel in our midst. By keeping Israel here it knows we must continue to fight, which means that our governments and our economies are diverted from their real task, which is to improve the fortunes of our people. As long as our economies remained weak because we were forced to spend most of our resources on defense, America thought she could impose her economic imperialism on us. But she has learned some hard lessons since last October. She has learned that the Arab world can weaken her own economy. So now she is having second thoughts about supporting Israel. Israel has been nothing to the United States except a wedge it has driven into the Arab world to keep it weak."

"Well, I think Israel has meant more to America than that," I said. "Whether right or wrong from your point of view, there has been a certain amount of idealism behind America's support of Israel. But let me get back to my original question. Now that America and Russia are here — and by here I mean in terms of money, arms, and so on — isn't it likely that they are here to stay for some time? Even if Israel is gone by tomorrow, they would simply not pack up and leave. So even with Israel gone, the Arab world would still not be sovereign and in complete control of its own destiny."

"That is where you are wrong," said Assad. "With the problem of Israel eliminated, we would be free to invite both America and Russia to compete in helping us enter the modern era. If they want to invest money here, if they want to build factories, dams, whatever it is, they are free to do so. But it will be on our terms. They will be here economically, yes, but it won't be in an imperialistic way because we will have full control over their presence. If there is no adversary military situation here, such as Israel creates, they won't be having to use them for our own strategic purposes, and they won't be having to use us for their strategic purposes. It will be more of a cooperative situation than an adversary one. And they will not be able to tell us what to do. We will tell them what we are going to do, and invite them to join us if they wish. That is the great difference between the Arab world as it is today and the Arab world as I see it should be. It is achieving the 'should be' that the Arab unity I talk about is dedicated to."

"As I understand it," I said, "Syria was the center of the revival of Arab unity. By that I mean political unity. It was here that the first ideas about a single great Arab nation were developed. And it was here that attempts were made to establish that nation at the end of the First World War. Does the idea of Arab unity mean that all the separate Arab states of today will eventually blend into one nation?"

"That is certainly possible. I believe, in fact, that it is probable. Perhaps not in my lifetime, for there are still too many differences between one Arab state and the next. But there is a strong feeling among Arabs, a spiritual feeling, that we are all a single nation of people. And so we are. But it will take a long time to convert that spiritual feeling into a material reality."

"And perhaps a good deal of turmoil," I suggested.

"Yes, but you see, turmoil can be good. It can be creative. As we revolutionize ourselves, we will unite materially as well as spiritually."

"But it is a long way off?"

"It is a long way."

"What do you see happening in the meantime?"

"Nothing can happen until the problem of Israel is eliminated. We Arabs have very much to offer the rest of the world. We have oil, we have gas, we have all these other great natural resources. And we have this vast land hungering to be developed. Think of how the rest of the world can benefit from what we are in a position to give it, and how we can benefit from what other parts of the world can give us. We could very well be the key to the world peace all your leaders always profess to desire. There could be such an interchange of riches between other parts of the world and here that everyone would benefit and no one would want to wage war. War comes when people feel deprived of their share of the world's bounty. When Israel is eliminated we will then be ready to share what we have in exchange for a share of what the rest of the world has. No one need feel deprived."

"Wars also come about because of power-hungry leaders, or because one political system seeks to dominate another."

"Ah, yes, but these leaders and these systems only arise because they appeal to deprived peoples who are frustrated with their misery. If a people is not deprived, they will not produce such leaders. That is why it is so important for the world — the West particularly — to realize what could happen here. The Arab people have been deprived for too long. It is how the West relates to us now that determines how the Arab world goes in the future. We will quickly be in a position to make life very difficult for the West. We do not need the West. But the West needs us. Oh, we can benefit from the West, I do not deny that. But we can also get along without it, if that is what it chooses."

"When you speak of the West, I assume you mean the United States."

"The United States, yes. You see, the United States has been the cause of all our recent problems. Had we been able to eliminate the Israel situation long ago, we would by now have solved many of our other problems. But the United States has prevented us from doing so. And I will tell you, the United States — we are giving it one final chance to abandon this course it has pursued. It is not just we Syrians who feel this way. It is all Arabs."

"Do you really expect that the United States will abandon Israel?"

"Abandon?" Assad said after a moment. "It is not a question of abandon. The United States could easily maintain its commitment to the Jews and still bring about justice here. We have no wish to destroy the Jews. The Jews have as much right to exist as any people. But not as a nation on Syrian soil. The United States could easily move this state called Israel elsewhere. If the Jews must have a nation, there are many places in the world they can have it without violating the territorial rights of other people. I am told that in the United States the government dispossesses thousands and thousands of people from their land to build motorways and great reservoirs. Let the United States do the same for the Jews. Take all the Jews from Israel who must have their own state and give them some land on the continent of America and let them call it Israel. And let those Jews who want to stay here, let them stay as citizens of Syria, of Palestine . . ."

"Wait a minute," I said. "Isn't that a bit unrealistic? After all, it's the Jews themselves who have determined where they live. They have shed a great deal of blood to preserve their state. They are not going to . . ."

"Ah, I just say that to show you that we do not take pleasure in killing Jews. I know how your propaganda works in the West. It makes us look as though we are bloodthirsty animals whose only pleasure in life is to slaughter Jews. It is absurd. Our only goal is to recover our land. Let the Jews stop conducting their aggression against us and we will be happy to leave them alone."

"That word 'aggression,' " I said. "We hear it a great deal from Arab leaders. What exactly do you mean by it?"

"Aggression," he echoed. "It is what the Jews have been doing for the last sixty years. The entire history of the Zionists here has been one aggression after another. They started with this much land . . ." Assad unclenched his hands and held up his thumb and forefinger, an inch apart. "And then they take this much land, then this much, then this much, until they are like this . . . " Now his hands were spread wide apart. "This is a clear proof of their aggression, and it is clear proof that they will not be satisfied until they have everything." His hands dropped, his fingers intertwined again. "They say that we are the aggressors. This is madness. We have been defending our land against Zionist aggression for fifty, sixty years. So, each time we fail. And the Zionists end up with more land. Let me ask you this: If some foreign power came to your country and took over one of your states, and then when you tried to get it back took over a second state, then a third, who would you say is the aggressor? The United States, for trying to recover its land? Or the foreign power, who keeps taking more of your territory?"

"I gather, then, that in spite of all the talk in the Arab world these days that you will allow Israel to exist in peace provided she returns the territories she captured in 1967, this is not really your intention. Your real intention is ultimately to eliminate Israel for good."

"This is a very complex question," Assad said. "I will admit that there is a mood in the Arab world to make some sort of settlement with Israel, to allow Israel to exist within certain frontiers. There is a great struggle taking place between the heart and the mind. In our hearts we say: 'No Israel, not on any terms.' In our minds we say: 'We must turn to other things, so let us give

Israel a chance to withdraw to its original frontiers, let us give it a chance to prove it will no longer try to expand.' It is a very difficult problem."

"The Israelis claim that their annexation of Arab territory does not come out of any expansionary desire, but that it has been forced upon them by the Arabs, that they do it to give themselves secure borders . . ."

"That is a lie, and the Israelis have proven it to be a lie. In a time of jets, rockets, long-distance missiles, there is no such thing as secure borders. Look at this, in 1967, when Israel claimed it had no secure borders, it won the war easily. But in 1973, when it had these 'secure' borders, it suffered great losses. So the idea of secure borders is a gross diversion. The Israelis use it to justify their expansionist policies, to hide from the world its true ambitions. You tell me, how does the Israeli possession of all of Jerusalem represent a secure border? Any nation that wants totally secure borders can have them only at the expense of its neighbors. And that is aggression."

"Well, then, on the question of whether you will let Israel exist in peace or not, provided that it withdraws, how do you feel personally?"

"I have been thinking of something that came about in your country some time ago. It was 1962, was it not? When your President Kennedy brought the world to the brink of nuclear war over the question of Cuba. Do you recall that?"

I recalled it very well. I especially recalled the sinking feeling, the profound sense of doom I and so many other Americans experienced as the Kennedy-Khrushchev confrontation approached its climax.

"Well, here was a dispute over 'secure borders,' " Assad continued. "The United States disputed the placing of Soviet missiles in Cuba. The United States considered this an aggression, and was willing to go to war unless the Russians withdrew. And finally the United States chased the Russians out. The United States was willing to permit Cuba to go on existing, but not when Cuba represented a clear threat to its borders and its sovereignty over the Americans. Do you see my point?"

"I'm not sure," I said.

"It is this. The United States feels it is justified to take military action against any foreign power that it thinks threatens the security of its national frontiers. It will go to any length to destroy such a threat. Once the threat is destroyed, it is willing to let the other people go on existing, such as was the case with Cuba. Cuba itself, without Soviet missiles, is no threat to America. The Cuban system is not approved of by America, the Cuban people are not friendly to America, but the United States permits them to exist. One day, thinks the United States, Cuba will again become a friend to America. In the meantime the United States works behind the scenes to overthrow Premier Castro so that Cuba can be brought back into the American sphere of influence.

"Now it is very similar between us and Israel. So long as Israel represents a threat to our security, so long as Israel continues to act as an aggressor against Arab sovereignty, we are justified in fighting to destroy it. Israel is to us as Cuba is to the United States. The Jewish people themselves, they are no threat to us. It is the Jewish state, backed up by United States arms and missiles. Before the United States it was Great Britain. You see? The United States is doing in Israel what the Russians did in Cuba. They are giving the Jews the means to threaten our security and sovereignty over our region. Except that this is not a crisis of only a few weeks, as it was in Cuba. It is a crisis that has been going on for more than fifty years. It was started by the British and has been continued by the United States. So long as the United States continues to put its weapons in Israel, which enables Israel to take more and more of our land and reduce our traditional and natural sovereignty, we will continue to fight, for by fighting the aggression of Israel we are fighting the aggression of the United States. Once the United States removes its arms from Israel, it will be the end of Israeli aggression. Then you will see, we will leave Israel alone. Let Israel return to what it was, and we will be inclined to leave it alone. Yes, we will work behind the scenes to overthrow the Zionist system of Israel, to bring about a just return of Arab presence there so as to make this land an integral part of the Arab world. But this will be done in the same way as you do what you do in Cuba . . ."

Assad unclasped his hands again and raised his finger in a pedantic gesture. "That is one possibility of the future, as I see it. If Israel withdraws to its original borders, we will not wage war against it. We will accept the United Nations resolutions of 1947 in the interest of getting on with other important business, and simply let nature take its course."

"What do you mean by letting nature take its course?" I said.

Perhaps Assad felt he was talking too much. He shook his head at the interpreter and mumbled something in Arabic. "The President feels he has mentioned enough about Israel," the interpreter said.

"Will he consider one last question?" I asked.

When Assad nodded, I said, "I assume by letting nature take its course you mean internal agitation against the Israeli government. I assume also that in granting Israel the right to exist without war, provided it goes back to its

1947 borders, you are acknowledging that there will be a Palestinian Arab state. From your point of view, then, wouldn't this Palestinian state merely be a base from which further agitation against Israel would be launched? And isn't that a good reason for Israel to resist the establishment of such a state?"

"A Palestinian state is inevitable," Assad replied. "Every Arab country wants it. It will relieve us of having to take responsibility for all the dispossessed Palestinians who are living under such terrible conditions in our countries. What occurs later no one can tell."

"But the Arab nations would certainly support a Palestinian state in its efforts to regain what it claims is the remainder of its territory in Israel, would they not?"

"I go back to Cuba again," he said. "How many Cuban refugees are there living in the United States — a million? two million?"

I had to confess I didn't know the exact number.

"If these Cuban refugees made a great effort to regain their land in Cuba, would the United States not support them? Did your country not try it once?"

"It's not the same thing," I said. "The Cuban refugees are not living under the same conditions as Palestinian refugees. They have prospered in the United States, or at least many of them have. Many have become citizens. I don't believe the United States would today support a Cuban refugee movement that sought to return en masse to Cuba."

"It would if the conditions were appropriate."

"All right, perhaps it would. But the situation is still not the same. What it comes down to with the Arabs is that in the long run you still mean to eliminate Israel — is that a fair conclusion?"

"The ultimate goal of all Arabs is an all-Arab world here. We do not know exactly how it will come about. But we know that it *will* come about. That is all I wish to say on the subject for now. Except for this. Once this problem is solved, then I can say that the Jews will be able to live here with no fears for themselves."

"As Jews, but not as Israelis," I said.

"That is correct."

"Well, on that I would frankly have to wonder," I said, broaching a subject I knew might bring an abrupt end to the interview. "It seems to me from what I've observed while I've been here that the Syrian people — especially your young people — have been imbued with a very deep hatred for the Jews.

Your schoolbooks, your newspapers, much of the material in your propaganda paints the Jews not as a national enemy but as a kind of racial scourge. From what I can gather, your people are being conditioned to hate the Jews in the most virulent of ways. On the one hand you say the Jews could live in peace as individual citizens in an Arab world. On the other you have created emotional conditions among your own people that would make that impossible . . ."

"You are saying that we do as the Nazis," Assad interrupted through the interpreter. I nodded.

"We have heard that many times," he said impassively, "and I'll tell you this. It is not something we encourage. But you must realize, where there is war, there is propaganda. Look at the propaganda of your own country during your war with Japan. Your propagandists made the Japanese people to look like scum, did they not? And yet today, once you made the Japanese realize that they could not take this land, that land, you are great friends with them. The same will happen between Arabs and Jews, once the Jews are made to realize that what they do to the Arabs is impossible to continue."

"Well," I said, "what about the Jews who remain in Syria?"

I should digress for a moment. The evening before I had toured the Jewish quarter of Damascus in the interest of learning whether the plight of Syria's small residual Jewish community was as bad as most propagandists for Israel made it out to be. I was driven to the quarter by a one-armed Arab taxi driver who spoke a bit of English and seemed rather proud — almost proprietous — of "our Jews."

The Jewish quarter — Harut al Yudah, as it is called — occupies a small portion of Old Damascus at the end of a street known as The Straight. Nestled between the Christian section and the predominantly Muslim mass of the Old City, and practically indistinguishable from them, the quarter is an assortment of artisan workshops, hole-in-the-wall souks, dilapidated buildings, dingy alleys and the incessant clamor of Levantine commerce. Because Syria's remaining Jews have developed a low-profile approach to life, the quarter looks a bit more forlorn and less busy than the rest of the Old City. But except for the ubiquitous secret police who were observable — as they are in all minority communities in Damascus — there was no evidence of an iron-fist approach to the Jews.

Before Israel came into being in 1948 there was a sizable Jewish population in and around Damascus as well as in Syria's second largest city, Aleppo. An

estimated 20,000 have left since then, most for Israel, and the Jewish population is now reckoned at just over 4,000 in Damascus and about 1,500
elsewhere. Apart from restrictions on travel — Jews must obtain a special
permit to travel beyond an approximately two-mile radius of their homes —
and a not too rigidly enforced ban on emigration, the community appears to
live unmolested.

This was not always the case. With a Christian Arab friend along to interpret, I managed to speak to about a dozen men on my tour of the quarter. A
couple told me of a few outbreaks of anti-Jewish sentiment in 1948 and again
in 1967 — broken shop windows, occasional beatings — but said that since
Assad took power conditions have improved and their lives are relatively
peaceful. Most of them were guarded in their response to my questions
concerning their desire to leave Syria for Israel, but behind the guardedness I
could detect no burning wish to emigrate.

Syria's Jews are theoretically eligible for military service, I was told, but
are never called up. They can practice trades and professions and enjoy
freedom of worship, but participation in government remains closed to them.
The community is self-contained. It has several synagogues, two schools, a
community council and a rabbinical court. Although clearly second-class
citizens, they are not, as one Jewish young man told me, the only ones who
suffer from official discrimination. Certainly there was no evidence that they
were required to wear yellow Star of David patches on their clothing, as was
the Nazi practice. Nor did they seem particularly depressed by their situation. The only thing they seemed to really fear was becoming pawns in the
Arab-Israeli propaganda war. "I am a Syrian," one senior inhabitant of the
quarter told me rather heatedly. "We are all Syrians. We stay because we
wish to stay. This is our home. The Israelis make life more difficult for us
than the Syrians. They are always on the radio,* preaching at us to sneak out
of the country to Israel, where we will no longer have to live under such
terrible conditions. But conditions here are not so bad. I know many Syrian
Jews who went to Israel, and now they are sorry. They are treated like
Arabs. So we are content to stay here. If only the Israelis would stop this
preaching on the radio. The Syrians listen to it too, and it makes them
suspicious of us . . . If the Israelis would leave us alone, the Syrians would do
so as well . . ."

Despite the lack of any evidence of harassment, Damascus's Jewish community was still popularly thought of outside Syria as being sorely op-

* The Arabic service of Radio Israel, which is beamed into Syria and other Arab countries.

pressed. True, the restrictions on Syrian Jews were ones that I would certainly chafe at were they applied to me, but they seemed of little concern to the men to whom I talked. Perhaps all that meant anything to them was the right to practice their religion; as long as that remained secure, it seemed secular restraints were of little moment.

But had I missed something? Was Damascus's Jewish ghetto made relatively free of oppression for the benefit of foreigners, while in the hinterlands, where no foreigners went, Jews suffered lives reminiscent of the Nazi era?

This was the question I sought the answer to when I asked Assad, "Well, what about the Jews who remain in Syria?"

"What of them?"

"I have seen some. All things considered, they seem reasonably well off. But in the West we are told that Syria's Jews suffer indescribably. Is there anything you can tell me about that?"

"Of course," he said. "Those are the lies fed to you by the Zionist propaganda machine. The Jews here in Syria listen to the Israeli radio tell them how badly they are being treated. The Jews look around at each other and say, 'Who, us?' "

"But still, you have special laws that apply only to Jews here."

"I will tell you," he said, "the Jews here are treated no better and no worse than Arabs are treated in Israel. An Arab, he must have special identity, he cannot go here or there, he cannot work here or there. Before Israel, there were no special laws for Arabs in that land. And there were no special laws for Jews in Syria. But then comes Israel, and it makes special laws for Arabs. So then we make special laws for Jews. Let the Israelis abolish all their special laws for Arabs. Then we will do the same for Jews."

"May I ask how you personally feel about Jews?"

Assad let a small sigh escape. "I think we have already talked too much about Jews. However, you want to know how I feel about Jews myself?"

"Yes."

"I feel this way. I have not known many Jews. I know you have a great number of Jews in America, that in Europe there are many Jews. In the Arab world there were many Jews. Jews are different from each other all over the world. They have their religion, yes, but they are different. Is that not true?"

"There's something to that, yes."

"What I mean to say is, the American Jew has nothing in common with the

Jew from Yemen, no? The British Jew, the French Jew, they have nothing in common with the Jew who lives in Syria, in Iraq."

"Except for religion."

"Religion, yes. But does this make the British Jew and the Yemeni Jew the same people? No. Do you think so?"

I didn't quite know how to answer him. "The Jews believe that their religious bond makes them one people," I said lamely.

"But this is ridiculous. I have a religious bond with people in many places outside the Arab world. But I do not feel that I am of the same people as them. By even the most liberal laws of logic, how can an American Jew say he is the same people as a Jew from Syria? He cannot. It is this religious obsession that makes it so. That is all it is, an obsession. It makes them blind to logic. It is illogical. And that which is without logic is false. So — you ask me what I feel personally about Jews. I feel they must be an obsessive people who are obsessed to destroy themselves. It is a great pity, I think. For I know that Jews have contributed much to the world."

"So you have no personal animosity toward Jews?"

"Indeed no."

"Then why do you permit the kind of literature I see all over Damascus?"

"I do not have any personal animosity against the Jewish religion, or the Jew as religious person. But the Jews of Israel, this is different. The Jews are our enemy. So how do you expect me to feel? I will feel about the Jew — the Israeli Jew, the Zionist Jew — in the same way I feel about any people who comes and takes my land, dispossesses my people. It is only because they are Jews, and because they have had a bad time of it elsewhere in the past, that they convince the rest of the world that to be their enemy has some racial meaning. In fact, they are the ones who are the racialists, with their doctrines of an exclusive Jewish state. We have heard their leaders say over and over again, 'The fewer Arabs here, the better.' Those statements are applauded in the West. But when we say 'The fewer Jews here, the better,' we are condemned. It is hypocrisy of the worst kind."

"But there seems to me to be deep, almost visceral hatred for the Jews here in Syria that goes beyond just national hatred."

"You mean this thing they call anti-Semitism?"

"Well, yes . . ."

"But, you see, the Jews themselves encouraged this," Assad said. "Here in Syria, they encouraged the Syrian Jews to believe that we hated them in order to get them to go to Israel and become soldiers for their army. It has been that way since the beginning. In Iraq the same. In Yemen the same. In Morocco the same. They sent in agents to stir up the Arabs against the native Jews, to make it so impossible for the Jews to stay that they would run off to Israel. What did they do this for? To get manpower for their army. It is even occurring today, in Russia, in Argentina. Do you know what is happening in Argentina? The Israelis say they are happy when there is an outburst of this anti-Semitism, as they call it, in Argentina. They encourage it, because they think it will force hundreds of thousands of Argentinian Jews to emigrate to Israel. They are obsessed with this anti-Semitism. They have half the world believing we want to kill Jews because we are anti-Semites. We no more want to kill Jews because they are Jews than we want to kill Hindus because they are Hindus. If a Hindu nation attacks us, we will kill Hindus because they are part of that nation. So we kill Jews because they are Israelis, not because they are Jews."

"In this context, would you care to explain why you are not willing to disclose the fate of the Israeli prisoners you have?"

Assad shook his head.

"Would you tell me anything about them? Many people are concerned about whether you in fact have any prisoners. There is a question about whether they have been killed in captivity."

"There is no cause for such concern. It is again the Israelis who make these defamations."

"I have seen Israeli soldiers who were obviously trussed up and shot after they were captured in the early days of the war," I said, sure that this would provoke Assad into terminating the interview. "I just wondered . . ."

"In war there are always atrocities. We find Syrian soldiers with hundreds of bullet holes in them. How many bullets does it take to kill a man? Besides, I know about those bound Israeli soldiers. That propaganda. The Israelis found the bodies of some of their soldiers killed in action. They then tied their hands, took photos of them and claimed that we killed them after they were captured."

"With their genitals stuffed in their mouths?"

"Who knows how far the Israelis go to gain sympathy? As I say, they are obsessed. If they choose to destroy themselves because of this obsession, we shall be happy to accommodate them. If they wish to live in peace and take their chances on surviving without war, we will also accommodate them."

"But you've implied — in fact, you've said — that without war they will not survive."

"The illegal state of Israel will not survive," Assad said, standing up to indicate the interview was at an end. "The Jewish people can survive, if that is their wish."

# 22.

# HISTORY: *Jordan*

NEXT TO PALESTINE-ISRAEL, the existence of Jordan has proved the most prickly internal political problem to face the combined Arab world during the past fifty years. Lopped by Britain, like Palestine, from the original Pan-Arab state envisioned by Hussein Ibn Ali and his sons at the end of World War I, this largely desert region was for most of its pre-1920 existence merely a sandy link between the Arabian peninsula to the south and the Mediterranean to the north.

Situated to the east of the Dead Sea and the Jordan River, in prebiblical times it was the home of the Moabites and Ammonites, nomadic tribes that had spilled out of Arabia like the Canaanites who settled the lands west of the river. In biblical times it was the seat of various other tribal societies, the most notable of which were the Nabateans, who brought a relatively advanced level of civilization to the area in the way of agriculture, commerce and writing.

Thereafter the region fell under the domination of the several European empires that followed one another in their attempts to control the Middle East. However, since the land's widespread aridity held little commercial promise except as caravan routes, foreign rule was only peripheral and the region remained neglected. During the early centuries of the Byzantine Empire it was merely a southern extension of Constantinople's Syrian province, its frontiers unmarked on any map and generally indistinguishable from those of the lands around it.

When the Islamic conquest began in the seventh century, the region's

Arabian-descended nomads, who made up most of its population, were among the first to be converted and enlisted in the march across the Middle East. Once Islam had cemented itself in the Arab world, with its headquarters at Damascus, the territory that is now Jordan, like Palestine, was a thoroughly integral part of the Arab Empire with no separate political identity of its own; it was the land bridge between Damascus and Mecca, across which tribal armies marched and pilgrims trudged.

The land remained much the same down through the centuries of Ottoman rule until the beginning of the First World War. Then its largely Bedouin population became embroiled in the Anglo-Turkish war and the British-backed Arab revolt of Hussein Ibn Ali. The revolt succeeded, but as we have seen, the British quid pro quo — a postwar Pan-Arab state to be headed by Hussein and his sons — was not fulfilled

The fallout from these events plunged most of the Arab world into the maelstrom of European power politics and brought about the arbitrary fragmentation of the Ottoman Arab province of Syria into four separate political entities: Palestine, Lebanon, Transjordan and the much-reduced Syria, with Lebanon and Syria going under French mandate and Palestine and Transjordan — a state that had not theretofore existed even in the imagination of the Arabs — falling to the British. Britain carved out this new country solely to serve its own strategic interests. Situated between the Mediterranean ports of Palestine and the British-controlled oil fields of Iraq, it was perceived as a vital land link between .the two. As well, it adjoined the Arabian peninsula, where the British anticipated extensive future oil exploitation. In the event of something happening to the Suez Canal, Britain would have this link across which to pipe its oil to tankers tying up in the ports of Palestine.

The creation of Transjordan — whose northern and southern boundaries extended, roughly parallel, from the bank of the Jordan River eastward along the frontiers of the new Syria and Arabia respectively, and then narrowed to form a panhandle abutting Iraq — proved additionally convenient to Britain because it gave the British an opportunity to salve Sharif Hussein's bitterness over the collapse of his ambition to rule over the vast Pan-Arab state promised during the war. Just as the British installed his son Feisal as king of Iraq after the French had been given Syria, so too did they install his son Abdullah as the ruler of Transjordan. As well, they expressed their approval of Hussein's proclamation of himself as king of the Hejaz. With Transjordan, Iraq and northern Arabia all in the hands of the ancient and respected Hashemite family, Britain's administrative and economic control of the region, stretching overland from the Nile valley and the Mediterranean to the Persian Gulf and the Tigris-Euphrates, seemed secure.

What Britain did not anticipate with sufficient foresight were the reactions of the Arab population to Zionism, the rebirth of the Wahhabi religious movement in Arabia, the accelerating nationalisms of all their mandatory territories, and the expansion of American interest in Middle East oil. During the interim between the two world wars, each of these parallel and often interweaving currents served to effectively erode the strength of the British grip on the region.

Yet during this period, while the rest of the Arab world sought to shed itself of European control, the Emirate of Transjordan — as it came to be called officially — developed a special relationship to Britain. This was of necessity. At its creation, Transjordan was economically and politically unviable. With its population largely Bedouin, most of it by now only semisedentary, the country had little industry and few resources. Emir Abdullah's only strength was the loyalty of his overwhelmingly illiterate Bedouin subjects — a loyalty freely given to a scion of the Hashemite family.

The family was not as respected in the more sophisticated precincts of the Arab world, however, particularly among the nationalist Arabs of Palestine and Syria who had been forced to stand by helplessly while, in their view, Sharif Hussein and his son Feisal permitted the British and French to parcel out Greater Syria between them and to reserve Palestine for Zionism. In the new Lesser Syria, Arab nationalist resistance to the French takeover resulted in the Hashemites losing their provisional throne; while in Palestine, increasing Arab resistance to Anglo-Zionist colonization, under the leadership of Amin Al-Husseini, soon to become grand mufti of Jerusalem, intensified Arab hatred for the Hashemites. Out of this atmosphere of distrust and betrayal originated an inter-Arab conflict that has continued to this day and has made the present Kingdom of Jordan — the only Hashemite country remaining in the Middle East — a kind of "odd man out" in the Arab world.

Transjordan remained quiescent during the two decades between the wars, while intense Arab nationalist activity went on all around it. The Hashemite throne of Emir Abdullah's father in northern Arabia was overthrown by the revivified Wahhabi movement led by Abdul Aziz Ibn Saud in 1926. In 1933 Adbullah's brother Feisal died, passing the Iraqi throne on to his son, who held it for only two years before he and his successor fell prey to a series of military dictatorships that left Hashemite power in Iraq virtually sterile. These events provoked in Abdullah a profound appreciation for the protection afforded him by the British; he thus kept Transjordan relatively free of any nationalist activity. In exchange, the British organized and trained a Transjordanian Bedouin army which quickly became the crack native military force of the Middle East and, given the Bedouin allegiance to the Hashemite family, Abdullah's intensely loyal personal police arm. When, in 1935, Britain opened a pipeline from its oil fields in Kirkuk, Iraq, to the port of Haifa on the Palestine coast — a line that transversed the northern part of Transjordan — the strategic importance of Abdullah's emirate to the British was assured. The British depended on the emir to maintain the security of the pipeline; the emir counted on the British to maintain the security of his regime from the threats that were constantly being voiced and manifested elsewhere by Arab nationalists. Abdullah was a nationalist, too, but only in the context of the nationalism of his father and brothers, which meant Hashemite dominion of sovereign Arab nations that might one day still merge into a single Pan-Arab Hashemite kingdom. Beyond that he was content with his own guaranteed position in Transjordan. In order to maintain his British economic and political support, he rejected the pleas of neighboring Syrian and Palestinian nationalists to join in the fight against British-Zionist and French encroachments on Arab soil.

It was particularly in Palestine that the ambitions of Abdullah most closely coincided with British policy during the years immediately prior to World War II. Amin Al-Husseini, now the mufti of Jerusalem — militantly anti-British, fanatically anti-Zionist, and ill disposed to the Hashemite tradition as well — was in control of the Palestinian Arab resistance movement. Any independent Palestinian state that might emerge from the various partition ideas being sponsored by the harassed British Colonial Office would surely have found Husseini at its helm. This was a prospect whose avoidance was imperative from the point of view of the British, the Zionists and Abdullah alike, for it would mean certain continued turmoil (Husseini, among other things, was demanding the reintegration of the territories adjoining the east bank of the Jordan River — Transjordanian territory — into the Arab Palestinian state). It was only when Husseini fell in with the Nazis and diverted his attentions to the establishment of a pro-Axis government in Iraq during the early stages of the war that British-Transjordanian pressure on the nationalist strivings of the Palestinians was relaxed.

The war, in fact, diverted the attention of all the principals in the Palestine controversy. With its end, however, and with the growing signs that Britain would throw the Zionist-Arab conflict into the lap of the West-dominated United Nations, the intensity of the issue became magnified.

The end of the war also brought the end of the British mandate over Transjordan. In March of 1946 Britain recognized Emir Abdullah as king of the independent state, but at the same time signed a treaty that pledged continuing British support and aid in case of threats to his regime. With the assurance of continued British protection, and with his Bedouin army still led by British officers, Abdullah hastily set out to mend his fences in the Arab nationalist world, especially among the increasingly violent postwar Palestinian leadership.

Of all the Arab rulers in the environs of Palestine, Abdullah had been the least vocal in opposition to Zionism. Indeed, since the aspirations of the Zionists had until the very end been supported by the British, he had said hardly a word against the Jews and had been disinclined to give sanctuary to Palestinian Arab nationalist fugitives from the British on his side of the Jordan River. Now, with Transjordan independent, and with renewed Arab nationalist agitation persuading the British and French to abandon all their mandate responsibilities in the Arab world, Abdullah would be dangerously exposed to hostile Arab groups despite his treaty with Britain and his loyal, highly proficient army. So he immediately joined the Arab League, which had been established in 1945 to act as a collective Arab counterforce against the continuance of European colonialism in the Arab world, but which quickly became an organization devoted almost exclusively to the prevention of the establishment of a Jewish state. He then began to lend his voice, if only hesitantly, to the general Arab polemics against the Zionists.

When the United Nations voted for the partition of Palestine in 1947, the Arab League announced that it would fight the creation of a Jewish state. As an alternative, it demanded independent Palestinian Arab dominion over all of Palestine, with the Jews to enjoy citizen status. But the momentum of events had gone far beyond the control of the Arabs, and when Israel proclaimed its existence in May of 1948, all that was left to them was to make good on their promise to fight.

Although the 1948–1949 Arab-Israeli war ended with an expanded Israel, it also concluded with an expanded Transjordan. The other Arab states were forced to retire in various states of disgrace over their inability to sack the underequipped but highly motivated Israeli forces. Transjordan, on the other hand, thanks mainly to its British-led troops, now occupied much of the territory on the west bank of the Jordan River that had been assigned under the partition plan to the Palestinian Arabs and would have constituted a large part of the independent Arab state of Palestine, had the Arabs chosen to accept partition.

The possession of a considerable chunk of Palestine — a fertile and economically productive one, at that, and one which included part of Jerusalem, the third holiest city of Islam — seemed to bode well for the fortunes of Abdullah. In fact it boded ill, for his unilateral annexation of the territory further incited the passions of the now-countryless Palestinian resistance movement — especially those of Amin Al-Husseini, who had returned to the Middle East from his captivity in France. All Palestinian territory was now under the domination of either Israel or Transjordan (with the narrow strip called Gaza, on the Mediterranean, under Egyptian administration).

At the conclusion of the war, Husseini had attempted to establish a Palestinian government over the Transjordanian West Bank. But Abdullah, perceiving that the retention of the fertile and populous West Bank would be highly salutary to his kingdom's treasury, and profoundly mistrusting the intentions of the anti-Hashemite Husseini, blocked the latter's bid for authority. Instead, with the approval of several thousand picked notables on the West Bank, he declared himself sovereign of the territory and incorporated it, along with his own larger but mostly arid land across the river, into a new state: the Hashemite Kingdom of Jordan.

Jordan was immediately a very different state from Transjordan. The number of its inhabitants more than doubled — not only through the annexation of the crowded West Bank but through the influx of many Palestinians who had become refugees from Israel after the war. Indeed, the Palestinian portion of Jordan's population now outnumbered the Bedouin among its citizenry. In addition, the Jordanian economy was transformed by the inclusion within the kingdom of a rich agricultural region, sites of traditional pilgrim-tourist traffic — particularly the Old City of Jerusalem (the West Bank was the heart of the biblical Holy Land for both Jews and Christians) — and communities with important and long-established commercial and professional resources.

King Abdullah was not to be around long enough to enjoy the anticipated fruits of his expanded kingdom. In the eyes of Husseini and his recalcitrant resistance followers, the king had betrayed the Palestinian cause even more heinously than had his brother Feisal thirty years before. He had not only deflated Palestinian nationalist intransigence, he was secretly meeting with representatives of Israel — a sure sign of an Israeli-Jordanian conspiracy to forever snuff out the Palestinians' hopes of one day regaining their land. The militant Palestinians had no greater enemy, therefore, than King Abdullah. He was as arch an enemy as Ben-Gurion and the Zionist leadership of Israel, at least in the immediate sense, for until he was eliminated there could be no continuance of the struggle to liberate Palestine.

Thus it was, then, that on July 20, 1951, Abdullah, Hashemite king of the newly formed Palestinian Arab State of Jordan (which, like Israel, had received diplomatic recognition from most of the great nations of the West) was assassinated in Jerusalem by an agent of Amin Al-Husseini.

The assassination shocked the Arab world, and its effects were diametrically opposite to those anticipated by Husseini. By then an aging man much reviled by those less fanatical than himself for his Second World War association with the Nazis, his role in the assassination put an effective end to his dominance of the leadership of the Palestinian movement. Certainly there were many militant Palestinians who applauded his action, especially among the hundreds of thousands who had been collecting in refugee camps in Lebanon, Syria and Gaza. But the refugees were without any political or economic resources; the real power of the Arab Palestinian population, including the power of public opinion, lay in the hands of those who had been living more or less free and prosperous lives on the West Bank under Abdullah's rule. Tired of the recent war and recognizing the reality of Israel's rapidly expanding military strength, they were inclined for the most part to forget their dreams of the liberation of Palestine and to forge their lives as citizens of Jordan. So, as if in silent agreement, they ignored the zealous calls to arms of the Husseini-ites and waited quietly to see what would happen with Abdullah's successor, his son Talal.

King Talal quickly proved mentally deficient. Within a little more than a year the Hashemite court, acutely anxious that Talal's unstable behavior would provoke a renewal of Palestinian dissidence in Cisjordan (as the West Bank came to be known), pressured him into abdicating and installed in his place his diminutive seventeen-year-old son, Hussein.* Thereafter, to the

---

* The coincidence in the names of Hussein Ibn Talal, the new king of Jordan, and Amin Al-Husseini, the man who inspired his grandfather's assassination, is just that. "Husseini" was the

present day, the fortunes of Jordan — and not a little of the turmoil of the Middle East — have revolved about him.

---

name of an old and widely entrenched Palestinian family from which the Palestinian leader was descended, thus the "Al-" before his name when it is written in full. "Hussein" is a name that is traditional to Bedouin society. Of course, the two names doubtless have a common origin in the ancient archives of the tribal tradition.

# 23.

# JOURNAL: *Hussein Ibn Talal*

NO PRESENT-DAY ARAB COUNTRY has been ruled longer by one man than has Jordan by King Hussein. His longevity is a testament to his political nimbleness, for not only has he had the problem of Israel to contend with, but also the plottings and schemings of various ideologues within the Arab world itself, plus the fact that his country has remained throughout its brief history almost entirely dependent on foreign subsidies. Such pressures — the now-forty-year-old Hussein has survived dozens of assassination attempts — would generate a deliberate and pragmatic nature in any man. It certainly has in Hussein, although much of his famed calm comes as well, as he himself suggests, from his Hashemite family heritage. His grandfather Abdullah, whose assassination he witnessed, his granduncle Feisal, and his great-grandfather Sharif Hussein Ibn Ali were all known to be cool and deliberate men.

For several years after his rise to the Jordanian throne in 1952 the adolescent monarch remained hardly more than a figurehead, supported politically by a powerful prime minister and militarily by his Arab Legion — the Bedouin army trained and led by the English army officer John Bagot Glubb.

During the mid-fifties Hussein came under the strong and rather conflicting influence of Egypt's Nasser, who was intent upon rallying all Arabdom into a unified and integrated federation that he would lead. Nasser's ambitions were never fulfilled, but in the process of dealing with the Egyptian leader, Hussein received a lasting education in the exercise of political power and the convoluted machinations of inter-Arab politics. On the one hand Jordan and its crack army were strategically vital to Nasser's plans; on the other, Nasser had to feed and expand anti-Israel sentiment in order to ascend to the forefront of Pan-Arab leadership. Such sentiment could only spill over onto Hussein who, like his grandfather, displayed little public concern over the presence of Israel and was in fact still suppressing the organized presence of liberationist passions among his large Palestinian population.

Rather than join Nasser in a political federation, and advised by politically wizened ministers who perceived well the long-term economic benefits of Jordan's continued possession of the West Bank, Hussein turned his attention to consolidating his position within his kingdom and to accelerating its economic development. He had been educated at England's Harrow School and at Sandhurst, the British military academy; this background not only refined his instinctive unflappability but also colored his Arab perspective with sophisticated political realities. He easily appreciated the still-unstable state of Arab politics and the increasingly strategic importance of the Middle East to the great powers. Rather than completely throw his lot in with other Arab governments, which might result in the eventual discontinuance of the Hashemite dynasty — a prospect that every ounce of his childhood training and instinct could not permit — he craftily chose to tread a middle road between anti-Western Arabdom and the West itself.

Thus in 1956, in a display of at least superficial Arab unity as Nasser prepared to nationalize the Suez Canal, Hussein dismissed John Glubb and took over personal command of the Jordanian army. Moreover, when the joint Anglo-French-Israeli force attacked Egypt he entered into a military defense pact with Egypt and Syria. He retained his own political sovereignty, however, and when the short-lived Suez crisis came to an end he returned his attention to Jordan's internal affairs.

His two principal problems were the further stabilization of his Palestinian population and the introduction of some level of prosperity, by way of agricultural and industrial development, in Jordan's Bedouin hinterlands, where his real constituency lay. He achieved the former to a certain degree by appointing to important posts in his government representatives of the large Palestinian bourgeoisie of the West Bank. He accomplished the latter by letting it be known in the West that his country was open to massive infusions of foreign aid in exchange for a Jordanian policy of "even-handedness" within the larger and by now virulently anti-Western North Arab world.

The West responded eagerly, particularly the United States. America saw the advantages of having an Arab friend in the middle of anti-American Arabdom. It hoped that by supporting an Arab country while at the same time supporting Israel, it could moderate the Arab-Israeli conflict and counter the rapidly growing Soviet influence in other parts of the Arab world.

By 1958 Jordan was at the top of the list of the world's recipients of foreign aid at $68.1 per capita. (In contrast, Israel in the same year received $46.8 per capita aid.) Some of this aid went, of course, to enriching Hussein himself, enabling him to live ever more regally than before, and to strengthening and expanding his army. But there was enough left over to be channeled into development projects, mainly in agriculture and in the mining of minerals. Soon the Jordanian economy began to expand and diversify — although to this day it still depends largely on foreign aid.

The early and middle sixties found Jordan at the beginning of what seemed would be an era of increasing prosperity. Indeed, by 1965 the United States started to cut back its assistance because the Jordanians were doing so well. In real terms, the Jordanian gross national product had been growing, between 1958 and 1965, at a rate of eight and one half percent — a very high rate of increase by any standard.

Nevertheless there remained strong undercurrents of displeasure with King Hussein in many quarters of the Arab world, especially over his less than enthusiastic support of the Palestinian nationalist cause and the moderateness of the few public statements he did make about the existence of Israel. Matters came to a head in 1964 when an Arab summit conference, convened by Nasser, sponsored the establishment of the Palestine Liberation Organization in an attempt to counter the new and vocal grass-roots Arab Palestinian liberation groups that had emerged in the wake of the 1956 Suez War. Arab leaders demanded that Hussein permit the new organization, under its Egyptian-appointed spokesman-leader, Ahmed Shukairy, to function on the West Bank. Hussein reluctantly agreed, although not before securing a written guarantee that the PLO would make no territorial claims on Jordan.

The PLO was basically a propaganda machine designed by Nasser to take the wind out of the sails of various small but clamorous liberation groups which had been born in the refugee camps. These groups had no connection with the Palestinian liberationism of the earlier generation of Amin Al-Hus-seini. Many were promoting a Maoist and Viet Cong political philosophy, and were criticizing the inaction of such Arab leaders as Nasser and Hussein in the "holy war" against Israel.

The chief among these evolving groups was Fatah, the brainchild of Yasir Arafat, an educated Palestinian who had become disillusioned with Nasser's ability and commitment to regain Israel as a result of Egypt's loss of the Sinai during the 1956 war. Arafat toured the Palestinian diaspora during the late fifties. His message, in recruiting support, was that the Palestinians would have to lead the drive to regain their homeland. By 1959 the revolutionary ideas of the movement began to take hold among the younger generations in the camps.

It was to counter the spreading influence of Fatah and similar groups that Nasser organized the PLO and got other Arab leaders to pressure Hussein into letting it operate on the West Bank. Hussein had already escaped several attempts on his life. But they convinced him of the necessity of taking a firmer stance vis-à-vis Israel. This necessity was reinforced by Israel's diversion of the headwaters of the Jordan River in 1964 — a move that not only reduced the flow of the Jordan but, in the view of Arab experts, in-creased its salinity and made it unsuitable for Jordanian irrigation.

The introduction of the PLO into the West Bank constituted the beginning of a process that utterly changed what had appeared to be Jordan's bright future under Hussein. The pressures of PLO propaganda and the counter-pressures brought about by increasing guerrilla activities against Israel on the part of rival revolutionary groups sucked the entire Arab world — Hussein with it — into the vortex that led to the 1967 war.

That war resulted in the Israeli takeover of the entire Jordanian West Bank, including all of Jerusalem. Within a few hours Jordan had lost half its economic resources. A third of its population was left under Israeli oc-cupation. And Jordan proper received the additional burden of 300,000 new Palestinian refugees — a fertile garden for further Palestinian resistance activity and opposition to Hussein.

The catastrophic outcome of the war for the Arab states thoroughly dis-credited the officially sponsored PLO and thrust Fatah and other small but active groups into the forefront of the Palestinian resistance. These groups, separately and collectively, were immediately able to expand their follow-ings. They received a marked increase in sympathy and financing by certain Arab governments, and began to receive arms, training, money and moral support from outside the Arab world, particularly from the communist bloc. By 1970 the guerrilla movement, led by Fatah, had virtually become a state-within-a-state in Jordan and posed a severe threat to Hussein's regime. When Hussein, for fear of massive Israeli reprisals, attempted to put the guerrillas under restraint in September of that year, a bloody civil war broke out between the Palestinians and the Jordanian army. Most of the surviving guerrillas were forced out of Jordan into the surrounding Arab countries. But once again a Hashemite ruler had become the bitter enemy of the Palestinian Arabs.

Hussein's expulsion of the Palestinian guerrilla movement, and his subsequent refusal to join Egypt and Syria in the 1973 war against Israel, put him once more on very shaky ground within the Arab world — among both radical and moderate elements. Indeed, his refusal to join the war in an effort to regain at least a sliver of the Jordanian territory occupied by Israel in 1967 left him, in the eyes of most Arabs, without a shred of moral claim to the West Bank. His decision to stay out (although he sent a token symbolic force to fight alongside the Syrians) was, of course, well considered from a military point of view, for his army had practically no chance of forcing a wedge into the West Bank — or so he thought at the time, based on his mistaken estimate of Israeli readiness. But from an Arab political point of view it was ill considered, for it gave widespread respectability to the Palestinian claim to the West Bank as the place in which to establish an independent Arab State of Palestine, and it effectively destroyed any hopes Hussein might have had for recovering it for Jordan.

Its ultimate effect, however, was to add a profoundly complicating ingredient to the Middle East problem and to prolong the possibility of its solution.

King Hussein is highly articulate, but he is not voluble, and this makes an interview with him rather frustrating. He has learned the art of noncommittalness well, perhaps through his extensive experience in the West, and he uses it skillfully to mask what one hears some of his acquaintances describe as an intense Arab emotionalism.

Although I had hoped to interview Hussein on his home turf, I was unable to make connections with him in the Jordanian capital of Amman. We met instead in London, where, through the offices of a friend-of-a-friend-of-a-friend, he agreed to give me a few minutes of his time. He had stopped there on his way back to Jordan from a trip to the United States during the period of intense comings and goings of Henry Kissinger and various Arab dignitaries between Washington and the Middle East during the summer of 1974. His visit to London was supposed to have been secret, but a lunch one day with British prime minister Harold Wilson had made his arrival public. We met that evening in the commodious flat of one of his mistresses, a dark and slightly eccentric Anglo-Italian woman who was a member in good standing of London's smart set — a fey mix of show business notables and the youthful cream of Britain's upper classes.

Hussein seemed not at all circumspect about the milieu in which we met. A tiny man (at least compared to me), there was little about his physical appearance that betrayed his regal position. He was slim — he might have been a Panamanian jockey, I thought — and was celebrated for his pursuit of risky sporting endeavors — driving race cars, piloting jets, parachuting. Yet he had a kindly mien, informal, almost self-consciously apologetic, and a thoroughly Western sense of humor. It was only when he spoke that I sensed his conception of himself. His voice, astonishingly deep and sober for so small a man — resounding like a bass drum — and his cautious, practiced precisioning of words in mildly accented English left no doubt in my mind that he carried on his shoulders a wearisome kingly weight.

At the beginning of our conversation my questions were aimed at plumbing his curious relationship (for an Arab) with the Israelis over the years. He replied in very general terms, saying that he had no personal animus against Jews but that, in Middle Eastern political terms, the existence of Israel made little sense and that he could understand the fifty years of hysteria in the Arab world over it. He said that he recognized the reality of Israel, however, and that the Arab dream of abolishing its existence had been irrevocably eroded by the harsh realities of time. He claimed that he had worked tirelessly during his reign to moderate Arab belligerency toward Israel and to encourage the development of an Arab modus vivendi with it, but he was sadly cognizant of the fact that his efforts had gone largely for naught. "And yet, you see, the Israelis made no efforts to help me in this," he concluded.

"What do you mean?"

"Take 1967, for instance. Here was a situation in which we were forced to go to war . . ."

"You mean your country," I said.

"Yes — we were forced into it not so much by the other Arab nations as by the Israelis. We knew that Israel would use the war as a pretext to take over Jerusalem and the West Bank. They kept saying they had no expansionist ambitions, but everything in the Zionist philosophy demanded complete Jewish possession of Jerusalem . . ."

"Wait a minute," I said. "It seems to me that by any objective standards the Arab countries provoked the war. Syria was sponsoring guerrilla raids. Guerrillas were operating from the West Bank. Egypt closed down the Tiran Straits and then sent great masses of armor into the Sinai."

"These were political maneuvers designed to increase Israel's discomfort and force the Jews to be more conciliatory. It was not our intention to go to war. It was our intention to persuade Israel to cease its reprisal raids against its neighboring states for the guerrilla incidents and to deal with the Palestinians directly, to settle the refugee problem, to consider repatriation and compensation . . ."

"But wouldn't you say all these Arab acts were justifiably seen by Israel as acts of belligerency, acts of war?"

"That is how Israel interpreted them, although that is not the way they were intended. Remember, in political disputes between nations, military movements, naval blockades — such things as these are accepted international practices in the pursuit of political and diplomatic ends."

"As far as I know," I said, "they are also considered preliminaries to war."

"Only when such actions put a nation's back so firmly to the wall that it has no other options. But our actions did not put Israel in that position. The Israelis had many options left besides going to war. But they chose war instead."

"What options did they have?"

"Well, they had the option of coming to terms with the entire Palestinian problem. Remember, it was not the Arab nations which created the refugee problem, it was Israel. Now, perhaps Israel did not do it all by itself. Perhaps certain Arab actions in 1948 encouraged it. But it came into existence primarily because of the establishment of Israel, and even more so because of the actions and attitudes of the Zionists prior to Israel's creation. So, it being a problem created by Israel, it was a problem to be solved by Israel. The problem of the refugees was causing serious complications in all the Arab states surrounding Israel, as well as farther away. The events of 1967, prior to the war, were our way of trying to induce Israel, to prod Israel, into dealing with the problem. They chose instead to ignore it and to use the political and diplomatic pressures we were placing on them as a pretext to go to war. I can tell you that it was a shock to all of us."

"Well," I asked, "how do you explain all the Arab propaganda prior to the war? I mean the genocidal stuff about driving the Israelis into the sea, wiping them off the face of the earth, and so on?"

Hussein smiled tightly. "That is deplorable, I concede. But you must be able to differentiate between propaganda and intention. This differentiation exists in every conflict between states. Take the Israelis, for instance. They have been saying all along that their intention has not been to annex more Arab land beyond what was given to them in 1947. But within Israel there are great elements in the society and government who propagandize intensely for the inclusion of all of Palestine in the Jewish state. And even some who go beyond that and say the Jewish state will not be complete until it embraces the entire Fertile Crescent. Now, if the Israelis say that Arab propaganda makes them anxious for their survival as a people, how do they think their propaganda makes Arabs feel? Particularly when, while saying they have no desire to expand, they do precisely the opposite. And you must acknowledge that this drive to spread the Jewish state far beyond its present borders has been a central feature of Zionist philosophy from the very beginnings of its presence in the Middle East, long before the Arabs had any awareness of it, before the Arabs began to resist it."

"So you think the 1967 war was really born out of Israeli opportunism."

"Yes, it was born out of a blind refusal on the part of Israel to confront its true problems as we were attempting to force it to do. In spite of the excesses of Arab propaganda, the Israeli government knew full well that it had little to fear from us in the sense of our being able to overrun the country. But it chose to play on the fears its own propaganda encouraged in order to expand its frontiers. . . . And that is not all. Before the war, Israel was in a very depressed state economically. It had lost many of its educated people through emigration to other parts of the world — people who did not like what Israeli society was becoming, which was predominantly Levantine rather than European. And it was suffering from very high unemployment, from social inequities, and a number of other internal problems. By going to war the government saw a convenient way of diverting the Israeli people's attention from these problems. Look at Israel after the war. Suddenly its economy was prosperous again. Money poured in from all over the world. Now, it is popular to think of Arab governments as being cynical. I say: What about Israel?"

"Getting back to the war itself," I said, "you say that you, that Jordan, were forced into it?"

"Yes, indeed. And that was Israel's greatest mistake. For even though they won the battle in the short term, they lost the war in the long term. And that is the weakness of Israel. This fanatical Zionist religious drive of the Jews causes them to be blind to the long-term political consequences of their actions."

"How is that?"

"Well, the situation with the West Bank, for example. They had no political reason to invade and occupy our territory . . ."

"What about their doctrine of secure borders?"

"That is a doctrine that went out the window with the invention of the rocket," Hussein said.

"I don't mean 'secure' against the attacks of another state. I mean against commando raids, guerrilla warfare, terrorist activities. I believe that is what Israel is talking about when it says 'secure borders.' "

"I know what Israel is talking about. And this doctrine of secure borders is a cover for territorial expansion. Look at it this way. Jordan proved in 1970, at great risk to ourselves, that we would not tolerate guerrilla activity from our soil. We proved that we had the means and the will to enforce that policy, and we did so. Israel could easily have withdrawn from our territory then — returned it to Jordan and pulled back to the 1967 lines — and it would not be facing the problems it is facing today. We have been attempting to persuade Israel to do so, but it has stubbornly refused to consider it. It is no longer really a question of a secure border with Jordan, it is a question of the Zionist policy of annexing the land it occupies."

"The Israelis I've talked to say they had little faith in your ability to maintain control over the West Bank."

"Look, we almost went so far as to propose a permanent peace with Israel, acting independently of the other Arab nations, in exchange for the return of our territory. Do you realize what sort of concession that is for an Arab head of state to make? We in Jordan realize the precariousness of our position. But we are prepared to take risks to achieve an accommodation with Israel. And yet the Israelis have consistently refused to compromise."

"You've been making proposals to Israel?"

"Of course," said Hussein.

"How?"

"Through intermediaries."

"Would you care to say who?"

"I would rather not."

"Kissinger is one?"

"That is well known. But I do not want to discuss Mr. Kissinger. And anyway, the 'who' is not the point. The point is that these initiatives have been taken by us, and they have been consistently rebuffed. I can understand Israeli fears about guerrilla attacks, but their fears are more than that. Their fears are simply the yielding of any territory whatsoever. Not for security reasons, but for reasons of Zionism. Let me say this. I accept that the entire history of this conflict has been brought about in large measure because of the mistakes of Arab leaders in earlier years. We Arabs have made many mistakes, and we have often sought to transfer the responsibilities for those mistakes onto the Jews. I have often mentioned this in my private talks with colleagues from other Arab nations. But the Jews have made one great mistake — one that I would say transcends all of our collective mistakes. And that is this. Zionism got them their nation. Once they had it, and once they successfully secured it — as they did in 1948 — they should have known enough to abandon their fanatically Zionist obsession and replace it with a modern one. Zionism is not a workable political philosophy. And yet it has remained all these years as the monolithic political rationale of Israel. It is a rationale that has its roots in the ancient Jewish tradition of conquest and expansion. It is built on the biblical Jewish nation, a nation that depended on military might and social superiority, a nation whose creation and existence were based on the principles of divine right and might makes right . . ."

"But Israel is not a state whose political rationale is Zionism. It is socialism, and parliamentary democracy."

"These are the methods it uses," Hussein replied. "But they are merely internal methods. The political institutions of Israeli society are still drenched in the Zionist obsession. It is as if an Arab country — no matter what its practical political system — were still living under the old Islamic obsession, the obsession that brought about the Arab conquests."

"But isn't that exactly what has generated Arab hatred for Israel all these years?" I asked. "Isn't the Arab desire to eliminate Israel motivated ultimately by the old Islamic obsession to conquer the infidels within their midst?"

"Not at all," Hussein answered with a wry smile. "If it were, then we would have been warring all these centuries against the Christians among us, the Copts, the Druzes. But we have left these people to be what they want. And that is my point. It is popular in the Western press to describe our reaction to Israel as a holy war. Yet I can tell you as a representative of an ancient Muslim family that for as long as I remember there was never any hint of holy war in this family's attitudes toward the Zionists. Islam long ago went through the process of adapting itself to modern realities. But Zionism has only transposed its ancient driving force into a modern guise. It still remains the Zionism of old. And that is the difficulty, the great mistake Israel has made. By refusing or being incapable of ridding itself of its Zionist character, its policies and goals remain identical to those of the ancient Hebrew community. History has shown what befell that community because of Zionist intransigence."

"It wasn't called Zionism then," I said.

"No, but it was the same thing."

"Are you saying, then, that Israel will eventually suffer the same fate as its biblical predecessor?"

"I cannot predict what will happen. But you will recall that the biblical land of Israel was swept away in the tide of time and events because it insisted on its exclusivity and refused to compromise with its neighbors. The modern state of Israel has proved to be no different."

"But what about the Palestinian refusal to compromise?"

"The elements among the Palestinian movement today who refuse to compromise represent only a very minor portion of the movement as a whole. Israel's refusal to recognize the Palestinian movement, even to acknowledge the existence of a Palestinian people, is the cause of the Palestinian movement. It is a grave mistake."

"But you don't exactly acknowledge the existence of a Palestinian people yourself, do you?" I said. "After all, the Palestinian movement wants to turn the West Bank into an independent Palestinian state. This means that you would permanently lose your most valuable piece of property."

"It is not that," said Hussein. "You see, we inherited the West Bank situation. It became an integral part of Jordan. We have tried to do our best with it. But we have to face two realities. One is that this land was originally set aside for the Palestinians. The second is that despite our very sincere efforts to have it returned to us, Israel has refused to do so. We still hope, but our hopes grow dimmer by the day. And here is where Israel engages in a persistent self-defeating practice. For every further day it prevents us from reestablishing our control, it brings itself closer to a confrontation with the Palestinians themselves. If they do not yield very soon, they will no longer have us to deal with, but will be required to deal with the Palestinian leadership. We are receiving at this very moment great pressures from other Arab governments to renounce our rightful control of the West Bank and deliver it over to the leadership of the Palestine Liberation Organization. We have made every attempt conceivable to encourage an Israeli withdrawal in our favor, and we have been rebuked at every turn. We have one final effort underway at the moment, with the help of Mr. Kissinger. If they refuse, they are digging their own grave. There comes a time when the Israelis must choose the lesser of two evils. From their point of view we are the lesser, but they refuse to make the choice. So, they will be faced with the greater — the PLO claiming the West Bank as the site of the Palestinian state. They cannot prevent it. And it makes one wonder if they want to. It makes one wonder if they do not, deep down in their hearts, want this confrontation with the Palestinians. For it surely will mean another war."

October 1974, three months after our interview. The Palestine Liberation Organization — not the original one founded in 1964 by Nasser to counter the revolutionary groups then forming around Yasir Arafat, but its successor, made up of these very groups and led by Arafat — had just been overwhelmingly recognized by the United Nations as the legitimate sole representative of the Palestinian people. The Israeli government reacted with shocked outrage. The United States expressed mild dismay. The Arab world was ecstatic.

Shortly thereafter, at an Arab summit meeting in Rabat, Morocco, the collective Arab leadership prevailed upon King Hussein to yield Jordan's twenty-four-year suzerain over the West Bank. And it gave its stamp of approval to Arafat and his Palestine Liberation Organization as the official government-in-exile of the independent State of Palestine — to be located within the Israeli-occupied West Bank. After twenty-seven years the Palestinians had gotten — at least in spirit, and at least in part — the independent state they had originally rejected. Did this mean an end was in sight for the problems of the Middle East? Or did it mean simply the beginning of a much greater problem?

# 24.

# HISTORY: *The Palestinians*

AT THE END OF WORLD WAR I there were approximately 644,000 Arab inhabitants in the land that was about to be carved out of southern Syria by Britain. There were also about 56,000 Jews of various ethnic identities, the majority of eastern European origin, as well as smatterings of non-Arab and non-Jewish groups. The ration of Arab to Jew was a shade over 11:1.

Under the mandatory rules of the League of Nations, whose international legal code provided the rational for the mandate system, Palestine, which had theretofore been more of an idea then a physical or territorial reality, was given borders, a national sociopolitical identity under British mandatory administration, and a form of statehood which, in accordance with the League's Covenant regarding the self-determination of indigenous peoples, promised an eventual self-governing independent and sovereign Arab State of Palestine. Thus the British, under the auspices of the League of Nations, created a body of people who could only be called Palestinians. The vast majority was Arab.

To most of the Arabs living in Palestine this demographic distinction meant little. If they thought at all in terms of a national identity, it was as Syrian. To most of the Jews it meant little too. They thought of themselves first and foremost as Jews, and perhaps secondarily as Poles, Russians, Hungarians, Ukrainians, and so on.

During the period between the world wars, although a rigorous Arab Palestinian nationalism grew up out of the native Arab resistance to Zionism, the majority of Arabs continued to think of themselves in terms other than Palestinian — as, of course, did the rapidly swelling Jewish population. It was only in the aftermath of the Arab-Israeli war of 1948–1949 that the great mass of Palestinian Arabs, by then numbering well over a million, began to perceive themselves as a "Palestinian" people.

By then, of course, they were no longer living in Palestine. Through the process of flight and exile — either voluntary or forced — approximately half of them had collected in miserable refugee camps on the territory of neighboring Arab states. Of the other half, about a fifth remained in the new state of Israel, while the remaining four-fifths either came under Jordanian rule on the West Bank or spread throughout the world as voluntary émigrés and expatriates.

By their flight, the Arabs eliminated for the Israelis one of the major problems of partition — an Arab majority in a Jewish state. Thereafter Israel was content to view its Arab "problem" as having been solved, and to turn its attention to the challenges of its own development. In defense of its disclaimer of responsibility for the Arab refugees, it contended that the Arabs of Palestine had been given every opportunity to have their own state according to the UN Partition Resolution. That under the prodding of surrounding Arab states they refused to accept it was no fault of Israel's, went official Israeli thinking. If you offer a hungry man half your loaf of bread and he throws it back in your face, it is his, not your, fault when he falls dead of starvation. This thinking has been at the heart of Israel's continued refusal to acknowledge the existence of a Palestinian people; by rejecting statehood in 1948, the Arabs of Palestine forever abrogated their right to be considered a distinct people.

But the notion of Palestinian peoplehood did not evaporate among the exiled Palestinians themselves. Israeli propaganda did everything it could to discourage non-Arab sympathy for the idea of a Palestinian people, and for a long time it succeeded. But its immediate success sowed the seeds of its ultimate failure, for the longer the outside world — especially the Western world, which was most responsible for creating the problem in the first place — remained antipathetic to the Arab cause and ignored the plight of the largely refugee Arab Palestinians, the more fertile became the collective mind of the Palestinians for the cultivation of ideas of a collective identity.

It was fashionable in the West for many years following the creation of Israel to think of the refugee populations of the various Arab countries surrounding the Jewish state as pawns used by the leaders of these countries to keep the issue of Israel alive within the Arab world and, by so doing, to secure their own credibility as leaders. The insistent claim of Arabs was, after all, that they were all brothers, all the same. If this was so, why, then couldn't the various Arab countries simply absorb their Palestinian refugee populations and be done with the problem — much as Israel was absorbing populations of Jews from the Arab countries — instead of keeping them isolated in filthy, disease-infested camps? Such thinking reflected the age-old Western ignorance of, and prejudice against, Arab culture. It was the very thinking that to a large degree spawned the Middle East problem to begin with.

In the first place, Arab slogans of homogeneity had long been rendered obsolete by the introduction into the Middle East of Western political institutions and values. At one time in the past they might have logically referred to a politically unified people — in fact, this concept had been the very engine of pre–World War I Pan-Arab nationalism. But the failure of the Arabs to achieve their Pan-Arab state, and the subsequent parceling up of that phantom state into real political entities, cast Arab nationalism into an entirely new (for it) frame of reference. The natural progress of events thereafter dictated the development of separate Arab political identities — Syrian, Iraqi, Jordanian, and the like — until the slogan "We are all brothers" was left with only a spiritual connotation. In condemning the Arab countries for not absorbing the refugee Palestinians, then, the West was condemning them for not doing something Western nations themselves would not have done. The Israeli absorption of Jewish populations — both refugee and non-refugee — was politically desirable for Israel, just as its absorption of a million Arabs in 1948 would have been politically undesirable.

My point is that all nations will seek to absorb refugee groups when it is politically desirable and will isolate or reject them when it is not. There are numerous enough examples of this in history to suggest it as an unwritten political law. For the Arab countries in 1948 and immediately thereafter, it would have been clearly politically undesirable to attempt to assimilate the hordes of refugees pouring across their borders. Each of these countries was still relatively poor, with not particularly large native populations, and the organized absorption of large masses of outside Arabs into their economies would have further impoverished them. But there was still an even more compelling reason for the political undesirability of absorption, from the Arab point of view, and that was the inherent illegality of the entire Western-sponsored disposition of the Palestine matter. Efforts to absorb the displaced Palestinians would have been tantamount to endorsing what the Arabs had for so long been protesting — the unilateral expropriation of territory that was by tradition and international law unquestionably Arab.*

The Arab refusal to assimilate the homeless Palestinians passed the responsibility on to the United Nations, which expanded the United Nations Relief Works Agency (UNRWA) — funded largely by the United States — to deal with them. Through UNRWA, a network of fifty-three residence camps was developed in Jordan, Syria, Lebanon and Gaza (which Egypt had annexed at the end of the 1948–1949 war). These camps became home for approximately 750,000 Palestinians, most of them uneducated, unskilled and without any cohesive political spirit. Another 450,000 found themselves suddenly Jordanians as a result of Jordan's annexation of the West Bank and part of Jerusalem, while about 160,000 remained behind to become citizens of Israel. Still others dispersed far beyond the immediate area, both within and without the Arab world.

The fragmentation and dispersal of the Arab population of pre-1948 Palestine had the effect of splitting and factionalizing the people to a degree that was well above the normal traditional factionalization of Arab society. For the most part a conservative people, the Palestinian Arabs lived through the 1950s in various stages of impoverishment, despair and resignation. Those among them who were politically minded left it to the Arab governments to eventually regain their homes for them. When the rather unrealistic promises of Arab leaders continued to go unfulfilled, however, there began to grow in the camps a deepening discontent — particularly among the less conservative youth — and an impulse to do something.

The impulse took shape around ideas and principles — mostly communist-inspired — that had emerged during the postwar period and hardened into the broad ideology of revolutionary nationalist liberation and self-determination. The outlines of this ideology, which have since become institutionalized under the general term "New Leftism," had already spread across the Arab world through such movements as the Baath party and the Algerian National Liberation Front. Moreover, they were beginning to bear fruit in other places in the world — black Africa, Cuba, the Far East. To a handful

* The one exception to the Arab refusal to absorb the Palestinians was, of course, Jordan. This exception came about precisely because, for King Abdullah, the absorption of the Palestinians was eminently desirable, politically, for it meant the profitable, if accidental, expansion of his own state. However, the bulk of the Palestinians absorbed into Jordan were the inhabitants of the West Bank. They were not, in the strict sense, refugees. Many of the actual refugees from other parts of Palestine were interned in camps.

of youthful Palestinian Arab refugees and enforced émigrés, they came to represent a potential escape from what otherwise appeared to be an endless future of misery and disenfranchisement.

In the hands of these sorely discontented young men, the radical outlines of the emerging ideology mingled with the basically reactionary and parochial principles of pre-1948 Palestinian Arab nationalism to produce a new sociopolitical movement dedicated to the *self-recovery* of all of Palestine. It was by no means a unified movement, however. Given the physically fragmented character of the dispersed Arab population of Palestine-Israel, given the diversity of fortunes among that population, and given the restrictions placed on it by Arab host governments — which made communication between one segment and the next difficult at best — the infusion and proliferation of the new liberationist ideas were as variegated as the population itself.

But proliferate the ideas did, in various guises, until they became a single idea, then a wish, then an expectancy, finally a demand. In the process the vague and general world perception of a faceless mass of refugee Arabs became transformed into a perception of a cohesive Arab entity that identified itself as the Palestinian people. That this people seemed to be comprised during the early 1960s of only a handful of outspoken leaders and their small and often-at-odds political cadres, whose principal activities consisted mostly of pathetic and ill-organized partisan warfare along the borders of Israel, was beside the point. The point was that now the Palestinians had an identity. The question then became: To whom would pass the responsibility of leading and representing them in the inevitable struggle for self-determination and territorial independence?

The bellicose Arab countries, particularly Egypt and Syria, had long sought to represent the displaced Palestinians, but they had managed more to obscure their identity than to clarify it. Their assertion was that only through the molding of Pan-Arab unity and the consequent expansion of Arab military might would the entire Arab Palestinian homeland be wrested from the Jews and restored to its exiled owners. Scattered throughout the Arab world and without a central authority of their own, the Palestinians had no choice but to accept this representation.

After the Suez War of 1956 it became apparent to the handful of new-generation Palestinians who had come under the influence of leftist political ideologies that the already-independent Arab nations would inevitably place their own interests before the Palestinians'. Slogans of Arab unity began to seem more a hollow device to keep the Palestinians quiet than an intrepid policy to liberate them. They also began to perceive that the Jordanian annexation of the West Bank and the incorporation of its large Palestinian population had the potential for thoroughly diluting the Palestinian cause. If Israel turned out to be unrecoverable, and the West Bank Palestinians became content to remain under Jordanian rule, there would never be an Arab Palestine to which the vast refugee population could return.

Out of these perceptions grew a reinvigorated sense of Palestinian nationalism modeled loosely on leftist revolutionary ideas and dedicated to bringing the Palestinian cause to the forefront of Middle East affairs. This sense was articulated most forcefully at first by a small group of Palestinian Arab friends who formed a tiny organization they called "Harakat al-Tahrir al-Filasteni" — the Palestine National Liberation Movement, or Fatah.* One of its founders was a young man named Yasir Arafat.

By the fall of 1959 Fatah was beginning to publish political tracts and to distribute them throughout the Palestinian diaspora. The essential point made by these tracts was that the hope of inter-Arab unity achieving the liberation of Palestine had been proven bankrupt, that liberation was primarily a Palestinian affair no longer entrustable to the Arab states, and that the Palestinians themselves must take the lead in the battle with Israel. The Algerian war of liberation, which featured terrorism and guerrilla warfare against the French, was often cited as an example of what would have to be done to liberate Palestine.

By 1960 the tactic of guerrilla warfare had become an acceptable one in the minds of those the world over who sympathized with struggles for independence on the part of peoples who had lived for centuries under various forms of colonialism. It is not surprising, then, that the tactical principles advanced by Fatah found an appeal among the dispersed and depressed Palestinians, particularly those of the young generation. By 1961 Fatah was a well-organized political and paramilitary organization, though still small. When Arab Algeria finally won its independence in 1962, however, its ranks began to swell with recruits who quickly became convinced of the virtues of the Fatah philosophy of guerrilla warfare.

Fatah was not the only liberation organization to benefit from the impact of the Algerians' success. Several other leftist groups had sprouted up among the Palestinian populations of Jordan, Syria, Lebanon and Iraq. Although

---

* Fatah is an acronym formed by reversing the order of the first letters of Haraket al-Tahrir al-Filasteni. In Arabic it means "conquest."

their ideologies differed in degree with that of Fatah — they were for the most part more radical — their goals were similar: the liberation and independence of Arab Palestine by the Palestinians, using the tactics that had proved so successful in Algeria. The Algerian victory swelled the ranks of these groups, too, although not to the extent it did those of Fatah, which, because it had been the first to materialize, was still considered the primary radical Palestinian liberation organization.

As Fatah expanded, it created a military arm — Asifah — to carry out its program of terrorism and guerrilla warfare against Israel. At the same time it began to formulate a broader political strategy, one designed to intensify the anti-Israel militancy of the Arab states and to force them into a confrontation with Israel.

In 1961 Syria had seceded from its union with Egypt in the quarrel over the nature of Nasserism in Damascus, thus damaging Nasser's policy of Arab unity and giving Fatah's national self-liberation program wider appeal. When Nasser saw in 1964 that the expanding influence of Fatah among the Palestinians had the potential of dividing the Arab world further, he called for a summit conference of Arab leaders and sponsored the establishment of the Palestine Liberation Organization, as we have seen. The new organization was to be headquartered in West Bank Jordan, filled with old-guard Palestinian nationalists, funded and otherwise supported by the Arab nations, and was to be the "official representative" of the Palestinian people. Guerrilla warfare was clearly not to be part of its program. Instead, a small conventionally trained and equipped army — the Palestine Liberation Army — was assembled and scattered throughout Egypt, Syria and Iraq.

To express its independence of Nasser's influence and to simultaneously fulfill what it saw as its historical responsibility to the Palestinians, Syria ignored Nasser's pleas that the Arab states unite behind the PLO so as to discourage the more radical guerrilla groups that were coming into existence. Instead, the Syrian government invited the various groups to operate from its soil in order to conduct raids into Israel. Fatah responded eagerly and soon spread its Asifah cadres along the Syria-Israel border and into Jordan, whence they mounted a series of sorties against Israel.

The raids, commencing in 1965, were only a minor nuisance to the Israelis, yet they served to increase popular Palestinian support of the guerrilla movement. But as the groups continued to expand, their leaders began to find themselves at odds over strategy and philosophy. Some, like Arafat, viewed guerrilla warfare as the best means of uniting the scattered Palestinian population; in his scenario, guerrilla warfare was to be the catalyst of Palestinian passions, out of which would eventually emerge a distinct and cohesive Palestinian political ideology. Others took the position that the waging of guerrilla war without first having formulated a clear political ideology was self-defeating, that guerrilla activity could not really be effective until the people were united behind a cohesive ideology (the liberation of Palestine was merely a political goal, not an ideology).

A representative of the latter view was George Habash, a Palestinian physician who had learned his politics at the American University of Beirut and who brought to his commitment to the liberation movement a decidedly Marxist orientation. He was interested not just in liberating Palestine, but in establishing there a militant socialist society that would eventually revolutionize the entire Arab world. He named his small band the Popular Front for the Liberation of Palestine (PFLP), sought to recruit followers by indoctrinating them in his political principles, and spent much of his time criticizing what he saw as Fatah's needless waste of valuable Palestinian manpower through futile and often suicidal commando raids on Israel.

By the beginning of 1967 Habash's arguments had begun to take hold within the Palestinian community, especially among young intellectuals, and they threatened to split the liberation movement, still dominated by Fatah. The outcome of the 1967 Arab-Israeli war intensified the split, for Habash and his followers saw in the overwhelming Arab defeat the abject failure of Fatah's guerrilla-first approach to the liberation of Palestine.

The war, however, was consistent with Fatah's objective of drawing the Arab regimes into a confrontation with Israel. The humiliating nature of the Arab setback provided the opportunity for the Fatah leadership to convince many Palestinians of the claims it had been making all along: that the outside Arab states had neither the will nor the capacity to liberate Palestine. Indeed, the Israeli takeover of the West Bank from Jordan and the Gaza Strip from Egypt underlined the contention. Fatah emerged from the war as one of the few active dynamic forces in the Arab world. With its prestige enhanced, it decided the time was ripe to step up its guerrilla activities.

The Israeli military occupation of the West Bank had driven tens of thousands of additional Palestinians into the camps of the East Bank as refugees. By now there was a total of about 700,000 Palestinians crowded into East Bank Jordan, by far the largest concentration of refugees in the Arab world. It was here that Fatah headquartered itself, recruiting mainly from within the camps but also drawing from the less-deprived and educated Palestinians who had managed to stay out of the camps.

Fatah received a significant boost in March 1968 when, in response to a series of commando raids, Israel sent a large armored reprisal force into the Jordanian town of Karameh. There a group of underarmed Fatah guerrillas, supported by Jordanian artillery, managed to stand off the Israeli attackers for twelve hours, destroy a few Israeli tanks and inflict heavy casualties. The battle of Karameh was a moral victory for Fatah. The leadership cleverly exploited it for recruiting purposes. Soon Fatah's ranks began to swell even further, until the organization came to constitute a formidable independent military presence within Jordan.

Karameh proved an additional bonus, for as Palestinian enthusiasm for Fatah spread, the Arab governments were forced to acknowledge its influence and pledge financial support. Shortly after Karameh, Yasir Arafat emerged as the chief leader-spokesman of Fatah, and by the summer of 1968 the organization's political stature was great enough for Egypt's Nasser to include Arafat as part of an official Arab delegation visiting Moscow for consultations about Russia's support in future Arab efforts against Israel.

But the growth of Fatah's popularity and strength entailed risks, as well. As it began to proclaim itself the only valid representative of the Palestinian people, it incurred the wrath of rival political groups that were expanding, or springing up anew, in the wake of the 1967 war. Fatah also became a source of growing concern to King Hussein and his Jordanian government, for with its deepening influence over Jordan's Palestinian population it was beginning to play a vital role in that country's internal political affairs.

By the end of 1968 Fatah sought to translate its numerical superiority into complete authority over the entire Palestinian movement. In early 1969 it managed to win control of the old Palestine Liberation Organization, which had lost much of its influence — even among older-generation Palestinians — as a result of its empty rhetoric prior to and after the 1967 war. Yasir Arafat was named chairman of the executive committee of the reconstituted PLO.

Thereafter, Fatah's mission became twofold: to continue its terrorism and guerrilla warfare inside Israel, and to bring the other liberation groups under its umbrella so as to present a united front. The first part of the mission was lessened by the effect of the second, however. The fragmentation of Palestinian society was simply too great to allow a single group to dominate its varied political impulses. The population of the original 1948 Arab Palestine was split into four basic groups: (1) those who had lived for some time within Israel; (2) those who were now living under Israeli military occupation on the West Bank; (3) those who were refugees and exiles in the neighboring Arab countries; and (4) those who were dispersed throughout the world beyond. Of the four, only the large refugee population represented a potentially unifiable force. The Arabs of Israel were generally indifferent to armed liberation movements; the West Bank Arabs were under the strong restraints of the Israeli military administration; and the Palestinians dispersed beyond the pale were generally out of reach of the organizational efforts of the guerrilla groups.

Even the refugees in the immediate neighborhood of Palestine were fragmented and factionalized. Their subjection to the political life of their host Arab countries for two decades had left many of them with divergent ideological orientations which heightened the obstacles to political unity. Moreover, the Arab host countries themselves had been further split from one another as a result of 1967. In their attempts to recover from the humiliation of their defeat, they began to maneuver more intensely, one against the other, to lead a general Arab resurgence. In so doing they sponsored competing liberation groups, which made it all the more difficult for Fatah to achieve unity.

By late 1969 the movement was riven with dissension in three principal quarters. The clearly radical groups were quarreling with one another over the proper ideological stance of the liberation movement. Then these groups, sometimes together and sometimes separately, were challenging the authority of the ideologically more moderate Fatah, which had a high degree of organization but little in the way of long-term strategy. And the entire movement itself was bickering with reactionary Jordan, which was attempting to put reins on its expanding presence there.

Suddenly intramovement discipline began to disintegrate. Most of the post-1967 action against Israel was forgotten as various guerrilla groups began to war seriously among themselves. In an attempt to outdo Fatah terrorism and to draw wider attention to their own aspirations, the more radical groups instituted a program of foreign terrorism which involved hijacking international airliners and shooting up airports. Prominent among the groups behind these operations were Habash's PFLP and an offshoot that had been organized by his one-time follower, Nayef Hawatmeh. Hawatmeh distinguished his band by calling it the Popular Democratic Front for the

Liberation of Palestine (PDFLP). Two intentions of this terrorist program were to embarrass Fatah, which was by then solidly and widely entrenched in Jordan, and to bring down on it the wrath of Hussein's army, which would, it was hoped, eliminate Fatah's leaders and open the door to the ascendancy of the more radical elements to the leadership of the movement.

In early September 1970 the PFLP carried out the spectacular hijackings of three international passenger planes, flew two of them to a remote airstrip in the Jordanian desert, and held their passengers hostage.* Three days later another plane also ended up in Jordan. This was enough for Hussein, who viewed these actions as an attempt on the part of the entire guerrilla movement to destroy his sovereignty. Arafat and the PLO leadership rigorously criticized the Habash program of terrorism, but when Hussein sent his army against Palestinian guerrilla outposts throughout the country Arafat was obliged to condemn the king in even stronger terms. What followed was a brief but vicious Jordanian war against the entire PLO and the Syrian forces sent to support it. At least 2,000 commandos and Palestinian civilians were killed and 10,000 wounded, with most of the movement's survivors taking refuge in Lebanon and Syria.

Since then, Jordan has been relatively free of a Palestinian guerrilla presence. Once again, however, King Hussein was cast in the role of Hashemite villain and betrayer of the Palestinian cause. His claims to being the proper representative of the Palestinians by virtue of Jordan's twenty-year possession of the West Bank would forever after possess diminishing credit in the minds of most Palestinians — even those moderates of the West Bank.

With much of its guerrilla force wiped out, the weakened PLO was forced to suspend most of its military activities against Israel and reorganize itself politically. Nasser had died the day after negotiating a ceasefire between the Jordanians and the guerrillas, thus removing from the scene a potentially valuable mediator and supporter. The liberation movement was thrust into isolation while the leaders of the still-vying factions resumed their struggle for authority.

Except for a steep increase in terrorism by small, ultrafanatical splinter groups and Israeli reprisals that brought about another guerrilla-Arab war — this time in Lebanon in 1972 — the movement continued to go largely ignored by the outside world. Within, however, the ongoing process of fragmentation and reconciliation, often erupting in violence between repre-

---

* The third plane, a Pan American 747, was flown to Cairo, where it was blown up moments after the passengers had disembarked.

sentatives of various factions, intensified. It was only when King Hussein extended his suppression of the guerrilla movement, while at the same time offering Israel a plan* which would take the energy out of Palestinian self-determination, that conflicting groups within the movement began to reintegrate. One thing the vying leaders by then were willing to agree upon was the absolute impossibility of allowing Hussein to rule the Palestinians. So they started to issue counterproposals — proposals that had as their ultimate aim the establishment of a secular Arab-Jewish binational state in all of Palestine in place of the present combination of the Jewish state of Israel and the Jordanian-Palestinian West Bank.

Israel, of course, would entertain no such proposals, and Hussein was no more enthusiastic. Yasir Arafat took advantage of the triple stalemate to propose to the other groups an interim solution which said, in effect: Let us deal with Hussein and the West Bank for now; we will deal with Israel later. Out of this grew a more or less consensus demand that Hussein relinquish his claim to the West Bank (and Egypt to Gaza) and that these two areas be acknowledged as the locus of a future independent Palestinian state.

The idea quickly gained currency in the Arab world. As a result, Arafat and other Fatah notables were thrust once again to the forefront of the Palestinian leadership. The 1973 war, and Jordan's refusal to join in it, further strengthened Arafat's hand and weakened Hussein's. Thereafter, Palestinian propaganda concentrated on the immediate creation of a Palestinian state out of the West Bank and Gaza, to which all the refugees from the various camps scattered throughout the other Arab countries would be repatriated. The idea appealed to the Arab governments if only because it would relieve them of the pressure of having almost one million refugees continue to live on their soil.

There was only one problem, however. Hussein refused to countenance the idea. If he were to lose the West Bank, his regime would not only suffer a grave loss of prestige, but Jordan would revert permanently to being a minor Arab state, less a kingdom than an emirate. Similarly, the leaders of Israel — if there was to be any Israeli withdrawal whatsoever in response to pressures being placed on it by the United States — would countenance nothing *but* a return of the West Bank to Jordanian rule, with a bundle of international guarantees thrown in.

The Arab governments solved their share of the problem a year after the

---

* In exchange for Israeli withdrawal from the West Bank and Gaza, Hussein would reorganize these areas into a combined Jordanian-Palestinian state under his rule.

war by coercing Hussein into relinquishing Jordan's claim to the West Bank and to the Palestinian people in general. At the Arab Summit Conference at Rabat in October 1974, they formally granted to Arafat and his regrouped Palestine Liberation Organization the exclusive authority to speak for the Palestinian people and to control any government set up to represent them. The inevitable had happened. It remained only to see how Arafat and the PLO would exercise their newly legitimized authority.

# 25.

# JOURNAL: *Yasir Arafat*

TRYING TO ARRANGE A MEETING with Yasir Arafat is like wending one's way through a dusty maze. I had embarked three times in the period of a week on complex journeys to meet and interview him — journeys made under the guidance of ostentatiously armed bodyguards and involving vehicle switches, roundabout routes, blindfolds, and all the other paraphernalia of dime-novel spy fiction — only to be told upon my arrival at some remote Lebanese destination that Abu Ammar* was unable to keep the appointment.

I had just about given up on my attempts when I received a telephone message in Beirut one morning that he would be able to see me in a few hours. I was instructed to go to a beach club on the southern outskirts of the city, rent a cabana, and wait inside for a code-knock on the door.

I did as instructed, thinking that a beachside cabana was as good a place as any to talk to Arafat. But our meeting was not to take place there. When the knock came and I opened the cabana door, I was confronted by a pudgy Arab girl in a bathing suit. She handed me a slip of paper and was gone. On the paper was another instruction: Put on a bathing suit, rent a deck chair, and sunbathe for an hour; then, at 2 P.M., return to the cabana, change, and leave

---

* Abu Ammar is Arafat's Fatah code name and the name he is generally called by his colleagues in the movement. Abu means "father of" in Arabic. It is a traditional practice among certain Bedouin tribes to refer to a man in this manner when his genealogy is unknown. When Fatah began to organize in the late fifties, all its leaders took such names to symbolize the shedding of their personal pasts and to express their solidarity and hopes for collective leadership.

the beach club by walking across the dusty soccer field that was situated between it and the main road.

I followed the routine, feeling slightly put out by now and vowing this caper to be my last. As I crossed the empty, grassless soccer field, baked hard by the sun, I was approached by a pair of teenaged boys, one of whom handed me another note. This instructed me to continue on to the main road, take a taxi to a haberdashery shop on the Hamra — the main commercial street in Beirut — and there tell the proprietor that I wished to purchase a maroon necktie.

When I got to the store and made the request, the man nodded me through a curtained doorway into the rear. There I encountered two sullen men in dark sunglasses who escorted me to a small Renault parked in the alley behind the store. After I got into the back of the cramped car we set off, winding through a series of narrow streets until we were in a teeming, garbage-littered quarter that I had never seen before. The driver negotiated a series of alleys, honking bedraggled pedestrians and donkeys out of his way, then pulled to a stop at a pockmarked building. The two men grunted me out of the car and told me to wait.

They entered the building. A minute later one of them stuck his head out the door and motioned me in. As I entered, my eyes trying to adjust to the dark interior, my arms were gripped by two pairs of hands and I was led down the hallway to an anteroom. There I was completely searched by two different men, also sullen, also wearing sunglasses, their faces scarred by what looked to be old wounds. After the search I was taken farther down the hallway to an elevator. One of the men pushed the button, then both proceeded to stare at me grimly while we waited for the car to arrive. When it did we got in. The elevator was hardly bigger than a telephone booth, and as we ascended the two men continued to stare at me.

We stopped at the top floor, the sixth. I was escorted down another hallway, this one lined with posters showing pictures of Palestinian guerrillas in various poses of attack. I was taken into an office and told to wait. Opposite me a swarthy young man, his right arm almost all scar tissue from wrist to shoulder, sat at a desk cutting articles from newspapers. He occasionally peered at me through his sunglasses. I ventured a smile. He frowned. A pistol lay on the desk.

Another man entered and impassively presented me with a cup of Turkish coffee. There was no hospitality in his face as I thanked him. I sipped the coffee, lighted a cigarette and waited. After a while the telephone rang. The man at the desk picked it up, listened for a moment, then put it down. He looked up at me and said something in Arabic. I shrugged to indicate that I didn't understand him. "Fife meenootes," he said.

Another half-hour went by, along with two more cups of coffee. Then a new man entered the office. In heavily accented English he said, "Come with me."

He led me back to the elevator. Uh-oh, I thought, here we go again — another wild-goose chase. We did not go all the way down to the street, however. Instead the elevator stopped at the second floor. My guide pointed me down a narrow dark corridor to a door where another man stood. Crooked in his arm was a lethal-looking AK-47, the Russian automatic rifle that is the staple weapon of the Palestinian guerrilla forces. I was handed over to the man with the gun, who opened the door and motioned me in.

It was another office. Here a group of men stood around talking, all wearing soiled short-sleeved shirts, tight black chino pants and narrow pointed loafers — outfits reminiscent of an American high school gang of the fifties. One of the men detached himself from the group and approached me. "Mr. Kiernan?" he said in confident English.

"Yes."

He extended his hand. "Welcome. I am Abu Assan. I shall be your interpreter. Come. Abu Ammar awaits."

He led me through another series of offices to a door, before which sat still another man with an AK-47. The man knocked, a voice came through the door, and we were admitted. Sitting on a ragged settee at the far side of the room was a dark, portly man in a casual shirt. Except for a fringe of hair at the sides of his head he was totally bald, the curve of his skull describing a graceful arc against the white wall. His eyes were large, wide-set, brown and liquid. His neck and fleshy cheeks were covered in a gray-tinged stubble, while a thicker beard and moustache framed his wide, heavy-lipped mouth. It was a thoroughly Arab face, a face that an American movie director dependent on stereotypes might cast in the role of an unctuous Levantine rug merchant, I thought. Although I was momentarily taken aback by his baldness — I had only seen pictures of him wearing his checkered Palestinian *keffiyah* — there was no doubt who he was: Yasir Arafat. I wondered at that moment of recognition how I would have felt had one or both of my children been victims of his guerrilla bands.

Arafat did not wish to talk about his past, he told me after announcing that he would speak in Arabic. (He said this in English, revealing a fair command of the language, and in fact lapsed more and more into English as our conversation progressed.) He confirmed that he was a relative of Amin Al-Husseini, the old Palestinian nationalist who had had such a checkered career during his years as leader of the resistance against the British and Zionists. But he said Husseini himself had had little influence on him, although other members of the family did.

Arafat was born in about 1928 in Jerusalem and passed his early years there. As a teenager, a year or so before the creation of Israel, he joined with his father in an Arab resistance group led by another Husseini relative, Abdelkader Al-Husseini. After Abdelkader was killed by the Israelis in 1948, Arafat fled with his family and thousands of other refugees to Gaza, where the Arafats owned some property. In Gaza he became associated with the Muslim Brotherhood, which had organized a volunteer guerrilla force to strike back at Israel.

At the time the Muslim Brotherhood was moving onto the center stage of Egyptian politics as Egypt drifted aimlessly in the grips of a decadent king and a corrupt government. Although Arafat claims never to have been a member of the Brotherhood, its militant political aspirations, molded on a powerful Islamic religious appeal, were a magnet for many politically minded young men who were part of the Arab world emerging from decades of colonial domination.

After the Arab-Israeli truce in 1949 Arafat enrolled at Cairo (then King Fuad) University to study engineering. In the early fifties he became president of the university's Palestinian Students' Federation, an organization that was beginning to simmer with leftist ideas. Then he entered the Egyptian army, serving as a lieutenant and demolitions specialist in the 1956 Suez War. It was the ease with which the Israelis captured the Sinai and marched to the banks of the Suez Canal that convinced Arafat and several other Palestinians who witnessed the advance that Nasser's promises regarding the Pan-Arab liberation of Palestine were impossible of fulfillment.

He left the army shortly after the war and went to Kuwait, where he entered a community of Palestinians drawn by the oil boom — an elite of skilled workers, technicians and teachers. He got a job as an engineer in the Ministry of Public Works and operated a contracting business on the side. He was doing well financially, but he still, like many of his fellow Palestinians, felt himself a homeless exile. Out of these feelings grew the organization that came to be called Fatah. Thereafter Yasir Arafat — Abu Ammar — gradually grew into a symbol of the Palestinians, at least in the Western world. Now he was about to be elevated to a position equivalent to what we like to call "the father of his country." I asked him if this had any weighty meaning for him.

"But we don't have a country yet," he replied.

"It seems that you will," I said.

"It is not something that is easy to come by, as you see," he answered. His large brown eyes glistened as he looked me over. A man who had spent much of his life threading his way through the Palestinian underground, living in caves and back rooms, ducking in and out of sight like a forest animal, fearing for his life more from Arabs, probably, than from Jews, he showed a surprising openness. He spoke quietly, and his voice had a gentle, almost fragile, quality. In repose his face seemed sad, concerned, rather than hard and militant. When he smiled, which was more and more often as the conversation progressed and he became more relaxed, his face turned almost boyish, conveying qualities of sweetness and shyness that were totally out of character with his reputation. At no time did I feel that he was expressing himself in any particular way for my benefit; his locutions, darting between quiet gravity and humor, seemed completely natural. I experienced an uneasy feeling, much as I imagined a reporter might have in the early 1930s interviewing the ascendant Adolf Hitler.

I had been assured that he would entertain any question except one about his pre-Fatah past and would not reject a question simply because it seemed unfair or distasteful to him. So I asked him, "You have been accused of being a bestial merchant of murder by Israel, and much of the Western world thinks of you the same way. Many say that this makes you unfit to be a spokesman or representative of the Palestinian people. How do you react to this?"

"I do not personally claim to represent my people," he said. "I am merely part of an organization that represents them."

"Okay, then," I said, "the organization is thought of as the sponsors of murder and so on . . ."

"Well," he said, "we cannot afford to spend our time worrying about what other people say about us. But the very fact that they say we are unfit to represent our people proves that today they acknowledge there is such a thing as a Palestinian people. Without the efforts and sacrifices we have made, the world would still be ignorant of the existence of the Palestinians. So, because we have forced the world to take notice of our people and the injustices that have been for so long imposed on them, we must be acknowledged as those who are most qualified to represent them. Who else do they have?"

"In traveling through the world of Palestinians," I said, "I have found great differences of opinion over who in fact should represent them. Many feel that you — your organization — cause more problems for them than you solve. Are you aware of these differences?"

"Of course we are. But unless you are a Palestinian yourself, unless you have endured all these years of deprivation and dispossession, you cannot possibly understand the great internal dilemma that faces our people today. There are three and a half million of us scattered about the Middle East and the rest of the world. A few of this three and a half million have managed to exist better than others. But by far the majority have suffered, and even here some have suffered less than others. Palestinians have always been a politically conscious people, so there are bound to be differences of opinion on such things as representation. That is another danger we face from the rest of the world. At first the world refused to acknowledge the existence of the Palestinian people. Now that it does, it seems to expect that all Palestinians should not be like other people and be subject to differences of opinion. When we do have internal differences, the world says, 'Oh, that is just those crazy Arabs, they cannot get along even with their own kind.' "

"So you think the majority supports you?"

"If that were not the case, then we would not be here today. Let's look at it this way. Of the three and a half million Palestinians, about three million live here in the Middle East. Of those three million, more than half live under refugee status. The rest live a little better, but still they live as second-class, third-class, fourth-class people in other countries, without the rights and privileges of those who are natives of these countries. Now we represent to them their only chance to get their own country. Their own country — it is a dream that they have lived for fifty years, and it is a dream that has been betrayed time and time again. Now we give them a chance for that country. Do you think they will disapprove of us? Of course, some would like to see their dream come true in a different way. Some are content to let Jordan be their country. Others will not be content until all of Palestine is their country, as it should have been many, many years ago. We represent the consensus, the majority, who want their country back. Any part of it will do for now. We believe in the democratic system — the majority rules. That is why we are still here today."

"Do you expect that, when and if you get your country, all Palestinians will return to it?"

Arafat shrugged. "That is unimportant, for we still have a long struggle ahead of us before we get it. But no, I do not expect all will return. However, most will. We will be a country of three million."

"You're talking now of the West Bank and Gaza connected into a single country," I said.

"And Hamma,"* Arafat added.

"Well, then, what are your plans after that?"

"Our plans are to establish our state. We will establish a democratic state and begin to build up our institutions."

"How?"

"How? We will have a constitution, we will have elections . . ."

"Are you thinking of a parliamentary system? Or would your leaders and ministers be elected directly by the people?"

"This is something we are working out," said Arafat.

"You have been — or I should say you and the PLO have been — receiving much aid and support from the Soviet Union. I assume that Russia would be highly instrumental in the setting up of a Palestinian state?"

"You are worried about Russian motives?" he replied.

"Well," I said, "the phrase 'democratic state' means different things to different people. You are certainly not unaware of Western concern, and Israeli concern, over what sort of state this would really be. And this goes along with other questions, questions about what your own ambitions are. For instance, is it your ambition to rule over this state?"

"I have no personal ambitions other than to see my people become a nation. What happens after that will be according to the will of the people. But I can assure you of this. The Palestinian people will never tolerate a dictatorship."

"Are you sure? Wouldn't the people tolerate anything after all the misery they've been through? Wouldn't the acquisition of a state of their own be enough to satisfy them? Wouldn't the nature and form the state takes be secondary?"

* Hamma is a tiny enclave at the juncture of the Syrian, Jordanian and Israeli borders, south of the Golan Heights, to which the Palestinians also lay claim.

"That remains to be seen. I am confident that we will create a state that is suitable to the needs and wishes of the people."

"But do you appreciate the concern of others about this?"

Arafat showed his only flash of impatience. "The concern of others is not for us to appreciate or understand, if by 'others' you mean America and Israel. 'Others,' as you call them, have showed no understanding or concern for us. We will determine for ourselves what we will be."

"But don't you think that by taking into account the concern of America and Israel you might be able to achieve your state in a faster and more orderly way? In other words, if you take a more conciliatory attitude toward your adversaries, isn't it likely that you will be quicker to get what you want?"

"That is nonsense. How can we take a more conciliatory attitude to the Israelis when they refuse to recognize our existence? When they simply dismiss us by calling us murderers and animals? They understand perfectly that this terrorism they accuse us of is a legitimate means of warfare for a dispossessed people to use to recover their land and to make a nation for themselves on soil that is theirs. Israel itself achieved its goal through terrorism. What is the difference between the Haganah of the Zionists and the Fatah of the Palestinians? What is the difference between the Irgun of the Zionists and the Black September of the Palestinians? They say that it was all right for them to kill Arab women and children because it was for a good cause. They say it is evil for us to kill Jewish women and children because ours is an evil cause. Now we do not like to see women and children killed, no matter who they are. But the Israelis must understand that the terrorism they accuse us of is the very same terrorism they condoned in themselves. When they are willing to do that, when they are willing to recognize that we are the Palestinian people, then perhaps we can begin to talk about conciliation."

"Are you planning to continue your guerrilla activities?"

"Our plans are to use all the means at our disposal to achieve our goals."

"Have you put any timetable on the achievement of these goals?"

"We have no timetable. We have been struggling for twenty-six years. We can keep on for another twenty-six, and longer if necessary. I can tell you that we will never give up. They may kill me, they may kill all of us, but there will always be people to take our place."

"Getting back to the Russians," I said, "can you tell me how much influence they have over the PLO? I mean, would an eventual Palestinian state be based on a Russian model?"

"The Soviet Union has been very helpful to us. Now we realize that they help us, acknowledge us, for their own global interests. So? If you are struck by a car and are lying in the road badly injured, and someone comes to you and helps you get to a hospital, you don't question his motives. You don't care whether he is doing it because he thinks it will earn him a medal or a reward that will enhance his own status in the world. You accept his help simply because you need it. Without it you will die. But accepting his help does not obligate you to submit yourself to him for the rest of your life."

"What about your divisions within your own organization?" I said.

"Again," he replied, "we have differences. They are well known."

"But wouldn't these differences be inclined to spill over into the government of the Palestinian state, once it was established? Don't your present differences imply a considerable amount of internal strife in the future state?"

"We are better united now than we were before, particularly since we have gained the worldwide recognition we have." He smiled. "You know, if what you say is true, it is a good reason for the Israelis to give our state back to us. We would be so busy fighting among ourselves we would have no time for Israel."

"On that point," I said, "as you know, the Israelis are worried that the establishment of a Palestinian state in the West Bank and Gaza will simply be a prelude to further Palestinian agitation against Israel itself. Much of your propaganda has supported that idea — that your long-term goal is to use the smaller state to eventually wipe out Israel . . ."

"This may or may not happen," he interjected in English. "Look, we know that a Palestinian state cannot exist in a vacuum. We know that once we become a fully accredited nation the situation will change, that we will be subject to various international pressures, just as any nation is. We are not going to slaughter the Jews; no one would allow us to. Once we get our state, even if it's only half a state, we will be too busy organizing ourselves to have enough energy to keep up a war with Israel. We are not intent on engaging in a war that will bring about mutual suicide. And once we get our state the world will say, 'All right, you've got it, so now let us turn to other things . . .' "

"Are you saying peace will reign over the land?"

"Let us say the situation will be defused. We are realists. We know that the entire focus of the situation is changing here in the Middle East. In time, Israel will disappear altogether as a Zionist state. It will either kill itself off trying to resist the closing in of Arabness from all sides on its Jewish identity, or it will submit peacefully. How can it be otherwise? How can Israel continue to exist as a Jewish island in an Arab ocean? It is like pouring a cup of cold water into a tub of hot water — the cold water from the cup will turn warm, then hot; it will not turn the hot water cool. That is Israel, the cup of cold water. This is my prediction of what will happen to Israel. They have five, ten, perhaps twenty years left to exist. Not as a people, but as a Jewish state. That is, if they hurry up and face reality. If they face reality and quickly give us our state, they will be able to live in relative peace and will have the opportunity to make a peaceful transition from a Jewish state of Israel to a larger democratic Arab state of Palestine where people of all religions can live as equals. But if they refuse to face reality, or if they refuse along the way to accept this inevitability, they will conclude by trying to destroy us. But they will only succeed to destroy themselves — as a state *and* as a people."

"You must admit," I said, "that the idea of the Israelis accepting the dissolution of their own state, however peacefully, is not something they are likely to look kindly upon."

"It does not matter, really, how they look upon it. As I said, a Palestinian state cannot exist in a vacuum. Neither can the Israeli state. Things will be so radically changed here in relation to the rest of the world that Israel will have no choice in the matter except either to kill itself off or to accept to be part of the Arab world in a different way — as an integrated people."

"Well," I said, "long-term predictions are fine, but what about the short term? What about next year, and the year after?"

"Next year, the year after — that depends most on the United States, doesn't it? The United States now has it in its hands to determine the immediate future. And I want to emphasize this if what I say is going to appear in the book you are writing. The United States must face its own reality."

"What is that?"

"It is that it can no longer expect to keep Israel as its client state here in the Arab world. Remember what we have been saying for the last twenty-six years. Everything we have been saying is beginning to happen. Nothing the United States has done has been able to prevent it from happening. The Palestinian people are now a reality. The Palestinian state is soon to be a reality. And the Arab world as a whole has begun to acquire unprecedented power. These are all great events that we have been predicting for many years, and now they have come true. No amount of Israeli military might or

American diplomatic interference has been able to stop it. So, what we are saying today about the future will also come true. It will be proved not to be just empty Arab propaganda. The United States will be no more able to stop the future than it was able to stop the present situation. America has a choice. Like the Zionists, it can continue to try to resist the future. Or it can join it. If it resists, it could very well bring about its own downfall."

# 26.

# JOURNAL: *The Future of the Arabs and the Israelis*

To TRAVEL THROUGH the Arab confrontation countries — as those which are in direct conflict with Israel have come to be known — and through Israel itself, interviewing, watching, listening, is to understand everything. At the same time it is to understand nothing.

The Middle East is a paradox. Whatever the rights of Israel, Arabs once possessed its land. Whatever the rights of the Arabs, Israel now possesses it. Instead of ghettos for the Jews, there are refugee camps for the Arabs. In place of a Jewish diaspora, there is an Arab diaspora. "Our hope is not yet lost to return to the land of our fathers . . ." These words are the beginning of the Israeli national anthem. Yet you see them slogan-scrawled on the stained walls of refugee huts wherever you go among the Palestinian camps. The Palestinian liberation movement, as it likes to say of itself, is the Zionism of today; today's Palestinians are the oppressed and homeless Jews of a European yesteryear.

The arguments that issue from both the Arab and Israeli sides over who is right, who is wrong — each have a compelling logic. Arab arguments are basically legalistic, turning on interpretations of international law that are hard to fault. Israeli arguments derive their nourishment principally from an emphasis on historical and moral imperatives: Even if, technically, the establishment of the state of Israel were not in total accordance with international law, there was a higher law at work — a moral law, God's law — which transcended the human dimensions of international law and in every respect justified the creation of Israel.

These arguments have through the years become institutionalized until they are now catechism, each for its respective side. Within this broad outline rage other arguments and counterarguments, these more specific, designed to attach or disclaim blame for this, that and the next thing that has happened between the two sides. These too have compelling logic. These too have become rote.

So, then, it is logic against logic, the validity of one claim against the validity of an opposite. And through the years the circle has spun with increasingly vicious rhythms, sucking into its vortex the larger and more dangerous ideologies of the outside world. The basic problem started because the Arabs of Palestine and elsewhere refused to accept the establishment of a Jewish state in part of Palestine. Why? Because, the Arabs said, aside from the illegality of it, most of the manifestos of Zionism indicated an ultimate intent to incorporate a generous part of the Arab world — "from the Nile to the Euphrates" — into a Jewish nation.

Now the pendulum has swung; the problem has reversed itself. Today Israel refuses to accept the establishment of an Arab state in part of Palestine. Why? Because, the Israelis say, most of the manifestos of Palestinianism indicate an ultimate intent to incorporate the Jewish world into an Arab nation.

There has similarly occurred another reversal of history, for the very forces of world public opinion that supported the successful creation of a Jewish state are now operating to breathe life into an Arab Palestinian state. Whether Israel likes it or not, whether Jews or others the world over believe in the legitimacy of a Palestinian people or not, the probability of a soon-to-be Palestinian state is even more certain today than the probability of a Jewish state was, say, in 1946. Yet that very certainty lends an even greater uncertainty to the future.

This state has been in a process of "becoming" for the past twenty-seven years. Through that time it has been cast into sharp focus as the central and fundamental factor in the Arab-Israeli conflict — just as the "becoming" of the Jewish state was the central and fundamental factor in the Arab-Zionist conflict during the previous twenty-seven years. The historical symmetry of these two processes raises a compelling question: Will the establishment of a Palestinian state mean another equivalent extended period of warfare between Israel and the Arab countries? Or will it sufficiently defuse the tensions in the region to permit the beginnings of some sort of lasting accommodation to take hold between the adversaries?

There are of course no simple answers to these questions. And not even the most complex speculation can be complete without taking into account the impact on the matter of such ever-present pressures and influences as those that spring from the internal politics of individual Arab nations, from the unity and diversity of political and economic interests that exist between these nations, from the political and economic relationship that is evolving between the Arab world and the outside big-power constellations, and from the competing tactical and strategic interests of the big-power constellations themselves.

Until 1973 the question of whether or not the establishment of an independent Palestinian state (along with attendant territorial adjustments between Israel and its other Arab adversaries) would induce a climate of peace in the Middle East was of little concern to most Westerners. The net effect of the October War of 1973 — regardless of who won or lost what — was to make that question suddenly the all-consuming one. This is because its answer has profound political and economic implications for the entire world.

The political implications relate most directly to the future of the West's — particularly America's — policies and actions within the international sphere. Put more bluntly, they relate to whether or not America (with or without the rest of the Western world) will find itself forced for one reason or another to engage in some sort of war.

The economic implications relate most directly to the future of the West's — again, particularly America's — economic and industrial health and to the future of just about every Westerner's traditional notions of comfort, security, mobility and freedom. The Arab world has found an effective means to bring the conflict between the Arab nations and Israel home to all of us, through its handling of its petroleum resources, and to present the West with some extremely difficult choices with respect to its own future.

Taken together, as they always must be, the political and economic impact of the October War on the West has made the question of whether war or peace is to be the future of the Middle East of crucial concern. It has thus made the question of how the establishment of an independent Arab state of Palestine will determine the region's future of equal concern.

Rather than attempt to provide an answer to the question myself (for it would be no more than speculation mixed with hope), I thought it would be more valuable to see if I could develop a consensus from a cross section of informed leaders in the Arab world, orchestrators of public opinion and political policy, as I made my way through it. In addressing the question to forty-three political and military figures, and others well connected to the leadership of the Palestinians and the various Arab countries, I posed it much as I have outlined it here, making sure the individuals I put it to understood that I expected them to take into acccount the international factors that went beyond the basic Arab-Israeli conflict. These included, for instance, the potential effect of the future on the political stability of their nations and the potential damages another twenty-seven years of Arab-Israeli hostilities (if that were to be the case) might inflict on the political stability of the world. I felt it important to emphasize these considerations in order to provoke answers that would be thought out and independent — or as independent as possible — of the traditional catechism of anti-Israeli propaganda. In other words I wanted to see if the people I asked, all of whom were thought of as responsible, educated and sophisticated wielders of power in the Arab world, were willing and able to think of *all* the possible consequences to the Middle East and the rest of the world, both favorable and unfavorable, of a continuation or escalation of Arab-Israeli hostilities once a Palestinian state was a fact.

The question thus took the following form: "It is generally agreed in all high-level political quarters that what happens here in the Middle East between the Arabs and Israel in the immediate future, and what happens between the Arabs — including an Arab Palestine — and Israel in the less immediate future, is no longer just a local problem, but is a pressing concern of all powerful nations for a variety of reasons, mostly having to do with their own strategic and pragmatic self-interests. Keeping this in mind, and keeping in mind all the possible political, economic and military consequences — good or bad, locally and worldwide — that you can imagine occurring as a result of the way things develop here in 1975 and thereafter, how do you think the situation will be resolved, if at all? Specifically, assuming that the Palestinians will eventually be granted independent statehood, do you see the situation between the Arabs and Israel getting better or worse until that time? And once Palestinian statehood is achieved, do you anticipate that things will veer more toward peace or toward an intensification of hostility and warfare?"

The answers I received were for the most part serious and well thought out, although not free of conventional Arab biases (what political analyses anywhere are free of the subjective national slants of those who voice them?). Taken together they did point to a consensus — one that for the United States, and Israel, could only be interpreted as gloomy.

Several were based on historical parallels. For instance, Amin Hafez, the former Lebanese prime minister who liked to steep himself in Arab history, compared the present situation to the time of the Crusades. "The Crusaders came here, occupied the land and tried to set up Christian states. The Arabs eventually drove them out. The Christians who had become members of these states, they were permitted to stay if they wished, as part of the Arab world. . . . It is similar today. The same impulses that provoked the Arabs to prevent the creation of European Christian states have been at work against the presence of a European Jewish state. History has a power of its own which is much greater than the power of individual nations. The United States, the Soviet Union — they can do all they wish to influence events here, but history will flow in spite of what they do, in spite of what pressures or threats they bring to bear. It is like trying to divert the course of a great river by putting up obstacles. Nothing can stop it. Such actions may alter it slightly, but if they slow down the current in one place they force it to go faster in another. The details of the conflict may change slightly here and there as history goes on, but the conflict itself cannot be stopped. . . . The Arabs will struggle until Israel is no longer a reality — even if this means a nuclear war that destroys half of mankind. For that is history. It is a pity the Jews cannot recognize this. . . . We have no desire to destroy Jews. Our wish is only to delete the Zionist state of Israel from the map of the Arab world. International Zionist propaganda has used the statements of a few extremist Arabs about driving the Jews into the sea to gain money, weapons, support, and so on. But this, I can guarantee you, is not the sentiment of the great, great majority of Arabs, not even of Arab Palestinians. We would welcome to have the Jews live among us, because they can contribute much to our civilization. Jews as Jews have nothing to fear from the Arab world. Look at the many Christians among us, they are not persecuted, they exist in peace. Jews could do the same. But, of course, they refuse. And they refuse an Arab Palestinian state. And yet history demands an Arab Palestinian state. So you can be sure that there will be more war, no matter what pressures are brought down on us by the outside world. . . ."

Abdallah Al-Ahmar, secretary general of the Syrian Baath party, also took a historical view, but compared the situation in the Middle East to the Europe of the 1930s. "It is a very similar pattern. The Zionists are acting just as the Nazis did.* First the Nazis said, 'We are a special people, a superior

---

* It has become fashionable in the Arab world to compare Zionism to Nazism. Ahmar did not mean his analogy in the philosophical sense, however, but in the tactical one.

race. We have been maltreated by the world, so we must remake our destiny.' That was Nazi racism. Then they began to plan how to remake their history, and they realized they could only do it through the acquisition of military might. That was Nazi militarism. And finally, when they had a certain degree of military might they began to use it to annex surrounding lands such as in Czechoslovakia, Poland, Alsace. They said this was their 'vital space.' That was Nazi expansionism. As the Nazis grew more powerful, their neighbors objected, so they proceeded to further annex their neighbors. Then they came to the conclusion that they would not be able to live in the peace they so constantly claimed was their desire until they annexed all of Europe. And what was the consequence of all this? The greatest war the world has ever known, a war that came about despite the efforts of nations to stop it with diplomacy and threats. It became the great nations of Europe, with America thrown in, against this relatively small state of Germany. . . . Now, I am not just parroting the opinion of many Arabs that the Zionists are the modern-day Nazis. I am simply pointing to the record. They say they are a special people who must have their own state in which they control everything. Is this not a copy of Nazi racism? The Nazis put out this nonsense that they were Aryans, the superior race. There was no such thing as an Aryan race, just as there is no such thing as a Jewish race. But the Zionists have convinced much of the world that the Jews are some special race who have exclusive title to this land of Palestine. So this is Zionist racism. And in order to secure that special title they have plotted and planned to accumulate military might. This is Zionist militarism. But even that is not enough. In order to contain all of the Jews of the world they must have their own 'vital space' — the little land of Israel is not enough. They keep calling for total immigration of all Jews, then they annex additional land through their militarism to contain them. This is Zionist expansionism. . . . Look at me, do I look like I am some bloodthirsty fanatic making up all these tales about Zionism? I will tell you, I will forget about the Arab side in this conflict, I will not even mention the illegal nature of Israel as we see it, I will not even talk about Arab humiliation, revenge — all those things the Jews accuse us of. I will just say, look at the record. And then tell me that there will not one day, sooner or later, be a monumental war here? . . . Zionist Israel will go the way of Germany. It will be conquered and wiped out. Then, as Germany was after World War II, it will be reconstructed according to the wishes of those who conquer it. And it will be allowed to develop again, but this time as a nation of many people — call them Palestinians, if you like, Muslim

Palestinians, Christian Palestinians, Jewish Palestinians. Or perhaps it will be reconstructed to resemble some nation like Belgium, with two distinct kinds of people, Arabs and Jews, two languages, but one central government. This is how I see the Palestine of the future, perhaps someday becoming part of a united or federated Arab nation. But first, the Arab world must be cleansed of the aberration of Zionism, just as Europe was washed clean of Nazism."

Adnan Abu Ouda was, when I put the question to him, the Jordanian minister of information. "The Israelis missed their chance at getting a settlement here when they refused to consider proposals to return the West Bank to Jordan. Which made us convinced that Israel does not truly want a settlement. Another thing that convinces us is their obsession with procedures. If you look closely at all the past discussions that have taken place concerning settlements, you will see that although the Israelis say they want to negotiate directly with the Arabs, the matter always comes down to procedures and techniques. They are forever releasing communiqués about how the negotiations should be conducted, who should sit where, who should speak first, who should speak for whom, what the agenda should be, and so on and so on. Not once do they offer anything of substance, anything that we can look at and say, 'Well, here is something they are willing to talk about, can we talk about it?' All they do is tell us how and where and in what order. Their refusal to talk to the PLO is simply another one of these procedural obsessions. They say the PLO does not represent the Palestinians, they say 'Who elected them?' Well, realistically speaking, who elected the Zionist leaders of the twenties to speak for Jews of the world? You know, of course, that there was great resistance to Zionism within the Jewish world in the early days. So who elected the Zionists to speak for all Jews? The Zionists elected themselves. . . . And then the Israelis say they will not talk to the PLO because they are terrorists. Well, what was the Irgun, the Stern Gang, if nothing but terrorists? And who is the leader of the party in Israel most adamant against the PLO? This man Begin, who was a leading Zionist terrorist — that is who. You might say it takes a terrorist to know one.

"The Israelis know that their own terrorism was very instrumental in getting them statehood, so they know that the PLO will achieve the same thing for the Palestinians. . . . It is all such a smokescreen for their hypocrisy. You know what hypocrisy is, it is saying one thing while doing another, often the opposite. And that is one big difference between the Jew and the Arab. When we say we want to do something, we will do it, or try to do it even if we don't always succeed. And we don't hide our intentions, we put them out on the table for everyone to see. But our experience with the Israelis proves to us that they hide their real intentions behind diverting words. That goes back to the beginnings of Zionism here, when the Zionists were telling us and the British they had no intention of trying to make a Jewish state, while they were secretly writing in their diaries and in their letters to each other about how cleverly they were building the foundations for a Jewish state. . . . So there will be no possibility of settlement until the Palestinians at least have their own state.

"At one time extremist Palestinians said they wanted to destroy Israel, to drive all the Jews out of Arab land. Now they say they only want to have Israel incorporated into a state that would include all Palestine — Arab Palestinians and Jews. You will see, as they gain more and more recognition they will become even more moderate in their demands, and that is because the majority of Palestinians are not extremist, despite the conditions in which they have had to live so long. The great majority want to give up wandering in misery and begin living in a land they can call their own. Once they get their own state they will treat Arafat the way the English treated Churchill after the war. They will say, 'Thank you, Arafat, you are a great hero and you have gotten us through this struggle, but let us now have the time to enjoy the fruits of our victory. We will make statues to you and the others, but go now to some nice hillside villa in a grove of olives and write your memoirs.' And he will probably do just that. Arafat has no desire to be the Ben-Gurion of his country, only the Weizmann, if you see what I mean. . . . So, I see peace coming out of a Palestinian state. The great majority of Palestinians will not tolerate a leadership that wants to just use a small state to wage further war on Israel to destroy it and make a larger state. The majority of Palestinians are willing to accept Israel and get on with their own nation-building. . . . However, the Israelis will not demonstrate an equivalent moderation, so there will be one, two, perhaps three more wars before the conditions are made right for Israeli acceptance, unless the United States can make Israel accept. But I don't think the United States will be able to do this. So, the Arab countries — and I can tell you this as fact — the Arab countries will continue to wage war until Israel has lost so many of its young men and has become so demoralized it will finally say, 'Okay, let us talk.' Of course, if these wars are necessary, I hate to imagine what else they will bring with them in respect to the outside world. The oil countries are thoroughly committed to using the oil weapon again and again against the West, and they are fully aware of what wrath this may bring down on their heads. But they will not back down. . . . So there you are. In many respects you can say the future of the world is in the hands of this tiny state of Israel."

Bassam Freiha is the head of one of the largest publishing companies in the Middle East, with newspapers and magazines distributed to almost every major Arab city. He is also an intelligent, aspiring politician and, because of his constant journeying throughout the Arab world to confer with national leaders of every political stripe, he reflects well the diverse and often clashing crosscurrents of public and private opinion and expectation. Like many a concerned American will about the U.S., Freiha will readily decry the weaknesses and moral diseases that infect his own society. But also like such an American, he will point proudly to its achievements and potential. "The Arab world as a whole is sick and tired of this never-ending conflict with Israel," he told me. "There is a genuine wish to get it over with and get on with our own development — even in the most private quarters where you Americans imagine all sorts of secret conspiracies to be going on to slaughter the Jews. But no matter how sick and tired we get, we will not rest until the Jews have returned to their original borders and the Palestinians have their state. These are the two keys. And don't tell me the Palestinians could have had their state twenty-five years ago because that is rubbish — they could no more have accepted partition in 1948 than your country could accept the annexation of part of Texas by Mexico. There are principles and rules involved in international affairs, after all. It is when these are violated that wars occur. But now they are ready to accept partition. They are realists, and they know they are not going to get all their land back. So they will take what they can get and leave it at that. Everything here on the Arab side is moderating. We have proved that we can make life very difficult for Israel. We have proved that the Zionists cannot come in here and kick us around forever. . . . But now Israel will not grant us our small victory and get going with the real work.

"We have both acted like children through all this. But the difference is, we are willing to admit it and the Israelis are not. The Israelis cannot go on forever against us, that is for sure. They have two options. One is to go for eventual destruction. The other is to take the risk of an immediate accommodation with us in the hopes of saving their state. And I can tell you, it is not that much of a risk. You would be surprised what peace does to people. But the Israelis won't take such a risk. Do you know why? Because they have grown used to the benefits of military power and military confrontation.

They are a military state — almost everyone in their government has a military background — and they are locked into this military mentality that says might makes right. No decision in Israel is made without its military ramifications first being considered. Israel is not a theocracy, it is a militocracy. I don't deny them their due — they are marvelous fighters, brilliant tacticians, why even I marveled at the way they crossed the Canal in the October War. What we wouldn't give to have a Dayan, a Sharon, leading our forces. But the very thing that makes them good fighters makes them poor politicians.

"Military might should be a political instrument, not a political philosophy. But that's the way it is. They spent so long, the Jews did, with the reputation of being nonfighters that their success as fighters has gone to their head. It has made them dizzy with power, and they can think only in one line. . . . But in the long run this is self-defeating. Their rigidity will eat them up. Now personally, I don't mind if the Jews eat themselves up. But if they do they will take a lot more with them than they themselves are worth — not as Jews, but as a state. . . . Yes, there will be more war. That is precisely why the Arab governments decided to recognize the PLO in Rabat. We realize that the Zionists will not acknowledge the Palestinians, the PLO. We realize that the PLO puts the Zionists in a position of having to start another war. And we realize that it will take another war, and all that goes with it, to get someone to pound some sense into the Israelis. We don't have to win the war, all we have to do is keep it going long enough. Our armies are much better trained now, our weapons are as good and as plentiful as the Israelis', and our pilots no longer automatically bail out when they see an Israeli plane flying nearby. . . . We would not have another war if we had the choice, but we don't have the choice. The Israelis do have the choice, but they want another war — well, perhaps not 'want,' but it is the only way they know how to respond to the prospect of peace. . . . Let me put it this way — they may not want war, but they certainly do not want peace either."

# PART FOUR

# 27.

# HISTORY: *"Eben Sihoudo"*

AT THE SAME TIME Great Britain and the United States were joined in their great alliance to snuff out Nazism, they were furiously maneuvering against each other for control of what few failed to recognize was to be one of the greatest spoils of the war: the oil of the Middle East.

Through its oil companies, Britain had laid solid claim to the oil of Iraq and Iran in the decade following the First World War. Thereafter it engaged itself in the process of extending its claims southward along the Persian Gulf shore of the Arabian peninsula, an area that had long been within its exclusive sphere of interest.

As a result of drawn-out and often bitter negotiations during the 1920s, American oil companies were given severely limited participation in the tapping of the largely British- and French-controlled oil resources within the boundaries of the old Ottoman Empire. But they soon began to chafe under the restrictions imposed on them. When Britain failed to vigorously explore the vast oil reserves that were suspected to exist along the northern shoreline of Arabia, American companies, led by Standard Oil of California (Socal), took up the search through a series of legal and extralegal ploys designed to sidestep the Anglo-French restrictions. Socal concentrated on the territory of the newly established Kingdom of Saudi Arabia. In 1933, by outbidding the British in an auction that featured ridiculously low prices (in retrospect) for concessions, the American company managed to secure from King Ibn Saud the exclusive right to search for and produce oil for sixty-six years. The final price was $175,000, which the king insisted be delivered in gold.* It was, and America found itself in business on its own in the Middle East.

Socal immediately began exploration under the name of the California-Arabian Oil Company, but it was not until 1938, after spending considerable sums of money, that it struck oil in commercial quantities. To share in the expenses of exploration it had brought in as a half-partner, in 1936, the Texas Oil Company (Texaco). This partnership would eventually expand to include other American companies and be reincorporated under the name of the Arabian-American Oil Company (Aramco).

The beginning of the Second World War brought an abrupt shutdown of Aramco's operations just at the time the company was about to considerably step up its drilling and transport. After finding its first productive oil field it was successfully discovering others, and the prospects of an endless supply of oil from Saudi Arabia seemed exceedingly bright. The cost of the concession, the cost of developing the oil fields, and the royalties to be paid to Saudi Arabia on each barrel of oil produced would together be minuscule compared to the income that would be realized in the increasingly oil-thirsty industrial world.

Thus, when the war brought about a suspension of production and the Saudi Arabian king began to complain about the poverty of his treasury, Aramco lobbyists in Washington brought the problem to the attention of high officials in the Roosevelt administration. They in turn persuaded the President that if the United States failed to subsidize the Saudi king in the absence of his oil-royalty income, the British would enter the breach with subsidies of their own, with a view to restoring their influence in the area after the war and thereby getting a piece of the oil action.

When it became evident early in 1943 that this was precisely Britain's aim, the behind-the-scenes sense of urgency in Washington intensified until Roosevelt finally twisted the terms of the Lend-Lease Act to provide the required subvention.

But even after this maneuver, suspicion over British intentions did not abate in Washington. The British tried to persuade the Roosevelt administration that the Middle East was of greater postwar importance to England

* The United States had just gone off the gold standard, and the exportation of gold was illegal without Treasury Department approval. When the Treasury Department dragged its feet at Socal's request for the transfer of $170,000 worth of gold to Saudi Arabia, Socal bought the gold itself in London — also illegal under the new American regulations. Such winking at financial laws was common in the development of the American oil industry in the early days, and was often done with the tacit approval of the government.

than to the United States, and to counter the Lend-Lease maneuver they privately offered the Saudis increased subsidies of their own. The alarm became so great that Secretary of State Cordell Hull told Secretary of the Interior Harold Ickes, who was also the head of the wartime Petroleum Reserves Corporation, that "there should be full realization of the fact that the oil of Saudi Arabia constitutes one of the world's greatest prizes." Hull demanded that measures be taken to ensure the proper protection of the United States against British long-term intentions "to build up their postwar position in the Middle East at the expense of American interests there."*

The alarm spread through the official halls of Washington, boosted not a little by the oil industry lobbyists. Shortly after the Hull message, Secretary of the Navy James Forrestal telephoned President Roosevelt to tell him that the oil people with whom he was acquainted were anxious to have the government further secure their interests in Saudi Arabia because they thoroughly coincided with the vital strategic interests of the United States. "The main thing," added Forrestal, "is that stack of oil is something that this country damn well ought to have, and we've lost, in the last ninety days, a good deal of our position with this sheikh — Eben Sihoudo, whatever his name is — and we are losing more every day."†

All this concern, culminating in the post-Yalta meeting between Roosevelt and the king of Saudi Arabia, ensured the maintenance of Aramco's and the United States' premier position in Saudi Arabia. The outcome of the war did the rest. As a consequence, American power, wealth and influence, internationally, were unprecedented in history. The reconstruction of Europe and the tremendously increased capacity of America's industrial complex outpaced all expectations about the demand for oil, and the race was on for the exploitation of all the untapped oil reserves in the Persian Gulf. With Britain and France, along with their oil companies, deterred by changing attitudes toward them in the Arab oil countries they had controlled before the war, the American companies, along with independent prospectors, were left with an almost free track in establishing themselves in the undeveloped areas of the gulf — even those areas still under paternal British protection.

Thereafter the story of the Middle East, at least from a Western perspective, gained a subplot. Still central was the Zionist-Arab conflict and

---

* These quotations are part of a communication from Hull to Ickes of November 13, 1943, which is contained in *Foreign Relations of the United States, 1943*, IV: 942–943.
† From the transcript of a recorded telephone conversation between Forrestal and Roosevelt of December 22, 1943. Quoted in Gabriel Kolko, *The Politics of War*, New York: Random House, 1968, pp. 298, and 649.

all its ramifications in the countries that surrounded Palestine. But as the story progressed, the development of the oil industry in the Arabian peninsula began to take on greater significance. To properly understand these developments, we must know a little more about the place in which they occurred quickest.

# 28.

# HISTORY: *Saudi Arabia*

SECRETARY FORRESTAL'S SUPERCILIOUS REFERRAL to "Eben Sihoudo, whatever his name is" in his 1943 conversation with Roosevelt sharply reflected the general state of contempt, ignorance and superior indifference that existed in the highest councils of the United States government vis-à-vis the Arab world in the 1940s. If such states of mind pervaded the government, as a plenitude of documentary evidence from the period clearly indicates, they were even more pervasive as a general bigotry throughout America itself. From the contemporary Arab point of view, the bigotry was totally undeserved, was at the root of America's postwar support of Zionism and Israel, and will prove to be a central factor in determining how the Arabs choose to deal economically with the West — particularly America — in the future.

Forrestal's reference was, of course, to Abdul Aziz Ibn Saud, the man who in the early part of this century incorporated most of the Arabian peninsula into the unified kingdom it is today.

Following the spread of Islam in the eighth century and the transfer of the caliphate to Damascus under the Ummayads, most of Arabia reverted to its timeless nomadism, with the vast oasis-specked inland region empty of any resource that would attract foreign interest. Similar was the situation of the peninsula's lengthy coastal periphery, from the top of the Red Sea, around the Indian Ocean, to the top of the Persian, or Arabian, Gulf. Here and there was found some minor commerce, and in the northwestern province of Hejaz there were the holy sites, but the entire peninsula went largely ignored during the golden age of Islam. Except in the Hejaz there was none but tribal rule, with various tribal sheikhdoms exercising their authority over the territories in which they lived. Occasionally one tribe, driven by famine and disease, would encroach on the territory of another, bringing about tribal wars and shifts in reigning clans. But aside from this, little happened of any note.

When the Ottomans took over the Arab world, however, foreign influences began to filter down the tribal latticework that connected Arabia to the Fertile Crescent. In the beginning these influences took the form of cosmopolitan revisionary religious ideas that confounded the simplicities of fundamental Islam. There followed a gradual loosening of Islamic discipline that spread among the tribal populace and manifested itself in different ways throughout the peninsula for several centuries. Then came the puritanical reform movement of Muhammad Abd-Al-Wahhab, who in the eighteenth century converted the leader of one of central Arabia's most powerful warrior tribes, Muhammad Ibn Saud, to his cause.

Ibn Saud took over the Wahhabi movement and conquered the Hejaz in an attempt to wrest Arabian Islam from the grip of the Turks and restore it to its Koranic fundamentals. As we have seen, when Ibn Saud and Wahhabism began to make inroads into the Ottoman province of Syria early in the nineteenth century, he and his Wahhabi ruling clan were thrown back into their homeland in central Arabia by the Turko-Egyptian viceroy, Muhammad Ali.

For almost a century thereafter the heirs of Ibn Saud remained embroiled in disputes with another powerful tribe, the Rashid, over control of the central Arabian territory of the Nejd, while the Turks consolidated their grip on the Hejaz and eventually restored the ancient Hashemite dynasty — which traced its connection directly to the Prophet — to power in Mecca.

In 1891 the Rashids drove the Wahhabi leaders of the Saud tribe out of the Nejd and into exile in what is now Kuwait — then one of many separate sheikhdoms strung out along the Persian Gulf coast of the Arabian peninsula. When the leader of the Rashids died in 1897, Abdul Aziz Ibn Saud, the youthful head of the exiled Sauds, made plans to recover his tribe's territory in the Nejd. Enlisting the help of the Sheikh of Kuwait, he recaptured the family's traditional capital, the mud-walled oasis town of Riyadh, in 1902.

There followed a renewal of the old tribal war between the Sauds and the Rashids. In this struggle the Ottomans backed the Rashids, who had been content with their rule over the Nejd and had made no claims to the Hejaz, where the Turks had installed the Hashemite Hussein Ibn Ali as grand sharif. Ibn Saud was not to be deterred, and by 1910 he had driven the Rashids out of much of the Nejd. In order to lessen the power of other nomadic chieftains and to increase his control of the Nejd territories whose sheikhs had acknowledged his leadership, he developed a unique system of agrarian settlement. In 1910 he organized the militant order of Ikhwan (the Brotherhood)* and sent its members into his newly conquered domains both as missionaries of Saudi Wahhabism and as agricultural settlers. The Ikhwanites impressed upon the less powerful tribes the virtues of the fundamentalist Wahhabi religious philosophy, and soon much of the central Arabian plateau existed in obeisance to Ibn Saud.

On the eve of the First World War, Ibn Saud spread his power into Arabia's Persian Gulf province of Hasa, the site of many of the later oil discoveries and then under nominal Ottoman control. Here he came in contact with the British who, about to embark on a war against the Turks, sought his favor. Although he remained neutral, he entered into a treaty of friendship with the British in 1915 as an expression of his contempt for the Ottomans, who were still supporting his keenest rivals, the Rashids. By this treaty Ibn Saud received British recognition as sole ruler of the Nejd and Hasa, the latter of which, bordering the gulf, was of vital strategic interest to England. By the start of the war, then, Ibn Saud controlled the central and eastern provinces of northern Arabia, while the Turkish-appointed grand sharif, Hussein Ibn Ali, held the western Hejaz.†

As we have learned, Hussein, along with his four Hashemite sons, had spent many years in Constantinople, had become exposed to Western political ideas, and was an ardent proponent of Arab nationalism. Ibn Saud, on the other hand, was strictly a traditional religious leader untouched by any interest in or familiarity with nationalist ideas and political theories. For this reason, plus the fact that they then considered the Hejaz to be the most important Arabian province, the British approached Hussein to engineer a midwar Arab revolt against the Turks, committing themselves to establishing an independent Arab state in his name once the war was over.

Ibn Saud watched these developments with mistrust and contempt. Although he had previously been satisfied to leave the Hejaz to the control of

---

* Not the same as the later Muslim Brotherhood that developed in Egypt.
† Southern Arabia, dominated by the vast and empty sand desert known as the Rub Al-Khali, was sparsely populated except for its coastal areas, which were divided into minor sheikhdoms. The most southerly part of the peninsula, separated from the Rub Al-Khali by mountains, was still parceled up among the descendants of the ancient kingdoms of Yemen, Aden and Oman.

Hussein, he recognized that the Hashemite design for a Pan-Arab state included the regions under his own dominion; and that if such a state came into being, with the Hashemites on its throne, his own power would be dissipated. Moreover, the revolt being orchestrated by Hussein was being subsidized by a Christian power, which in Ibn Saud's fundamentalist view was a profound violation of the precepts of Islam. Thus, although he had signed a friendship treaty with Britain and had little affection for the Turks, he refused to take part in the Hashemite revolt. Instead he used the time to reinforce his power over the Nejd and Hasa and to extend his sway to the borders of the Hejaz.

When the war ended and the Pan-Arab state failed to materialize, the northern part of the anticipated state was instead cut up into various provisional Hashemite monarchies under European mandate — Transjordan, Syria, Iraq — while in the south Hussein was acknowledged as king of the Hejaz. The rest of Arabia, except for coastal areas that remained under British protectorate, was left to Ibn Saud.

The Hashemite domination of Arabian Islam had become cosmopolitan and revisionary compared to Wahhabi fundamentalism. Having disposed of the Rashid dynasty and brought most of the lesser tribal families under Wahhabi influence, it was only natural that Ibn Saud would look upon the conquest of the Hashemite Hejaz — the center of Islam — as the next logical step in his drive to reform Arab life. His expansionary impulses were given a decided boost by the actions of Hussein immediately after the war.

When Hussein's son Feisal represented his father at the Paris Peace Conference in 1919, he succeeded in having a piece of territory along the indistinct border between the Hejaz and Nejd assigned to Hussein. When Hussein sent troops to occupy the territory, Ibn Saud, who saw in the action an attempt to weaken his territorial prerogatives, sent his own fanatical Ikhwan forces to drive the Hejazians back. This was the first installment in a series of widening skirmishes between the Hashemites and the Wahhabites that were to climax in the eventual Wahhabi conquest of the Hejaz in 1925. Once the conquest was completed and Hussein and his son Ali were banished, Ibn Saud demanded recognition from the British as king of the Hejaz and got it. By 1927, having cleaned out all remnants of Rashid and Hashemite power, Ibn Saud was master of approximately two-thirds of the Arabian peninsula. He was then faced with the problem of securing his power and organizing his still tribally diverse territorial possessions into a manageable political entity.

Ibn Saud was generally ignorant of the modern world and all his values were still deeply rooted in the matrix of Bedouin tradition. For instance, he was the husband of numerous wives and the father of countless children.* He thought the world flat. He was astonished to learn that Americans spoke English and not some native Indian language. He understood nothing about political concepts and still less about foreign affairs. In the old-time Arab Islamic perception, politics was religion and religion was politics, and it was merely the province of that tribe which had proved its superiority to administer these identical categories.

Yet socially he was farsighted or intuitive enough to realize that the exercise of power for the purpose of achieving stability could not rest alone on the wandering sword, but depended on a certain cohesive sedentary element as well. Using the methods of agrarian settlement that had served him earlier, he instituted a program designed to settle the Bedouin on the land in a network of agricultural colonies that would promote both obedience to the Wahhabi version of Islam and loyalty to the Saud dynasty.

The ruling classes of Mecca and Medina were exceedingly dubious about Ibn Saud and Wahhabism, however. They were accustomed to the luxuries and self-indulgences that had been afforded them during the previous centuries and had little taste for the rather stark way of life of the Wahhabis. Ibn Saud, once he was in control of the Hejaz, sensibly sought to soften the harder edges of Wahhabism so as not to excessively alienate the Meccan establishment. This brought a reaction from the fanatical Wahhabi religious leaders, who had a deep contempt for the traditional profligacy of the Meccans. They provoked elements within the theretofore loyal Ikhwan to revolt against Ibn Saud, thus preoccupying him until 1930 when he finally managed to silence the dissidents. Thereafter he was confronted by a revolt of a group of tribes in northern Hejaz. Upon putting this down in 1932, he incorporated all the territory now under his control into the single Kingdom of Saudi Arabia and declared himself king. He then became embroiled in a dispute with the ruler of Yemen over control of the southern Arabian Red Sea province of Asir. After two years of sporadic warfare this struggle was settled by a treaty whereby Asir was added to Ibn Saud's kingdom.

When Ibn Saud came out of Kuwait to recover Riyadh in 1902, he and his clan were impecunious, having for more than ten years been without the

---

* Ibn Saud, although celebrated for his virility and sexual drive, also used marriage for what can be regarded as political purposes. By marrying maidens from various tribes, he bound many tribes to the Saud family. He is said to have wed close to three hundred women and to have sired almost as many children.

tribute due the ruling families of various regions from its lesser tribes. His conquest of the Hejaz and his assumption of the kingship of the new Saudi Arabia improved his financial position only slightly, for although he was now entitled to income from poll taxes and the pilgrim trade, much of that modest treasure was siphoned off by the traditionally corrupt ruling class administrators of Mecca. Thus, when the first British and American oil prospectors approached him, he made sure that all dealings would be directly between them and himself, with no old-style Arabian intermediaries who might apply their long-honed skills at making money disappear.

Oil had already been discovered beneath the sheikhdom of Bahrain, a group of islands off the Arabian coast in the Persian Gulf, by the time California Standard Oil began vying with the British for concessions in Saudi Arabia in the early thirties. The $175,000 Ibn Saud received in gold from Socal was expected to tide him and his large family over until the oil beneath the sands of Hasa province began to flow, after which they would begin receiving royalties. Getting the oil up took longer than anticipated, however, and when it finally did begin to flow in commercially exportable quantities, in 1938, production was almost immediately forced to a halt by the Second World War. Ibn Saud had run through the gold he had received in 1933 as well as the brief spurt of royalty money he got during the short period of active prewar production. With an ever-expanding royal family to support in increasingly regal style, and with dissident tribal elements still striving for a voice in his rigidly autocratic government, he got Britain and the United States into their wartime competition for his favor in hopes that loans and subsidies would secure their respective positions after the war.

The United States, as we have seen, won. Once the threat of an Axis presence in the Middle East was disposed of, Aramco returned to Saudi Arabia to find its concessions still safe. The company immediately geared up its production facilities and shipping terminals. Even before the war was over, Saudi oil was gushing up out of the earth again along the Persian Gulf.

For the next seven years most of the history of Saudi Arabia was made by Aramco, whose royalties on spiraling production turned the kingdom of Ibn Saud into the second richest in the world. Local conditions did not change appreciably with the influx of all this money, however. Ibn Saud continued to rule according to the precepts of austere Wahhabi religious fundamentalism. His government consisted of himself and a handful of sons and relatives. The country's law was the rigid religious code of the Islamic Sharia. And the quality of life of its seven million inhabitants remained still profoundly rooted in the Bedouin tradition. Except for its oil and the rapidly expanding Aramco facilities along the eastern coast, Saudi Arabia remained a political and economic cubbyhole on the world stage.

This situation began to change when Ibn Saud died in his palace at Taif, the cool mountain town near Mecca, in 1953. The king's last three years had turned him into an increasingly senile old man. During that time he had lost control of his government to the various princes of the realm — his sons — many of whom, like many sons of strict fathers, had long chafed at the bit of their own father's old-fashioned ways. Attempting to express themselves, and scheming one against another for position and influence, they saw their father's senility as license to release themselves from the moral strictures of Wahhabism. Dipping into the seemingly bottomless family treasury, they soon spread a blanket of corruption, waste and wanton profligacy across the kingdom, an approach to life that has lasted until this day despite later attempts to check it.

By the time Ibn Saud died, the kingdom's treasury was sorely depleted, in spite of increasing oil revenues, and the bulk of the country's population still existed at a subsistence level. There were schools, but they had been built and staffed by Aramco; there were hospitals, but they were built and staffed by Aramco; there was even a railroad between the central capital city of Riyadh and the Gulf, but that too was built and maintained by Aramco. Where Aramco had no oil or administrative facilities there was poverty and disease. Aramco's royalty payments, some of which might have gone into public welfare, were being squandered through the unprecedented waste of the numerous princes and their entourages.

The princely profligacy was symbolized by the man who succeeded to the throne upon Ibn Saud's death — his oldest son, Saud Ibn Abdul Aziz al-Saud, who became known as King Saud. The new king made the monarchy a marvel of grotesque extravagance, highlighted by immense jerry-built concrete palaces, glittering with gold and neon and housing his hundred successive wives. The swindlers of the Arab Levant descended upon Riyadh and ensnared the royal family in an expanding web of fraud and corruption. Other Saudi princes ventured more and more frequently to the fleshpots of the West, where they squandered fortunes on women, whiskey and gambling and from which they returned with shiploads of Cadillacs, perfumes and high-priced British and European courtesans.

Saud's rule proved to be an unmitigated disaster for Saudi Arabia. By 1958 the monarchy was bankrupt, and in an attempt to restore the kingdom's finances he was constrained to install his half-brother and Ibn Saud's second son, Prince Faisal,* as prime minister.

If Saud reflected the dissolute side of his father's character, Faisal incorporated all his austere traits. He was frugal, intellectual, deeply religious and thoroughly Wahhabist in his outlook. He drove a Chevrolet, rather than a Cadillac, and lived frugally and monogamously in a villa, not a palace. Born about 1905, he had led a post–World War I royal mission to England while still an adolescent, then commanded one of his father's armies in the struggle with Yemen during the early 1930s, then became viceroy of the Hejaz. Once appointed prime minister, he immediately set out to reform the monarchy and restore it to its original Wahhabi ideals.

A pious man with the fierce features of the falcons that were the favorite sporting creatures of desert royalty, Faisal pursued an unconventional vision. His travels around the world as Saudi Arabia's head minister impressed him with many things Western, although he remained convinced, as befitted a man who knew the Koran by heart and was intimately conversant with the hair-splitting niceties of the Sharia, that there was much about the West potentially destructive of the ascetic purities of Islam.

Faisal proved to be a conscientious administrator and statesman. When King Saud, in 1964, was unable to cope with the country's increasing political involvement with the outside world — particularly with Egypt's (Nasser's) endeavors to gain influence there — Saud was deposed by senior members of the royal family and Faisal chosen to succeed him. Inheriting a kingdom still in the throes of economic want, Faisal set out to prove that moral rectitude and fantastic wealth could flourish together. He was determined to put strict controls on oil revenues, to avoid an irreparable collision of Western materialism with his own provident Islamic code, and to lead his people to universal prosperity while insulating them from what he saw as the confusion of socialism, the godlessness of Communism, and the decadence of democracy. He would bestow on the kingdom all the blessings of technology, while retaining the Koran as the law of the land and the autocracy of the Saud dynasty as its organizing spirit. In short, he would be a despot of progressive and benevolent persuasion.

There can be little doubt that Faisal was an effective ruler; in the eleven

* To keep the distinctions clear, I should note that Prince Faisal, the son of Ibn Saud, bore no relation to Prince Feisal, the son of Hussein Ibn Ali, who later became king of Syria, then of Iraq under the British. The former was a descendant of the Nejdian House of Saud and a Wahhabi; the latter was a descendant of the Hejazian Hashemite line, and it was his father who lost the Hejaz to the Saudis under Ibn Saud.

years of his reign he gained a popularity among the rank-and-file Saudi Arabian populace that bordered on adulation. During the past decade, through strict controls and increasingly imperious negotiatory methods, he enriched the Saudi treasury to unimagined proportions. But he did not, like several of his predecessors in other Arabian principates, hoard most of these riches for his own personal use. Instead, in the 1960s he began to scatter thousands of miles of asphalt roads across the desert to connect the major cities and towns and spent untold sums to develop the beginnings of a modern social, political, economic and military infrastructure. His government has built seaports, airports, refineries, industrial complexes, hospitals, clinics and schools with gathering speed out of the ballooning sums from the proliferating oil production of Aramco and from increased Saudi participation in that production.

During the past five years the kingdom's economy has been carefully planned with the help of American- and European-educated Saudis and advisers from other areas, most of them Palestinians and Lebanese. The government has assumed responsibility for the huge tasks of national education, social welfare, heavy industry, and the like. In other matters the economy is consigned to the private sector. Perhaps nowhere in the world is the American method of free enterprise imitated with such devotion; Saudi and foreign businessmen are free to pursue whatever profit the marketplace will countenance, although often with funds provided or guaranteed by the government.

Today the two main commercial cities of Jiddah and Riyadh, little more than mud-brick enclaves twenty years ago, glint with glass-sheathed apartment buildings, skyscrapers and supermarkets. Corroded tin shacks and scarred wooden shanties still blemish the spaces in between, but even the primitives who inhabit them seem soon destined to be engulfed by a torrent of plenty. Indeed, Saudi Arabia's possibilities boggle the mind. It is a land of a mere seven to eight million people, yet it is fast becoming a major repository of the Western world's monetary assets. And what it isn't managing to suck into its treasury in the way of foreign funds, other smaller Arab oil states, along with non-Arab Iran, are.

It is by no means inappropriate that the name Faisal could be translated into English either as "arbiter" or as "a sharp sword." Both names aptly symbolized the Saudi king's lofty position in the Arab world, as well as the power he possessed, above all others, to bring about a solution to the Middle East puzzle and the problem it has created for the rest of the world. How he intended to use that power in the little time left to him — he was seventy years old and in chronic ill health — remained one of the most fascinating and crucial questions of all just prior to his death.

Before trying to gain an accurate from-the-horse's-mouth perspective on that question, it would first be helpful to gain some understanding of the scope of Faisal's — and Saudi Arabia's — power.

# 29.

# HISTORY: *Money, Oil and the Arabs*

MOST OF US ARE ACCUSTOMED TO THINKING of the value of money in the context of our own personal spending and earning needs. Some still relate to money in terms of single dollars. Others have become used to thinking in terms of tens or even hundreds of dollars. To a few of the more materially fortunate among us the image of a thousand, or several thousand, is conceptually comfortable. To those more fortunate still, tens of thousands, possibly even a hundred thousand, are figures that have realistic meaning. Traditionally, of course, the figure of a million dollars has always been the idealized standard of monetary achievement in our society, based on the idea that the possession of such a sum provides one with the freedom, purchasing power and mobility to exist free of care and inconvenience — to do, in short, whatever one wants.

What is a million dollars? We all have an idea, more or less. Whether we conceive of it in terms of some simple mathematical equation (it is ten units of $100,000 each; it is a hundred units of $10,000 each), or in an equation related to our own lives (it is fifty years of work at $20,000 a year), or in some equation symbolizing its purchasing power (it will buy 166 fully equipped American cars at today's average prices, build about 33 average-priced family-sized houses), or simply in terms of an abstract figure — however we conceive of it, it has an identifiable reality.

Try now to form an image in your mind of a billion dollars. It is difficult, is it not? No matter how you try to conceptualize it, the figure seems to recede into some kind of haze of inconceivability. (I except bankers and other financial professionals from this test on the grounds that it is their business to think in such sums.)

How do you relate to a billion dollars? You can, of course, add three zeros to a million, but what does this tell you? In the American system of financial mathematics a million dollars is equivalent to a thousand thousand; thus a billion is the same as a thousand million. A thousand million. Does this help? Not much, as I'm sure you'll agree.

Try it another way. Apply the equations I used to define a million dollars. A million dollars will buy 166 fully equipped American automobiles at today's average prices. But a billion dollars will buy 166,666 such cars. That's 166,500 more cars than you could get for a million dollars. The average parking garage in any big city holds about 166 cars. To hold all the cars a billion dollars could buy, a city would need a thousand such garages.

A million dollars will build 33 average family-sized houses — about the number of homes in a typical American suburban housing development. A billion dollars will build 33,333 such homes, which taken together would comprise a fair-sized city. If you live in an average housing development, think of the difference between owning all the homes in that development and owning all the homes in a city of about 250,000 population. That is the difference between a million and a billion dollars.

Or look at it this way. At a salary of $20,000 a year, it would take you 50 years to earn an aggregate of one million dollars — a period of time that is about ten years longer than the average career lifespan. To earn an aggregate of a billion dollars, you would have to work for 50,000 years or 1,250 lifetimes.

Such are the metaphors for a billion dollars. And such are the reasons why we are not accustomed to thinking in these terms. Governments and nations are, however, particularly those of the industrialized and resource-rich world, and it is here that the parameters of today's international problems broaden.

What does a billion dollars mean to a nation? Let us take the United States, by far the richest nation in the world. To the United States, one billion dollars represents about a thousandth of the total Gross National Product of just over one trillion dollars in 1974 — one trillion being a thousand billion.* (There is no convenient way of measuring the total dollar worth of the

---

* The actual fraction is a shade more, but for ease of understanding I shall keep to the nearest round numbers.

United States, so I will use the GNP, which reflects the worth of the economy at any given time, as an index.)

When you delineate billions in thousandths, it is similar to delineating units of a thousand in ones. Thus, if you carried around with you a wad of dollar bills totaling a thousand and suddenly discovered you'd lost a single dollar from it, you would probably shrug it off. If you lost ten dollars, you would be concerned. And if you lost, say, a hundred, you would be downright anxious and depressed.

To a nation like the United States, a billion dollars has the function in the overall trillion-plus economy that a dollar has in your wad of a thousand. A billion-dollar loss or a billion-dollar gain is of little significance except as a possible indicator of an economic trend. Ten billion dollars lost or gained is a source of national concern or gratification. And a hundred billion lost or gained becomes an occasion for deep anxiety or celebration.

What is a billion dollars? A billion dollars is one three-hundredth of the total United States budget for 1974–1975. A billion dollars is the cost of about fifty DC-10 jumbo jetliners, enough planes to take care of the airborne equipment needs of all the long-haul airlines in the country together. A billion dollars is roughly the aggregate wholesale cost of the total gallonage of petroleum products consumed in the United States each month.

If these figures are too esoteric, let me put it another way. A billion dollars is what it would take to support 100,000 people in this country in very comfortable style for a full year. And for a billion dollars the basic needs of food, shelter and clothing for one *million* people could be guaranteed for the same amount of time. For two million people, the provison of these needs could be accomplished with two billion dollars. As for the entire 250 million people of the United States, their basic needs could be provided for with 250 billion dollars. This is roughly one-fourth the value of the American economy. It is the amount that most economic experts agree will pour into the Saudi Arabian treasury, in the form of oil revenues, within the next five years. It is also almost as much as the total supply of money in the United States.*

Following World War II, the major international oil companies expanded their operations in the Arab nations of the Persian Gulf until by the early

* The nation's money supply in the week ended November 6, 1974, according to the *New York Times* of November 15, 1974, averaged $282 billion.

1950s they were virtual states within states. They dictated the oil and foreign policy of each Arab government. They set the prices at which the oil they pulled from Arab ground would be sold. And they kept the feudal Arab governments content by paying them sums sufficient enough — under the royalty terms of contracts executed before the war — to maintain the rulers and their courts in a style befitting their nobility and superiority.

The first reaction to the foreign domination of Persian Gulf countries came in 1951 against Britain, and it came not from an Arab country but from Iran, where the British-controlled Anglo-Iranian Oil Company had been active since the early years of the century. Revolutionary Iranian nationalists, behind the by now familiar slogans of anti-imperialism, set out to eject the major source of British influence by nationalizing Anglo-Iranian, despite the fact that the Iranians themselves had little of the technological know-how necessary to assume the efficient management and field operations of the company.

The events in Iran had few immediate political repercussions across the gulf in Saudi Arabia, which was then still the only major source of oil on the peninsula. The autocratic Saudi government, in the person of King Ibn Saud, had no interest in revolutionary nationalism. Their concern was money. Although they had earned hundreds of millions of dollars in oil royalties since the war, they were spending it faster than it came in and were running up rapidly expanding foreign debts. However, as effective control of the Saudi court passed from the senile Ibn Saud to his son Saud and to the new, more self-indulgent generation, the Saudis began to put pressure on Aramco for a larger monetary share in the oil the American consortium was producing. The pressure became an outright demand when the Saudis learned that Aramco was paying more to the United States in income taxes than it was to Saudi Arabia in royalties. The fact that the Saudis were receiving less from the exploitation of their own mineral wealth than a nation thousands of miles away sat not at all well with Saud and his advisers.

Aware of the potential threats to their present very profitable position and to their future exploration rights in the gulf should Saudi demands remain ignored, Aramco turned its attention to the problem. To increase payments to the Saudis out of their own earnings would, of course, decrease their profits. The participating parent companies back in the United States, which divided the profits among themselves according to their share in Aramco, would not look kindly on that type of solution.

So, with the cooperation of the United States government, another solution was embraced. This called for Saudi Arabia to institute an income tax system on oil so that in addition to paying a per-barrel royalty, Aramco would be required to pay a per-barrel tax as well. This, Aramco lawyers and American diplomats pointed out to the Saudis, would effectively double their revenues. At the same time it would have no effect on Aramco's profits, for the American oil consortium could simply write off the taxes it paid Saudi Arabia against its taxes in the United States.

The Saudis were pleased with the solution and readily accepted it — indeed, they even asked Aramco's lawyers to write up the tax law for them. Aramco was equally pleased, for it would cost them not a penny to double the Saudis' revenues. It was only later that the American government — when it realized it was losing in the neighborhood of $200 million in tax revenues annually from American oil companies operating in the Middle East — began to have second thoughts about the wisdom of the solution.

The gulf's political tensions, unleashed by Iran in 1951, were calmed in 1954 when the Iranian revolutionary nationalist government was overthrown by the American CIA and access to the country's oil was restored to a complex consortium of British, French, Dutch and American companies. The calm was short-lived, however, for in 1956, when Britain joined France and Israel in the attack on Egypt over the Suez, anti-British rioting broke out in the tiny oil sheikhdom of Kuwait,* which had long been under British colonial control and had become a major oil producer after Britain's access to Iran had been shut off in 1951.

Kuwait, situated at the top of the Persian Gulf, was for centuries a kind of sandy no-man's-land between the mouth of the fertile Tigris-Euphrates valley of Mesopotamia and the wastes of Arabia to the south. During the middle of the eighteenth century two clans of the northern Arabian Anaza Bedouin tribe — the Sabah and Khalifa clans — drifted into the region. Attracted by the presence of a fine natural harbor along the coast, the land's only evident resource, the Sabahs settled there and began to build a tribal town while the Khalifas moved farther south to settle the island archipelago of Bahrain.

During the next hundred years the Sabahs grew into a dynasty and built the town of Kuwait into a thriving port and commercial center. In 1865 a British traveler, W. G. Palgrave, noted its prosperity in a report he sent back to London, attributing it to the "skill, daring and solid trustworthiness" of the Sabahite mariners and the "good administration and prudent policy" of

* The word Kuwait is a diminutive of the Arabic *kut*, meaning "fort."

the rulers. The sheikhdom's principal industries were pearling, fishing, boat-building and the transshipment of goods to and from India and the Orient.

By the late nineteenth century Kuwait became caught up in the conflicting great-power pressures of faraway Europe. Britain had been acquiring bases throughout the Persian Gulf, first to protect its sea routes to India, then to expedite its oil activities in Persia and Mesopotamia. In 1899 Kuwait's ruler followed the example of other gulf sheikhs and signed a treaty of protection with Britain, which lasted until 1961. The British connection proved useful to the Sabahites in preventing Kuwait from being overrun by desert warriors during the rise of Ibn Saud in Arabia proper. The fact that the Sabahs had given sanctuary to the Saudi leader and had aided him in his recovery of Riyadh in 1902 was of little consequence to Ibn Saud; when he later conquered the province of Hasa, his original intention was to incorporate adjoining Kuwait into it.

The link also proved profitable to the British, for in 1934 it helped to ensure that the concession to explore for oil in Kuwait territory went to a company in which the British-owned Anglo-Iranian Oil Company had half a share. (The other half was held by the American-owned Gulf Oil Corporation which, shut out of the competition for Saudi Arabian oil by California Standard, joined the British in the international petroleum quest.)

The Kuwait Oil Company, as the British-American venture was called, first struck oil in large quantities in 1938, but drilling was stopped in 1941 because of the war. Although it was resumed in 1945, the Kuwait oil boom did not begin in earnest until 1951, when Britain stepped up production in response to its loss of access to its fields in Iran. Thereafter, with the help of the same kind of income tax scheme first devised by Aramco in Saudi Arabia, Kuwait's oil income rose at a rate of about $130 million per year — a handsome sum for a land with a population of only 300,000. During the same period the income of Saudi Arabia, whose population was over seven million, was rising at a rate of only $110 million, and most of that was being squandered through corruption and the reckless acquisition of redundant personal material luxuries.

The beginning of the oil boom coincided with the accession to power in Kuwait of Sheikh Abdullah Al-Salim Al-Sabah, who was a more democratically minded ruler than his Sabahite predecessors. As if prophetically fulfilling the observations of the British voyager Palgrave a century before, Sheikh Abdullah resolved to apply the vast income to the benefit of his entire people rather than just to his own family. Accordingly, he established an elected council that had some say in the spending of oil revenues. Thus, while Saudi Arabia was wasting its new riches, Kuwait embarked on a program to employ them in a responsible manner. Thenceforth the tiny land was to rapidly evolve into an independent nation whose extravagant revenues would turn it into a welfare state the material and financial dimensions of which were beyond anyone's imagination at the time.

During the early 1950s the port town of Kuwait was transformed into a city that, in a frenzy of building activity, crept farther and farther into the desert. Schools, hospitals, apartment houses, boulevards, handsome squares and lavishly planted traffic circles began to rise out of the sand, and cars flooded in to clog them with traffic. The money filtered down from Sheikh Abdullah's treasury to almost every native Kuwaiti in one form or another — either directly or in the form of other benefits — in proportion to his status, so that by 1955 no Kuwaiti citizen was without at least rudimentary luxuries.

There was only one problem with Abdullah's munificence: The advantages and benefits that accrued to the native Kuwaitis were theirs solely because of their Kuwaiti citizenship. The construction boom was bringing into the country waves of immigrants — Egyptians, embittered Palestinians and others from the overcrowded northern Arab world — in search of work. There was certainly no shortage of employment in the rich new welfare state, but because they were not citizens (and could not become citizens until they had lived there for fifteen years), except for their wages they derived no benefit from the largesse. They were poor Arab servants in the rich Arabs' house. Class distinctions were quickly established by the native Kuwaitis to set themselves off from the immigrants, and immigrant resentment soon began to smoulder. It came to a head in 1956 when Britain — still exercising its protectorate control over Kuwait — parachuted troops into Egypt to meet up with Israeli forces streaking across the Sinai.

The Suez invasion brought a violent outburst of anti-Western and anti-Israeli agitation on the part of the large Egyptian and Palestinian population swelling Kuwait City. The most convenient target was the half-British-owned Kuwait Oil Company, and soon pipelines leading from the wells in the desert to the loading facilities in the port were being blown up by the dozens. Residual violence spilled over onto the Kuwaitis themselves because of their cavalier treatment of the immigrants and because of what the dissidents' propaganda claimed was Kuwait's acquiescence in continued British and Western "imperialist exploitation of the Arab world."

Although order was eventually restored, Kuwait was shaken by the incident. Abdullah, suddenly realizing that his sheikhdom had become a hotbed of political activism and anxious to keep his reign secure, began to utter mild anti-Western epithets to at least partially appease the dissidents without overly alienating the British and American interests that kept his realm in gold.

Of course, the reaction in Kuwait to the Suez War was nothing compared to the reaction elsewhere in the Middle East. The British involvement reflected with utter clarity Britain's frustration over its waning influence in the region; at the same time it confirmed the irrevocable loss of that influence. Nor was the United States exempted from the orgy of Arab anti-Western sentiment in the wake of the war. Although America had attempted to dissuade Britain from the Suez adventure, it had earlier in the year reneged on its commitment to underwrite the construction of the huge Aswan Dam along Egypt's Upper Nile. So it too got rained on in the storm of Arab propaganda.

Although the 1956 war represented another Arab military humiliation, in accordance with the often paradoxical pattern of Middle East politics its outcome was transformed into a political victory for Nasser and the cause of Arab unity. The Arab world rallied behind him, and in his euphoria he conceived his grand design for a vast Pan-Arab socialist union with Egypt at the helm. The necessity of coopting the politically backward but economically wealthy Arabian peninsula in order to effect this design did not escape him, and soon he had agents circulating throughout the peninsula states drumming up enthusiasm for his vision.

Concentrating his efforts in the most southerly — and perhaps the most backward — state of Yemen, he quickly involved Egypt in a civil war there between revolutionary forces and its traditional royal rulers. This thrust Saudi Arabia into a defensive position. The Saudis, although in no sense Pan-Arabists themselves, had to acknowledge Nasser's Pan-Arab aspirations. On the other hand they were monarchists, and since Nasser had repeatedly condemned monarchism as a hindrance to his Arab-socialist dream, his ambitions could only redound unfavorably upon themselves should his attempts to overthrow Yemen's royal regime be successful. So, taking the long view, they threw their lot in with Yemen's royalists, supplying them with troops, weapons and money in the fight against the Nasser-backed revolutionists.

The struggle in Yemen did not divert the Saudis' attention from the main issues at hand, however. This was oil, and here again, in concert with the increasing anti-Western sentiment in the Middle East, new developments were about to emerge that would further change the nature of the relationships between the oil companies and their host governments. Here again, too, the developments were to originate in the non-Arab state of Iran.

The American-engineered overthrow of the Iranian nationalist government in 1954 had restored to power Shah (King) Pahlevi, a weak and indecisive young man who had inherited the throne from his tyrannical father and who had sat by helplessly while the revolutionary nationalists took over his country in 1951. Propped up by the United States, and with several years in office under his gilded belt, the shah decided in 1957 that the time had come to test his authority. The result of this decision was the passage of a new petroleum act into Iranian law. It was an act that revolutionized the oil industry, for it made all future concession agreements between Iran and the international oil companies contingent upon an at least fifty percent ownership in any company by the Iranian government. What this meant, simply, was that the profits of international oil companies exploring for and producing oil under new concession agreements would thenceforth be halved. Not only would the companies be required to pay for concessions and pay royalties and taxes, they would also have to distribute half their profits, after all these other items were taken care of, to Iran. And this included profits not only from the production of oil, but from every aspect of its marketing in various product forms. The Iranians called their new law the joint-venture law.

At first the American oil companies interpreted the law as the manifestation of an Iranian impulse to commit economic suicide. With oil throughout the world in plentiful supply — indeed, with oil reserves and surpluses elsewhere apparently endless — no one thought that any oil company would be so foolish as to enter into such a restrictive arrangement. They were, of course, wrong. When Iran announced that it was offering a previously unexplored area of the country for exclusive concession and exploration on a joint-venture basis, fifty-seven companies from nine different nations sent in their bids. The winner was the Standard Oil Company of Indiana. The Middle East oil business would never be the same again.

By now the international oil consortiums were sending their agents farther southward along the Arabian Gulf coast and into the tiny obscure sheikhdoms that had, with the help of the British, remained independent of Saudi Arabia when that country was formed in the early thirties. With the success of the Iranians, the sheikhs began to repeat the phrase "joint venture" as if it were inscribed in the Koran. The oil companies, sensing trouble ahead, started to broadcast the word back home of potential future oil-supply crises.

Although the oil companies did their best to remain apolitical, oil was becoming more and more of a political issue in the Middle East. It was tied not so much to Western support for Israel as to Western domination and manipulation of the Arabs' greatest natural resource. Although the West had removed its troops and its colonial administrations from the Arab world, its economic imperialism, in the view of increasing numbers of Arabs, was even more insidious. The years 1958 to 1960 brought the issue bubbling to the surface. First, a revolution in Iraq in July of 1958 brutally deposed its Hashemite rulers and established an anti-Western military government that loudly threatened Britain's long-standing control of the country's considerable oil reserves. The revolution brought about brief but rapidly executed military occupations of Lebanon and Jordan by American and British troops, respectively. These occupations were ostensibly conducted to calm the insurrectionary moods the Iraqi revolt had unleashed in these countries and were done at the request of the host governments, but they were interpreted by more radical elements in the Arab world as bald expressions of the still-vibrant Western imperialistic impulse. Then, in 1959 the oil companies complicated matters further by unilaterally slashing the "posted" crude oil prices because of the surpluses of oil that were flooding the market.

Here we should pause briefly to examine the history and technique of oil pricing in the Middle East. When the international oil companies began to operate in the Arab world they formed local subsidiary companies to carry on the actual work of exploration and production. The Iraq Petroleum Company was made up of British, French, Dutch and American companies. Aramco was shared by four American companies. The Kuwait Oil Company was coowned by a British and an American company. These local consortium companies were formed simply for the purpose of producing the oil for the home-based companies that had a share in them. They sold the crude oil to the parent companies, who would then refine, market and sell it to the outside world. In the old days the subsidiaries would sell crude oil to their parent companies at low prices and pay royalties based on a percentage of those deliberately low prices to the governments of the countries in which they operated. The parent companies would then sell this cut-rate oil at the prevailing world prices, which were based on the much higher costs of producing oil in the United States. The result was low royalties for the Arab producing countries and high profits for the international parent companies.

When the system of payment to the Arabs was changed from royalties only to royalties plus taxes, the Arabs insisted that a standard price be established upon which the royalty and tax percentages could be based. In this way, the Arab governments could accurately anticipate their revenues and arrange their budgets accordingly. The oil companies agreed, and thus a "posted price" was set for all oil produced in the Arab countries.

The posted price was an artificial price. With the increasing glut of oil on the market in the fifties, the "real" price — the price at which the local producing companies sold the oil — descended well below the posted price. Nevertheless the taxes and royalties paid by the consortiums remained based on the posted price, which meant that although the Arab governments were receiving the steady income guaranteed by the posted price, the oil companies were earning less and less on each barrel of oil produced and sold to their parent companies, which in turn meant a shrinkage in the profits of the parent companies.

In 1959 the world oil glut reached a peak. Oil was in such plentiful supply and demand was so weak* that the real price of Arab oil had plunged sharply below the posted price. More money was going to the Arab governments in royalties and taxes than was going into the coffers of the companies. To counter this situation, one of the partners in Aramco — Standard Oil of New Jersey — reduced the posted price without consulting any of the governments concerned. The other companies followed suit.

The cut came at a time when the parsimonious Crown Prince Faisal had been appointed by the Saudi royal family to reverse the fiscal mismanagement of his half-brother King Saud. Despite Saudi Arabia's considerable tax and royalty earnings, the kingdom was functionally bankrupt, with debts of close to $500 million. Faisal had already instituted a program of fiscal reforms which, based on future oil-revenue projections that were accorded by the posted price system, would erase the debt in a few years and put Saudi Arabia back on a healthy economic footing. At one stroke the oil companies' price reduction slashed Saudi Arabia's income by $30 million for the following year. The Saudi reaction was pained and vocal. It was soon joined to a chorus of protest from all the Arab oil governments, for each had learned to depend on what they thought was a guaranteed yearly income based on an inviolable posted price and to fix their budgets accordingly.

* You might recall the furious advertising and promotional campaigns of American oil companies in the fifties and sixties to get you to buy your gasoline at their service stations, campaigns that promised such premiums as highball glasses, china sets, stuffed pandas, and the rest.

The move confirmed in the mind of one Saudi the innate capacity for selfish treachery on the part of America. His name was Abdullah Tariki. The son of a respected Saudi government official, he was a thirty-four-year-old graduate of Cairo University, where he had taken a degree in geology and had dabbled in the radical, nationalist, anti-Western student politics of the day. Slender, dark, as handsome as a movie idol, he followed his Cairo education with a year of petroleum studies at the University of Texas and then went into a year's training program with the Texas Oil Company, one of the principal shareholders in Aramco. While in Texas he repeatedly experienced examples of what he considered to be the kind of blustery, paternalistic, anti-Arab bigotry that was endemic to Aramco's Middle East operations. He found Texans loud, coarse and as monetarily greedy as the wasteful Arabian princes they were so prone to condemn in their barely comprehensible dialects, and each time he heard himself referred to as "our little Aye-rab friend" he shuddered with contempt.

Offered a job with Aramco when he returned to Saudi Arabia, he turned it down and took a position instead as a specialist on natural resources in the Saudi government, where he immediately began to agitate for a stiffer Saudi approach in its dealings with the American oil companies. He rose rapidly in the Saudi hierarchy during the 1950s until, by the time the companies cut the posted price, he was director general of the kingdom's ministry of petroleum and minerals. His rise in station was accompanied by an increasing bitterness toward the United States — Aramco officials tended to treat him as an enemy — and he talked more and more of "American economic imperialism" and the need for Saudi Arabia to get out from under the yoke of American control of its only significant natural resource.

Tariki had already, in 1959, negotiated a new kind of contract with a Japanese company for the rights to crude oil off the Arabian shore. Many of the major American companies and several independents had competed for it, but the Japanese, whose country had no oil resources of its own, were the only ones willing to meet Tariki's rigorous demands. The contract represented a coup for Tariki's radical ideas on dealing with foreign oil companies, for it gave Saudi Arabia fifty-six percent of all profits made, and these profits were to be calculated not only on sales of oil from the wells but on all sales that took place farther down the marketing line, no matter where and in what form they occurred. Moreover, the Japanese were forbidden to sell the concessioned oil to "enemies of the Arabs."

With this revolutionary contract, which gave the Saudis better than equal participation in profits while protecting them from any capital risks — usually implied by the term "joint venture" — Tariki became an influence to be reckoned with in the politics of oil. Anti-Western feelings were running high throughout the Arab world in the wake of the bloody Iraqi revolt, and when the oil companies cut the posted price of Persian Gulf crude the move turned Tariki feverish with ambition to further stem the power of the Western companies. He rushed to Iraq in 1960 to urge the military junta there to nationalize the foreign-owned Iraq Petroleum Company. Oil ministers from other producing countries, fired by Tariki's anti-Western polemics, followed him to Baghdad in a show of solidarity. Once gathered there, Tariki called them all into an emergency congress in which he urged them to join together in an association to combat the monopolistic practices of the oil companies. Out of the congress came the formation of the Organization of Petroleum Exporting Countries (OPEC), a cartel of nations that was to gradually but profoundly alter the balance of economic power in the world.

The birth of OPEC was at first looked upon almost smilingly by the oil consortiums like Aramco and the nations of their parent companies. Its initial membership consisted of Saudi Arabia, Iran, Iraq, Kuwait and Venezuela. Such a makeup boded ill for its chances of surviving beyond infancy, many oil analysts opined: How often before had the nations of the Middle East tried to band together in a united front only to see their initial fervor dissolve into rivalry and dissension? Not only that, but the presence of Iran and Venezuela — both non-Arab countries, one Western — would further complicate matters.*

The primary demand to come out of the first OPEC conference, which was orchestrated by Tariki, was for stability in the posted prices and an immediate restoration of the original price. The members additionally insisted that no further cuts in the posted price be made without prior consultation with the producing nations. They acknowledged certain obligations to the oil companies, such as the security of existing concession contracts, but warned that these obligations would continue to be honored only if the companies met their demands. They pledged among themselves to maintain their solidarity and remain united in the face of counterpressures, and to reject any special advantages that might be dangled in front of one of them by the foreign consortiums for the purpose of provoking a break in organization ranks.

* The oil sheikhdoms along the gulf coast of the Arabian peninsula joined OPEC a little later, followed by Libya, Algeria, Egypt, Nigeria, Indonesia, Tobago and Trinidad.

The oil companies reacted by collectively announcing their intention to ignore OPEC. They stated that they would continue to negotiate with the individual oil-producing countries and would in no instance deal with any combined organization. In the beginning OPEC seemed indeed to justify the oil companies' scorn; during its first year or so it served primarily as a talk forum for Tariki's anti-Western and anticompany sentiments. But out of these discussions came loud and clear signals which presaged the future course of oil dealings between the companies and the Arabs: partnership. Previously the Arab countries had been independently powerless to force a revision of existing concession contracts — many of which ran until the end of the century — calling for a true, across-the-board fifty percent participation in the exploitation of their resources. Now, however, acting as a united bloc, they became convinced they were in a position to do so. True, they needed the money their oil brought them. But the companies — and the industrial world — needed the oil even more. If they acted in concert, steadfastly refusing to negotiate with the companies except as a unit, and if the companies continued to refuse such negotiations, the resulting shutdown in production would precipitate a severe fuel crisis in the Western world. With this strategy in hand, then, they served notice on the companies. "It was," an American Aramco official of the time recently remarked to me, "the Arabs' first discovery of the art of blackmail. And all because of that goddamn Tariki!"

Tariki did not stay around long enough to savor the triumph. By 1962 the spendthrifts of the Saudi Arabian royal family had gotten the upper hand again and the country's treasury was again fast depleting. Prince Faisal was called in once more to put the fiscal house in order. A conservative man, he did not interpret the time as being ripe for Tariki's repeated explosive threats to cut off oil production, but rather favored a more conciliatory approach. Tariki was dismissed from his post as Saudi oil minister and invited to take up his cause elsewhere. He exiled himself to Beirut as an oil consultant, and the Saudi oil ministry passed into calmer hands. Tariki not only lost his job, but with it his leading voice in the still youthful OPEC. His mantle there was passed to Fouad Rouhani, a quiet, urbane, cultivated Iranian with a decided liking for things Western.

The Saudi cause was taken up by Tariki's youthful replacement — a Harvard-trained expert in international law named Ahmed Zaki Al-Yamani. In 1963 Yamani, a plumply handsome, soft-spoken negotiator, persuaded Aramco to give at least token recognition to OPEC. "Once we are strong enough to shut down all the wells and shut off the pipelines," Abdullah Tariki had been quoted as saying while still OPEC's voice, "the companies will see a great light. The world can not live without Middle East oil."* Although Yamani was not the type to resort to such bluster, he let that threat dangle vaguely in the background as he attempted to transform the companies' token recognition into a real one. By the end of 1966 Libya and Abu Dhabi — one of the Arabian coastal sheikhdoms newly found to be rich in oil reserves — had joined OPEC, and the organization's bargaining strength was further reinforced. The OPEC members looked toward 1967 as the year of change in the oil companies' attitudes. Beginning with Saudi Arabia, now recognized as the possessor of the greatest oil reserves of all, it was anticipated that each oil state would markedly improve its financial arrangements with the companies operating within its borders — all others standing resolutely behind it — first to force, and then to sustain, the negotiations.

Nineteen sixty-seven was indeed a year that induced a change. But it came from an unexpected source — the outbreak of the Arab-Israeli Six-Day War — and it did not bring about the change anticipated. In fact, the 1967 war served more to reveal the weaknesses of OPEC than to provide it with an opportunity to display whatever strength it had.

The war touched off various reactions among the OPEC countries. The Iraqi government — by then a hard-line Baathist regime dedicated to revolutionary Pan-Arab socialism — shut down Iraq's production in order to deny petroleum to the "imperialist Western aggressors" who were in sympathy with Israel. Now, although the OPEC countries had vowed not to let their differing political systems interfere with united action, politics reared its head. The Arab gulf oil countries followed Iraq's example, more from fear that militant Arab saboteurs would shut down production than from any compelling sympathy for the left-wing countries engaged in the struggle with Israel. Iran, however, a Muslim but not an Arab nation, had no quarrel with Israel's existence. Thus it stepped up production to take advantage of the shortages occasioned by its Arab OPEC confreres and by the closing of the Suez Canal. The result was a tremendous increase in Iranian sales to Britain and Germany, the two principal targets of the Arab embargo.

Venezuela likewise accelerated production; although the primary market for its oil was the United States, it also increased its shipments to Europe. And Libya, which was ruled by a corrupt, reactionary monarchy that held the radical politics of Egypt and its allies in little favor, stepped up its

* *Saturday Evening Post*, February 17, 1962.

production and sales to Europe sufficiently to override the effectiveness of the Arab boycott.

The boycott, which only remained in force for a week in the Arabian peninsula, cost Saudi Arabia over $30 million in revenues, while Kuwait, the second largest oil producer, lost more than $7 million. Moreover, so rapid was the income and outgo of oil revenues that by the end of the week the Saudi treasury was empty, whereas Iran's was spilling over. The failure of the non-Arab OPEC countries to back the Arab embargo, and the haste with which they went about enriching themselves in the bargain, were sobering realizations to the Arabs. The idea of using their oil as a political weapon against the West and its producing consortiums, first articulated by the nationalist firebrand Abdullah Tariki, appeared hollow indeed. The sharpest sufferers from the boycott were the Arab oil states themselves.

Later that summer the Arabs met in Khartoum to hash the matter over. Everyone agreed that the entire affair had been poorly handled. "Injudiciously used, the oil weapon loses much if not all of its importance and effectiveness," Oil Minister Yamani of Saudi Arabia had declared. "If we do not use it properly, we are behaving like someone who fires a bullet into the air, missing the enemy and allowing it to rebound on himself."*

The convening Arab oil states discussed the possibility of banding themselves into an Organization of Arab Petroleum Exporting Countries (OAPEC), to be separate from the larger OPEC and to coordinate their own oil policies so that in the event of some future boycott they would be able to bring pressure to bear on noncooperating non-Arab oil nations. They also agreed — or at least Saudi Arabia and Kuwait did — to provide Egypt and Jordan with substantial subsidies to help rebuild their armed forces. The rest of the time they spent mourning the opportunity they had missed in impressing the oil companies with the solidarity of OPEC and criticizing King Idris of Libya for his less than inspired behavior during the boycott. Little did they know that the deflated Arab oil power was about to get a new boost from that very same country.

If Libya's actions during the boycott angered the Arabs, they positively infuriated a handful of desert-born pro-Nasser officers in the Libyan army, among whom was a certain ascetic, handsome, burning-eyed captain, still in his twenties, by the name of Muammar Al-Qadhafi (often spelled Kaddafi).

* *Middle East Economic Survey*, July 21, 1967.

Up to 1965 Libya was still trying to struggle into the twentieth century after years of oppressive Italian colonial rule. Vast quantities of oil were discovered beneath its sands in the mid-1950s, but its inexperienced king, the aging scion of the land's ancient ruling Senussi tribe, was no match for the foreign oil company agents who trooped to his palace bearing concession contracts. King Idris delegated the responsibility for granting concessions to ministers whose venality and corruption knew few bounds, and for ten years Libya gushed oil under financial terms that were manifestly unfavorable to the country as a whole, although highly profitable to individual ministers.

Instead of granting widespread exclusive concessions, the ministers realized that much more personal, under-the-table income could be derived by playing the old established companies off against the newer, smaller, independent operators who were beginning to enter the Middle East oil picture. They thus parceled out several districts among the major companies and the independents for large advances but at royalty and tax schedules that were well below the norm of the gulf countries.

By paying further bribes, the oil companies persuaded the Libyan ministers to keep their country out of OPEC for as long as possible so as to maintain their low oil payments. But pressures from the other oil states became too great, and in 1965 Libya joined the association. Once in, it was constantly reminded of the inequities in the concessions its ministers had granted. Eventually, under OPEC prodding, the Libyans finally forced the companies to accept oil payment rates that were on a par with those remitted to the gulf states.

The new rates did not put an end to Libyan corruption, however; it was precisely that corruptibility that was responsible for Libya's continued shipments of oil to Germany, whence much of it was reshipped to Britain, during the short-lived 1967 boycott. As a result, the clique of disgusted, fanatically religious army officers, led by Captain Qadhafi, began to mutter among themselves with ferocious disapproval.

Their disgust was compounded by the oil bonanza that descended on Libya in the wake of the 1967 war. The closing of the Suez Canal had caused a rise in the cost of transporting Persian Gulf oil to Europe; tankers were now required to take the much longer route around Africa. This provoked a rise in the price of petroleum products in Europe. Libya, situated a relative stone's throw from Europe, suddenly found itself in a highly favored position, with its oil in far greater demand than ever before.

The boom brought with it spiraling corruption. With high government officials showing the way, Libyan civil servants, police, customs agents and others in positions of petty authority got into the act by demanding higher and higher bribes for their services. By 1969 oil men and tourists were doing a popular turn on the country's motto: "The Land of the Date Palm." It was now being called "The Land of the Greased Palm."

In 1969, with the Libyan oil circus at its peak, the young Qadhafi witnessed an event that sparked a resolve to do more than just express his private disgust. By now furiously pro-Nasser and always a highly orthodox Muslim, he despised the modern West and equally those Arabs who emulated Western ways, associated with Western women, or in any other way subscribed to Western values. Thoroughly inspired by Nasserite propaganda, he reserved his most extreme hatred for Jews who, through the instrument of Israel, he saw as the embodiment of Western evil and the most ruthless defamers of Islamic sanctity in the Arab midst.

In the spring of 1969 the American-owned Occidental Petroleum Corporation, an independent concessionaire in Libya, finished a pipeline from its inland wells to the Libyan port of Cirte on the Mediterranean. King Idris was invited to preside over the ceremonies marking the opening of the pipeline, and the event was turned into a state occasion, with all the colonialist pomp and ritual involved in such events. A large honor guard from the Libyan army was trotted out for the rite, and among its officers was Captain Qadhafi. The young, stern-faced captain had a close view of his country's king and courtiers arriving in their sleek limousines and fawning over the visiting American contingent of Occidental executives and board members led by the company's president Armand Hammer, a Jew.

Six months later, while King Idris was on a visit to Turkey, Qadhafi and his fellow officers, calling themselves the Revolutionary Command Council, staged a totally unexpected coup d'état. In its aftermath they abruptly changed the face of Libya. By mid-1970 the country had been cleansed of most of the pernicious foreign influences Qadhafi had so detested, including American and British military bases. With Libya recomposed into a much more fundamentalist Muslim society, all that was left for now-Colonel Qadhafi to do was to bring his ax down on the foreign oil companies.

His first impulse was to express his contempt for them by summarily nationalizing the entire Libyan oil industry. But his second-in-command on the Revolutionary Command Council, Major Abdessalem Jalloud, dissuaded him with the argument that there were not enough trained Libyan personnel to run the production facilities. Instead the two devised a tactic designed to appreciably increase Libya's oil revenues until such time as sufficient Libyan citizens were trained in the technology of oil.

The oil companies, aware of the pending crisis, united in their resolve to hold onto their properties without being forced into paying more money. Their view was that, as in the other oil states, a past contract was a contract, and no amount of pressure should be permitted to breach it. They waited, anxious but en bloc, to hear Qadhafi's proposals.

There were no proposals. Instead, Qadhafi and Jalloud summoned representatives of just one company, Occidental, the same company the religion of whose president and founder so nettled Qadhafi. Of all the independents operating in Libya, Occidental was the most vulnerable to the presentation of a Hobson's choice, for it possessed no other sources of supply but its Libyan concession. Moreover, it had $450 million in capital invested in new facilities. To be forced into closing down would be tantamount to putting an end to its corporate existence. It could not even afford a cutback in output, and any thoughts it might have had about remaining united in its resistance with the other companies were quickly discarded when Qadhafi ordered Libyan troops into its oil fields and instituted an immediate cut of thirty percent in the company's production.

In mid-1970 Occidental announced that it had reached a compromise with the Libyan government and would sign a new contract that called for a substantial increase in taxes, royalties and posted prices. With Occidental giving in, the other companies had no choice but to follow. For the companies it might have been a compromise, but for the Libyans it was a triumph, for they had succeeded in breaking the tradition of ironclad, nonrenegotiable contracts on existing concessions.

The other Arab oil governments watched the proceedings in Libya with a heightening appreciation for what they foresaw for themselves. They then called an OPEC meeting in Teheran and there confronted the major oil companies with demands for huge increases in revenues. The companies balked, but in the end they had to give in under the threat of nationalization of their operations. The new 1971 agreements generally doubled the income of the Arab states. The oil companies, of course, passed their increased costs into the consumer chain.

But that was not to be the end of it. Emboldened by their newfound ability to impose their will, the Arab gulf countries, led by Oil Minister Yamani of Saudi Arabia, now began to demand participation in all phases of the companies' existing operations. This the companies flatly rejected.

Libya responded by seizing all the British Petroleum Company's facilities in its territory and threatening to nationalize Standard Oil of New Jersey's operations as well. Iraq made even more bellicose gestures. Kuwait talked about nationalizing.

By 1972 OPEC was polarized between the militants, led by Iraq and Libya, and the moderates, whose spokesman was Yamani. The Saudi argued for patience, claiming that for the Arab gulf states to nationalize then would be premature and costly. And if all the OPEC countries nationalized it would be the end of OPEC. Individual oil-producing governments would be forced into competition with one another to sell their oil, which would mean a nosedive in prices as they sought to undercut each other, and a severe reduction in revenues. Some might benefit, but others would lose. Better to remain united, went Yamani's argument, for this way all the countries would benefit in proportion to their resources.

Yamani continued to press for participation into 1972. In February Aramco finally agreed to sit down and discuss the matter. Yamani requested that Aramco sell Saudi Arabia a twenty percent interest in the company and its existing producing concessions, with the percentage to increase in gradual increments over the future. Aramco said no, but came back with a counteroffer: fifty percent participation in the operation of its undeveloped concessions in the future.

The offer had to be a temptation to the Saudis, for Aramco held concessions to vast reservoirs of untapped oil which only it had the economic means and technical know-how to develop. Nevertheless Yamani declined. None of the other Arab countries had such proven undeveloped reserves which could be exploited under such fifty-fifty arrangements; their only hope for real participation lay in an insistence on a twenty percent share of the existing production within their borders. To accept the Aramco offer would sabotage the aspirations of the other nations and destroy the solidarity the OPEC ministers had pledged themselves to.

Yamani instead came back with a veiled ultimatum from King Faisal: Either voluntarily deal us in for twenty percent of your existing operations, or else we will enact legislation which will force you under Saudi Arabian law to do so. In March 1972, Aramco grudgingly agreed, its chief executives muttering sourly about the Saudi definition of "voluntary."

Aramco's accession was the climax of the fifty-year-old Middle East oil drama. Its denouement is well known. Other oil companies in other Arab countries were forced to follow suit, and the process of ending Western domination of Arab oil resources began to pick up pace. The Arab states established schedules for legislated incremental increases in their share of ownership of the consortiums (Saudi Arabia, the pacesetter, as of this writing owns sixty percent of Aramco and will soon own a hundred percent). Then came the 1973 Arab-Israeli war, the second Arab oil boycott, the advent of the energy crisis in the West, further production cutbacks, and a sudden quadrupling of prices and a dizzying increase in revenues to the Arab states in the aftermath.

Today the Arab oil-producing nations have enough monetary reserves in their treasuries to shut down petroleum production for three years without having to suffer. Storage stocks of oil in the energy-hungry West range from only a week's worth or so in the United States to about two months' worth in Europe. Of course the Arabs are not going to shut down their oil production, for they derive their own energy from it. But as they proved in 1973, they are capable of manipulating their oil resources in a number of ways to impose their will — political and economic — on the world that has long and often cynically dominated them.

In traveling about the Arab world, as I have elsewhere indicated, one often hears the Arabic equivalents of such English phrases as "the chickens have come home to roost" and "the tables have turned." These phrases, carrying with them a certain tone of vindictiveness, are usually uttered by people who have little or no real say in the official policies of the oil states. However, their frequency and intensity are, it seems to me, an accurate measure of Arab public opinion. But do they represent the ambitions and intentions, overt or covert, of the nations to whom so much economic power has been in the process of shifting? Are there secret plots and conspiracies forming within or among the oil kingdoms and sheikhdoms to exercise that power in ways dictated by the ancient tribal revenge-ethic of an arm for a hand, a leg for a foot? Are the Arabs really driven by an impulse to bring the West to its knees? It was to get an indication of the answer to such questions that I made my way into Saudi Arabia and Kuwait, one the star and the other a chief supporting actor in the new drama that is unfolding between the Arab world and the West.

# 30.

# JOURNAL: *Faisal and the Saudis*

THANKS TO THE FOURFOLD RISE in Middle East crude oil prices after the 1973 war, Saudi Arabia's revenues leapt to $21 billion in 1974. The earnings of all the Middle East oil-producing states rose correspondingly, but the Saudi revenues were by far the most voluminous — almost twice as much as those of Iran, the second leading oil producer. In 1975, barring boycotts or calamities, Saudi revenues will be $30 billion or better. During the next five years they will continue to rise until all the Arab states will have between them, theoretically at least, $280 billion of the world's $400 billion in monetary reserves. Of this, Saudi Arabia will have about $100 billion — about one-eighth of the total capitalization of the publicly owned American business and industrial complex. In ten years, assuming a continued world-wide demand for Middle East oil, total Arab accumulations will mount almost to $600 billion — enough, theoretically, for the Arab world to buy its way into majority ownership of America.*

The people of the United States and western Europe experienced the initial effects of the 1973 oil embargo at their gasoline and petro stations. Whether the fuel shortages and rationing programs of late 1973 and early 1974 were a direct result of the Arab embargo, or more the consequence of a cabal among the oil companies to jack up their prices, has been argued feverishly since. The question is academic. The real issue is that oil, although in plentiful supply, has had its character completely transformed in the

* All these figures are based on estimates provided by the World Bank and the International Monetary Fund.

scheme of things in the Western world. Arab oil is no longer simply a cheap, viscous black fluid the flammable properties of which, in various hydrocarbonic manifestations and combinations, are the fundamental catalysts of the West's material progress and plenitude. Oil is now a potent instrument of Arab ideology and political will. The Arabs can and will use it in much the same way the United States has for so long used its own abundance of money and material resources for foreign aid — selectively, its purposes primarily political and only secondarily humanitarian.

This idea was put to me by Anwar Ali, the suave, polite Pakistan-born head of the Saudi Arabian Monetary Agency. It was early fall of 1974, and I had heard on good authority that Saudi Arabia was about to pledge several billion dollars to Egypt, Syria, Jordan and the Palestine Liberation Organization.* We had been discussing in general terms the question of the financial balance the Saudi government intended to strike between its commitment to the Arab side of the conflict in the north and its own worldwide economic aspirations.

"It seems to me," I said, "that your country could be painting itself into a corner of its own. If it gives three or four billion to Egypt, Syria and the others, most of this money will go to buy arms. The money comes from the West in the form of oil payments and becomes part of Saudi Arabia's enormous monetary surplus. Then it goes to Egypt and the others. But it does not stop there. From there it goes to Russia to pay for the arms. So what has happened is that you have taken three or four billion dollars from the West and transferred it to the Soviet Union, instead of reinvesting that money back into the West. Aren't you afraid that the money might come back to haunt you? After all, you are spreading it through a chain of revolutionary socialist political systems which do not look kindly upon capitalist monarchies such as Saudi Arabia."

"From the point of view of economics," Ali replied, "there is no great problem. Much of that money which goes to Russia will not terminate there. With the increasing climate of détente and trade between America and Russia, the Soviet Union will use that money to purchase goods from the West. You see, we plan these things out carefully. We ask, what is of more importance to the United States, peace with Russia or that Israel remain the bête noire of the Arab world? And we decide it is peace with Russia. Now in America you still have your senators and congressmen who would support

* The pledge was subsequently announced at the October 1974 Arab Summit Conference at Rabat, Morocco.

Israel at any cost. These people are presently making it difficult for the United States to accept a wider détente and wider trade with Russia. We know that much of the money we give to the Arab countries in the north will go to Russia. But we also know that the United States will not want that money to stay there. They will want it to come back to the West so that the West will have it to buy even more oil. So what will happen? The United States will recognize this reality and pressure will build to get this money back. How? By increasing trade. And increased trade is based on increased détente. That is why your Mr. Kissinger is so adamant in improving relations with Russia."

"But doesn't that just start another round-robin?" I said. "I know this is all a bit oversimplified, but say the United States gets much of this money back in the form of exports to Russia. We can then use it to make more arms to send to Israel, or to support Israel in other ways."

"Ah, but you forget the law of diminishing returns," he said. "We would then continue to send money to Russia via the Arab countries, as before. But in each transaction the quantity of the money diminishes. Let's take the four billion figure. It starts here as four billion. By the time it leaves Egypt or Syria it is only three billion, for these countries will keep a billion for their own domestic purposes. It arrives in Russia as three billion, but by the time it leaves Moscow to go back to the West in trade it is down to, say, two billion, for the Russians will keep a billion for *their* internal needs. Not all of this will go to the United States — perhaps only one billion. So what began as four billion in oil payments from the United States comes back as one billion a year or so later. This is not sufficient, and your leaders will recognize it. How to get more? You must increase trade with Russia. Which means increasing détente. So that practical people in your government will recognize the realities of America's primary needs and will overcome the impractical supporters of Zionism. There will be no more arms to Israel. Israel will have to come to terms with the Arab states if it wishes to survive. You see, there are many ways of fighting a war. And there are many ways to use the oil weapon. You in the United States have fought many of your wars with foreign aid. Why should we not? You have been struggling for years, with great outlays of money in other parts of the world, to make the world safe from Communism, as you say. But when you reduce this slogan to its essentials, you are really interested in making just the United States safe from Communism. This is exactly what we wish to do. We wish to make the Arab world safe from Zionism."

Dr. Ali scoffed good-humoredly when I asked if there were an impulse operating within Saudi Arabia to use its burgeoning wealth, either singly or in concert with other oil states, to buy effective control of the West's industrial and capitalistic complex. "It is not a bad idea," he said. "But no, I do not see that as a grand design. Why should we want to lumber ourselves with such headaches, anyway? We can achieve all the prosperity we need over the next fifty years with our money."

"With all due respects," I replied, "you are a Pakistani. I've gotten a distinct impression from many of the people I've talked to that among the Saudis there is an idea of this nature percolating. I get it in different forms, but they all boil down to the same thing. They see themselves one day presiding over board meetings of IBM and General Motors."

"It is not likely to happen," Ali said, "for I'll tell you this about the Saudis. They are fundamentally a lazy people. With the exception of a few, they have a long way to go before they are capable of dealing with modern business concepts. They have little sense of Western organization and managerial disciplines, to say nothing of technology and the drive for hard work. And these things are the keys to the success of the American system. They are smart enough to recognize this, and are content enough to simply sit back and enjoy the fruits of other people's labor and invention. No, it will not happen, at least not in my lifetime."

Anwar Ali was in his early sixties. Two months after our conversation he was in Washington, where he died. I had sought out Ali because I was told that he, as one of the principal managers of Saudi Arabia's mounting monetary surpluses, was a symbol of the responsible Saudi approach to the handling of that money. The problem was as exquisitely simple as it was complex, he explained. Between 1970 and the end of 1975 Saudi Arabia will have earned $60 billion in oil revenues, most of them from the West and Japan. Out of that sum about $12 billion will have been invested in the development of the industrial and commercial infrastructure of the country itself (transportation facilities, municipal improvements, health care, roads, communications, education, and the like). This is all the country will have been able to absorb in the period — it can build only so many hospitals and schools before there are more beds and classrooms than there are people in the country; it can build only so many roads before roads are so numerous they end up going nowhere. Since the country has hardly anything in the way of its own technological and industrial development resources, these must be hired from the industrialized world, principally the West. Thus, about $12 billion has or will find its way back to the West in exchange for the importation of Western technological and industrial development and the services that go with it.

That leaves the Saudi treasury with $48 billion. Deduct from that the $3 billion pledged to the Arab confrontation countries and $1 billion for the personal treasury of the king and his government, and the Saudis will be left with $44 billion in net monetary surpluses.

Saudi Arabia's surpluses represent, in round numbers, fifty percent of the total net cash surplus of all the Arab oil-producing countries combined. Thus, by the end of 1975, the total Arab real-net monetary reserves would be close to $90 billion — almost one-fourth of the entire monetary reserves of the world.

If the Arabs choose to hold on to this, it would mean chaos for the economies of the Western world. This is due simply to the basic law of economics — supply and demand — and to the meaning of money. Money is not only the primary instrument of value and exchange between people and nations, it is even more fundamentally the single most important commodity in existence, with its own specific value. In this sense it is like any other essential commodity. When it is in short supply the demand for it increases; similarly, when demand for it increases in one place and that demand is provided for, it becomes in short supply in another place. When a commodity is in short supply, the demand increases its cost. When its cost goes up, the costs of everything else involved in its production go up correspondingly. The result is economic inflation.

Although I am vastly oversimplifying a complex process, this is what has been happening during the past few years. In our global economic system, the value of one nation's money is measured against the values of all others'. And this is where the balance of monetary reserves plays a crucial role. Ideally, when the world's monetary reserves are in balance, there is no overabundance of supply of one nation's money in any other nation or nations. Thus there is no excess demand within that nation for its money, and the cost of the money remains settled according to its ordinary value.

But as often happens, international monetary reserves do not remain in balance. Poor nations endeavoring to develop themselves are often required to import more materials and services than they can export. They therefore have to pay more of their money out for imports than they get back for their exports, either in cash or credit. This increases their supply of money abroad while decreasing it at home, and is known as an unfavorable balance of payments. This in turn increases the demand for the money at home, which increases its cost. But while the cost of the money at home increases, the money that is out in the rest of the world lessens in value, which is due simply to the classic rule of supply and demand (where there is more supply for a commodity, there is less demand for it and its value lessens in the place in which the oversupply exists.)

Yet there is demand in the nation in which the money originates. So three processes usually follow. The first is that the nation of origin devalues its monetary system in an attempt to reduce the difference between the value of its money at home and its value abroad, thus making it easier to retrieve the money at more equitable rates. With devaluation comes an expansion of credit granted to the nation from other countries for the purpose of allowing continuity of trade. If this doesn't solve the problem — as it often doesn't — then the nation whose international payments are out of balance resorts to the creation of more money on its own in order to reduce some of its debt and remain solvent. But this has the effect of spreading more of the nation's money abroad, thereby further reducing its value in the international marketplace and making it even more costly to retrieve.

Of course these processes do not occur in a vacuum. Other nations go through similar experiences, and the international balance of payments is never in an ideal state of adjustment. All nations would basically prosper if such were the case. When such is not the case, which is always, then some nations prosper and others don't. But when the major industrial countries find their balance of payments unfavorably adjusted for any length of time, the effects are felt around the world. The effects are not just localized inflation, but inflation on a global scale.

Anwar Ali told me that the Saudis were acutely aware of the economic perils that would be created if Saudi Arabia kept its $44 billion share of the Arab world's $85 to $90 billion in monetary reserves from returning to the industrialized countries. "Aside from the $12 billion we will be sending back in the form of imports of goods and services, we are sending much of this back as investments and deposits. It is not our intention to destroy the Western nations' economies, for where would that then leave us? Who would buy our oil? No, what we want to do is to benefit from your economies. If you stay strong, then we will become strong. If you collapse, then we collapse."

"But doesn't that imply that if you sense us collapsing you will move in with your money to shore us up?"

"It could happen. But it doesn't mean we now have a design to take you over. I grant you, some hotheads among the Arabs may have such delusions of grandeur, but I can assure you that they do not control the purse strings. And the country you should really worry about is Iran, not Saudi Arabia. The Iranians are the ones with the real delusions, not the Arabs. That is why the United States must cooperate with us. Look at the way the Shah is building up his armed forces. You should not be here writing a book about the Arabs' intentions, you should be writing about Iran's intentions."

"What are their intentions?"

"In another year he will be able to conquer us all."

That was not the first hint of Arab Iranophobia I encountered in the ministries and palaces of the gulf countries. Indeed, it was everywhere, humming in the background with the same intensity of concern about Arab intentions that seemed to infect the squads of American businessmen — their briefcases bulging with elaborate investment proposals, their falsely supplicatory manners aggravatingly self-conscious — that I met on the circuit, particularly in Riyadh.

Riyadh is the once-dusty oasis village of the tribal Al-Saud clan, the fiercest warriors of the central Arabian desert. It is situated on the eastern edge of the scrubby upland plateau that separates Arabia's Red Sea and Persian Gulf coasts. Today a four-lane, tree-lined boulevard leads into the heart of the city from the airport to the north. The boulevard is flanked by modern government buildings, air-conditioned ministries of steel, glass and concrete that stand like sleek sentinels in the sun and whose curving entryways are clogged with Cadillacs and Rolls-Royces. Inside, their marble lobbies are cool and dark.

Farther into the city, near the bazaar and the old Friday Mosque, all sense of the calm institutional order symbolized by the ministries disappears. Here one encounters a densely packed jumble of mud-brick buildings and alleys barely wide enough for two camels to pass. Nowhere in the world does the clash between past and present confront you the way it does in the Arabian peninsula.

The clash was further accented as I waited in the anteroom of one of the ministries for my appointment with a deputy finance minister — one of King Faisal's brothers, or nephews, I'm not sure — who had agreed to talk with me.* An old man, dark, frail, bent, lost in his soiled white robes and Bedouin headdress, suddenly shuffled into the pristine room with a tray of mint tea. He offered it to me with a toothless grin and a breathless spurt of Arabic. He shuffled out again, but the room remained choked with his odor. He returned in a few minutes and led me down a marbled corridor to the deputy minister's office, walking spasmically, talking all the while in bursts of spittle. As I followed him, the cool currents from the central air-conditioning ducts wafted his odor into my face, and I felt as though I were trailing a herd of camels.

The deputy minister, youthful and good-looking, did not laugh off my inquiry about Arab financial intentions in the West. Instead he picked up a pile of charts and spread them across his desk. "Look here," he said. The charts were financial breakdowns of eleven major communications companies in the United States. "I have just returned from New York with these."

"What do they mean?"

"These are your leading communications institutions. I spent several years at one of your universities. I saw how the bulk of American public opinion is shaped. It is stacked overwhelmingly in favor of Israel and totally against the Arabs. Wouldn't you agree?"

"I wouldn't say overwhelmingly," I replied. "But I agree, I think Israel gets the better of it. What else would you expect?"

"Exactly," he said, calmly but with intensity. "And this sympathy is disseminated largely through these institutions. For instance, let there be an Arab commando raid on an Israeli town. What happens? Every news show on television, every newspaper, features pictures of the victims and interviews with the survivors. But let there be an Israeli air attack against a refugee camp in Lebanon. Then what do you see? Nothing. No pictures of victims, no interviews with survivors. Just communiqués from Tel Aviv about chasing down so-called Arab terrorists wherever they can be found. Are Arab women terrorists? Are Arab children? No. But you don't get to see the Arab women and children who are mangled and burnt beyond recognition by Israeli jets. You only get to see Jewish women and children."

"What does that have to do with these charts?" I said, although I suspected what he was leading to.

"These companies are the ones responsible for such an imbalance. Do you know what it would cost us to buy all of these institutions?"

* I promised not to identify him, for his views are at variance with those of the more senior officials of the ministry.

"Do you intend to buy them?"

"I did not say that. But do you know how much it would cost us?"

"I have no idea."

"Look," he said, beckoning me closer. "Here are your three major radio and television networks. Look at the total number of common public shares there are of CBS, and then look here at the price per share. What is it worth on the market? Here is your answer. Some $790 million. A year ago, before we put the oil embargo on, it was worth considerably more. You see? But all your major institutions have come down in value since then, have they not? Right now we could buy majority ownership in CBS, for $395 million. If there is another war, another boycott, your market will go down even more, and we'll be able to get it for much, much less. But take these figures for now. You agree, do you not, that fifty-one percent ownership in CBS would cost us no more than $395 million?"

I did a fast double check on his figures and agreed.

"And what would we be getting for that? Look here. Five major television stations and more than two hundred subsidiary stations. Fourteen major radio stations, and then all these affiliated stations that broadcast the CBS news and cultural programs." His fingers danced over the chart. "And here, we would gain control of a major publishing company. And all these other communications-industry subsidiaries."

"Quite impressive," I said. "But as I understand it, the United States government does not permit its communications systems to be owned by foreign interests."

"My friend," he came back, "do you think we are fools? Do you think we are not aware of this? And do you think there are not ways around this law? We could easily make such an acquisition through American representatives, or through other methods. Do you know what they say in your country? Money talks. Now look here . . ."

He passed on to the chart captioned NBC-RCA. The charts had obviously been printed up somewhere; they were formal and official-looking, not like casual memoranda. When he turned the CBS chart over I could see that it was duplicated in Arabic.

Majority control of NBC he showed me, could be bought for $825 million. It would mean buying fifty-one percent of RCA which, at $11 a share and with 150 million shares outstanding, was worth $1,650,000,000. More television stations, more radio stations, more book publishing companies, plus worldwide telegraph and satellite communications systems, military electronics manufacturing, and others, would come with it.

"Again," I said, "I believe there's a law that prohibits more than a certain small amount of ownership of a company involved in American military and defense projects."

He smiled beneath his moustache. "And now to ABC, your third major broadcasting corporation." For $143 million Saudi Arabia would own the remaining major television and radio stations in the United States.

He went on to publishing empires. The *New York Times*: about $45 million to gain control. With it went eleven other newspapers, a radio station and a television station, plus a syndicated news service and a share in the Paris-based *Herald Tribune* — the paper most Americans living in Europe get their news from.

The *Washington Post*: just over $36 million. Included in this package would be *Newsweek* magazine, four television and two radio stations, and additional newspapers, including another share of the Paris *Tribune*.

The deputy minister went on, and now the charts were flying. Time Incorporated: $165 million. The Los Angeles Times-Mirror Company: $155 million. The two largest independent newspaper chains, with papers in major cities all over the country, plus other vital communications assets: $135 million. Dow Jones and Company, publishers of the *Wall Street Journal* and several other influential publications, including the final share of the Paris *Tribune*: $270 million.

"Now," exclaimed the deputy minister, "do you know what that amounts to?" He didn't give me a chance to reply. "It amounts to just over $2 billion. Think of it. For $2 billion and some small change this country alone could effectively own the great bulk of the American communications industry. For another $300 million we could get most of the rest of it. For instance — the motion picture industry, the highbrow opinion magazines, a few more large book publishers. Throw in another $50 to $100 million for the fees and services we would have to pay to acquire this industry. The total cost to us would not be more than $2½ billion. Do you realize what a small portion of our total dollar surplus that is?"

"About five percent."

"Close. It is even less."

"Then why aren't you doing it?" I said. "Why aren't you out there buying up America?"

He looked at me and smiled. Then he gathered his charts back into a pile and shook it at me. "You don't think we make up these things for our own amusement, do you?"

"You mean you are buying?"

"That I am not permitted to tell you. But I will say this. We are increasing our test investing in various American industries. It is no secret."

I noticed on the long table behind him dozens of other piles of charts. "I don't get it," I said. "Are you showing me all this to prove you do intend to take over control of these industries or not?"

"We have not yet decided what we are going to do. I am showing you these charts simply to prove to you what we *can* do. Much depends on the coming year, on whether there will be a need for another embargo, on whether your stock market goes down further, on whether your press adjusts the slant of its coverage away from the Zionists, on whether your public opinion changes. We receive each day here every publication that is released in America. We have a room up above where a dozen men analyze these publications for what they say about us. We get a weekly report . . ."

He went on for fifteen minutes detailing the studies, analyses and reports being made in the Finance Ministry of every corner of American enterprise. Finally I said, "Well, are you willing to declare that your government *does* have a plan to gain economic control of the United States?"

He held a finger to his lips. "Financial people do not talk about their plans. I would not say it is *a* plan. It is one of many contingency plans in various stages of preparation. Once we have all our plans collected, we will then decide on a master plan."

"I assume you would think of getting involved in other countries, too."

"Of course. We already are. Look what Kuwait is doing, look what the emirates are doing . . . ."

"But supposing you did make these monumental buy-ins, who would you get to run all this?"

"To you it is monumental. To us it is not so monumental. But it doesn't matter. Who will we get to run everything for us? Why, there is no shortage of managerial expertise in the United States, in Britain, in France."

"So the Arabs would stay behind the scenes."

"We pay very well for good talent, you see."

"And then?"

"Gradually, as our own people became educated and skilled in these things, we would start moving them into positions of managerial authority."

"All right," I said, "but how do you buy the really big industries — the ones that have the defense connections, the ones that fall under the non–foreign ownership rule, the television companies?"

"When you return to the United States I suggest you go to your immigration department and find out how many Arabs have become citizens of America during the last three or four years."

"You mean you are planting agents there?"

"Let us simply say they are there. Many of them, ironically enough, are Palestinians. Palestinians are very intelligent in financial matters."

"Okay," I said. "But suppose the United States doesn't like the idea of being taken over by Saudi Arabia. Have you considered the remedies the American government might take. Freezing of Arab funds? Nationalization?"

He shrugged. "You tell me. If you are propping up the rest of the Western world, and between you and the rest of the Western world you require eighty percent of our oil and gas resources, would you take such measures? Could you afford to? What would happen to all your alliances? Your NATO and so on? No, my friend. We've got you over a barrel, if you will pardon the pun. If you nationalize, if you freeze, you get no more oil from us. Last year you took ten percent of our oil. This year you are taking fifteen. Next year it will be twenty. In 1976 it will be thirty. By 1976 you will still have no alternate sources of energy. Can you imagine, in 1976, the United States having to reduce its energy output by thirty percent? You would have riots in the streets. If you take such measures, we will simply stop selling you our oil. It will hurt you much more than us. We will simply sell it elsewhere. Or perhaps we won't sell it at all. We will keep it in the ground. We will still be selling enough to keep us going in very high style. And remember, the more oil is needed, the higher goes the price."

His eyes were positively glinting with pleasure as he stared into the middle distance. Then he looked at me. "But come, my friend, why are we talking of such unpleasant prospects. Look at it this way. You need us, we need you. Why can't we talk about that? We are perfectly willing to cooperate. If it only wasn't this business with the Jews . . ."

"But it's this business with the Jews that has put you in the favorable position you're in today."

"Ah," he exclaimed. "The Jews have only made it happen sooner. But don't talk to me about the Jews. It is all such hypocrisy in your country. Just last week I was in New York. Do you know who I was spending most of my time with? Loeb, Rhodes. Kuhn, Loeb. Lazard Freres. Goldman Sachs. Lehman Brothers. Do you know who comes knocking at our door when we go to London? The Jewish banks. They are all eager to take our money. And then they take part of their commissions and pledge them to donations to Israel . . ."

"There are ironies," I said.

"Ironies! Let me ask you. How many Jews in America?"

"Six million or so?" I guessed.

"Do they all drive cars?"

"Most of them."

"That means they must buy petrol. Tell me, when they pull into their petrol stations to fill up their tanks, do they realize that each gallon they buy is going to pay for another Palestinian rifle? All your American Jews who rant and rave about Palestinian terrorism. Do they know that by buying their petrol from Exxon or Texaco or Mobil or Shell they are indirectly contributing to the loss of another Israeli life? It is all hypocrisy, this political business. After your American Jews stuff their bellies and their petrol tanks, *then* they scream about the Arabs. It is all very noble. But it is phony. As I say, in the end, all that talks is money."

"Nonsense," said Saudi Foreign Minister Omar Al-Saqqaf when I put the question to him. "We are flexible. We will take the course that best suits our needs, but we have no economic designs on America."

"It could happen, it couldn't happen," said Oil Minister Yamani. "Frankly, we do not object to Israel's existence within borders specified in 1947. But we are growing weary with America's unflagging support of Israel's expansionism. We will continue to step up our economic pressures on the United States until it sees the light. I can guarantee this: Nothing positive will happen in the American economy until it forces Israel to respect and honor Palestinian claims, and the claims of other Arab countries. I don't say this in diplomatic language. I say simply and directly that we are thoroughly committed to see the Arab cause through. If the West goes down because of that, it is the West's problem, not ours. If Italy falls to Communism, then Britain, then France, and so on, because even though their economic systems collapse, these countries will still need our oil. We won't lose, only the West."

Another Saudi Arabian deputy finance minister is Abdul Aziz Rashid. "The problem is," he told me, "that the United States is six or seven years behind the times. The survival of Israel ceased to be an issue of any consequence after 1967. The issue now is the survival of the West and its institutions. No matter how the cards are dealt, we have the upper hand. It is only a matter of how long it takes the West, the United States, to confront the issue. If there is another war, there will be another boycott. The war will last much longer, as will the boycott. But it is not the boycott that will hurt you. It is what happens afterwards. A further price rise. Why? Because we — the Arab oil countries — will have to increase our subsidies to our brother countries. There can be no doubt of the outcome. We are now in a position to price Israel out of existence. We do not want that. We want this to be over as soon as possible. As long as the Palestinians achieve their state, that is all we wish. Once that happens, they will be so busy constructing themselves they will have no time to think about Israel. And with prosperity and independence, their anger will fade. But the longer Palestinian statehood takes, the closer the West will come to economic chaos."

"I am an economist," said Emir Musaed Ben Abdul Rahman, the Saudi finance minister. "So I can tell you we do not have to buy America to enforce the Arab viewpoint in this business with Israel. We intend to re-create America here. But, you know as well as I that everything in this world can be reduced to a single common denominator. And that is economics. When you have a political enemy who seeks to overthrow you, humanistic idealism can be wonderful and can justify foregoing certain economic luxuries for a time. But we are not your political enemies. We have expressed no desire to overthrow you. We have committed no crimes against you. So you and your people have no reason to mount an idealistic political crusade against us. True, we might be your economic enemies, but if we become so it will only be because you have stupidly chosen to make us so. . . . The only political enemy we have at the present time is Israel. But the United States is not Israel. Why should the people of the United States choose to suffer economically because of Israel? Ah, but they do. However, we are confident that they will be willing to suffer only so much. Then they will choose between their own economic well-being and some distant political idealism. Which do you suppose it will be?"

Sheikh Muhammad Abdul Kheil, minister of state for finance, did a variation on the same theme. Then he added, "You know, hundreds and hundreds of Israelis, thousands — men, women and children — kill and mangle themselves each year in auto collisions. I am told they are very poor drivers. So what is this business when a couple of people get killed in an Arab commando raid? It makes great headlines. I'll wager you something. I'll wager that more innocent people in Ireland and England are killed by Irish terrorism than Israelis are killed by Palestinian terrorism. But who hears about these poor Irish and English? They die, and no one raises their voice. A few Israelis die and the world shakes. That is something I don't understand about you people in the West. The Jews have become like a sacred cow to you. You should all begin to look into the question of why. What makes a Jew so special, even a Jewish woman, a Jewish child? Why is a slain Jew so much more worthy of your attention than a slain Irishman? When you discover the answer to that question, you will know what you have to do if you — I mean you, Americans — if you yourselves wish to survive."

All over the Arabian peninsula — in the official chambers of the Saudis, of Kuwait, of Abu Dhabi, Dubai and Bahrain, I found the attitude toward Israel sardonically distasteful, but without any virulent rancor. Conventional defamations of the Jews (Zionists, Israelis, take your pick) were repeated almost, it seemed, as if by rote, but without the stridency of Arabs in the confrontation countries. Indeed — and you will have to take my word for this — whatever paranoia exists in the mind of Arabian officialdom, the obsessions are first with Communism, then with Iran, then with Arab revolutionary movements such as exist among the Palestinians, and only then with Israel. The ultimate obsession, of course, is money, which was demonstrated to me by none other than the king of Saudi Arabia himself.

My audience with King Faisal was instructive in an unsettling way. For when I met with him, I was struck by the realization that all those ministers and deputy ministers who sat in their plush, modern Riyadh offices were not terribly unlike sinecured sons and cousins in a family business run by a patriarchal grandfather. Oil ministers, finance ministers, foreign ministers, domestic ministers — all could inflate their importance with political discursiveness and the state jets at their disposal, but none made a move, none had the authority to make a move, without the king's imprimatur.

I had been told that Faisal had two pet subjects when talking to Americans: his admiration for the United States and his aversion to Communism. From the latter he usually proceeded to express his distaste for Zionism, equating it with Communism and reminding his visitor that Karl Marx was a Jew. This was exactly how he opened our conversation.

I had not gotten to see Faisal at his mountain residence at Taif, above Mecca, but encountered him later at his pink concrete working palace in Riyadh. After being ushered into his modern, teak-paneled office by one of his giant, sworded African bodyguards and assuring the translator that I would not directly quote him, I was served tea. Faisal entered moments later in a swish of white robes, his dark, crenellated face framed by a gold-banded head drape. He sat at his desk and nodded at me stonily, his astoundingly large and wide-set eyes hooded, his mouth set in an avuncular scowl. He was smaller and slighter than I had anticipated.

In response to my first few questions he spoke in the manner I had been told he would — America, Communism, Zionism. His voice was surprisingly high-pitched, its cadence tinged with lamentation. He answered my questions without analysis, merely uttering brief responses that had an air of regal fiat about them.

When I asked him if another oil embargo was in the offing in the event of a future Arab-Israeli war, he said that the rules of the game had been set and that all the players were well acquainted with them.

Was it possible that the Arab countries would start another war simply to bring about another embargo?

Anything is possible, he said.

How much control, then, did Saudi Arabia have over events in the Middle East if it could be used by other countries for their political purposes?

The political purposes of all Arab countries coincided when those purposes were related to Zionist expansion, came the answer.

"In America," I said, "we hear much about you wanting to be able to pray in Jerusalem before you die. Is this true? Or is it just a myth that has become accepted as fact?"

It was true, he said. There was no reason for the Jews to be in Arab Jerusalem.

"I have also heard that you bear a special personal hatred for Jews that goes beyond your political feelings about Zionism," I then said.

His scowl froze, his heavy eyelids narrowed. Jews meant nothing to him, he replied, except insofar as they encroached on the sanctity of Islam, which they were doing in Jerusalem.

I remarked that Jews — even non-Israeli Jews — had never been permitted to be employed by Aramco. Was there any relation between that and his personal feelings about Jews? He brushed the question aside. So I proceeded to one of the questions I had really come to ask.

"Can you tell me this?" I said. "It seems to me that with all the economic power at your disposal you could bring about a resolution of this problem in the Arabs' favor very quickly. I am told you and the other Arab oil states now have enough money to prevent oil from going to the United States and Europe for more than a year. I was wondering why you have not continued to use the oil weapon to force a quick resolution."

He responded by saying that as king he had to balance the interests of all the Arab nations with the particular interests of Saudi Arabia. A favorable resolution would be reached in time, but he did not wish to create enemies where enemies did not exist. As an Arab, he believed in persuasion over the sword, and would only use the sword — in this case, oil — in the most extreme situations. And then only to intensify the forces of persuasion.

"Do you fear Western retaliation in the event you use the embargo again?"

He did not. With retaliation, only the West would lose. Besides, the United States was as interested in keeping its Arab oil-producing friends free from Communism as it was in supporting Israel.

I said that I had heard from some of his ministers that there was a fear in Saudi Arabia of an Israeli-Iranian alliance, abetted by the United States, that would take over the Middle East. Was there any substance to this fear?

There would always be nations who would covet Allah's gift to the Arabs, he answered cryptically.

But was this Israeli-Iranian prospect being seriously considered? I pressed.

Suddenly Faisal became loquacious, saying that the Arab oil nations faced a great threat from Iran. Saudi Arabia, he said, had been endeavoring to act responsibly in all matters concerning oil, trying to keep the price reasonable, even reduce it to take some of the economic pressure off the West. It was Iran, he claimed, that was keeping the price high and threatening to raise it further, yet it was the Arabs who were taking the blame for it. The possibility that this might be a tactic on the part of the Iranians to bring the wrath of the world down on the Arabs had not escaped his attention. He expressed a concern with the rate at which Iran was expanding its armed forces and said he was dismayed at the almost exclusive United States' participation in the buildup.

But you are building up your armed forces as well, I suggested.

In no way like Iran, he rejoined with some heat. Iranian intentions were not something he contemplated with pleasure.

Could he give me an authoritative idea of what shape Saudi fiscal policy was going to take vis-à-vis the United States and other Western countries? I mentioned the various and sometimes contradictory schemes I had listened to. Did Saudi Arabia intend to achieve a major stake in the United States? Or was it content merely to import what it wanted of the American way of life into Saudi Arabia?

A smile flickered in his eyes. He said he couldn't understand all the worry that had been voiced over the possibility of Saudi Arabia investing heavily in America. After all, the United States had something like $150 billion of its own invested in foreign countries. Why shouldn't Saudi Arabia do the same thing in the United States? Wasn't that the essence of world trade and the free enterprise system? When countries have active trade and investment between them, such activities go a long way toward making friendly relations and international cooperation. And only through these mechanisms will peace and stability be achievable.

Finally I asked him what he thought would happen in Saudi Arabia once he was gone — he was seventy and was said to be in chronic ill health, a fact I thought was confirmed by the habitually pained and furrowed expression on his face. I had met the brother who had been designated to be his successor, Prince Fahd, a man who in his personal life was said to be as self-indulgent and licentious as Faisal was austere. The king swung slowly in his chair and stared through the French doors of his office to the straggly garden outside. I thought he was pondering my question. Then I felt a hard tap on my shoulder. I turned and saw two of the bodyguards standing over me. The translator nodded to me. The interview was over.*

---

* A few months later, early in 1975, King Faisal was murdered by an allegedly deranged nephew. It was not Prince Fahd but another of his brothers, Rashid Ibn Saud, who was named to succeed Faisal as king. According to most knowledgeable observers, however, although the title went to Rashid, the real power of the Saudi throne was assumed by Fahd.

# Epilogue

## CONCLUSION: *The Inverted Pyramid*

A POPULAR AXIOM AMONG DIPLOMATS is that "a nation has no friends or enemies, only vital interests." Over and above whatever sentimental factors contributed to it, the creation of the State of Israel in 1948 was the result of nations then in possession of preeminent world power exercising their vital interests.

Another maxim is that the vital interests of nations inevitably change, and with them international friendships and enmities. The truth of this has never been proven with more alacrity than in the relationship between the nations of the Middle East and those of the rest of the world.

Still another favorite rule of thumb, coined almost two centuries ago by the French diplomat Talleyrand, holds that "the art of statesmanship is to foresee the inevitable and to expedite its occurrence." Many experienced observers, conscious of history, would dispute the wisdom of this concept. They would do so on the grounds that if what Britain's Chamberlain achieved at Munich in 1938 was an expression of the art of statesmanship, then the function of statesmanship is nothing less than to expedite war.

A final adage beloved by political practitioners is that "war is the failure of diplomacy." Some prefer to put it differently: "War is the *extension* of diplomacy." Either interpretation is historically valid.

In the light of these notions, what does the present state of affairs in the Middle East portend for the future — for Israel, for the various Arab nations, for the world at large?

Predicting the future is, of course, a fruitless business — except perhaps for whatever gratuitous pleasure it provides those who engage in such speculation. A reasonably accurate shape of future events may be gleaned, nevertheless, from an informed consideration of the vital interests of the diverse national blocs involved in the Middle East situation. The projection that follows, dealing with the near future, is constructed out of a series of analyses and estimates I have gathered and collated from inside sources in all the governments concerned. It may at first glance seem far-fetched, but I can assure the reader that it represents a reliable consensus of the views and expectations of those close to or at the heart of the policy-making centers of the various governments. This is not to say that what I am about to describe will absolutely happen. It is what is most likely to occur within the coming year or so, barring a sudden and improbable reconciliation of differences in the region. The scenario is predicated upon a curious kind of limited, non-nuclear semi–world war involving the United States and the Soviet Union, a war that will be in the interests of practically all parties concerned. Here is how it is expected to develop.

Between Israel and the Arab confrontation countries at least one more formal war is inevitable. Such a war will be in the interests of Israel, for above all else it will compel for the first time the introduction of a large-scale American military presence into the region. Israel will initiate the war on preemptive grounds and the United States will join it so as to forestall Israel's use of its nuclear weaponry and to guarantee the security of its borders.

The next Arab-Israeli war will be in the interests of the United States as well. Once introduced into the northern sector of the Middle East, America will have a base from which to expand its military presence into the Arab oil states of the Persian Gulf. Should the oil states institute another embargo, as anticipated, this would be even more in the interests of the United States, for it would provide it with the justification needed to seize control of Arab oil production until the oil-producing states were persuaded to adjust their ruinous oil prices downward to a level commensurate with what the West adjudges to be equitability.

The war will also be in the interests of the Palestinians, for it will guarantee the fulfillment of their dream of statehood as the United States and the Soviet Union orchestrate a postwar peace settlement. One of the absolute conditions of such a settlement will be Israeli recognition of a Palestinian state in exchange for an American guarantee, by way of a joint defense pact, of Israel's future sovereignty.

The war will be in the interests of the Arab confrontation states — Egypt,

Syria, Jordan — for it will remove from them the burden of the Palestinian question and secure the return of their territories as part of the necessary postwar settlement.

The war will be equally in the interests of the Arab oil-producing states along the Persian Gulf. Although the temporary American takeover of their production facilities will result in a considerable reduction in revenues, a more workable balance will be restored to the international economic system which, in the long run, will accrue to their benefit. The rate of economic growth of these sparsely populous states will fall more into line with what they are able to absorb. Moreover, the tribal monarchies will be preserved, at least for a time, and Iranian designs on the Arabian peninsula will be rendered obsolete.

The war will be in the interests of the European bloc and Japan, for it will relieve the pressure of out-of-sight oil prices under which they, as the primary consumers of Arab oil, are presently suffocating.

But how about the Soviet Union? Well, goes the consensus (some of which was contributed by Russian officials I spoke to), the war will be as much in its interest as it is in America's. The Russians too will be able to justify an open and large-scale military presence in the region. The Soviet Union and the United States will, in effect, trade off prerogatives. The Russians will acquiesce in the American occupation of the Arabian peninsula; the United States will in turn acquiesce in the introduction of Russian forces into Syria and Iraq. Thereafter, between them, the two superpowers will work out a final settlement of the Arab-Israeli and Israeli-Palestinian questions. Once this is accomplished, each will settle back with more or less equal amounts of hegemony in the Middle East, each permitting the other to manipulate their respective, carefully demarcated sectors in whatever ways they choose. An extended period of peacefulness will ensue, however uncertain it may at times appear.

Beyond that the script does not go. I am oversimplifying it, of course, but in its bare outlines the scenario does represent the large majority of informed intimations I have received of things to come. The only important nation whose interests would suffer is Iran. Iran's imperial designs on the Arab world would be neutralized both by the Russian presence at the top of the Persian Gulf, in Iraq, and by the American presence along the length of its western shore. Although armed to the teeth, Iran would have little choice but to pull in its wings.

Surprisingly, I found that the above projection, or some slight variation of it, was most widely anticipated in the Arab world. "The situation here is a tightly tangled web of numerous conflicting interests that grows more dense with the passing of each month," a high-level Egyptian diplomat told me. "It will require a powerful outside force, an explosion of mighty wills, to untangle it. A force whose interests transcend all others. There is no doubt about it. No matter how much Kissinger, no matter how much Brezhnev, the situation will not be straightened out without, ultimately, a military confrontation between Russia and America." His prediction, in varying shades of calmness and despair, was repeated by dozens of government figures I talked to in different Arab countries.

And what of the future beyond the immediate scenario, should it indeed be the one to be played out? Again, prediction is fruitless. "Educated" prognostications nevertheless continue to fill the air.

"The evolution of events in the Middle East during this century can be likened to the construction, if you can imagine it, of an inverted pyramid. The capstone, which in the case of such a pyramid turns out to be its base, was formed out of the inevitable conflict between foreign Zionist need and ambition on the one hand, and local Arab pride and aspiration on the other. As the pyramid grew, the stones in each of its successively widening tiers had added to them further elements — the passions and needs of other foreign interests, the passions and aspirations of other national groups within the Arab world. Each succeeding tier sucked more of the world into it. Now the pyramid is finished. And there it stands, incongruously balanced on its point, its four sides reaching up and out into every corner of the world."

The speaker of these words was a senior American State Department official who has played a central role in the mediatory efforts of Henry Kissinger during the past two years. He was responding to a question I had put to him concerning the scenario and about whether the intensifying Middle East political conflict, with its attendant economic ramifications, would be resolved without a worldwide cataclysm.

"We all know," he went on, "that it is impossible for a pyramid to stand freely in such an upside-down manner. So far it has been supported on its four corners by the rest of the world. Although it has precariously tipped now and then, it has managed to remain more or less upright. But the effort to keep it upright has imposed greater and greater tension on those who support it. Tension is resolved in two ways, our psychologists tell us. One way is through outburst. The other is through withdrawal. The fight-or-flee mechanism which is part of every human being's reaction system. Now, you tell me. Will it be resolved peacefully? Or will it take a world war to bring about a resolution?

"I gather from your analogy," I said, "that you see it as a world war."

"If my analogy is correct, there can be no question of the ultimate outcome. One way or the other — whether one side or the other relaxes its support of the pyramid and withdraws, or whether one side or the other chooses to eradicate its tension through outburst — the pyramid will lose its balance and come tumbling down. Either way, the resolution of the situation will come out of the dust and rubble of the collapsed pyramid. The Israeli-Arab conflict, the very thing that started it all, will be forgotten. East and West will be left to pick over the remains like buzzards dining on carrion. That is, if there still is an East and West."

# Acknowledgments

There are dozens of people I should publicly thank for their help and cooperation in easing the way for me in my travels about the Middle East to research this book. However, because of the parlous politics of the region and the possibly unhappy reception the book might receive in certain quarters there, many have expressed a desire not to be mentioned. Not to mention some would in my view give disproportionate credit to others. So my thanks to all equally, albeit anonymously. They know who they are.

Notwithstanding the above, my special appreciation goes to the management and staff of *Dar Assayad*, the large Beirut newspaper and magazine publishing organization whose documentary and photographic research facilities were generously put at my disposal in the preparation of this book; and particularly to Messrs. Bassam Freiha and Wajih Abdallah, who provided me with many valuable perspectives in the course of our discussions.

# INDEX

# INOEX